A History of Churches

The Survival of New Testament
Christianity Against Overwhelming Odds

Dr. Lester Hutson

A History of Churches: The Survival of New Testament Christianity
Against Overwhelming Odds

Cover photo: Tower of David located in the Old City of Jerusalem

ISBN: 978-0-9836802-6-0

www.lesterhutson.org

Acknowledgments

This project has consumed a huge block of my life for over seven years. The amount of time spent in research and reading has been great, but there's far more to writing a book like this than time spent in books and libraries. The writes and rewrites, refining and more refining, input from trusted colleagues; it's all very taxing and time-consuming. Getting a book ready to publish is no small task.

For me it would have been impossible without support. My dear wife Margaret has tolerated hours upon end of me sequestered in my office with a book in my face or behind a keyboard. Thank you dear love of my life! Sometimes my friends and family have thought I didn't want to see them; time writing a book means you are often not available for other things. I truly appreciate the understanding of people who wanted a share of my time, but who didn't get it.

The person who has given the most hands-on help for this book is unquestionably Philip Rice. He has provided countless hours of input. He has put every chapter in the crucible. He has questioned my claims, challenged my logic, asked me to rewrite whole sections and held me to an ever higher standard. I thank him for that. He's the consummate editor, but he's also the expert in formatting and industry standards. Most of all he has a hunger for the truth and is committed to excellence. This book has his fingerprints all over it. Without his help, I can't imagine it becoming a reality.

Many others have also helped in a variety of ways. Several critiqued the book and offered very helpful input and suggestions. Thanks to each of you and especially to Raleigh Estes Campbell. His detailed input greatly improved the book. I am also indebted to

James Peterson who proofread every chapter to make sure all Scripture quotes were correct.

What a debt of gratitude we owe to those faithful souls who sacrificed so much to give us the heritage we have! They are a great host who century after century suffered and often gave their lives that we might know the truth of God's Word and His work on our behalf. I am humbled by their commitment and sacrifice.

Above all I acknowledge the great God of this universe who let me complete this work. He provided the health and resources necessary for the task. I am privileged that He would allow me to be His tool for such an undertaking. I trust that He is honored and exalted as a result of this endeavor.

Table of Contents

Foreword

During a lifetime of personal ministry in and among churches that believe and practice first-century Christianity, I have painfully observed that the overwhelming majority of Christians know almost nothing of their spiritual heritage. Jesus is the founder of Christianity. He established His first church in Jerusalem, Israel. Many Christians claim to be a member of an unbroken line of churches after the order Jesus established. They date their heritage back to Him, but offer little or no evidence to support their belief. It is somewhat embarrassing and self-incriminating to dogmatically embrace a belief with little evidence to support it. Today it is rare to find Christians (including pastors) who are knowledgeable of their heritage of Christianity after the end of the first century.

This book was written to help those who need a simple, working knowledge of their heritage since the end of the New Testament. The book is not exhaustive. Rather it is intended to present a concise historical overview in simple language in a reasonably short treatise. From Jesus' earthly ministry to the present is a long period of time. During those years, Christianity has been the most defining influence on the history of the entire world. The presentation of a working knowledge of this long era of time and events from the standpoint of true New Testament Christianity is challenging. Hopefully this book will present it in an easy-to-understand manner.

The main goal of this book is to show that the brand of Christianity presented in the New Testament has continuously existed from Jesus Christ to the present. This book names the people who embraced New Testament Christianity century by century and tells where they lived. Apart from a basic understanding of enormous on-going efforts to eradicate them from the face of the earth, it is doubtful that anyone could appreciate their continuous existence. Only God could have made it happen. Otherwise first-century, New Testament Christianity would have surely perished. This book presents both a look at the continuous existence of New Testament Christianity through the ages and a look at some of the astounding, massive and cruel efforts to eradicate it.

I acknowledge that the factual claims and information of this book are not new or original. This book is based on secondary, not primary sources. Many great historical works establishing the validity of the claims made here already exist. Because they were not written according to modern standards, they are widely condemned and discounted by many modern scholars. Some of these great historical works are quite lengthy, hard to read and out of print; however, the facts are undeniable that they are thorough, well-documented and authoritative. My attempt in this book has been to summarize what many have already said very well. My effort has been to credit each source.

My heart is to give the common man a glimpse of his great heritage as a New Testament Christian. The references anchor the claims to a great reservoir of supporting evidence and establish their authority. They also enable the reader to both verify the claims and pursue deeper, more exhaustive studies. The scholarship of this book will stand inspection; however, it was written for the common man who needs and desires a working knowledge of his connection to the Christianity of Jesus Christ and the church He built in Jerusalem.

My prayer is that God will use this book to inform you, strengthen your faith and enhance your appreciation for all that has been passed on to you at an enormous price. I pray also that it will help prepare you for the ominous days that seem to be heading our way.

Lester Hutson

Chapter 1

A Book About Churches over the Centuries

The history of churches through the centuries is not as simple as it might seem. There have been and are churches like the one personally established by Jesus Christ and then there are others — many others. Some of them are not at all like the one He established in Jerusalem, Israel. Yet, they call themselves the church of Jesus Christ. To say the least, it can be confusing. Many godly Christians know very little of their spiritual heritage past the end of the New Testament. By the time you finish this book that will not be your case.

PREVIEW

You are about to look at 2,000 years of church life and activity. It is obvious that a one-volume book on this subject will not be exhaustive. The scope of this book is broad; however, this book will give you a broad overview as well as insight that will help you sort through the mountain of information on this subject. These lessons will enlighten you, enhance your knowledge, strengthen your faith and cause you to appreciate your spiritual heritage; but they will not make you an authority on the history of churches.

The word "church(es)" is used in this book in two main senses: (1) in reference to true churches that Jesus recognizes to be His own and (2) in reference to churches that have departed sufficiently from Jesus' idea of what a church is so as to no longer be recognized by Jesus as His own. In each case the context will help you distinguish the sense in which the term is used. The word "church" will not be used in the improper sense that all professing Christians constitute one body or unit called "the church," implying that one individual church (visible or invisible) has continuously existed since the time of Christ. An unbroken line of churches has existed from Christ to the present in an institutional sense, but not one church in a particular sense. Hence this book is titled *A History of Churches,* not *Church History.*

This book examines many developments that relate to Christianity since the establishing of the original church by Jesus Christ. Its main thrust is to identify the continuous existence of true churches which have embraced New Testament positions from Christ to the present.

As you read through these pages, you will become familiar with many key aspects of history that have had a direct bearing on current conditions and life. You will encounter the names, writings, actions and influence of some of the outstanding Christian leaders from the end of the New Testament to the present. You will learn of the severe persecution of Christians by pagan Rome followed by more persecution of those who practiced first-century Christianity once the Roman government in A.D. 323 made Christianity its official religion. You will learn of false doctrine and huge doctrinal controversies faced by early Christians, the origins and formation of the Roman Catholic and Greek Orthodox Churches, the birth and rise of Islam, the Crusades, the rise of European states, the Protestant Reformation and the proliferation of Protestant denominations.

UNDERSTANDING WHAT A *"CHURCH"* IS

It is important to understand Jesus' definition of the word *church.* When Jesus established His church, He called it an *ekklesia.* This compound Greek noun comes from ek meaning "out of" and kaleo meaning "to call." Thus a church of Jesus Christ is literally *a called out assembly.* [1] Of the total usage of the word *ekklesia* in the

New Testament, three times it is used in reference to the assembly of city leaders in Ephesus, **Acts 19:32, 39, 41**, and once in reference to the *"assembly"* of Israel at Mount Sinai under Moses' leadership, **Acts 7:38**. Every other time it is exclusively used in reference to Jesus' church. [2] In each case where *church* is used in the Christian sense, it refers to either (1) a specific congregation or (2) churches in an institutional sense. [3] There are no exceptions. Some misunderstand Paul's use of the word *"body"* in connection with the church, **Colossians 1:18, 24, Ephesians 1:22-23, 5:23**, to imply some broader sense than a local congregation. The term *"body"* is simply used in a metaphorical sense. [4] The connection between one's head and the rest of the body is paralleled between Christ who is the head of each church and the members whom He calls His body. Christ is the head and He directs and saves each true church. [5] No change in the definition or application of *ekklesia* is implied by likening it to a body. Each *ekklesia* (church) is like a body. **1 Corinthians 12:13-27** makes that fact abundantly clear.

Definition

In the biblical sense, "A New Testament Church is a company of baptized believers voluntarily associated together for the maintenance of the ordinances and the spread of the gospel of Jesus Christ." [6] This is the definition of John T. Christian and it is a succinct statement of the true meaning of church as seen in the Scriptures. [7]

Ramifications

There are inescapable ramifications of this definition. If this indeed is the true definition of *church* as set forth in the Bible, then:

1. All true churches have their origin in Jesus Christ.

2. A true church is a visible assembly.

3. All true churches are located somewhere on earth.

4. All true churches are independent and self-governed congregations.

5. A person must be saved before he is eligible to become a member of a true church.

6. A person must be baptized (immersed) in water to become a member of a true church.

7. A true church is made up of saved members in covenant relationship.

8. True churches keep the ordinances in memorial of their relationship to Christ, not in order to obtain salvation.

9. True churches are evangelistic and missionary. [8]

This book assumes this definition and these ramifications of what a true church is.

The Foundational or Core Beliefs of the Church Jesus Originated

As this book examines the history of churches throughout the centuries since the church Jesus personally established in Jerusalem, Israel, it is important to know where His original church stood on key issues. A working knowledge of His true church will serve as a measuring or evaluating device. With it one can easily see who stayed true to His pattern and who went astray. In one format or another this information will be repeated several times in this book; however, while defining the word *church*, it is also important and appropriate to define its fundamental beliefs. The list given here reflects the more foundational or core beliefs of Jesus' original church. It is not intended to be fully comprehensive.

- Jesus Christ personally founded His church.

- Jesus Christ is deity, God and He alone is the head of the church.

- Jesus' church has two permanent offices: pastors and deacons.

- The government of Jesus' church is congregational.

- All churches are to be autonomous and self-governing.

- Jesus' churches are to be entirely separate and independent of the state.

- Jesus' churches are to assemble on Sunday and keep the ordinances of baptism and the Lord's Supper.

- Salvation is exclusively by grace through personal faith in Jesus Christ alone.

- Only saved persons are to be baptized and baptism is by immersion.

- Only saved persons can be members of a church.

- Every believer is of equal worth to God and there is to be no ecclesiastical hierarchy in the church. This theological position is known as the priesthood of every believer.

- The Scriptures and only the Scriptures are inspired of God.

- The Scriptures are the final rule of faith and practice for believers and the church.

Jesus' Personal Promise Regarding His Church

Jesus said that from the day He personally established this institution which He called *"My church,"* it would continuously exist until His return. *"I will build my church; and the gates of hell shall not prevail against it,"* **Matthew 16:18**. This is a divine guarantee of church perpetuity and historical evidence will validate Jesus' claim. This book will highlight churches throughout the years that exhibit the characteristics of Jesus' original model. The definition of *church* means its history is a study of individual, specific churches at different locations and times throughout history. It is not the study of one giant entity of which all Christians are a part.

SOURCES FOR THE HISTORY OF CHURCHES

How do we know what happened 1,800, 1,000 or even 500 years ago? As we shall see, powerful entities deliberately attempted to destroy all evidence unfavorable to their positions and actions. In spite of massive efforts to erase forever from history much of the truth, many writings of a personal nature survived. Individuals left diaries, journals and personal letters. Christian leaders wrote explanations and defenses of true, biblical Christianity and many of those writings survived. Through the years there have been thousands upon thousands of pastors and churches. Church and pastor records abound: of their decisions and sermons, accounts of meetings between pastors and other church people and minutes recording church meetings and beliefs. Great numbers of church hymnals, creeds and teaching materials survived. There are countless records from secular courts, rulers and writers. [9] Accusations of persecutors tell us what the issues were and where both accusers and the accused stood on the issues. [10] Furthermore historical writings abound.

PREVAILING INFLUENCES AT THE INCEPTION OF THE FIRST CHURCH

Before we launch into this historical journey, we would be wise to consider some of the more powerful prevailing influences at the time of Jesus on earth and immediately following. These are influences that God allowed, influences that He used to shape and forge the direction of early Christianity and the churches.

An Oriental (Eastern) not Occidental (Western) Society and Culture

Jesus was an easterner, not a westerner. The entire Old Testament and almost all of the New Testament were written by easterners. It is difficult to grasp the story of Christianity, particularly in its early days, apart from an understanding of eastern history, culture and thinking. Much of that influence is integrated into and explained in this book.

Greek Influence

Just prior to the Roman rule of New Testament days, Philip of Macedon and Alexander the Great had conquered and ruled the entire Mediterranean World. Greek influence was profound and continued under Roman rule. The influence of renowned philosophers such as Socrates, Plato, Aristotle, Zeno and Epicurus moved masses of people. Some of their thinking was absorbed by segments of Christianity and lead to much heresy and false doctrine. Materialistic and sensuous Greek culture (called Hellenism) was highly appealing to the flesh and permeated the Roman Empire. The religion of the Greeks was adopted by the Romans. The Romans renamed the Greek gods and made them their own. The masses identified with the gods who were enormously powerful super humans full of human weaknesses such as anger, lust, greed, jealousy and every imaginable vice. Against this backdrop entered the pure, wholesome, moral message of Jesus Christ. Another powerful Greek influence was the Koine Greek language which was common to the entire Empire. It would be difficult to overstate what this common language meant to the spread of the Christian message. The Scriptures were brought into Koine Greek. Throughout the Empire, people received the Christian message in their own language.

Roman Rule (From 63 B.C.)

Rome ruled the entire Mediterranean world. There was one government, not many. It was the most elaborate, organized and powerful government the world had ever seen. The icon of Rome was *Pax Romana* meaning the peace of Rome. Rome ruled with an iron fist and ruthless cruelty; men feared to challenge Rome. As harsh as it was, the government of Rome meant peace throughout the Empire. Furthermore a superior communication system meant the wide spread flow of ideas and information. Highly developed roads and a good courier system meant relatively safe travel. Christianity and churches proliferated.

Another powerful Roman influence upon Christianity was the Roman system of gods. As mentioned, the official Roman religion was worship of the adopted Greek gods; however, the Romans also believed in Emperor Worship. In early Christianity, that Roman stance was to become a major obstacle; for rejection of this Roman position, many Christians paid the ultimate price. A third aspect of Roman religion was her Mystery Religions. The people conquered by the Romans had religions and systems of gods. The Romans allowed the conquered to keep their religions and gods as long as those people also accepted emperor worship, the official

Roman gods and the gods of others. The Romans prided themselves in *Religio licita* or "freedom of religion."

The Jewish Diaspora

Jews were spread (dispersed) throughout the Roman Empire. A Jewish colony existed in almost every major population center of the Roman Empire. This paved the way for the spread of Christianity which sprang from the Jews and was initially propagated by Jewish evangelists.

REASONS FOR THE RAPID SPREAD OF EARLY CHRISTIANITY AND THE PROLIFERATION OF CHURCHES

Like a wildfire spread by high winds, Christianity spread exponentially. There are many reasons why this happened.

Spectacular Initial Events

The ministry of Jesus Christ was nothing less than miraculous. He was God with us and He performed true miracles, not merely superhuman acts. Multitudes including His apostles saw them. They knew He was God and not a mere man. The biggest miracle of all was the resurrection of Jesus Christ. They saw Him die in crucifixion; He rose in three days and they spent the next 40 days with Him. They knew He was no fluke. They believed His message and were willing to export it regardless of the cost.

The Apostolic Witness

The apostles were eye witnesses of the work and ministry of Jesus Christ. Their reports were not hearsay. Their zeal and passion were beyond adequate description. They also experienced the Day of Pentecost at which time the Holy Spirit of God anointed and empowered them in a miraculous way. They knew that God was with them. Furthermore the apostles were given the power to perform miracles. They were able to validate their messages and claims with miracles. The impact was phenomenal. Additionally they were divinely inspired by the Holy Spirit. God gave them their messages, and in the receipt of the Scriptures they were infallible. These realities fanned the fires of Christianity.

Opposition and Persecution by Jewish Leadership

Strangely the vile hatred of most Jewish leadership for Jesus Christ, His message and those who followed Him became a major factor in the rapid spread of Christianity. It started in Jerusalem where the Jewish hierarchy was headquartered. As evidenced by their role in the death of Jesus Christ, the Jewish leadership had enormous political power. The book of *Acts* records their vicious efforts against Christianity. They were set on silencing and eradicating Christians.

Saul of Tarsus, a highly intellectual and powerful young Pharisee, was one Jewish leader, **Acts 8:1**. He made it his personal mission to destroy Christianity which he viewed as a heretical affront to Judaism. His vicious efforts against Christians spread them far and wide throughout the Roman Empire. Wherever they went, they were like seeds and planted churches which grew and won more to Christ.

The Conversion of Saul of Tarsus

Soon Saul of Tarsus was miraculously saved. The same zeal and passion he formerly used against the Christians were now turned to bring men to Christ. Paul's message struck the heart of Judaism's mistaken concepts. Multitudes turned to Christ. Paul exported the gospel message and planted churches in strategic nerve centers far and wide within the Empire.

Other Evangelism by the Apostles and Others

Paul was not alone in his mission and success. Peter zealously exported the message of Christ. God revealed to him that Christianity is not limited to Jews; it is also for Gentiles. God sent Peter to the Gentile, Cornelius who was gloriously saved, **Acts 10-11**. This opened the door wide to the Gentiles. Soon thereafter Barnabas went as a missionary to Cyprus Island, **Acts 15:39**. There is reason to believe that Thomas took the gospel to India and that Mark took the message to Egypt and North Africa. Evidence also indicates that Pudens and Claudia exported the message to Britannia (Wales), **2 Timothy 4:21**. (Welsh historical records indicate that Pudens and Claudia were from Wales.) It is likely that Christianity had reached Britannia (England) before the end of the first century.

Churches were planted in nerve centers throughout the Empire (Antioch, Corinth, Ephesus, Rome, Philippi, etc.) The main vehicle that seems to have spread Christianity throughout the empire was Paul's success in winning his Roman guards to Christ. As these guards were assigned other tours of military duty, they took Christianity with them. Converts were made and churches were established wherever they went, which was from Babylonia to Britannia (Wales) and North Africa to Macedonia (the Balkan States).

The Destruction of Jerusalem in 70 A.D.

The destruction of Jerusalem in 70 A.D. broke the back of Jewish resistance and Jewish control of Christianity. With the conversion of thousands of Gentiles, Christianity became less and less an exclusively Jewish religion, **Acts 15**. Gentile churches proliferated.

With this background information in mind it is now time to move forward. In chapter two we will begin a look at how Pagan Rome persecuted the early Christians.

---

[1] W. E. Vine, *An Expository Dictionary of New Testament Words*, s.v. "ekklesia," (Nashville, Tennessee: Thomas Nelson Publishers, 1985), 42-43.

[2] George V. Wigram and Ralph D. Winter, *The Word Study Concordance*, (Wheaton, Illinois: Tyndale Publishing House, 1978), 227-228.

[3] I.K. Cross, *The Battle for Baptist History,* (Columbus, Georgia: Brentwood Christian Press, 1990), 10-11.

[4] Ibid.

[5] Elmer L. Towns, *Theology for Today*, (Orlando, Florida: Harcourt Custom Publishers, 1997), 457.

[6] John T. Christian, *A History of the Baptists*, vol. 1, (Texarkana, Ark.-Tex.: Bogard Press, 1922),13.

[7] It should be noted that Dr. John T. Christian was a chief historian of Southern Baptists whose two volume history of Baptists was the chief textbook in Southern Baptist seminaries for many years.

[8] J.R. Graves, *Old Landmarkism: What Is It?*, (Texarkana, Texas: Bogard Press, 1880), 25-72.

[9] Carl Deimer, *Church History* class notes, Lesson 1.

[10] It should be noted that the winners kept most of the records. Both Roman and church state persecutors (1) destroyed the records of true Christians and churches and (2) wrote skewed and biased accounts of their own.

The Proliferation of Churches

Year (in A.D.)	
Feb 27	First Church established (Matthew 10:1-14, 16:18-19; 1 Corinthians 12:28)
Apr 27	The Cross (Matthew 26-27)
Jun 27	Pentecost (Acts 2)
36	Paul saved (Acts 9)
41	Cornelius Gentiles Acts 10
43	Antioch (43)
45	Paul sent from Antioch Acts 13 — Galatian Churches (45-47), Troas
50	Philippi (50), Thessalonica (51), Corinth (52-53), Colossae, Cenchrea, Rome (Mid 50s), Crete
54-57	7 churches of Asia (54-57): Ephesus, Smyrna, Pergamos, Thyatira, Sardis, Philadelphia, Laodicea
60	Alexandria, North Africa
70	Churches proliferate Acts 8:4 — Bithynia, Britannia (Wales), Britannia (England), Gallia (France), Abyssinia (Ethiopia), Spain

[1] Edward Reese, *The Chronological Bible,* (Nashville, Tennessee: E.E. Gaddy and Associates, Inc. Publishers, 1977)

Chapter 2

Persecution by Pagans

Paul predicted, *"Yea, and all that will live godly in Christ Jesus shall suffer persecution,"* **2 Timothy 3:12**. Though zealous persecution of Christians has continued to the present, the years immediately following Paul's prophecy continuing until the Edict of Milan in A.D. 313 constitute one of the most striking eras of persecution against Christians to ever occur. (After defeating rivals in northern Rome at the battle of Milvian Bridge, Roman generals Constantine and Licinius met and formed an alliance. A part of their agreement was that the persecution of Christians would stop. As we shall later see, this did not fully end the persecution of Christians by Rome; however, for a brief period of time government persecution was greatly diminished. [1]) The official stance of the Roman government and society was the worship of many gods, all considered to be pagan in light of biblical Christianity. Thus during this time, Rome was considered to be a pagan society with a pagan government and a pagan system of religion. Thus this era of Roman persecution against Christians who strictly adhered to first-century Christianity is commonly called *pagan persecution* as opposed to the era of *Christian persecution* that followed. Centuries of horrendous persecution against those who stayed with first-century Christianity continued after Rome officially became a *Christian* nation. The two eras of major persecution should not be confused.

Here are key points to keep in mind as we move through this presentation:

1. We are considering an era of almost 300 years. Conditions, situations and persecution were not uniform throughout the period. Toward the end of the era the picture was much, much different than it was early in the era.

2. As a general rule, persecution grew more widespread and progressively worsened throughout these years.

3. Beliefs within the Christian community were not uniform. Do not assume that all who called themselves "Christian" held the same beliefs. There was great diversity of opinions, and the general drift was progressively away from biblical Christianity and its beliefs.

4. Persecution prevailed across belief lines. Sound believers and churches and those that strayed far from the apostles' doctrine suffered persecution side-by-side.

5. There never ceased to be a Christian community or churches that insisted on biblical beliefs and Christianity. Even within this tighter circle there was diversity; however, these more or less embraced the core beliefs and practices of Christianity espoused by Jesus and the apostles.

6. In addition to persecution, many other titanic struggles were going on in the Christian community. Some of these will be examined in other chapters. This chapter is limited primarily to the persecution of Christians in the years before Emperor Constantine professed to be a Christian and made Christianity the official religion of the Roman Empire.

> **Paganism is the embracing of gods other than the God of the Bible**

INITIAL PERSECUTION BY THE JEWS

Until A.D. 70, persecution against Christians came mainly from the Jews. Roman leaders viewed Christianity as a part of Judaism. Theirs was a *hands-off* policy except as it became necessary to keep the Jews from rebellion and civil strife. That the Romans were not interested in the Jew's religion is well illustrated in Gallio, the Roman magistrate in charge at Corinth. When local Jewish leaders made insurrection against Paul for preaching Christ and brought him to the Judgment Seat, "*Gallio said unto the Jews, If it were a matter of wrong or wicked lewdness, O ye Jews, reason would that I should bear with you: But if it be a question of words and names, and of your law, look ye to it; for I will be no judge of such matters. And he drave them from the judgment seat*," **Acts 18:14-16**. ("Drave" is from the Greek word <u>apelauno</u> which means *to drive*.) ²

The early Christians did not see themselves as detached from Judaism; rather they viewed Christ and all that goes with Him as the fulfillment of Old Testament claims and prophecies. They saw themselves as the inseparable extension of Old Testament teachings.

Whereas the Romans viewed Christianity as a part of Judaism and Christians saw themselves as the fulfillment of God's salvation plan for all men, the Jews did not. To orthodox Jews, Christianity was something wholly different. In fact, they saw it as a direct affront, a corruption of their religion and a threat. To them Jesus' claim that He was God was blasphemy, **Matthew 26:65**. In their opinion if Jesus was God, He was a second and separate God from Jehovah. To them Christianity meant more than one God (polytheism) as opposed to their monotheistic concept, **Deuteronomy 6:4**. Furthermore the Christian stance that Jewish customs such as circumcision and the keeping of the sabbaths were fulfilled in Christ and were not necessary for salvation was considered a direct affront to Judaism, **Colossians 2:16-17**.

The Jewish leadership beat and threatened the apostles, **Acts 5:40**, stoned Stephen to death, **Acts 7:57-60**, "*and Saul was consenting unto his death. And at that time there was a great persecution against the church which was at Jerusalem; and they were all scattered abroad throughout the regions of Judaea and Samaria, except the apostles. And devout men carried Stephen to his burial, and made great lamentation over him. As for Saul, he made havock of the church, entering into every house, and haling men and women committed them to prison. Therefore they that were scattered abroad went every where preaching the word*," **Acts 8:1-4**. Once Paul converted to Christianity and began to evangelize the Christian message, he too became a target of Jewish persecution, **Acts 18:12-17; 21:26-31, 24:1-9, etc**.

When the Romans destroyed Jerusalem and the Temple in A.D. 70, the Jewish leadership was broken and dispersed abroad. By this time Christianity was increasingly composed of Gentiles (non-Jewish people) and Gentile churches moved away from Jewish power and influence. Jewish domination of Christianity and church life waned rapidly.

> **A.D. 70 was a major mile marker in Jewish and Christian history**

PERSECUTION BY PAGAN ROMANS

How Pagan Persecution Developed

Jews hastened to tell Roman authorities that Christians were not a part of the Jewish religion. This is evidenced by Turtullus' speech to Felix, the Roman governor at Caesarea, **Acts 24:1-9**. Subsequently, Rome began to recognize Christianity as a force of its own, a movement that was not identical to Judaism. At first heathen statesmen and authors "considered the Christian religion as a vulgar superstition, hardly worthy of their notice." [3]

Once Rome came to view Christianity as a separate religion from Judaism, she began to persecute Christianity as a *religio illicita* or "illegal religion." [4] Tertullian, who was born about A.D. 150, said of Christians, "we are held to be wicked, senseless, worthy of punishment, deserving of ridicule." In his fourth apologetic defense, Tertullian accused Roman magistrates of decreeing against Christians, "It is not lawful for you to exist." [5] This "was the constant reproach of Christians." [6]

Despite her claims and practices of religious tolerance, Rome was fundamentally intolerant. The Roman state was thoroughly interwoven with heathen idolatry and made religion a tool of the state. The Roman state was considered the highest good, and there could be no religion outside the recognition and control of the state. "There could be no private religion." [7] The state must control all religion, but Christians saw God as in control. Their allegiance was first to God and then to the state. A clash was inevitable.

16

> **Religious allegiance is an issue with which secular states have struggled throughout history**

Reasons Why Pagans Persecuted Christians

- **Christians accepted one and only one God**

  Rome took great pride in its *religio licita* or "religious liberty." When the Romans conquered the Greeks in the first century B.C., they adopted the Greek religion as their own and simply renamed the Greek gods. Soon the Roman Emperors were seen as gods and as such were to be worshipped. Furthermore the people groups conquered by Rome had gods and religious systems of their own. Rome officially recognized and accepted all of these religious systems along with their gods. These were known as *mystery religions*. An individual could embrace whichever religion or sect that he might wish; however, he must acknowledge all of the others as legitimate. He must also believe in the entire Roman Pantheon of gods. He must also offer to and worship the Emperor. As long as one properly expressed allegiance to all of the official Roman gods and religions, he was free to worship his own god(s) and practice his preferred religion as he might see fit.

  Christians believed there is only one true God and Savior and that He is Jesus Christ, **Acts 4:12**. They refused to worship or acknowledge any other god as legitimate, **Exodus 20:3-5, Matthew 4:10**.

  That Christian stance directly clashed with Roman beliefs and practice. For example, Roman authorities saw worship of the ruling emperor as a both a means of unity and a test of loyalty. [8] Christians consistently refused to offer to and worship the emperors. They were thus accused of disloyalty and sometimes of treason. Christianity was not recognized as a legal sect by the Romans and was thus an illegal religion. It was seen as a private and secret society. In the Roman mind there could be no private religion. Thus Christianity became increasingly perceived by Rome as an affront and a threat to the state. [9]

- **Christian practices often generated suspicions and antagonism**

  Christians had no visible god to add to the Roman Pantheon. They stood and prayed with their eyes closed; and they had no altars, idols, priests, processionals and no visible object of worship. To the Romans this was nothing but atheism. Before Polycarp was burned at the stake in Smyrna, the judge ordered him to cry, "Out with the atheists." Polycarp turned to the huge crowd in the arena and said, "Yes. Out with the atheists." The judge promised to free him if he'd simply acknowledge the emperor and other gods. Polycarp said these words, "For eighty-six years I have served him, and he has done me no evil. How could I curse my king, who saved me?" [10]

  Some Christians were not sure about military service. This coupled with their refusal to worship the emperor created suspicions of disloyalty to Rome. Christians were sometimes not allowed to serve as soldiers.

  Furthermore the secrecy of the meetings of the Christians generated suspicions, antagonism and charges of immorality. Their *eating and drinking* the body and blood of Jesus during the Lord's Supper brought charges of cannibalism. Their practice of greeting each other with a holy kiss was twisted into charges of incest, homosexuality and other activities repugnant to the Roman mind. That these charges were untrue was of little consequence to the Romans. [11]

- **Christians were enthusiastic, zealous and evangelistic**

  Zeno's philosophy of Stoicism and no emotion permeated Roman society. Christians were warm, hospitable and emotional people who were excited about their relationship to Jesus Christ. This brought them the scorn of many Romans. [12]

  Christians actively recruited new believers to their faith. To Romans this was offensive.

- **Christians believed in the equality of all men before God**

  Paganism insisted on an aristocratic structure in which the privileged few were served by the lower class and slaves. [13]

Christianity placed masters and slaves on equal footing and of equal worth before God. In Christ there is no distinction between males and females or the rich and poor. This brought the ire and scorn of the rich, privileged and class-conscious Romans. [14]

Additionally Christians tended to separate themselves from pagan gatherings at temples, theaters and places of recreation. These non-conformist practices brought the usual resentment and scorn that go with non-conformist ways. [15]

- **Christian principles sometimes restricted the economy**

Paul's teachings against the worship of idols and the use of images hurt the business of the silversmiths in Ephesus, **Acts 19:27**.

"Priests, idol makers, soothsayers, painters, architects and sculptors" are some of those whose livelihoods were threatened by the teachings of Christianity. [16] It is not difficult to see why these groups were angered by the spread of Christianity and why they were quick to oppose and persecute it at every opportunity.

- **Romans believed Christians were responsible for natural disasters**

The Romans adopted and re-named the Greek gods whom they believed to be in charge of every element of nature. The twelve Olympic gods constituted their official Pantheon of gods. [17] It is noteworthy that Romans also believed in many lesser gods and goddesses.

Greek name	Roman name	Area of control
Zeus	Jupiter	Supreme ruler of all gods, sky and rain
Hera	Juno	Zeus' wife; goddess of marriage and wives
Poseidon	Neptune	God of the seas
Athena	Minerva	Goddess of wisdom, cities and agriculture

Aphrodite	Venus	Goddess of love, desire and beauty
Ares	Mars	God of war
Apollo	Apollo	God of truth, light, healing and music
Artemis	Diana	Goddess of wild things; the huntsman
Hermes	Mercury	God of speed; the messenger
Hestia	Vesta	Goddess of the hearth. Never let fire go out
Hades/Pluto	Dis Pater	God of the underworld and wealth
Hephaestus	Vulcan	God of fire; the volcano his furnace; ugly

When natural disasters occurred, Romans believed one or more of their gods were angry. They blamed the Christian God for making their gods angry. They thought their gods resented people turning from them to Christianity and retaliated by causing earthquakes, storms, famines and other natural catastrophes. Thus Christians were blamed for natural disasters and punished and persecuted as the cause (the indirect perpetrators thereof). "In North Africa arose the proverb: 'If God does not send rain, lay it to the Christians.' At every inundation, or drought, or famine, or pestilence, the fanatical populace cried: 'Away with the atheists! To the lions with the Christians!'" [18]

- **Many Christians were poor people of low social rank**

Such names as "*Tertius*" which simply means "third" in Latin [19] and "*Quartus*" which means "fourth," **Romans 16:22-23**, testify of the Roman disregard for poor people and those of low social rank. Often slaves were simply given numbers instead of names. [20] The fact that Christians gave them respect agitated many Romans.

It should be noted that especially in the earlier years of Christianity opposition to and persecution against Christians was not limited to the leadership of the Roman state. The Roman populace as a whole was against Christians and took advantage of every opportunity to persecute them. Christianity took issue with the concept of false gods which was thoroughly integrated into Roman society. The Christian lifestyle was a daily affront to the morally corrupt lifestyles which characterized Rome from the emperor's house to that of the common man. Christianity intimidated Rome, and Rome rose up to persecute it both informally and formally.

> **The Roman people as a whole were very negative toward Christianity**

Christians in Pagan Courts

When Christians were taken into court, legal reasons were needed to convict them. A legal system for this purpose was developed by two pagan Romans named Lucian and Selcius. Three charges constituted the basis for much of the official persecution of Christians by Roman officials.

- **Atheism**

  Because Christians rejected the myriad of other gods embraced by Romans, they were accused of being atheists.

  Because bystanders could not see the Christian God and Christians had no symbols of him, they were accused of having no God and consequently of being atheists.

- **Treason**

  Christians refused to worship the emperor. They were thus accused of being disloyal and guilty of treason.

- **Immorality**

  The Lord's Supper was called a love feast. The Christians observed this feast once every week.

Though the Lord's Supper is a spiritual feast of love for Jesus Christ, the Romans accused the Christians of practicing regular sex orgies between themselves. Among their charges was the charge of incest. The fact that Christians often met in secret to avoid persecution and death was interpreted by the Romans as confirmation of their suspicions that Christians were practicing immorality.

Furthermore, when the Romans heard that the Christians were eating the body of Christ and drinking his blood at their love feasts, they accused the Christians of cannibalism. [21]

THREE LEVELS OF PAGAN PERSECUTION

For approximately 250 years pagan Rome persecuted Christians. Historians have largely divided these persecutions into ten groups. Persecution was constant and continual from Jesus onward and is difficult to catalogue; however, examination reveals three main patterns, and these patterns generally break down by centuries. There were two emperors of major significance in the first century who persecuted Christians. There were six in the second century and two in the third century.

Note that this part of the discussion refers only to official, government-led persecution.

Sporadic

This means persecution against Christians was not universal, and it was not continuous. During this time Christians were officially persecuted here and there occasionally. There were intervals in the official, government-orchestrated persecution; however, most Christians were constantly persecuted by their neighbors and the general populace of the empire.

This type of persecution was headed by two Roman emperors, Nero (54-68) and Domitian (81-96).

Organized

This means persecution became orchestrated and organized by imperial decree. Policies against Christians were made official throughout the Empire; however, these oppressive policies were not uniformly enforced.

This type of persecution occurred under six Roman emperors. They were Trajan (98-117), Hadrian (117-138), Antoninus Pius (138-161), Marcus Aurelius (161-180), Commodus (180-193) and Septimius Severus (193-211).

Universal

This means persecution was everywhere throughout the empire all of the time.

This was the worst time of persecution to date for Christians. There were two main periods. The first was under Decius (249-251). The second and worst period was led by Diocletian (284-305).

---

[1] Justo L. Gonzalez, *The Story of Christianity*, vol. 1, (San Francisco: HarperCollins Publishers, 1984), 107-108.

[2] James Strong, Strong's Greek Dictionary of the New Testament, (New York, Abingdon Press, 1958), ref. 556.

[3] Philip Schaff, *History of the Christian Church,* vol. 2, (Peabody, Massachusetts: Hendrickson Publishers, 2002), 40-41.

[4] Carl Deimer, Professor, *History of Christianity I*, Video Lecture 6, Liberty University DLP, 2004.

[5] Tertullian, *The Apology* 4, <u>Ante-Nicene Fathers</u>, ed. Alexander Roberts and James Donaldson, (Peabody, Massachusetts: Hendrickson Publishers, Inc., 2004), 21.

[6] Schaff, 41.

[7] Earle E. Cairns, *Christianity Through the Centuries: A History of the Christian Church,* 3rd ed., (Grand Rapids, Michigan: Zondervan, 1996), 87.

[8] Gonzalez, 16.

[9] Cairns.

[10] Gonzalez, 44.

[11] Cairns, 87-89.

[12] Deimer.

---

[13] Cairns, 89.
[14] Deimer.
[15] Cairns.
[16] Ibid., 90.
[17] David A. Fiensy, *The College Press NIV Commentary: New Testament Introduction,* (Joplin, Missouri: College Press Publishing Company, 1994). 185.
[18] Schaff, 43.
[19] Strong, ref. 5060.
[20] Deimer.
[21] Ibid.

Three Levels of Pagan Persecution

Years of Reign	Emperor	Persecution Level
27 B.C. – A.D. 14	Augustus	
14-37	Tiberius	
37-41	Caligula	
41-54	Claudius	
54-68	Nero	Sporadic persecution
69-79	Vespasian	
81-96	Domitian	
98-117	Trajan	Organized persecution
117-138	Hadrian	
138-161	Antoninus Pius	
161-180	Marcus Aurelius	
180-192	Commodus	
193-211	Septimius Severus	
222-235	Decius	Universal persecution
284-305	Diocletian	

[1] Justo L. Gonzalez, *The Story of Christianity,* vol. 1 (San Francisco, California: Harper-Collins Publishers, 1984)

Chapter 3

Pagan Persecutors and Their Tactics

In this chapter we shall look at the state-orchestrated persecution of Christians during the era of pagan Rome. Please keep in mind that this accounting covers the better part of three centuries and is far from comprehensive. As you will see, through this era the persecution of Christians gradually worsened and intensified.

Before we look at the ten predominate eras of pagan persecution, we should consider the brutality and cruelty that prevailed more or less throughout the entire period. John Foxe wrote these words, "The tyrants and organs of Satan were not contented with death only, to bereave the life from the body. The kinds of death were divers, and no less horrible than divers. Whatsoever the cruelness of man's invention could devise for the punishment of man's body, was practiced against the Christians – stripes and scourgings, [sic] drawings, tearings, stonings, [sic] plates of iron laid unto them burning hot, the teeth of wild beasts, gridirons, gibbets and gallows, tossing upon the horns of bulls. Moreover, when they were killed, their bodies were laid in heaps, and dogs there left to keep them, that no man might come and bury them, neither any prayer obtain them to be interred." [1] Mr. Foxe's account of those who martyred a man named Lawrence reflects the prevailing attitude of the Roman populace toward Christians. One of Lawrence's executioners cried, "Kindle the fire – of wood make no spare. Hath this villain deluded the emperor? Away with him, away with him: whip him with scourges, jerk him with rods, buffet him with fists, brain him with clubs. Jesteth the traitor with the emperor? Pinch him with fiery tongs, gird him with burning plates, bring out the strongest chains, and the fire-forks, and the grated bed of iron: on the fire with it; bind the rebel hand and foot; and when the bed is fire-hot, on with him: roast him, broil him, toss him, turn him: on pain of our high displeasure do every man his office, O ye tormentors." [2]

THE SPORADIC ERA

Nero (54-68)

Nero came to power in Rome in A.D. 54. At first he was reasonable and popular; however, he dreamed of grandeur and lusted for pleasure. He surrounded himself with a court to satisfy his every whim. Within ten years, rumor was that he had gone mad. [3]

On the night of June 16, A.D. 64, a great fire broke out in Rome. The fire burned for six days and seven nights and then flared sporadically for three more days. "Ten of the fourteen sections of the city were destroyed." [4] The pagan Roman historian, Tacitus, said that Nero had wanted to rebuild Rome and that while the fire raged, he burned the part he wanted to rebuild. Rumors that Nero started the big fire and that he spent most of his time in a tower dressed as an actor and playing his lyre spread rapidly.

Two areas that did not burn had high populations of Jews and Christians. Nero, needing a scapegoat, blamed the Christians for starting the fire. He then proceeded to take revenge on them by a massive persecution that was centered in the city of Rome but which spread to many other cities in the empire.

Even Tacitus, who hated Christians and thought they deserved scorn and punishment, was shocked at Nero's tactics. Please note that the following account is a purely secular source testifying to the existence of Christ and Christians in the early sixties A.D. Also bear in mind that this essay by Tacitus reflects the attitude of the day toward Christians.

"In spite of every human effort, of the emperor's largesse, and of the sacrifices made to the gods, nothing sufficed to allay suspicion not to destroy this rumor, Nero blamed the Christians, who are hated for their abominations, and punished them with refined cruelty. Christ, from whom they take their name, was executed by Pontius Pilate during the reign of Tiberius. Stopped for a moment, this evil superstition reappeared, not only in Judea, where was the root of the evil, but also in Rome, where all things sordid and abominable from every corner of the world come together. Thus, first those who confessed (that they were Christians) were arrested, and on the basis of their testimony a great number were condemned, although not so much for the fire itself as for their hatred of humankind . . . Before killing the Christians, Nero used them to amuse the people. Some were dressed in furs, to be killed by dogs. Others were crucified. Still others were set on fire early in the night, so they might illumine it. Nero opened his own gardens for these shows, and in the circus he himself became a spectacle, for he mingled with the people dressed as a charioteer, or he rode around in his chariot. All of this aroused the mercy of the people, even against these culprits who deserved an exemplary punishment, for it was clear that they were not being destroyed for the common good, but rather to satisfy the cruelty of one person." [5]

It was during this persecution that both Paul and Peter lost their lives at the hands of the Romans. Note also that Nero was in power when Paul wrote Romans 13 calling for Christian subjection to civil authorities.

Domitian (81-96)

Domitian was "a suspicious and blasphemous tyrant, accustomed to call himself and to be called, 'Lord and God.'" He treated the embracing of Christianity as a crime against the state.

Domitian put many Christians to death including his own cousin, Flavius Clemens, who was an official. He sent Clemens' wife, Domitilla, into exile. He confiscated the property of Christians. He destroyed as many of the surviving descendents of King David as he could find and tried to eradicate the family of Jesus Christ. He is credited with the deaths of Andrew, Mark, Onesimus and Dionysius the Areopagite. [6]

Though some think it was Nero who banished John to Patmos, early tradition accredits the exile to Domitian. [7] *Tradition* is the general historical opinion on such matters; however, adequate documentation does not exist to settle such matters conclusively.

THE ORGANIZED ERA

Trajan (98-117)

Trajan was a strong military man who had nothing personal against the Christians. [8] During his reign, Christianity was spreading across the empire. Without any official policy, local magistrates were dealing with Christians on a helter-skelter basis. By issuing a policy for dealing with Christians, Trajan became the first to bring about their persecution by imperial policy.

The matter of dealing with Christians was brought to a head by Pliny the Younger, who from A.D. 109-111 was governor of Bithynia in Asia Minor. Pliny noticed the phenomenal growth of Christianity and commented that the pagan temples were mostly forsaken and that the sale of sacrificial animals had dried up. To stop the progress of Christianity, Pliny condemned many Christians to death. [9]

Pliny wrote to Emperor Trajan for a clarification on how to deal with Christians. Here is Trajan's answer.

"You have taken the right line, my dear Pliny, in examining the cases of those denounced to you as Christians, for no hard and fast rule can be laid down, of universal application. [2] They are not to be sought out; if they are informed against, and the charge is proved, they are to be punished, with this reservation – that if any one denies that he is a Christian, and actually proves it, that is by worshipping our gods, he shall be pardoned as a result of his recantation, however suspect he may have been with respect to the past. Pamphlets published anonymously should carry no weight in any charge whatsoever. They constitute a very bad precedent, and are also out of keeping with this age." [10]

Hadrian (117-138)

Hadrian was of Spanish descent; he was a very educated and scholarly man. However he was morally corrupt and very moody. He ultimately succumbed to utter disgust of life. [11]

Rome prided herself for her religious tolerance and different religions were known as *religio licitas* or legal sects; [12] however, Hadrian was particularly offended by circumcision and didn't like the Jews. In A.D. 135, a significant Jewish insurrection was led against Hadrian by Bar-Kokba. Hadrian thought Christians were not much different than Jews and thus persecuted them along with Jews. Christianity was seen as a *religio illicita* or illegal sect or religion. [13]

Public sentiment against Christians was particularly high during Hadrian's reign.

Antoninus Pius (138-161)

The reign of Antoninus Pius was characterized by a large number of natural disasters. The people of Rome were filled with fury against the Christians and their *religio illicita*. The Romans were sure their gods were angry and causing these disasters because so many people were deserting them to become Christians and practice Christianity. Outbursts and vigilante activities against Christians were widespread. These were allowed by Antoninus Pius; however the persecution of Christians could have been much worse had he actively cultivated it. [14]

Philip Schaff claimed that Polycarp was burned at the stake in Smyrna in A.D. 155. [15]

It was at this point that Christians began to explain themselves in writings known as *apologies*. Christians did not want to be confused with other foreign religions. They explained their beliefs and practices in their own words. These give a look at Christians from their own perspective and constitute a very significant contribution to the historical record. Among other explanations, they made clear that they were not causing the natural disasters. [16]

> **The apologists began to emerge during this period**

Marcus Aurelius (161-180)

Marcus Aurelius was a Stoic. Stoicism is a Greek philosophy which holds that wise men should be free from passion and unmoved by either grief or joy. Marcus Auerlius didn't like Christian emotion which he saw as weakness. Because of their refusal to worship him, he considered Christians disloyal. To him loyalty to the emperor was a top priority.

He encouraged the people to take advantage of every opportunity to persecute Christians. "The apologist Melito wrote, 'The race of the worshippers of God in Asia is now persecuted by new edicts as it never has been heretofore; shameless, greedy sycophants, finding occasion in the edicts, now plunder the innocent day and night.' Furthermore the empire was visited at that time by a number of conflagrations, a destructive flood of the Tiber, an earthquake, insurrections and particularly a pestilence which spread from Ethiopia to Gallia. This gave rise to bloody persecutions, in which government and people united against the enemies of the gods and the supposed authors of these misfortunes." [17]

The famous apologist Justin Martyr was put to death in Rome during this time (A.D. 166).

Commodus (180-193)

Commodus was a brutal military man. The Roman Empire was in obvious decline. A scapegoat was needed and Commodus made Christians that scapegoat. [18]

"Only an affection he had for a Christian named Marcia abated his wrath and brutality against Christians somewhat." [19]

> **The Roman Empire had degenerated greatly by this time**

Septimius Severus (193-211)

Faced with an empire filled with dissident groups and the constant threat of civil war, Septimius Severus adopted a policy to bring about religious harmony. He proposed to bring all his subjects together under the worship of *Sol invictus*, "the Unconquered Sun." All other gods were to be accepted as long as one acknowledged the Sun that reigned above all. [20] This policy was known as syncretism. Christians absolutely refused this idea and practice.

In 202, Septimius Severus "enacted a rigid law against the further spread of both Christianity and of Judaism." [21] Serverus thought this law would stop Christians from proselytizing and thus end the spread of Christianity. It was the first attempt to silence Christians. [22] The attempt failed miserably.

Severus' response was brutal and the widespread persecution of Christians ensued. Clement of Alexandria wrote, "Many martyrs are daily burned, confined, or beheaded, before our eyes." [23]

THE UNIVERSAL ERA

Decius (249-251)

Decius resolved to return Rome to her old religion and to root out Christianity as an atheistic and seditious sect. In A.D. 250, he published an edict to all the governors of the provinces enjoining them to return to the state religion under the heaviest penalties. "This was the signal for a persecution which, in extent, consistency, and cruelty, exceeded all before it." [24] This persecution was the first to cover the entire empire and consequently produced a far greater number of martyrs than any former persecution.

The edict required every Roman citizen to annually sacrifice to (1) the Roman gods and (2) the Roman emperor. When anyone sacrificed to the gods, he was given a signed certificate called a *libellus* which said he had sacrificed to the gods. A *libellus* was a certificate of allegiance and compliance with the religious stance of Rome. Without a *libellus*, one was subject to execution. [25] "What the authorities did was to arrest Christians and then, through a combination of promises, threats and torture, try to force them to abandon their faith." [26] Many did but multitudes did not.

This persecution lasted only until the death of Decius in 251; however, many were maimed for life and many died as a result of it.

Diocletian (284-305)

After Decius there was a lull in the persecution for almost forty years. Then came Diocletian, a strong military leader whose ambition was to restore Rome to her former glory. Diocletian ended rule with the Senate and became a total dictator. At first he was sympathetic to the Christians, but his adopted son, Galerius, convinced him that Christians were a great threat to the restoration of the empire. Galerius was a radical, cruel and fanatical heathen. [27]

Despite the fact that his wife, his daughter and many of the most loyal and faithful people in his court were Christian, Diocletian determined that he would completely destroy Christianity. His goal and intent was to eradicate Christianity from the earth. He determined to destroy every Christian building, kill every preacher, confiscate and burn all Scriptures and Christian materials and turn every human from Christianity by either recanting or death. [28]

This greatest era of persecution began in the army. Most church leaders of the time thought Christians should not be soldiers; however, there were many Christians in the Roman legions. Around A.D. 295, a number of Christians were condemned to death, some for refusing to join the army and others for trying to leave it. Galerius supposed that at a critical moment of combat Christian soldiers might not obey orders. Zealous commanders ordered Christians soldiers to recant. When they refused, many in the army of the Danube were executed. Diocletian ordered that all Christians should be expelled from the legions. Things worsened and spiraled downward for Christians everywhere. [29]

In 303, Diocletian issued in rapid succession three edicts, each more severe than its predecessor. His eastern counterpart issued the fourth and worst of all on April 30, 304. "Christian churches were to be destroyed; all copies of the Bible were to be burned; all Christians were to be deprived of public office and civil rights; and last of all, without exception, were to sacrifice to the gods upon pain of death." [30]

Church leaders were hit first and hardest. As Christians fled, hid and refused to recant and surrender their sacred writings, chaos erupted. Diocletian intensified the persecution and Christians "were tortured with refined cruelty and eventually killed in a variety of ways." [31] The *libellus* was resurrected and used to enforce the persecution. It was during this time that the killing of Christians became a sport in the Coliseum and other amphitheatres throughout the empire. [32]

A.D. 303 was the greatest year of persecution. In 304 Diocletian became ill. Galerius went to Diocletian, forced him to abdicate and seized the throne. However this was unpopular in the legions, many of whom were loyal to Constantine. Civil strife grew so intense that Galerius went back to Diocletian and asked him to restore order. Diocletian refused and said that "he was quite happy growing cabbages in his retirement." [33]

The persecution continued but without the former intensity. Galerius became ill with a painful disease. Many think that the Christians convinced him that his disease was punishment from God. On April 30, 311, he made a proclamation that Christians be pardoned and that they could again worship and practice Christianity. [34] Two years later, Constantine and Licinius issued the Edict of Milan formally ending the policy of persecution. Even after this edict, persecution continued throughout the empire for several years.

> **Three million killed plus the broken and maimed**

RESULTS OF PAGAN PERSECUTION

In spite of the extent and cruelty of the pagan persecution of Christians, there were far more Christians than ever when it ended. Estimates vary that by A.D. 300 between 10 and 15 percent of the population of the empire professed Christianity. That's approximately 10 million Christians. [35] Approximately three million people died martyr's deaths during this era of persecution. [36] This is not to mention the multitudes of others who were broken, maimed and scarred in one way or another as a result of torture and abuse.

There were positive, negative and mixed results of the persecution of Christians by the pagan Romans.

Positive

The vast majority of Christians remained true to the faith. Persecution weeded out the pretenders.

The Scriptures were canonized. Christians had to decide which *sacred writings* for which they would die.

Christianity grew and churches proliferated.

Negative

Three million died for the faith in the span of about 300 years.

Many surrendered their Scriptures. Irreplaceable records were lost forever.

Deep divisions among Christians were created mainly because of the stance to be taken toward those who fell away and those who denied the faith.

An abnormal attitude and desire for persecution developed. Many thought martyrdom would earn them a better position in heaven.

Mixed

While thousands fled persecution, the gospel was spread far and wide.

While about three million died for their faith, they provided a very effective witness. Many came to Christ as a direct result of the willingness of those Christians to give their lives for the cause. Multitudes who watched from the stands as Christians laid down their lives for Christ were deeply convicted. It was common for them to ask, "What in my life is important enough to die for?" [37]

---

[1] John Foxe, *Foxe's Book of Martyrs*, ed. W. Grinton Berry, (Grand Rapids, Michigan: Fleming H. Revell, 2000), 18.

[2] Ibid., 30.

[3] Justo L. Gonzalez, *The Story of Christianity*, vol. 1, (San Francisco: HarperCollins Publishers, 1984), 33.

[4] Ibid., 34.

[5] Tacitus, *Annales,* xv. 44, *Documents of the Christian Church, New edition,* eds. Henry Bettenson and Chris Maunder, (Oxford and New York: Oxford University Press, 1999), 1-2.

[6] Philip Schaff, *History of the Christian Church,* vol. 2, (Peabody, Massachusetts: Hendrickson Publishers, 2002), 44-45.

[7] Ibid., 45.

[8] Carl Deimer, Professor, *History of Christianity I*, Video Lecture 6, Liberty University DLP, 2004.

[9] Schaff, 46.

[10] Trajan to Pliny, *Plin. Epp. X. xcvii, Documents of the Christian Church*, 4-5.

[11] Schaff, 49.

[12] Earle E. Cairns, *Christianity Through the Centuries: A History of the Christian Church,* 3rd ed., (Grand Rapids, Michigan: Zondervan, 1996), 87.

[13] Deimer.

[14] Ibid.

[15] Schaff, 51.

[16] Deimer.

[17] Schaff, 54-55.

[18] Deimer.

[19] Ibid.

[20] Gonzalez, 83.

[21] Schaff, 57.

[22] Deimer.

[23] Schaff, 57.

[24] Ibid., 60.

[25] Deimer.

[26] Gonzalez, 86-87.

[27] Schaff, 66.

[28] Deimer.

[29] Gonzalez, 103-104.

[30] Schaff, 66.

[31] Gonzalez, 104.

[32] Deimer.

[33] Gonzalez, 105.

[34] Ibid., 106.

[35] Cairns, 93.

[36] Deimer.

[37] Ibid.

Roman Emperors and Persecution

Years of Reign	Emperor	Events
27 B.C. – A.D. 14	Augustus	Jesus
14-37	Tiberius	
37-41	Caligula	
41-54	Claudius	
54-68	Nero	Fire in Rome; Deaths of Paul and Peter
69-79	Vespasian	Fall of Jerusalem
81-96	Domitian	John in exile
98-117	Trajan	State wakes up to Christianity
117-138	Hadrian	The Bar-Kokba revolt; *religio illicita*
138-161	Antoninus Pius	Natural Disasters; Christians blamed
161-180	Marcus Aurelius	Thought Christians were disloyal
180-192	Commodus	Rome in decline; Christians were scapegoats
193-211	Septimius Severus	Forbade evangelism
222-235	Decius	Return Rome to former glory; *libellus*
284-305	Diocletian	His goal: eradicate Christianity

[1] Justo L. Gonzalez, *The Story of Christianity,* vol. 1 (San Francisco, California: Harper-Collins Publishers, 1984)

Chapter 4

Something Went Terribly Wrong

TARES AND WHEAT FROM THE START

Jesus prophetically announced that error would infiltrate Christianity. He likened the spread of Christianity to a wheat field (true Christians and Christianity) interspersed with a flourishing crop of tares (false pretenders and error), **Matthew 13:24-30**. From the days of Christ and the apostles, the truth of this prophecy is evident. True Christianity found itself under general rejection and scorn. Jesus was crucified, the apostles were violently opposed, Christians were generally held in contempt and counterfeits quickly infiltrated Christianity. Paul warned, *"For I know this, that after my departing shall grievous wolves enter in among you, not sparing the flock. Also of your own selves shall men arise, speaking perverse things, to draw away disciples after them,"* **Acts 20:29-30**. *"But evil men and seducers shall wax worse and worse, deceiving, and being deceived. But continue thou in the things which thou hast learned and hast been assured of, knowing of whom thou hast learned them,"* **2 Timothy 3:13-14**. The apostle John wrote, *"Little children, it is the last time: and as ye have heard that antichrist shall come, even now are there many antichrists; whereby we know that it is the last time. They went out from us, but they were not of us; for if they had been of us, they would no doubt have continued with us: but they went out, that they might be made manifest that they were not all of us,"* **1 John 2:18-19**. *"And every spirit that confesseth not that Jesus Christ is come in the flesh is not of God: and this is that spirit of antichrist, whereof ye*

38

have heard that it should come; and even now already is it in the world," **1 John 4:3**. The apostles were still alive and *already* compromised; error and departure from the truth were in full stride. That trend has never stopped; it escalated over the centuries.

These counterfeit Christians and churches made it increasingly difficult to distinguish real Christians and true churches from pretenders that deviated to varying degrees from true biblical Christianity. Within a few years, the ranks of professing Christianity had separated into two primary divisions: (1) churches true to the teachings of Christ and the apostles and (2) churches that had largely departed from those teachings. There was a great variety of differing positions and practices even within these two classifications. Such has been the history of churches and Christianity.

TRUE, LEGITIMATE CHURCHES

When people are training to spot counterfeit money, they do not spend time studying counterfeit money. Their training is consumed with becoming experts with legitimate, genuine money. Once they become experts with the real thing, it is easy to spot counterfeits. We will apply this principle to churches. The following is a snapshot of the church in Jerusalem, the one personally established by Jesus Christ during His earthly ministry. Many churches sprang up shortly thereafter. This snapshot is indicative of most churches until the turn of the next (second) century.

The Name

- Simply *"church"* or *"body of Christ."*

- In the New Testament, the name "church" was used in two, and only two, senses.

  One hundred times it was used to refer to specific churches such as *the church at Ephesus, the church at Corinth* or to *"the churches of Galatia,"* **1 Corinthians 16:1**.

39

It was used fourteen times in a general or abstract sense in reference to the institution, just as one might speak of the car, the horse or the peanut; *"I will build my church,"* **Matthew 16:18**; *"Unto him be glory in the church,"* **Ephesians 3:21**. Wherever there's a church, He's to receive glory in it!

The Relationships Among Members

- **Each member had an inner, or personal, relationship with Jesus Christ.**

Salvation was not by association with the church or by sacramental rituals.

- **Members had an outer relationship with other members.**

They were an organized body of believers banded together to keep the ordinances and carry out the great commission. **Matthew 28:19-20**

They met together regularly for worship and fellowship. **Acts 2:42**

- **The members had a relationship to the whole world.**

Their ministry was to evangelize the world. **Acts 1:8**

They viewed reaching the world as their task. They were not isolated and detached from the world.

The Government of the Churches

- **The pastoral leadership was chosen by God.**

Pastors and missionaries didn't call themselves. *"The Holy Ghost said, Separate me Barnabas and Saul for the work whereunto I have called them,"* **Acts 13:2**. *"And I thank Christ Jesus our Lord, who hath enabled me, for that he counted me faithful, putting me into the ministry,"* **1 Timothy 1:12**.

- **Each church chose its own general servants.**

Deacons. *"Wherefore, brethren, look ye out among you seven men of honest report, full of the Holy Ghost and wisdom, whom we may appoint over this business,"* **Acts 6:3**.

Note: (1) honest with good reputations, (2) spiritual men and (3) wise.

- **No hierarchy**

  There was no ranking of believers. There were different offices and ministries, but all members were equally important to God. The pastors were no more precious to God than the weakest member.

  There was no idea of apostolic succession. According to this concept, only those who received authority from a successive line of church bishops dating back to the apostles were allowed to serve as priests or bishops. Those in this hierarchy were considered to be direct spiritual successors of the apostles and were viewed as separate and above common members. This hierarchy controlled church leadership and passed it from generation to generation. In true churches, God sometimes selected the least likely candidates for church leadership roles. **1 Corinthians 1:26-31**

The Ordinances of the Churches

- **Ordinances were memorials (regular reminders).**

  They were never intended to convey or guarantee salvation or the grace of God.

  To qualify, an ordinance had to meet three tests.

  o It had to be commanded by Christ.

  o It had to present the gospel.

  o It had to be practiced by the early church.

- **The churches in A.D. 100 kept two ordinances plus Sunday worship.**

  Baptism (Emphasis on the burial of Christ)

  o Who? Only believers. No infants

  o How? *Baptizo*. Always immersion

41

o No waiting period. **Acts 16:33**. *"Straightway"*

o Always considered the door to the local church

The Lord's Supper (Emphasis on the death of Christ)

o Who? Only members of a local church

o The elements were never considered to be literal.

Sunday worship (Emphasis on the resurrection of Christ)

o Always Sunday and every Sunday. **Hebrews 10:24-25**

o Other meeting times were never a substitute for Sunday.

The Worship of the Churches

• The meeting places were anywhere and everywhere, including homes. At that time the idea of big, nice church buildings didn't exist.

• **There were five formal acts of worship.**

They sang. *"Let the word of Christ dwell in you richly in all wisdom; teaching and admonishing one another in psalms and hymns and spiritual songs, singing with grace in your hearts to the Lord,"* **Colossians 3:16**.

They prayed. *"When they had prayed, the place was shaken where they were assembled together; and they were all filled with the Holy Ghost, and they spake the word of God with boldness,"* **Acts 4:31**.

They gave. *"Upon the first day of the week let every one of you lay by him in store, as God hath prospered him, that there be no gatherings when I come,"* **1 Corinthians 16:2**.

They observed the Lord's Supper. *"And upon the first day of the week, when the disciples came together to break bread, Paul preached unto them,"* **Acts 20:7**.

They preached God's Word. Preaching was first and foremost. *"It pleased God by the foolishness of preaching to save them that believe,"* **1 Corinthians 1:21**. *"I charge thee therefore before God, and the Lord Jesus Christ, who shall judge the quick and the dead at his appearing and* *his kingdom; Preach the word; be instant in season, out of season; reprove, rebuke, exhort with all longsuffering and doctrine,"* **2 Timothy 4:1-2**.

The gospel was central. Meetings didn't count if the gospel was absent.

THEIR CORE BELIEFS

There was a uniformity of beliefs among churches from the start. That is not to say that every church believed exactly the same on all points. A look at the seven churches in Asia Minor, **Revelation 2-3**, shows serious differences; however, there was a core of central beliefs held in common by all. At the beginning all churches and Christians believed that:

- Jesus Christ was the founder of the institution and the head of each church in particular. **Matthew 16:18; Colossians 1:18**

- The Bible was the only rule of faith and practice for Christians and churches. **2 Timothy 3:15-17**

- The name of the institution and individual congregations was "church." **Matthew 16:18; Revelation 22:16**

- The government of the church was congregational. **Acts 6:2-6**

- Salvation came only by grace through personal faith in Christ. **Ephesians 2:8-9**

- The membership of each church was to consist of only persons saved by a personal relationship with Jesus Christ through faith. **Acts 2:47**

- Believer's baptism was essential to membership in a church. **Acts 2:41**

- Only believers were eligible for baptism. **Acts 8:36-37**

- Baptism must be by immersion. **Acts 8:38-39**

- The ordinances of the church were memorial, not redemptive, **1 Corinthians 11:24-25**, and they consisted of believer's baptism followed by the Lord's Supper. They also kept Sunday as their day of worship. **1 Corinthians 16:2**

- The permanent officers of each church were pastors and deacons. **Philippians 1:1**

- The mission and work of each church was to get people saved, baptized and taught to maturity. **Matthew 28:19-20**

- God's plan for financing the church and its work was tithes and offerings from the membership. **2 Corinthians 9:6-7**

- Each church was to be autonomous from external control, both ecclesiastical and secular. **Matthew 22:21**

- The weapons of Christian warfare were spiritual, not carnal. **2 Corinthians 10:4; Ephesians 6:10-20** [1]

A SNAPSHOT OF COUNTERFEIT CHURCHES IN A.D. 325

In less than 300 years, a large number of Christians were drifting away from the original moorings of Christianity. Here is a look at widely embraced core beliefs and practices by multitudes of professing Christians and churches by the year A.D. 325. Please note the amazing contrast with first-century Christianity. **Note well** that this represents many churches and professing Christians, but not every individual church and Christian. There were vast numbers that stayed true to first-century Christianity.

Sacramentalism (A change in the nature of faith and salvation)

Sacramentalism is the belief that salvation comes through baptism and the Lord's Supper. Salvation had become institutional through a church instead of through an individual's faith in Christ.

Baptism became essential to salvation; it was no longer only a picture of the death, burial and resurrection of Christ and the door to church membership.

Baptism by sprinkling. By this time three methods of baptism were being practiced: affusion (pouring), aspersion (sprinkling) and immersion (dunking).

Infant baptism. Since many believed that baptism saves, they deduced that babies must be baptized in order to be saved. They worried that small babies might drown, if immersed. For safety they turned to sprinkling babies. Sprinkling was then applied to the sick and elderly. With time the practice became common.

Last Rites or Extreme Unction. This was a baptism at life's end just to be sure the individual was saved. It was administered in case the first baptism was invalid or salvation had been lost along life's way.

Sacerdotalism (A change in the nature and perception of *ekklesia* or church)

Sacerdotalism is the idea that a set of special priests is necessary to administer the sacraments. Sacramentalism demands Sacerdotalism.

The New Testament speaks of the priesthood of every believer. **Revelation 1:6**. However the new way of thinking reasoned that a select group of church leaders would be priests who would administer salvation to individuals through baptism and the Lord's Supper.

This reasoning was followed by the belief that there should be a bishop over the priests. Then came the Metropolitan bishops (authority over two or more churches in one city), the Archbishops (authority over the Metropolitan bishops of several cities or regions) and the Cardinals (over a large region of Archbishops). Later came the Pope who was the head of the whole system.

A hierarchy was thus established in churches. All members were no longer equal before God; some were more important than others. The Pope was over the Cardinals who were over the Archbishops who were over the Metropolitan bishops who were over regular bishops who were over the priests who were over the elders who were over the deacons who were over the men in the pew.

Ritualistic Worship (A change in the way worship was conducted)

The pastor became a priest. A priest is one who stands between man and God. The belief evolved that a man could only get to God through a church priest. The priests assumed power to cut men off from God. From this, "Auricular Confession," meaning to confess to the ear of a priest, was born. The idea is that worshippers must go through a church priest to have their sins forgiven.

The Mass was born. Mass is from the Latin word <u>missa</u> which means "to dismiss." The priests conducted a worship service which included singing, a message and a celebration of the broken body and shed blood of Christ. At a point in the service, the common people were dismissed with the exhortation to go in peace. In time the entire worship service became known as "the Mass" which is the name for the dismissal.

By the 13th century, the Mass had fully developed with the use of full pomp and ceremony and became the main part of the worship service. Throughout Europe it was always said in Latin even though those of other languages did not understand Latin. The priest customarily took the bread during the Mass, turned his back to the audience, lifted the bread to the altar and said *hoc est enim corpus meum* meaning "for this is my body." At that point the bread was thought by some magical means to literally become the body of Christ. This is where some believe the term *hocus-pocus*, the term for "magic," originated. [2]

POINT BY POINT CONTRAST

The deep departure of many churches from the core beliefs and practices of biblical Christianity is evident when the original churches are compared with those of 300 years later.

ORIGINAL CHURCHES	CHURCHES IN A.D. 325
Church and churches	Church visible and universal
Jesus the head of each church	Church headed by a system of priests
Each member equal; no hierarchy	Members not equal; hierarchy
The Bible the only rule of faith and practice	Tradition, the chief rule
Congregational government	Episcopalian government
Salvation by faith in Christ alone	Salvation thru rites and rituals
Membership of saved only	Membership of partakers of rituals
Members consisted of baptized believers	Membership by baptism, not belief
Only the saved eligible for baptism	Faith in Christ not a baptism prerequisite
Baptism only after a profession of faith	Infant baptism
Baptism by immersion	Baptism by sprinkling or pouring
Ordinances memorial	Ordinances redemptive
Permanent officers: pastors and deacons	Permanent officers: a system of priests
Freewill giving	Forced giving
Each church autonomous	State church
Spiritual warfare	Physical force

---

1 J.M. Carroll, *The Trail of Blood*, (Lexington, Kentucky: Ashland Avenue Baptist Church, 1992), 4-5.

2 Carl Deimer, Professor, *History of Christianity I*, Video Lecture 11, Liberty University DLP, 2004.

Core Beliefs of True Churches

Matthew 16:18	Jesus Christ is the founder and head of each church
2 Timothy 3:15-17	The Bible is the only rule of faith and practice for Christians and churches
Revelation 22:16	The name of the institution and individual congregations is church
Acts 6:2-6	The government of the church is congregational
Ephesians 2:8-9	Salvation comes only by grace through a personal faith in Christ
Acts 2:47	The membership is to consist of only persons saved by a personal relationship with Jesus Christ through faith
Acts 2:41	Believer's baptism is essential to membership in a church
Acts 8:36-37	Only believers are eligible for baptism
Acts 8:38-39	Baptism by immersion
I Corinthians 11:24-25	The ordinances of the church are memorial, not redemptive, and consist of believer's baptism followed by the Lord's Supper
I Corinthians 16:2	They kept Sunday as their day of worship

The History of Churches

Core Beliefs of True Churches

Philippians 1:1 — The permanent officers of each church are pastors and deacons

Matthew 28:19-20 — The mission and work of each church are to get people saved, baptized and taught to maturity

2 Corinthians 9:6-7 — God's plan for financing the church and its work is tithes and offerings from the membership

Matthew 22:21 — Each church is to be autonomous from external control either ecclesiastical or secular

Ephesians 6:10-20 — The weapons of Christian warfare are spiritual, not carnal

The History of Churches

Chapter 5

The Rise and Ramifications
of False Doctrine
and Practice

We have considered the fact that from the time of the first church in Jerusalem and those apostolic churches that proliferated in the first century to the time of the Nicene Council in A.D. 325, something went terribly wrong. Doctrine radically changed and so did policies and practices. This chapter will take a look at some of the specific changes for the worse. It will demonstrate the truth of Paul's prophetic claim in **2 Timothy 3:13**, *"But evil men and seducers shall wax worse and worse, deceiving, and being deceived."*

The sentiment of the general Roman populace was overwhelmingly anti-Christian. With the passing of time, the Roman government officially persecuted Christians and warred against Christianity. Christianity also faced opposition and corruption from within its ranks, from those professing to be Christians. Keep in mind that these internal struggles were going on at the same time external persecutions were widespread and intense. The internal attacks and the corruption of pure, biblical Christianity can be loosely grouped under four broad headings, which are heresies, pagan corruptions, false views of Christ and the Trinity, and lowered Christian standards.

HERESIES

From a biblical standpoint, heresy is a view contrary to the Scriptures. Peter said, *"But there were false prophets also among the people, even as there shall be false teachers among you, who privily shall bring in damnable heresies, even denying the Lord that bought them, and bring upon themselves swift destruction. And many shall follow their pernicious ways; by reason of whom the way of truth shall be evil spoken of,"* **2 Peter 2:1-2**. Many historians have skewed the true definition. They define heresy as a view contrary to the positions embraced by orthodox Christianity. [1] A heretic is thus viewed by such thinkers as someone who does not hold the positions of orthodox Christianity and "orthodox Christianity" is thought to be the positions and practices of those with the most power and the biggest operations. A person may fully subscribe to the positions of the Bible, but if his positions are in conflict with the positions of those who claim to be orthodox or mainline, he is labeled as a heretic. His views and practices are viewed as heresy. The pattern of history has been that professing Christians in positions of greatest power have defined *heresy* and *heretic* to their own suiting and acted against their opposition accordingly. Those in power always see themselves as the *orthodox* Christians and what they say to be right. Those who oppose them are viewed as the *heretics*.

In this study, the word *heresy* is used primarily in the biblical sense, which is the belief that any view contrary to Scripture is heresy. The word *heretic* is used in reference to a person who embraces a view contrary to Scripture.

Heresy is a view contrary to scripture.

A heretic is a person who embraces a view contrary to scripture.

Two major types of heresy soon sprang up in the early days of Christianity. One was Jewish; the other was Gentile. Both began to invade and corrupt Christianity.

Jewish Legalism

The Jewish heresy was legalism. Judaism taught that salvation came by keeping the Levitical Law. Many Jews rejected the Christian concept of grace, which is God's free gift of salvation to each individual through belief (faith) in Jesus Christ as personal Saviour. They insisted that in order to be saved a person must keep certain aspects of the Law such as circumcision and the Sabbath. Ideas on how exacting the legal requirements must be varied, but the general belief of Jewish religious leaders was that salvation was not possible by grace alone through faith in Christ. Legalism is the concept that there is something that one must do in order to achieve a right relationship with God. Legalism embodies the concept of works. It is based on the belief that God recognizes the good things people do and gives them credit toward salvation for their works. It is the key idea and element of all worldly, human-conceived religions that salvation is in what man does for God.

This concept says salvation is not by grace through faith alone. It fully contradicts the vintage Christian teaching that salvation is neither achieved by what man does for God nor is it maintained thereby. A key idea and element of Christianity is that salvation is what God does for man.

A form of legalism continues to flourish throughout professing Christianity. In the early days of Christianity, there were two groups of Jewish legalists.

> **Legalism is a concept of works**

- **Judaizers**

  Judaizers were Jews from Judah who taught that salvation was impossible apart from keeping certain parts of the law. They taught that faith in Christ is not enough apart from certain works. They are identified and briefly described in **Acts 15:1**, *"And certain men which came down from Judaea taught the brethren, and said, Except ye be circumcised after the manner of Moses, ye cannot be saved."* Their main points of emphasis were that salvation depends on (1) obedience to the law, (2) circumcision and (3) baptism.

The book of Galatians is devoted largely to a rebuttal of the Judaizers.

- **Ebionites**

These Jews carried the "works" heresy into the second century. *Ebionite* is from a Hebrew word meaning "poor." It is believed that they assumed their name from **Matthew 5:3**, *"Blessed are the poor in spirit: for theirs is the kingdom of heaven."* They saw themselves to be exclusively the poor and needy of whom Jesus spoke.

The main characteristic of the Ebionites was their denial that Jesus was virgin born. They thought Jesus was the Messiah, but that He had an ordinary birth and was not divine. [2] They argued that acceptance of Jesus as God was a belief in two Gods. To them Jesus had to be less than God. [3]

Ebionites believed that a divine power came on Jesus at His baptism because of His perfect holiness but that this divinity left Him when He died on the cross. They accredited His miracles and divine wisdom to this divine power. [4]

Ebionites rejected all New Testament books and embraced only one book, a spurious book called *The Gospel to the Hebrews.* They believed that circumcision and keeping the whole law were necessary to salvation, that Paul was an apostate and heretic, and that Christ would soon come again and set up the Millennial Kingdom. [5] This heresy kept many Jews from coming to Christ.

Gentile Philosophy

In the early days of Christianity, three main false Gentile philosophical heresies infiltrated Christianity. There were others.

- **Gnosticism**

Gnosticism was the most wide-spread, corrupting heresy of early Christianity. Well before the end of the New Testament, the seeds of Gnosticism were taking root. Gnosticism is from the Greek word for knowledge which is gnosis. Gnostics claimed to have higher knowledge than anyone. Theirs was a *We know what you don't know* mentality. Their source was a mystery; however, they claimed superior knowledge. Paul warned about this problem. *"O Timothy, keep that which is committed to thy trust, avoiding profane and vain babblings, and oppositions of science falsely so called: Which some professing have erred concerning the faith,"* **1 Timothy 6:20-21**.

Gnosticism centered around the question of evil and its source. Gnostics claimed to know the answer. They said evil is resident in material things. Thus, material things are bad and spiritual things are good. They allegorized the Scriptures and imposed hidden meanings. They misinterpreted the biblical use of *the flesh* to mean *the actual tissue*, not the old nature. They argued that since Jehovah made the flesh, Jehovah was bad. They were thus anti-Jewish and anti-Old Testament. They particularly rejected the creation and God's creating of the natural world.

Gnostics believed there is a good god but that he is not Jehovah. They thought the good god predated Jehovah and the Scriptures. They said that over time the good god generated a line of spirit beings among who was the female Sophia (wisdom). They said Sophia had a miscarriage which resulted in the *Demiurge* which is identified with Jehovah. Since Jehovah is the source of all matter and matter is evil, they believed Jehovah is the ultimate evil and the source of all evil. [6]

They believed in Christ but not Jesus. They said Christ was pure because he was a spirit, but Jesus was evil because He was flesh. They did not believe that Christ became flesh. To them Jesus Christ was really just a phantom; He only appeared to be flesh. This belief is called "Docetism" from the Greek word dakeo which means "I seem to be but I'm not." Thus Gnostics believed Christ had no incarnation, no human life, no body, no crucifixion, no death, no burial, no resurrection and no ascension. Neither did they believe in his second coming. Gnostics were thus ascetic, denying the body to enhance the spirit. [7]

Marcion was the champion of the Gnostics. For rearranging the Scriptures and establishing a canon of his own liking, Marcion was excommunicated from the church in Rome in A.D. 144. (By this time the mother church in Rome had assumed control over most churches in the city and they were viewed as part of one church in Rome. This is commonly known historically as *the Church of Rome.*) Marcion rejected all of the Old Testament and removed from the circulating New Testament books all parts that he deemed to be Jewish. He then "formed a canon of his own which consisted of only eleven books, an abridged and mutilated Gospel of Luke, and ten of Paul's epistles." [8]

Valentinus followed Marcion and was the most influential of the Gnostics. He established a school in Rome and spread Gnosticism widely in the west. [9] He is the author of the infamous and spurious *Gospel of Thomas.* [10]

As corruptive as it was, Gnosticism resulted in three good impacts on Christianity.

o   It forced Christianity to define itself doctrinally.

o   It brought about Christian schools such as the one in Alexandria, Egypt.

o   It spawned the movement that resulted in the canonization of the New Testament.

Gnosticism also instigated a very negative trend in Christianity. Some Christian leaders began to look to other places than the Scriptures for direction and guidance. This trend led to Apostolic Succession. Some Christian leaders claimed to be in a direct line of succession to the apostles. They argued that this gave them greater authority and power than those who are not in the apostolic line of succession.

- **Neoplatonism**

    Neoplatonism (New Platonism) began with a man named Plotinus, a third century teacher in Rome. Plotinus claimed to have improved on Plato.

    Neoplatonism is a form of mysticism in which the flesh is a bad thing. It contends, much like Hinduism, that one day we will all be swallowed up in the great "all" which is purely spirit. The objective of those who embrace this is to purge themselves of everything physical. [11] It too is an ascetic system of belief.

This stands in opposition to Christianity, which promises the resurrection of the body.

- **Manichaeism**

  In many respects Manichaeism was very similar to Christianity, which is one of the reasons it was so dangerous and infectious.

  o   It was sacramental in that it believed certain acts were sacred.

  o   It was ascetic and did not appeal to the flesh.

  o   It claimed to be Christian but was not Christian at all. [12]

  Its Persian founder was Mani who claimed to believe in Jesus Christ. He also claimed to be the *Paraclete* (an intercessor like the Holy Spirit) promised by Christ and to have divine revelation. Manichaeism's foundational teaching is that the real powers are light and darkness and the main issue of life is the struggle between the two. This belief led his followers to a very moral and ascetic lifestyle. They met to worship on Sundays, but their worship was not of the risen Savior; they worshipped the sun. [13]

  Its main impact upon Christianity was negative. Sacramentalism (salvation through baptism and the Lord's Supper) was growing and Manichaeism fostered that growth. It turned men from faith in Christ alone for salvation and made them feel that they could have salvation by doing something such as perform a sacred right or sacrament. The idea of law over grace continually asserts itself throughout the pages of history.

PAGAN CORRUPTIONS

Christianity was rapidly spreading. People throughout the Empire, who for generations had practiced all sorts of false worship, embraced Christianity. Many of them did not completely abandon their old falsehoods; they brought them right into churches and Christian circles.

There were many of these corruptions; we will consider only those with the greatest ramifications.

Fetishism

Fetishism is the placing of great emphasis upon the importance of physical objects such as a shroud, bones or the cave of a dead saint. The Catacombs of Rome are an example of undue emphasis upon a burial place.

Fetishism also places great stress on signs such as the sign of the cross and on objects of worship such as crucifixes and other religious symbols. These signs and symbols became a part of their religious life.

Female Deities

There were goddesses in almost every pagan religion. The Gnostics believed the goddess Sophia had a miscarriage which produced Jehovah. Isis was believed to be the wife of the chief Egyptian god, Osiris. Hera was the wife of the top Greek god, Zeus. People in Asia Minor where Paul did so much of his missionary work believed Cybele was the great mother of all gods. [14]

Pagans coming to Christianity were ripe for a female goddess in Christianity. They gravitated toward worship of the Virgin Mary. This corruption spread and grew rapidly.

Professionalism

Professionalism is the existence of a religious hierarchy. Unlike churches after the New Testament order, the pagan religions had hierarchies or leaders who controlled the religion. This hierarchy of leadership determined who could and could not become a leader. In churches after the New Testament order, God chose leaders who were confirmed in a congregational, democratic way by the membership, not by a self-selected and preserved group of leaders.

This corruption took hold in Christianity and soon there were bishops, who were above presbyters (pastors), who were above deacons, who were above the people. Once the idea of a professional class took root, it grew. Ultimately bishops were under archbishops, who were under cardinals, who were under a pope.

Sacramentalism

Sacramentalism is a view toward church ordinances. The pagan religions all had sacred rites and rituals. Many preachers and churches catered to the desires of incoming converts. Soon the memorial ordinances of baptism and the Lord's Supper were seen by many as sacred rites with saving powers.

Within time they were no longer viewed as memorial ordinances but as sacraments essential to salvation. This soon led to the baptism of babies in order to guarantee them salvation. These rituals went by various names, but the end result was that they were empty and could not save. Only a personal faith in Jesus Christ can bring about and guarantee salvation.

Sacerdotalism

Sacerdotalism is a big word for "priestism." [15] If sacramentalism is accepted and certain sacraments bestow the grace of God, then the right persons must administer the sacraments (the Lord's Supper and baptism). This means that only a pre-select class of officers can administer the sacraments. Sacerdotalism is a necessary accessory of sacramentalism.

This is in direct contradiction to the priesthood of every believer concept as taught in Scripture. *"And from Jesus Christ, who is the faithful witness, and the first begotten of the dead, and the prince of the kings of the earth. Unto him that loved us, and washed us from our sins in his own blood, And hath made us kings and priests unto God and his Father; to him be glory and dominion for ever and ever. Amen,"* **Revelation 1:5-6**.

> **A sacrament is something essential for salvation.**
>
> **An ordinance is a memorial.**

FALSE VIEWS OF CHRIST AND THE TRINITY

From the start, false views of who Jesus Christ was began to develop. Who Christ was continued to be a matter of controversy throughout His earthly ministry. He claimed to be God for which many accused Him of blasphemy. See **Matthew 26:64-65**.

The heart of this matter is the issue of monotheism. Could the Father be God and Jesus be God and there still be only one God as declared in **Deuteronomy 6:4**, *"Hear, O Israel: The LORD our God is one LORD?"* This one God clearly said, *"Thou shalt have no other gods before me,"* **Exodus 20:3**.

An understanding of the Father, the Son and the Holy Spirit being one God has troubled Christians from the beginning to the present. Four major views developed within the first few years of Christianity. Each was woefully inadequate.

Alogi

Alogi is a transliteration of the Greek word <u>logos</u> in its plural form with an alpha primitive ("A") which negates the word. Logos means "word" and it is used in the Bible to refer to the Word of God. Jesus was the Word of God incarnate. The Alogians were a group of professing Christians that simply rejected the claim that Jesus was God. [16]

Adoptionism

Adoptionism is the belief that Jesus was the adopted, not the eternal, Son of God. The Adoptionists thought that He became God at some point in time. It's the idea that God is one, but for short periods of time He becomes two.

Adoptionists thought Jesus became God at His baptism and ceased to be God when He went to the cross as evidenced by His statement, *"My God, my God, why hast thou forsaken me?"* **Matthew 27:46**

Adoptionists had no explanation for the virgin birth, the resurrection, the ascension and the second coming. [17]

Modalism

This is called Modal Monarchianism with "monarchianism" referring to the unity of God. It is sometimes called Sabellianism after its chief proponent, Sabellius. Sabellius (or Cybillias) lived about A.D. 200.

Modalism is the idea that in Christ, God the Father simply changed names and assumed the name Jesus. This view says God is not three persons but rather one person who changes forms to suit His purposes. [18]

Subordination

Subordinationism said Jesus was deity but a subordinate and lesser kind of deity than the Father. It was the idea of Jehovah as a capital "D" deity and Jesus as a little "d" deity. This view says Jesus was not equal to the Father. [19]

The biblical view of God is that He is a Trinity, one God in three persons. Jesus is always in voluntary submission to the Father. That does not imply that Jesus is in any way inferior or unequal to the Father.

LOWERED CHRISTIAN STANDARDS

Not only did many Christians and churches fall to false doctrine and heresy in the early days of Christianity, Christian standards of practice were also greatly compromised. Many Christians began to disassociate themselves from those who were slipping so far from the apostolic model. Some of these Christians were over-zealous and there was considerable diversity between different preachers and their followers, but they recognized the false doctrine. Some of them strayed on peripheral issues but generally stayed true to the original core teachings of Jesus Christ. Even so, an unbroken allegiance to the core teachings of Jesus Christ and the apostles is clearly identifiable within them. This allegiance to those core beliefs is traceable in differing groups (many times identified by different names) from the church in Jerusalem to the present.

Later in this book, many of these early Christians and churches will be identified along with their offspring to the present. We will look more deeply into what they believed and at much of the evidence that says they are our spiritual forefathers.

Let it be emphasized here that from the start, multitudes of Christians and churches went astray, many into total heresy. Let it be equally emphasized that not all Christians and churches went astray. Multitudes stayed true to the faith as set forth in the Scriptures. As error proliferated and more professing Christians who went astray came to power, the price of staying true to the Word of God grew increasingly costly. Not only did the pagan Romans (the populace and the government) persecute them, heretic Christians also persecuted them. Even so, multitudes never bowed their knee to pagan Rome. Furthermore they refused to follow those who deserted the faith but held on to the name of Christian.

---

[1] Carl Deimer, Professor, *History of Christianity I*, Video Lecture 7, Liberty University DLP, 2004.

[2] J.E.H. Thompson, *The International Standard Bible Encyclopaedia*, ed. James Orr, vol. 2, s.v. "Ebionism," (Grand Rapids: Wm. B. Eerdmans Publishing Co., 1956), 890-891.

[3] Deimer.

[4] Thompson.

[5] Philip Schaff, *History of the Christian Church,* vol. 2, (Peabody, Massachusetts: Hendrickson Publishers, 2002), 433.

[6] Deimer.

[7] John Rutherfurd, *The International Standard Bible Encyclopaedia*, ed. James Orr, vol. 2, s.v. "Gnosticism," (Grand Rapids: Wm. B. Eerdmans Publishing Co., 1956), 1244-1245.

[8] Schaff, 485-486.

[9] Ibid., 472-481.

[10] Deimer.

[11] Ibid.

[12] Ibid.

[13] Schaff, 500-508.

[14] Justo L. Gonzalez, *The Story of Christianity,* vol. 1, (San Francisco: HarperCollins Publishers, 1984), 15-16.

[15] Deimer, Lecture 8.

[16] Ibid.

[17] Ibid.

[18] Ibid.

[19] Ibid.

The Development of Heresies

Year (in A.D.)	
27	First Church established in Jerusalem
Before 48	Legalism - Salvation by works; keeping some aspects of the law. (see Galatians and Acts 15)
Before 61	Christ Was Not Deity - Docetism means Christ was not in a body. Asceticism means all material things are bad. (see I Timothy 6:20-21)
107	Sacramentalism Baptismal Regeneration - Ignatius of Antioch. Ordinances have saving power and are essential to salvation.
Early 2nd Cent.	Sacerdotalism - Only special priests can administer the sacraments.
2nd Century	Hierarchy - Episcopal system > metropolitan > patriarchal > papal
	Female Deities - Gnostic Sophia, Egyptian Isis and other pagan goddesses paved the way for worship of Mary.
Around 155	Universal, Visible Church View - Transitioned from local, visible view.
	Fetishism - The worship of martyrs, heroes, and relics.
About 170	Unitarianism - Alogi (Christian heretics in Asia Minor) - Rejection of the doctrine of the Trinity.
About 180	Tradition + Scripture - Departure from 100% dependence on the Scriptures.
Before 200	Infant Baptism - No certain date, but grew out of baptismal regeneration.

[1] Philip Schaff, *History of the Christian Church,* vol. 2, (Peabody, Massachusetts: Hendrickson Publishers, 2002)

[2] J.M. Carroll, *The Trail of Blood,* (Lexington, Kentucky: Ashland Avenue Baptist Church, 1992)

The Development of Heresies

Year (in A.D.)	
About 200	Modalism - God is not three in one but one who merely changes forms.
235	Mysticism with Nature - Manichaeism (major dualistic religion). Fostered sacramentalism.
Before 258	Baptism by Pouring and Sprinkling
270	Adoptionism - Jesus adopted at baptism. He was not the eternal Son.

The History of Churches

Chapter 6

A Recognized Central Authority

The vast majority of Christians in the first three centuries believed the 27 books that we now recognize as the New Testament were divinely inspired Scripture. Some who called themselves Christians didn't. As heresies and controversies proliferated, the need for a central authority became increasingly obvious.

Before the turn of the first century, the 27 books of the New Testament had been written. The Christian community and the churches overwhelmingly recognized and accepted them and them alone as divine and authoritative. Copies were circulated and read among the churches. In his letter to the Colossians Paul instructed, *"And when this epistle is read among you, cause that it be read also in the church of the Laodiceans; and that ye likewise read the epistle from Laodicea,"* **Colossians 4:16**.

It should be kept in mind that during these years the books were not yet canonized and viewed as one finalized document consisting of 27 separate books. Each was a separate book circulating on its own.

This chapter will deal with the need and circumstances which resulted in the New Testament.

UNDERSTANDING THE CANON

We use the word canon to communicate the idea that along with the Old Testament we accept the 27, and only the 27, books of the New Testament to be divinely inspired. These 27 books have been brought together as one unit and constitute the highest and final rule of faith and practice for Christians.

The word canon comes from the Greek <u>kanon</u> and is used metaphorically in reference to a measure, norm or standard. [1] The apostle Paul used the word in reference to the standard or *rule* of conduct expected of believers, **Galatians 6:16**. Athanasius [2] mentioned the "books which have been canonized." [3] This is a use of the word canon in the sense of a standard of authoritative, divinely revealed documents. [4] Most of Christianity has agreed for centuries on the books that form the New Testament. Only a very small number disagrees.

EARLY RECOGNITION IN THE CHRISTIAN COMMUNITY

Soon after the earthly life and ministry of Christ, books were written and some were almost unanimously recognized as authoritative Scripture. Acceptance of canonical books was not the work of councils; it was "a spontaneous process that went on throughout the church." [5] Towards the end of the first century the four Gospels were written and "appear to have been brought together in one collection." [6] Acts shared the same authority as Luke. From their initial writing, possibly a few years earlier than the Gospels, Paul's letters to the churches were circulated and read among the churches, **Colossians 4:16**. Paul's letters were gathered in a collection bearing the title *The Apostle.* [7] Peter mentioned multiple writings by Paul, all of which he assumed to be authoritative, **2 Peter 3:15-16**. Of the seven general letters known as the catholic letters, 1 Peter and 1 John were without substantial question. James, 2 John, 3 John, 2 Peter and Jude struggled for acceptance, and many churches, particularly in the East, rejected the Revelation. [8] All books of the New Testament were complete, or substantially complete, by A.D. 100. The majority of the writings were in existence twenty to forty years earlier. [9] Debate over James, 2 John, 3 John, 2 Peter, Jude and the Revelation continued for over 200 years, but there was wide acceptance of all except these six books. The fact is that these six books were only questioned, not rejected, by the majority.

MARCION AND THE GNOSTICS

Even before some of the New Testament books were written, the heretical theology of Gnosticism emerged and those who embraced it claimed to be Christians. Gnosticism drew elements from Judaism, eastern religions and Christianity. [10] In the early second century Marcion was the charismatic leader of the Gnostics. He was famous and highly influential. Marcion was in Rome in A.D. 140. It was then and there that he drew up the "the earliest list of New Testament books of which we have definite knowledge." [11] Marcion was passionately anti-Jewish. His canon included only eleven of the New Testament books, and even the ones he included were stripped of everything Jewish and all vestiges of creationism. It is presumed that he brought with him to Rome the New Testament text that he had used in the Black Sea area where he grew to adulthood. [12]

After Marcion's death, his followers formed a very influential group for many years. They attracted a large following, many from old-line churches. In light of Marcion's bold initiative in announcing a canon and its influence in the Christian world, Christian leaders saw the necessity of explicitly defining a true canon of New Testament Scripture. Marcion's canon necessitated a countering. [13] His canon made the need for a true canon obvious.

THE NEED FOR A CANON

One should not jump to the premature conclusion that the establishing of a New Testament canon was only a response to Marcion. There were many other factors.

False Doctrine and Practices Within the Ranks of Christianity

For example, some Montanists (not all) emphasized continued prophesying. This strong influence forced other church leaders to declare what was legitimate and illegitimate prophecy. [14] Many heresies were infiltrating Christianity. The need for a standard rule of faith and practice stood out.

Persecution and Martyrdom

The persecution and martyrdom of multitudes of Christians intensified the climate for the clear identification of a standardized body of accepted Scriptures. During the hundreds of years of great persecution, Roman authorities demanded that Christians surrender their writings. To the Romans it was important to destroy these Christian writings. Furthermore the Christian community viewed surrender of the Scriptures to the authorities to be a grievous sin. The pressure on Christians to decide what was Scripture and what was not was great. Often writings considered non-canonical were surrendered to Roman authorities while those believed to be Scripture were hidden.

Constantine's Call for Multiple Copies

Another force that heightened the need for a clearly recognized canon was Constantine's (Roman Emperor in A.D. 306 to 337 who was a Christian) call to multiply copies of the Scriptures. It is obvious that identifying what they were became highly important. [15]

OTHER FACTORS THAT LED TO A CANON

There were external factors accenting the need for a canon, but "external factors did not determine that there would be a New Testament canon nor dictate its contents. However, external factors influenced the process of definition and likely hastened that process." [16] The canon was well on its way to taking clear shape before Marcion's activity began. [17] Some of the factors that led to a canon include:

The Need for an Authoritative Standard

Christianity needed authoritative materials for various purposes, such as guidance in the moral lives of members, confessional materials and worship practices. "Material accepted as divine revelation would have been authoritative from its reception." [18] Thus, "handed down" or "received" became standard language used by the first Christian writers about the canonical books. [19]

The Passing of Time

The inspired writers and those who followed them began to die off. "The increasing of time decreased direct contact with living witnesses and put more premium on written records as aids to memory and a standard by which to evaluate teachings." [20]

Historians trace three phases in the process of canonization.

- First, certain documents of the New Testament were collected locally and quoted in works of theology without any thought of having to argue their genuineness.

- Second, in response to Marcion and the spurious Gnostic texts, Christian leaders began to investigate the canon and publish lists of genuine books.

- Finally, church councils met to validate genuine books and expose those that were spurious. [21]

THE BASIS OF AUTHENTICITY

How did early Christians know a book was divine? The books that make up the New Testament were accepted as Scripture by the vast majority of Christians and churches from the time they were written. Many other books that came on the scene were not. What was the basis by which early Christians made such judgment calls?

To be considered Scripture, a book had to meet three main tests.

Apostolic Authorship

Apostolic authorship was the first and main criterion for acceptance of a book. The apostles claimed divine inspiration. Jesus promised the apostles that he would reveal His truths to them by His Holy Spirit. He said, *"Howbeit when he, the Spirit of truth, is come, he will guide you into all truth: for he shall not speak of himself; but whatsoever he shall hear, that shall he speak: and he will shew you things to come. He shall glorify me: for he shall receive of mine, and shall shew it unto you. All things that the Father hath are mine: therefore said I, that he shall take of mine, and shall shew it unto you,"* **John 16:13-15**. Early Christians accepted that as authentic. Paul captured the sentiment of that day in his letter to the Thessalonians. *"For this cause also thank we God without ceasing, because, when ye received the word of God which ye heard of us, ye received it not as the word of men, but as it is in truth, the word of God, which effectually worketh also in you that believe,"* **1 Thessalonians 2:13**.

It was not always necessary for the apostle to personally write the book. For example, Romans includes the acknowledgment that Tertius actually penned Romans; however, the words are those of Paul. *"I Tertius, who wrote this epistle, salute you in the Lord,"* **Romans 16:22**. Neither Mark nor Luke were apostles; however, they were contemporaries who were deeply involved in the lives of an apostle (Mark with Peter and Luke with Paul). Thus the books of Mark, Luke and Acts were readily accepted as Scripture. If a book was not written by an apostle, to gain acceptance it had to have been written by someone very close to the apostles.

Pseudonymous books were regarded with great skepticism, if not rejected altogether. [22]

Pseudonymous is a reference to an anonymous author

Conformity to the Rule of Faith

As important as apostolic authorship was, it is evident that it was not the sole ground for acceptance of a written document as divine. Another requirement was *Conformity to the rule of faith,* which was "conformity between the document and orthodoxy, that is,

Christian truth as normative in the churches." [23]   It was generally recognized in the Christian community that any book that failed to meet the common standards of faith and practice was not accepted as Scripture.   There were other writings that were considered good and profitable; however, neither were they regarded as Scripture nor were they given the same position of authority.   In the earliest days the association between most churches was sufficiently tight to enable them to generally accept certain beliefs and practices as normative. In most churches, straying from that norm was usually perceived and rejected.   That can be said to be true through most of the first century, at which time all of the New Testament books were being written.   It should be noted that this condition of a normative rule of faith and practice among the churches evaporated quickly after the death of the apostles.   Many churches continued thereafter to embrace this normative standard which conformed to the apostolic pattern; a growing number did not.

A major guide along these lines was the internal make-up and claims of a book.   The book must be internally in harmony both with its own self and with the general apostolic stance.   It must bear the earmarks of divinity.   A book's authority "must be confirmed by the internal testimony of the book itself." [24]

Widespread and Continuous Acceptance and Usage in Churches

A third, but less important, criterion was a document's widespread and continuous acceptance and usage by churches everywhere. [25] Jerome accepted both Hebrews and the Apocalypse (Revelation), "in part because many ancient writers had accepted both of them as canonical." [26]   The canonical books were read widely in the churches, but other non-canonical books were read also which may help explain why some early manuscript copies of the Scriptures have non-canonical books bound with the canonical ones. [27]   It is noteworthy that inspiration was not a conscious consideration in determining the canonical status of a book.   There did not seem to be significant questioning of the divine inspiration of the apostles or of what they wrote.   The early Christians assumed that the apostles, and those close to them who wrote, were inspired. [28]

QUESTIONABLE AND SPURIOUS BOOKS

When the canon was eventually closed it included the 27 books that make up the English New Testament. There were far more books than these, and many Christians were led astray by spurious books which they mistakenly thought to be canonical. For example, Marcion claimed his mutilated book of Luke was canonical, and his followers accepted it as such. With the progression of time and the proliferation of books, the issue of which books were authoritative Scripture and which were not grew.

To make them seem authoritative, many books were accredited to one of the apostles by those who wrote and/or endorsed them. Around A.D. 120 the *Didache*, also known as *The Teaching of the Twelve Apostles*, was regarded by Clement of Alexandria and by Origin [29] as holy Scripture. [30] Early writings regarded by some as Scripture included the *Epistle of Barnabas, The Shepherd of Hermas,* the *Apocalypse of Peter* and the *Acts of Paul.* "These books hovered on the border of Canon in some sections of the country for a time, but were all rejected by and by. Many other later Gospels, Acts, Epistles, and Apocalypses appeared under the names of the Apostles which did not receive the serious consideration of the Church." [31] Eusebius [32] subdivided the disputed books into three divisions. He classified James, Jude, 2 Peter, and 2 and 3 John as generally accepted books. Into a category of books that are not genuine, he put *Acts of Paul, Shepherd* of Hermas, *Apocalypse of Peter, Epistle of Barnabas* and the *Didache.* He was uncertain about the Apocalypse. His third category, embracing clearly heretical writings, included gospels such as those of Peter and Thomas, acts of Andrew and John and similar writings. [33] It is obvious that determining canonicity became a growing problem. The potential for confusion grew. The need for an authoritative canon became increasingly clear.

ACCEPTANCE OF THE NEW TESTAMENT BOOKS

Do not assume, as many modern skeptics have, that some group of Christian leaders got together and randomly decided which books should and should not be a part of the New Testament. That simply didn't happen and no valid evidence supports the contention that it did. The evidence does prove that long before Marcion, and with acceleration thereafter, the need not only for authoritative books, but also for an authoritative set of books, grew. "Generally speaking, from the time of Irenaeus on the New Testament contained practically all the same books we receive today, and were regarded with the same reverence that we bestow on them today." [34] Irenaeus lived from approximately A.D. 130 to A.D. 200. [35] Even before Irenaeus, Polycarp used much of the New Testament in his letter to the Philippians. The *Didache* of A.D. 120 alludes to most of the New Testament books. Melito, who was pastor of Sardis in the second century, quotes from all the books of the New Testament except James, Jude, 2 John and 3 John. Lucian's Antioch Canon, which is believed by many to be the parent of the great majority of present Greek manuscripts, includes all books of the New Testament except the Apocalypse, 2 Peter, 2 John, 3 John and Jude. Eusebius seems to have accepted all 27 books, although he was uncertain about the Apocalypse. [36]

The Muratorian Canon, named after Lodovico Antonio Muratori who discovered it, is a list of canonical books originating in Rome about A.D. 190.[37] It mentions Luke as the third Gospel, apparently an acknowledgment of Matthew and Mark. It also "mentions John, Acts, Paul's nine letters to churches and four to individuals (Philemon, Titus, 1 and 2 Timothy), Jude, two epistles of John, and the Apocalypse of John and that of Peter. The *Shepherd of Hermas* is mentioned as worthy to be read (i.e. in church) but not to be included in the number of prophetic or apostolic writings." [38]

It is obvious that with the passing of time, consensus was growing in the Christian community as to which books were canonical. Even most of the preachers and churches that were departing from the beliefs and practices of the Scriptures were in general agreement on which books were authentic and which were spurious. There was a mounting recognition of an accepted canon or body of books considered to be authoritative Scripture.

CLOSING THE CANON

As long as the list was open, there were individual books of Scripture, but there was not yet an authoritative collection of books, a canon. [39] Essential elements in the concept of canon are reflective judgment and an exclusively closed list of books. As long as these elements were missing, the Christian community had a collection of authoritative books of Scripture, but it did not yet have a canon. [40] The need for a divine standard of faith and practice could not be denied.

The collection of the current 27 books of the New Testament into a canon was the work of the early Christians. These books are different from the books that were apocryphal, pseudo-apostolic or orthodox yet merely human productions. In performing this work they were "likewise guided by the Spirit of God and by a sound sense of truth." [41] The sifting, rejecting and collecting of books was not a series of sporadic events. It was a long, continuous process. Instead of being the result of a deliberate decree by an individual or a council near the beginning of the Christian era, the collection of New Testament books took place gradually over many years by the pressure of various kinds of circumstances and influences. [42] One thing must be emphatically stated: the New Testament books did not become authoritative because Christian leaders included them in a canonical list; on the contrary, Christian leaders included them in the canon because they were already regarded as divinely inspired. They recognized their innate worth and general apostolic authority, direct or indirect. [43]

The first list that includes all and only the twenty-seven books of the New Testament is the Easter Letter by Athanasius to the Alexandrians in 367. This letter is prescriptive rather than descriptive. [44] He wrote, "Again it is not tedious to speak of the [books] of the New Testament. These are, the four Gospels, according to Matthew, Mark, Luke, and John. Afterwards, the Acts of the Apostles and Epistles (called Catholic), seven, viz. of James, one; of Peter, two; of John, three; after these, one of Jude. In addition, there are fourteen Epistles of Paul, written in this order. The first, to the Romans; then two to the Corinthians; after these, to the Galatians; next, to the Ephesians; then to the Philippians; then to the Colossians; after these, two to the

73

Thessalonians, and that to the Hebrews; and again, two to Timothy; one to Titus; and lastly, that to Philemon. And besides, the Revelation of John." [45]

Two prominent and very influential early Christian leaders had a tremendous bearing on the closing of the New Testament canon and the acceptance thereof. One was Jerome who was born in A.D. 346. He was a highly educated and brilliant scholar. He lived in Bethlehem from A.D. 386 until his death in A.D. 420. In A.D. 384 he finished a translation of the New Testament into Latin. It "contained the books which we use, and, as it came more and more to be accepted as the chief Latin version, the books it contained became the generally accepted books of the Western Church." [46]

The influence of Augustine was even greater than that of Jerome. Augustine was born in A.D. 354 and became the bishop of the city of Hippo in A.D. 395. In his famous treatise on Christian learning, he listed the current 27 books of the New Testament. The greater part of this document was written in A.D. 396-397. [47]

The great debate of so many generations was practically over, but it remained for someone to say that it was over. It was Augustine who, in three provincial synods, cast his weight for the twenty-seven books now known as the Christian Scriptures. Three synods were held, one in Hippo in A.D. 393, one in Carthage in 397, and the last in Carthage in 419. [48] The synod at Carthage in A.D. 397 stands out. Augustine was there. The twenty-seven New Testament books were officially recognized and declared. [49] "The opening words of the statute on the canon are straightforward and forthright: 'Besides the canonical Scriptures, nothing shall be read in church under the name of divine Scriptures.'" [50] Other books could be read, but not as Scripture. "Twenty-seven books, no more, and no less, is henceforth the watchword throughout the Latin Church." [51]

It would be a mistake to imply that the decision of this council finally settled the issue of canonicity in all Christian communities. It did not, particularly in the East. [52] There are still several segments within Christianity whose canons differ slightly from the standard twenty-seven. Minor debate continues. "Nevertheless the worldwide church almost universally came to accept the same twenty-seven books." [53]

74

> **A synod is a meeting of church officials.**
>
> **In A.D. 397, the Synod at Carthage recognized all twenty-seven New Testament books.**

SUMMARY

No person has impacted the world like Jesus Christ. He dramatically and radically changed lives. He came, not for one generation only, but for all men. His stories and sayings must be told and preserved in writing. God raised up men for that very purpose and guided them by His Spirit in the undertaking which was His and not theirs.

The New Testament canon is the work of God. Not only did He use human instruments to bring it into existence, but the writing of the books and the gathering of them into a closed canon was clearly not orchestrated by any person or group of persons. Over several hundred years players entered and exited God's grand stage, but His project continued. He was determined to give, then consolidate and preserve, His Word.

From the first, the Christian community knew what Jesus did and said and recognized the truthfulness of the twenty-seven books as they were written. They also recognized that many writings with claims of inspiration were spurious. The passing of time made it increasingly evident that an authoritative set of documents must be officially declared. The vast majority had long recognized which ones they were. Therefore, declaring them was not a difficult task. It was simply a matter of making the obvious official. Once that was done, most of the Christian community recognized the declaration to be correct and in touch with reality. Most accepted the canon and the debate was over. Just as selecting the individual books took many years, amalgamating them under one cover that was generally recognized and accepted as authoritative and final took time, but it happened. The historical evidence supporting the authenticity of the formation of the canon is strong, and the internal evidence of the New Testament that it is the work of God remains as evident and convincing as it was to the early Christians. From its start Christianity needed a commonly recognized set of authoritative and trustworthy written documents, which is exactly what it has in the New Testament.

[1] Henry Clarence Thiessen, *Introduction to the New Testament*, (Peabody, Massachusetts: Hendrickson Publishers, Inc., 2002), 3.

[2] Athanasius was an early influential Christian leader from Alexandria, Egypt.

[3] Athanasius, *Athanasius: Select Words and Letters, Letter XXXIX, Nicene and Post-Nicene Fathers*, eds. Philip Schaff and Henry Wace, vol. 4, 2nd series, (Peabody, Massachusetts: Hendrickson Publishers, Inc., 2004), 552.

[4] Thiessen, 4.

[5] Ibid., 26.

[6] F.F. Bruce, *The Books and the Parchments*, (Old Tappan, New Jersey: Fleming H. Revell Company, 1984), 98.

[7] Ibid.

[8] Kurt Aland and Barbara Aland, *The Text of the New Testament*, trans. Erroll F. Rhodes, 2nd ed., (Grand Rapids: William B. Eerdmans Publishing Company, 1995), 49.

[9] F.F. Bruce, *The New Testament Documents: Are They Reliable?* (Downers Grove, Illinois: InterVarsity Press, 1981), 7.

[10] Hans-Georg Link, *Glossary of Technical Terms, New International Dictionary of New Testament Theology*, ed. Colin Brown, vol. 1, s.v. "Gnosticism," (Grand Rapids, Michigan: Zondervan, 1986), 58.

[11] Bruce, *The New Testament Documents*, 17.

[12] Aland, 54.

[13] Bruce, *The Books and the Parchments*, 100.

[14] Everett Ferguson, *Factors Leading to the Selection and Closure of the New Testament Canon: A Survey of Some Recent Studies, The Canon Debate*, (Peabody, Massachusetts: Hendrickson Publishers, Inc., 2004), 315.

[15] Ibid., 316-320.

[16] Ibid., 295.

[17] Bruce, *The Books and the Parchments*, 100.

[18] Ferguson, 296.

[19] Ibid., 295.

[20] Ibid., 296.

[21] David A. Fiensy, *The College Press NIV Commentary: New Testament Introduction*, (Joplin, Missouri: College Press Publishing Company, 1997), 369.

[22] Kent D. Clarke, *The Problem of Pseudonymity in Biblical Literature and Its Implications of Canon Formation, The Canon Debate*, 454-455.

[23] D.A. Carson, Douglas J. Moo, and Leon Morris, *An Introduction to the New Testament*, (Grand Rapids: Zondervan, 1992), 494.

[24] Philip Schaff, *History of the Christian Church*, vol. 1, (Peabody, Massachusetts: Hendrickson Publishers, 2002), 572.

[25] Carson, Moo and Morris, 495.

[26] Ibid.

[27] Bruce, *The Books and the Parchments*, 102.

[28] Bruce M. Metzger, *The Canon of the New Testament: Its Origin, Development and Significance*, (Oxford: Clarendon Press, 1997), 254-257.

[29] Clement of Alexandria and Origin were well-known and influential early Christian leaders.

[30] Thiessen, 6.

[31] Ibid., 7.

[32] Eusebius wrote early in the 4th century and is regarded as the father of church history.

[33] Carson, Moo and Morris, 493.

[34] Thiessen, 10.

[35] Hans-Georg Link, s.v. "Heilsgeschichte," 59.

[36] Thiessen, 12-19.

[37] Aland, 48.

[38] Bruce, *The New Testament Documents*, 17-18.

[39] Eugene Ulrich, *The Notion and Definition of Canon, The Canon Debate*, 32.

[40] Ibid., 32-33.

[41] Schaff, 572.

[42] Metzger, 7.

[43] Bruce, *The New Testament Documents*, 22.

[44] Carson, Moo and Morris, 493.

[45] Athanasius, 552.

[46] Metzger, 234-235.

[47] Ibid., 236-237.

[48] Ibid., 237-238.

[49] Carson, Moo and Morris, 493.

[50] Metzger, 238.

[51] Ibid.

[52] Ibid.

[53] Carson, Moo and Morris, 494.

The New Testament Canon

Year (in A.D.)		
27	First Church established, The Cross, Pentecost	
36	Paul saved	
41	Cornelius Gentiles	
45	Paul sent from Antioch	James (Mid 40s)
50	Many spurious books written during this time with escalation thereafter	Galatians (48)
		1 Thessalonians, 2 Thessalonians (52)
		1 Corinthians (55) 2 Corinthians, Romans (56)
60		Matthew, Mark (60) Luke, Acts (Early 60s)
		Colossians, Ephesians, Philemon, Philippians (61)
65		Hebrews (62) 1 Timothy, Titus (62/63)
		1 Peter (60s) John (65-70)
		2 Timothy (67) 2 Peter (68s)
70	Churches proliferate Acts 8:4	1 John (About 70)
		2 John
		3 John
80		Jude (Before 80s)
90		
100		The Revelation (95-96)

[1] Edward Reese, *The Chronological Bible,* (Nashville, Tennessee: E.E. Gaddy and Associates, Inc. Publishers, 1977)

[2] D.A. Carson, Douglas J. Moo, and Leon Morris, *An Introduction to the New Testament*, (Grand Rapids Zondervan, 1992)

Chapter 7

Big Names, Early Writings and a Steady Drift
Part 1

We step back to look at the earliest days of Christianity from a different perspective. Already it is clear that long before A.D. 325, multitudes of Christians and churches had departed far from *"the faith which was once delivered unto the saints,"* **Jude 3**. Jude's next statement summarizes the departure from truth that was in progress then, and which escalated dramatically over the coming years. He said, *"For there are certain men crept in unawares, who were before of old ordained to this condemnation, ungodly men, turning the grace of our God into lasciviousness, and denying the only Lord God, and our Lord Jesus Christ,"* **Jude 4**. Many of those men truly fit Jesus' prediction of *"ravening wolves"* in *"sheep's clothing,"* **Matthew 7:15**. They claimed to be Christians of great learning and authority and were held in highest esteem by masses in the Christian community. All the while they were turning multitudes of Christians and churches away from the teachings of Jesus and the apostolic faith.

Do not assume that everything they taught was a sudden departure from the biblical stance. It was not. The drift away from truth was gradual, subtle and imperceptible to most people. The differences were not enough to make a difference to the majority of professing Christians, and the drifters became quite antagonistic against those who resisted, especially those who publicly or loudly protested. To this day most of those who led much of professing Christianity away from God are held in the highest esteem. A look at the drift of Christianity away from the truth in the second, third and fourth centuries is truly a lesson in how *"a little leaven leaveneth the whole lump,"* **Galatians 5:9**.

In this chapter we will look at some of the better-known leaders of early post-New Testament Christianity. We will briefly consider a few of the key points in their writings, with emphasis upon their departures from the apostolic standard. Keep in mind that most of these early writers were pastors who wrote under enormously adverse conditions. Many of them were persecuted and lost their lives because they were Christians. Also, keep clearly in mind that this is only a miniscule sampling. There were hundreds, and soon thousands, of other churches and pastors that drifted from the faith. As we will see in following chapters, large numbers of pastors and churches stayed true to the faith that was once delivered. They never embraced the falsehoods that came to characterize what has become known as *mainline Christianity;* however, the ones we examine here are better known and exercised inordinate influence and power over the direction of mainline Christianity. They are generally known as *church fathers* or "Patristics." [1] The study of their writings is known as Patrology. Those who lived and wrote before the Council of Nicea (A.D. 325) are known as the *ante-Nicene fathers*. Those who wrote at the time of the Nicene Council are called *Nicene fathers,* while those who followed are called *post-Nicene fathers*.

UNDERSTANDING EARLY CHRISTIAN WRITINGS

In describing the general character of Ante-Nicene Christianity, Philip Schaff said, "We now descend from the primitive apostolic church to the Graeco-Roman; from the scene of creation to the work of preservation; from the fountain of divine revelation to the stream of human development; from the inspirations of the apostles and prophets to the productions of enlightened but fallible teachers." [2] He continued, "The stream of divine life in its passage from the mountain of inspiration to the valley of tradition is for a short time lost to our view, and seems to run underground." [3] Within a few decades, Christians began to write again.

The Ante-Nicene writings can be organized into four main types. They overlap time periods.

Edification (90-150)

The emphasis of the writings of this period is on edification (to teach or enlighten with the intent and hope of strengthening and encouraging). Severe persecution was growing. Believers needed encouragement. These writings are characterized by their practicality. They are informal and generally free of pagan philosophy that had not yet infiltrated Christianity. They reflect a great reverence for the Old Testament. The writers of this period are called the Apostolic Fathers because they knew the apostles. [4]

> **Edification is writing to encourage**

Apologetic (140-180)

Do not misunderstand the use of the word "apology" which is defined two ways. It is not only used to express sorrow for wrongdoing; an apology is also defined as "a statement that defends some idea, religion, etc." [5] These early writers were not expressing sorrow for Christianity; they were defending it.

The documents they wrote explain how Christians responded to their persecutions. During this time, Christians were widely accused of being atheists, cannibals, traitors and immoral people. The apologists refuted these claims. They explained what a Christian is, what a church is, who Jesus was, what it means to be converted, how Christians are to act and what they believe. It is noteworthy that they begin to quote from the New Testament books. The infiltration of Christianity with pagan philosophy and ideas is increasingly evident in these writings. By this time the Roman state was orchestrating the persecution of Christians, so these apologetic writings were addressed to political leaders, particularly to the emperors.

> **Apology is writing to explain and convince of legitimacy**

Polemic (180-260)

Polemic writings are a different genre. Webster defines polemic as "of or having to do with argument or dispute." [6] By this time, major controversies and heresies had developed within the ranks of professing Christianity. These writings are against those believed to be heretics. The New Testament books are quoted often. Most of the polemic writers were westerners who wrote in Latin.

It is noteworthy that this is the period when the idea of an orthodox (the approved form of doctrine) church had its origin. A series of departures from church truth emerged. First, the biblical idea of churches being local and independent was gradually replaced with the view that Christianity is one giant universal church. From this false concept another belief developed. It was the concept that the bigger, stronger churches that agreed on doctrine and practice constituted the true, Orthodox Church. It followed that what these churches declared to be orthodox and true was orthodox and true. All who disagreed or opposed this growing coalition were considered heterodoxical (opposed the accepted doctrine) and false. No longer did Scripture alone constitute truth, and no longer was the Word of God the final standard for truth. What *the church* (those in power) declared to be truth was considered to be truth. *The church* became the standard for truth; it determined what was right and what was wrong. Those disagreeing with *the church* were heretics. Thus, a whole new definition of orthodoxy and heresy emerged. In the new way of thinking, orthodoxy and heresy are not what the Bible says they are; they are what *the church* says they are. Very soon, *the church* with the backing of the state would start persecuting those whom it deemed to be heretics. It would do so with a cruelty that made many of the tactics of pagan Rome seem docile.

> **Polemic is writing to argue and defend against heretics and pagans**

Systematic (200-260)

During this period systematic theologies first appeared. Systematic theology tries to find all information about theological topics (like Christ, Angels, Sin, etc.) and organizes each subject into a system of study that is cohesive throughout. In reality, these *theologies* are efforts to undermine the theology of the Bible. They are full of pagan philosophy. When they deal with the Scriptures, they use the Allegorical method of interpretation. Rather than seek the literal sense of Bible words and passages, this method seeks for hidden meanings. It imposes preconceived notions upon the Scriptures and attaches all sorts of speculative, baseless and hidden meanings.

Two such theologies were written. Both authors were from Alexandria, Egypt.

Systematic theology is a planned, ordered setting forth of all theological disciplines of the Scriptures in a systematic, harmonious way

---

A CAUTION ABOUT TERMINOLOGY

Over time, the understandings of words tend to shift. This can be a natural occurrence reflecting changing social trends or it can be a deliberate alteration of the true meaning of a word. As the drift away from first-century Christianity progressed, the meaning of the word *church* shifted.

The Word Church

A case in point is the use of the word *church* and the titles given to the chief mortal officer of a church. Jesus Christ was always considered to be the head and chief officer of every church, **Ephesians 5:23**. In the Bible, the word *church* used in the main sense always refers to one local assembly of baptized believers covenanted together to keep the ordinances and carry out the great commission. [7] First century Christians understood *church* in that sense. Two or more congregations were *churches*, not *church*, **Galatians 1:2**. Thus, when they spoke or wrote about the chief mortal officer of a church, they had in mind the chief officer of one and only one church, not two or more. The concept of one man having authority over more than one church or assembly was foreign to them. It is not in the Bible. It was during Jesus' earthly ministry that He personally originated His church, **Matthew 16:18**. It did not exist prior to Jesus.

The Chief Officers of the Churches

As the New Testament defines and explains Jesus' churches (the first one promptly multiplied into many), mention is made of their chief mortal officers (some churches had more than one). "There are at least seven titles for the man of God who leads the New Testament church: (1) elder, (2) bishop, (3) pastor, (4) preacher, (5) teacher, (6) servant and (7) messenger. Each title describes a different qualification of the man and leads to a distinct duty." [8]

- **Elder**

  Elder conveys the idea of spiritual maturity. It is from the Greek word prebusteri. Thus, many early church leaders were known as presbyters. The word occurs first in **Acts 11:30** and 22 times thereafter.

- **Bishop**

  With bishop comes the connotation of oversight. This word occurs five times in the New Testament. In giving the qualifications for this office, Paul used this word in **1 Timothy 3:2**. It simply meant the chief mortal officer of one local church.

- **Shepherd**

  Shepherd is from the Greek noun poimen. It conveys the idea of looking after sheep. Since a church is sometimes seen as a flock, **Acts 20:28-29**, the word *shepherd* is a fitting title for its chief officer.

- **Pastor**

  In **Ephesians 4:11**, the King James translators translated poimen as *pastor* (the literal translation of poimen is *shepherd*). This title gained common use and has continued to the present. Among those who continue to practice first-century Christianity, this is the most common title in use to refer to the chief officer of a local church.

- **Preacher**

  Preacher connotes one who publicly proclaims the Word of God. Since the main function of the chief officer of a church is preaching, **2 Timothy 4:2,** he is sometimes referred to as the preacher. The chief officer is an explainer of the Scriptures. He is thus called a teacher, **Colossians 3:16.**

- **Servant**

  Because he is a minister to all, the Scriptures call the chief leader of a church servant or minister, **1 Corinthians 9:13-14.**

- **Messenger**

  Finally the title of *"stars"* or messengers is given to the men of God who lead New Testament churches, **Revelation 1:16,20.** The Greek word is aggelo. In the King James Bible, seven times aggelo is translated as *"angel"* in reference to the chief officers of the seven churches of Asia, **Revelation 2-3.**

The Priesthood of Every Believer

It is noteworthy that first-century Christians never referred to their church leaders as priests to denote their office in the church. As we will shortly explain, all believers are *priests* before God. Regular, ordinary members are priests just as are church leaders. In churches after the New Testament order, there is no hierarchy. Under the Old Testament Levitical system, there was a priest's office, **Exodus 28:1.** One job of the priest was to offer sacrifices, primarily lambs. These sacrifices looked forward to Jesus' sacrifice to pay our sin debt, **Hebrews 10:1-2, 10-14.** When Jesus consummated His work of redemption, there was no more need for the priest's sacrifice. In view of His work on the cross, Jesus Christ once and for all fulfilled the prophetic picture of the sacrificial lamb. He is the one and only high priest. *"...We have such an high priest, who is set on the right hand of the throne of the Majesty in the heavens; A minister of the sanctuary, and of the true tabernacle, which the Lord pitched, and not man. For every high priest is ordained to offer gifts and sacrifices...,"* **Hebrews 8:1-3.** No man can come to God except through Christ. He said, *"No man cometh unto the Father, but by me,"* **John 14:6.** This high priest is only in Heaven and not on Earth,

85

"For if he were on earth, he should not be a priest, seeing that there are priests that offer gifts according to the law," **Hebrews 8:4**.

Jesus Christ fulfilled the office of high priest; however, the Bible says every believer (not only church leaders) is a priest. This Bible doctrine is known as *the priesthood of every believer*. *"And from Jesus Christ, who is the faithful witness, and the first begotten of the dead, and the prince of the kings of the earth. Unto him that loved us, and washed us from our sins in his own blood, And hath made us kings and priests unto God and his Father; to him be glory and dominion for ever and ever. Amen,"* **Revelation 1:5-6**. That all believers are priests is stated again in both **Revelation 5:10** and **Revelation 20:6**. As priests, all believers (not only chief church officials) can bring offerings and sacrifices directly to God through Jesus their high priest. They do not bring animal sacrifices since these were fulfilled in Christ. *"For Christ is the end of the law for righteousness to every one that believeth,"* **Romans 10:4**. In view of Christ's finished work of redemption, believers offer a different sort of sacrifices and offerings. *"By him therefore let us offer the sacrifice of praise to God continually, that is, the fruit of our lips giving thanks to his name. But to do good and to communicate forget not: for with such sacrifices God is well pleased,"* **Hebrews 13:15-16**. Paul spoke of items sent by the Church in Philippi to meet his material needs as, *"an odour of a sweet smell, a sacrifice acceptable, wellpleasing to God,"* **Philippians 4:18**. In general, saved people are to offer their lives as *"a living sacrifice, holy, acceptable unto God, which is your reasonable service,"* **Romans 12:1**.

The idea that ordinary church members could not reach God apart from a mortal church official to intercede for them was in total opposition to the Bible. It was a total departure from *"the faith which was once delivered unto the saints,"* **Jude 3**.

The Shifting of Definitions and Applications

With the passing of time, those drifting from New Testament Christianity compromised the correct definitions and applications of these and other Bible words. Whereas *church* originally was a reference to one local church or body, many began to incorrectly define and use the word to refer to two or more local churches. In less than two centuries, they openly wrote that all churches constituted one church, which is the idea of a universal church.

With the change in definition of the *church* also came changes in reference to the chief mortal officers of the churches. Those drifting away from New Testament Christianity increasingly referred to chief leaders as bishops. This is partly because one man had ultimate authority over more than one congregation or church. Pastors or presbyters no longer had ultimate authority and leadership over their own local congregations. Keep in mind that not all churches followed the drift away from first-century Christianity. They retained the original definitions and applications of *church, pastor* and other such terms.

Shifting definitions can be confusing. It is important to consider who is using a given term and in what sense. The retroactive use of terms is fundamentally dishonest. Consider the term *pope* which was not used in reference to a church leader until several hundred years after the end of the New Testament. The term never appears in the Bible. The word cannot legitimately be applied to Peter or any of the early bishops of the Church in Rome. Through the centuries, those who stayed true to first-century Christianity have faced an unending battle with terms and definitions. Many Bible words have been high-jacked and turned to mean something very different from the Bible definition. This has made it difficult for those true to the Scriptures to communicate their identity.

In this book, it is my intention to use words in the biblical senses and applications.

THOSE WHO WROTE AND THEIR WRITINGS

The Edification Era

- **Clement of Rome** (30-100) [9]

  It is believed that Clement was with Paul in Philippi in A.D. 57. He supposedly became the third bishop of the church in Rome. Without solicitation, he wrote a short letter to the church at Corinth. The Corinthians were still experiencing the same problems which Paul addressed in his letters. The letter written about A.D. 96 is known as *I Clement* or *First Clement*. [10]

  The letter was sweet and kind and was sent in the name of the local congregation in Rome; however, "it can hardly be denied that the document reveals the sense of a certain superiority over all ordinary congregations." [11] The root idea of a church system dominated by superior authority had already come into being. It would grow into a world-wide *church* controlled from Rome, Italy. At the time of Clement, the church in Rome had a domineering, superior, hierarchical spirit. Within 100 years, the bishop of the Roman church (Victor) would "excommunicate the churches of Asia Minor for a trifling difference of ritual" in his own name. [12]

Roman Catholics consider Clement to be the fourth pope. They say Peter was the first pope, and that he was followed by Linus, who was followed by Anacletus, who was followed by Clement. The fact is that there is zero evidence to indicate that Peter was ever the pope of the church in Rome. The existence of Linus and Anacletus is in serious dispute. In chapter five of his letter, Clement mentioned that Peter and Paul were dead. He does not say how and where they died, let alone that Peter was pastor, bishop or pope of the church in Rome. Even so, Catholics conclude from the letter that Peter was the first pope and that he died in Rome. [13]

- **Ignatius** (30-107) [14]

Ignatius is believed to have been a disciple of John and a colleague of Polycarp. Fifteen letters bear his name. [15] There is no universal agreement that all are his. His writings are known as *The Epistles of Ignatius.* He was bishop of the church in Antioch. [16]

In letter nine, Ignatius wrote about church schisms and encouraged members to look to their pastor. "His view begins to extend just beyond the head of a local church. He suggested that there is a difference between a bishop and a presbyter (pastor)." [17] The fact is that there is nothing in the New Testament to support such an idea. Ignatius laid the groundwork for a hierarchy above and beyond the confines of a local church. Here is a good example of the subtle and gradual departure from the teachings of Scripture. Note well these profound departures from truth in Ignatius:

- o The concept of a clergy separate from and in some spiritual sense elevated above and superior to the people

- o The idea of a bishop outside of a local church but with authority over it and its pastor

- o The concept that "the clergy" is "the necessary medium of access for the people to God" [18]

- o The concept that the bread and wine of the Lord's Supper are the flesh and blood of Jesus Christ and become a part of the means of salvation [19]

- **Other documents**

  - o *The Didache* (120)

    This document is also called *The Teachings of the Twelve Apostles;* however, it was not written by the twelve. The author is unknown. Eusebius referred to this document, although it was not discovered until 1875. It was found in Constantinople. It is noteworthy that *The Didache* talks about how baptisms and the Lord Supper were conducted at the time but suggests that these ordinances have nothing to do with salvation. [20]

  - o *The Epistle of Barnabas* (130)

    This writing is infected with Gnostic tendencies and is antagonistic toward the Jews.

  - o *The Shepherd of Hermas* (140)

    This is a collection of visions, mandates and parables in which a supposedly divine shepherd gave personal lessons to a man named Hermas. Most of this book was written as an allegory.

The Apologetic Era

- **Aristides** (c. 117-137)

  Aristides "was an eloquent philosopher at Athens who is mentioned by Eusebius as a contemporary of Quadratus." [21] Quadratus was bishop of a church in Athens, and his apology along with that of Aristides is testimonial that the work of Paul in Athens took root and produced fruit.

Aristides, like most of the apologists, was a very learned man who became a Christian as an adult after a careful examination of Christian beliefs and practices. His apology to the emperor Hadrian is pure New Testament theology. He compared Christianity to heathenism and found it infinitely superior. [22] His work is known as *Aristides' Apology*.

- **Justin Martyr** (c. 100-175)

This man was a prolific writer who wrote to Antoninus Pius between 138 and 161. He grew up in Samaria and studied in search of truth at the feet of many top religious leaders. As a mature philosopher, he saw no need for God. One day in a solitary walk, he encountered a simple, elderly peasant man who confronted Justin with the weaknesses of his beliefs. He was stunned and driven to the Scriptures where he found Christ. He became a staunch defender of Christianity. Justin asked why Christians were treated differently than other people. He argued that they were denied equal treatment under Roman law. He showed how Christianity was the superior faith and described how Christians worshipped. He gave detailed accounts of how they conducted the Lord's Supper, baptized, preached, sang and fellowshipped. He explained why they met on Sundays, how they assembled and the purity of their daily lives.

Perhaps Justin Martyr's most famous writing is his *Dialogue with Trypho*. Trypho was a Jew but little else is known about him. In this apology, Justin explained how he was saved.

Justin never fully exorcised his Platonic philosophy. He tended to be very Pharisaical; however, he was Christianity's strongest voice to the Romans during his time. He was ultimately martyred for his Christian stand. [23]

The Polemic Era

The men mentioned here were bishops of large churches. They wrote many things and influenced the course of history in tremendous ways. It is sad to say that much of their influence was extremely negative to the cause of Christ.

- **Irenaeus** (130-202) [24]

  Irenaeus was only two generations removed from the last apostles. He was born in Smyrna and was a disciple of Polycarp who was a disciple of John. [25] Irenaeus became bishop of a church in Lyon, Gallia (France) in 178. Later tradition holds that in 202 he died a martyr in the persecution of Septimius Severus. [26]

  Irenaeus was a strong proponent of orthodoxy; however, his idea of orthodoxy was not solely the Word of God. To him orthodoxy was determined by three tests.

  o **The Scriptures**

    By the Scriptures Irenaeus meant both Old and New Testaments. He referred to 25 of the 27 books of the New Testament. In his opinion, they were inspired.

  o **The Rule of Faith**

    The Rule of Faith is the name given to an early confessional. It was earlier than the Apostles' Creed and was considered by many to be an expression of apostolic confession and beliefs.

  o **Apostolic Succession**

    Irenaeus believed that church and pastoral legitimacy and authority depended upon the ability to trace spiritual lineage back to an apostle. In one of his books, Irenaeus "emphasized the organic unity of the church through apostolic succession of leaders from Christ and a rule of faith." [27] The negative biblical ramifications of this stance are enormous. He claimed the church in Rome could trace its lineage back to Peter. He is the man who gave names to those whom he supposed to have been the first three bishops of the church in Rome. He claimed that Paul and Peter founded the church in Rome and that Peter was the first pastor or bishop. These claims cannot be validated and the evidence does not support such claims. Paul could not possibly have founded that church. Paul wrote a letter to the church in Rome, **Romans 1:7**, and said therein that he longed to come there, **Romans 1:11**. The church in Rome was obviously in existence before Paul arrived, and there is no hard evidence that Peter went there; however, the Catholic Church uses Irenaeus' claims as proof that Peter was the first pastor or bishop of the Church in Rome. Since the inception of the Papacy, popes have claimed their position, power and authority come from a direct line of bishops of the Church in Rome starting with Peter. The Catholic Church then retroactively declared Peter a pope, which was not valid since there was no legitimate evidence to substantiate that claim.

More than any other, Irenaeus laid the groundwork for the Catholic Church.

- He changed the definition of orthodoxy from that which the Scriptures teach to Scripture plus what the ruling majority declares it to be.

- He elevated tradition to the level of Scripture.

- He is the first one to refer to the Catholic Church with a capital "C." [28]

- He fostered the concept of church hierarchy and the dominance of the bishop over the church. His dominance also fostered the dominance of big churches over smaller ones.

- Additionally he changed the Bible definition of "bishop." Biblically a bishop is the pastor of one congregation. Irenaeus held authority over many pastors and many congregations. He greatly fostered the concept of the Episcopal system of church government.

- He taught that the bread and wine of the Lord's Supper are the body and blood of Jesus Christ and that receiving them "strengthens soul and body (the germ of the resurrection body) unto eternal life." [29]

- In the mind of Irenaeus, baptism and regeneration were intimately connected. [30]

[1] Carl Deimer, Professor, *History of Christianity I*, Video Lecture 9, Liberty University DLP, 2004.

[2] Philip Schaff, *History of the Christian Church*, vol. 2, (Peabody, Massachusetts: Hendrickson Publishers, 2002), 7.

[3] Ibid.

[4] Deimer.

[5] *Webster's New World Dictionary with Student Handbook: Young People's Edition*, s.v. "apology," (Nashville, Tennessee: The World Publishing Company, 1973), 32.

[6] Ibid., s.v. "polemic," 535.

[7] Elmer L. Towns, *Theology for Today,* (Orlando, Florida: Harcourt Custom Publishers, 1997), 452.

[8] Ibid., 485.

[9] A. Cleveland Coxe, *The Apostolic Fathers with Justin Martyr and Irenaeus,* vol. 1 of *Ante-Nicene Fathers*, eds. Alexander Roberts and James Donaldson, (Peabody, Massachusetts: Hendrickson Publishers, Inc. 2004), 1.

[10] Deimer.

[11] Schaff, 158.

[12] Ibid.

[13] Deimer.

[14] Coxe, 45.

[15] Ibid., 46.

[16] Deimer.

[17] Ibid.

[18] Schaff, 125.

[19] Ibid., 241.

[20] Deimer.

[21] Schaff, 709.

[22] Deimer.

[23] Coxe, 306.

[24] Deimer.

[25] Earle E. Cairns, *Christianity Through the Centuries: A History of the Christian Church*, 3rd ed., (Grand Rapids, Michigan: Zondervan, 1996), 107-108.

[26] Schaff, 748-749.

[27] Cairns, 108.

[28] Deimer.

[29] Schaff, 242.

[30] Ibid., 260.

Early Christian Writings

Edify

96 The letter, *I Clement,* was sent to the church in Corinth

? *The Epistles of Ignatius*

120 *The Didache* talks about baptisms and the Lord Supper

130 *The Epistle of Barnabas*

140 *The Shepherd of Hermas*

Apologetic

? *Aristides' Apology* (c. 117 - 137)

? *Dialogue with Trypho* by Justin Martyr (c. 100 - 175)

178 Irenaeus became pastor of a church in Lyons, Gaul

Polemic

202 Irenaeus died a martyr in the persecution of Septimus Severus

? *One God in three persons* by Tertullian (145-220)

? Clement of Alexandria (160 - c212) wrote a soul-winning tract and a discipleship manual

Systematic

248 Cyprian (200-258) became bishop of Carthage

? Origen (185 - 254) wrote *Hexapla,* a six-columned translation of the Old Testament

Year
90
100
110
120
130
140
150
160
170
180
190
200
210
220
230
240
250
260

Chapter 8

Big Names, Early Writings and a Steady Drift
Part 2

This chapter continues a look at key leaders in Christianity who lived and wrote before the Council of Nicea (A.D. 325). They are known as the *ante-Nicene fathers*. Please keep in mind that these were desperate times as the persecution of Christians by the state and the common populace raged across the Roman Empire.

Remember that the ante-Nicene fathers and their writings can be organized into four main types: (1) edification, (2) apologetic, (3) polemic and (4) systematic.

The Ante-Nicene writings overlap time-periods. In the last chapter, we considered the edification writings of Clement of Rome and Ignatius. Both men began to influence Christianity away from its moorings in Christ and His apostles. We also considered the apologetic writings of Aristides and Justin Martyr. We looked at Irenaeus who wrote polemics that are systematic arguments. There were two other famous men who wrote polemics during this era.

The Polemic Era

- **Tertullian** (145-220) [1]

    It is believed that Tertullian was a native of Carthage in North
    Africa. While in Rome, he converted to Christianity when he
    was about 40 years old. His legal mind suggests that he was a
    lawyer. [2]

    Tertullian is best known for his explanation of the relationship
    between the Father, Son and Holy Spirit. During his time
    major controversy raged over who Jesus was in relationship to
    the Father. The doctrine of the Trinity was a matter of heated
    debate. Tertullian said the Trinity is one substance in three
    persons and that Jesus Christ was one person and two
    substances or natures, the divine and the human. [3] It is from
    this man that we got the phrase, *One God in three persons: Father,
    Son and Holy Ghost.*

    Tertullian was "a fiery champion of orthodoxy against every
    sort of heresy." Ironically, his ideas fostered the growing
    religious establishment against which he rebelled. He left the
    vast number of churches that were unifying across the Roman
    Empire to join the Montanists who emphasized prophecy and
    who believed that Christ would soon return. [4] The Montanists
    were not heretics (believers who differed greatly with the
    teachings of the Scriptures) but were schismatic (believers who
    differed with the unscriptural doctrinal drift of the church).

    They did not go along with the establishment churches in the
    drift away from biblical Christianity. [5] Tertullian thought that
    departing churches were heretics and argued that "the heretics
    have no right to use the Bible. They are latecomers who seek
    to change and to use what legally belongs to the church. In
    order to show that Scripture belongs to the church, it suffices
    to look at the various ancient churches where Scripture has
    been read and interpreted in a consistent manner since the
    times of the apostles." [6] He went on to argue that Rome could
    point to an uninterrupted line of bishops from his own time
    back to Peter. Tertullian was inconsistent. On the one hand he
    advocated strict adherence to the Scriptures; on the other hand
    he supported the concept that the community of older

churches should decide what the Scriptures meant. Inadvertently he supported both the authority of Scripture and the authority of church tradition. As the community of drifting churches grew stronger, Tertullian's writings strengthened their position of tradition over Scripture.

Though Tertullian was at deep odds with many church leaders, he was in philosophical agreement with them on the issue of succession and tradition. His was a clear departure from the apostolic concept of the sole authority of Scripture. His writings were in Latin and extremely convincing. From his statement "what legally belongs to the church," it is obvious that Tertullian viewed the church to be in some sense universal. In a rather nebulous sense, there seemed to him to be a core of Christians who had legal ownership of what was Christian and whose collective opinions constituted what was true, orthodox and right. This view suited the growing establishment well. It enabled the older, larger, stronger churches to decide what orthodoxy was and to declare as heretics all who disagreed. No longer was truth determined by Scripture; orthodoxy was whatever *the church* said it was.

In spite of Tertullian's strong support of many truths, he aided many corruptions.

- "Tertullian was the first who expressly and directly asserts sacerdotal claims on behalf of the Christian ministry, and calls it *sacerdotium*." [7] *Sacerdotium* is the office of priests that administer the sacraments in order to provide salvation.

- His assumption of a ministerial hierarchy above the people gave great support to its development.

- Though unwittingly, he greatly influenced the idea that orthodoxy can be found outside the Scriptures.

- His belief in the primacy of the church in Rome was support and groundwork for the power and supremacy of that church above all other churches.

- Tertullian leaned "towards the notion of a magical operation of the baptismal water." [8] He definitely leaned toward baptismal regeneration (salvation through baptism).

o Tertullian, though not a supporter of infant baptism, suggested that it had biblical grounds because Jesus said, *"Suffer little children to come unto me, and forbid them not,"* **Luke 18:16**. [9]

**Tertullian coined the phrase
"One God in three persons: Father, Son and Holy Ghost"**

• **Cyprian** (200-258) [10]

Cyprian was the highly educated son of a well-to-do pagan family of Carthage. He became a Christian in 246 and then the bishop of Carthage in 248. He continued as bishop until his martyrdom in 258. At that time Stephen, the bishop of Rome, claimed supremacy over all bishops; Cyprian opposed him. [11] Cyprian was "at the same time placed at the head of the whole North African clergy." [12] His strong support for ecclesiastical hierarchy is obvious.

Each new generation of establishment leadership increasingly viewed Christianity as one universal church. Unity among all local congregations and central control by some authoritative system became the passion and effort among the larger, more unified congregations. Efforts to impose orthodoxy (that which the more powerful church leaders defined as orthodox) increased, and severe moves were made against heretics (those determined as such by the dominate leaders).

Cyprian was passionate about unity in Christianity, which he viewed as one church. He "made a clear distinction between bishop and elder and emphasized the bishop as the center of unity in the church and a guarantee against schism." [13] When the Novations opposed the unscriptural trends of the day, Cyprian viewed them as a severe threat to the unity of the church and wrote against them.

Cyprian was equally passionate in his belief in a universal, visible church and that salvation was impossible apart from it. Historian Philip Schaff summarized Cyprian's position. "As the one Catholic Church is the sole repository of all grace, there can be no forgiveness of sins, no regeneration or communication of the Spirit, no salvation, and therefore no valid sacraments, out of her bosom." [14]

This man was a chief architect in leading multitudes of professing Christians away from the teachings of the New Testament. He significantly established the foundations of the Roman Catholic Church. For example, Cyprian said, "No man can have God as his Father without the Church as his mother," and "Where the bishop is there's the church." [15] This is like Sacerdotalism in which a bishop controls a person's relationship with God. Cyprian didn't directly say that a person couldn't come to God apart from a bishop; however the implication is unavoidable.

Some of his more glaring corruptions include:

o The concept of a Catholic Church with a capital "C"

o The strong elevation of *Church positions* to orthodoxy

o All who opposed orthodoxy as defined by the church were denounced as heretics

o The exaltation of a church hierarchy and priesthood

o The apostolic succession of the bishops in Rome from Peter

o The primacy of the church in Rome over all other churches

o Belief that the clergy has sacrificial priests (those that oversee the sacraments) who offer Christ's body and blood in the Communion service. This idea later developed into the concept of transubstantiation (a doctrinal concept which claims the bread and wine offered in the sacrament literally turn into the body and blood of Jesus). [16]

o The concept that salvation comes through the church and that man cannot have salvation apart from the bishop of Rome and thus the Roman Church [17]

o The concept of baptismal regeneration. In Cyprian's testimony of salvation, he wrote that "by the aid of the regenerating water, the stain of my former life was washed away." [18]

The Systematic Era

- **Clement of Alexandria** (160-c212) [19]

  Clement of Alexandria is not to be confused with Clement of Rome. Clement was converted by a man who started a Christian school in Alexandria. There was also a Christian school in Antioch of Syria and a few smaller ones elsewhere. Many of the doctrinal controversies that plagued Christianity in the years that follow this period grew between the theologians at Alexandria and those of Antioch.

  Clement was eloquent and speculative. He wrote a soul-winning tract titled *Address to the Greeks* and a discipleship manual titled *The Instructor*.

  Clement's theology is "a confused eclectic mixture of true Christian elements with many Stoic, Platonic, and Philonic ingredients." [20] Clement also elevated the office of the bishop and supported the contemporary doctrinal drifts of his day. He was against the Montanists who opposed the corruptions that were infiltrating Christianity. [21]

  > **Clement elevated the office of the bishop and supported the contemporary doctrinal drifts of his day**

- **Origen** (185-254) [22]

  Origen was born of Christian parents in Alexandria, Egypt. He professed Christ at an early age and was very devout. When his father, Leonides, was martyred, Origen, who was 17, sought to die as a martyr with him; however, his mother thwarted his efforts by hiding his clothes. [23] Origen was a brilliant scholar. He quickly became a renowned scholar with expertise in Hebrew and Greek. He lived a very ascetic life and even committed the act of self-emasculation in his efforts to separate himself from the world and secure himself against female temptations. [24] Because of this, he was excommunicated from the Church in Alexandria and made his way to Jerusalem, where he was severely tortured during the Decian persecution. Due largely to the violence against him, he died at age 69. [25]

Origen was an intense genius who lacked common sense. He is the author of the *Hexapla,* a six-columned translation of the Old Testament. He wrote commentaries on many books of the Bible and a systematic theology titled *De principiis (On First Principles).* Like many leading preachers of his day, Origen believed all of Christianity was really one church. His theology is riddled with Greek philosophy. Though he is considered by far the most powerful theological voice of his day, his anti-biblical stances include:

o   The ascetic (self-denial) philosophy of Plato

o   Denial of the material resurrection of Jesus Christ

o   The extension of the work of redemption to the inhabitants of stars

o   The final restoration of all men and fallen angels

o   The Son was a subordinate being to the Father. [26]

o   The validity of infant baptism [27]

Though most historians regard Origen as a maverick, there can be no legitimate denial that he fostered the development of a one-church system and many of the heresies that developed with it. He saw all churches as one unit and cooperated with the anti-biblical hierarchal system of government and control that was emerging.

STEADY DRIFT

Even before the writing of the final books of the New Testament, the fulfillment of Paul's prophecy to Timothy was in progress. *"Now the Spirit speaketh expressly, that in the latter times some shall depart from the faith, giving heed to seducing spirits, and doctrines of devils; Speaking lies in hypocrisy; having their conscience seared with a hot iron,"* **1 Timothy 4:1-2**. By 325 heresies had exploded to staggering proportions. Christianity as a whole was riddled with false doctrine and practice. More and more it came to be viewed as one mighty entity to be controlled and governed by a ruling majority. The steady move was toward centralization of authority; not based upon the

Scriptures, but upon the opinions and traditions of the strongest and most influential. The ruling majority increasingly viewed itself as *the orthodox, true church.* Dissenters were viewed as *heretics.* Specific departures from the teachings of the New Testament are too numerous to catalogue in this study; however, it would be in order at this point to name a few. Let it be remembered that not every preacher and every church departed from the faith and subscribed to these heresies. Even in this era of enormous drift, many remained true to God. These shall be addressed in coming chapters; however, at this point it behooves us to summarize some of the major departures from the Christian faith that took root and grew from approximately A.D. 100 to 325.

- The episcopal system of church government.

  o "The distinction of clergy and laity, and the sacerdotal view of the ministry becomes prominent and fixed; subordinate church offices are multiplied; the episcopate arises; the beginnings of the Roman primacy appear; and the exclusive unity of the Catholic church develops itself in opposition to heretics and schismatics." [28]

  o "The consolidation of the church and its compact organization implied a restriction of individual liberty, in the interest of order, and a temptation to the abuse of authority." [29]

  o "The idea and institution of a special priesthood, distinct from the body of the people, with the accompanying notion of sacrifice and altar." [30]

  o There was a proliferation of new church offices and officers. In addition to the bishops, presbyters and deacons, in many churches there were sub-deacons, readers, *acolyths* or *acolytes* (attendants of the bishops in their official duties and processions), exorcists, *precentors* (for music), sextons (janitors), *catechists* (teachers) and interpreters. [31]

  o The power, authority and control of large churches over smaller, weaker ones were "possibly the first serious departure from the New Testament order." [32]

  o The rise of bishops occurred. This system became the germ of the Papacy. Many of the big-name church leaders

(Clement of Rome, Ignatius, Irenaeus, Tertullian, Cyprian and others.) supported and fostered the episcopal system. [33]

- There arose bishops who ruled over groups of rural and small village churches and pastors. The bishops interfaced between them and the larger city churches.

- There arose city bishops who ruled over all the churches and pastors within their cities.

- There arose metropolitan bishops who rose above and ruled over the rest because of their residence and prominence in the capital cities of the provinces.

- Above the metropolitan bishops were the bishops of the *apostolic mother-churches.* (Jerusalem, Antioch, Alexandria, Ephesus, Corinth and Rome).

- Increasingly the church in Rome rose in prestige and power. It ultimately prevailed over other churches and became the head of the Roman Catholic system, which was drifting away from true, original Christianity.

• The embrace of tradition and majority opinion (not Scripture only) became the final authority for truth and orthodoxy.

• The concept of the church to mean more than one local congregation prevailed.

• A consequent concept developed that church discipline is not an action by one local congregation against one of its members, but rather that church discipline is the action of a universal church against a person. [34]

• The concept of institutional, ritualistic salvation developed. This is the idea that salvation is not in a personal relationship with Jesus Christ, but rather in something one does in connection to the church.

  o The view that salvation is tied to the Lord's Supper.

    - The development of the idea that the bread and wine of the Lord's Supper actually become the body and blood of Jesus Christ.

- The development of the idea that salvation is tied to eating the Lord's Supper.

- The Lord's Supper became viewed as a sacrifice, first as a *thank-offering* then as a *sin-offering* and no longer as a memorial ordinance. This led to the Catholic Mass. [35]

o The view emerged that salvation is tied to baptism.

- The development and acceptance of baptismal regeneration.

- The concept that baptism washed away sins but only those sins committed before the baptism. "Deathbed baptisms were then what death-bed repentances are now." [36]

• The introduction of infant baptism.

o Since erring churches decided that baptism is essential to salvation, they concluded that the sooner one is baptized, the sooner he is saved. Hence arose infant baptism.

o It was assumed by some that a baby might be drowned by immersion. [37] Shortly thereafter written references to sprinkling and pouring began to appear, especially related to babies.

---

[1] A. Cleveland Coxe, *Latin Christianity: Its Founder, Tertullian,* vol. 3 of <u>Ante-Nicene Fathers</u>, eds. Alexander Roberts and James Donaldson, (Peabody, Massachusetts: Hendrickson Publishers, Inc. 2004), 3.

[2] Justo L. Gonzalez, *The Story of Christianity,* vol. 1, (San Francisco: HarperCollins Publishers, 1984), 73-74.

[3] Ibid., 77.

[4] Ibid., 76.

[5] Carl Deimer, Professor, *History of Christianity I,* Video Lecture 10, Liberty University DLP, 2004.

[6] Gonzalez, 74.

[7] Philip Schaff, *History of the Christian Church,* vol. 2, (Peabody, Massachusetts: Hendrickson Publishers, 2002), 26.

[8] Ibid., 253.

[9] Ibid., 259.

[10] Coxe, vol. 5, *Introductory Notice to Cyprian,* 263.
[11] Earle E. Cairns, *Christianity Through the Centuries: A History of the Christian Church*, 3rd ed., (Grand Rapids, Michigan: Zondervan, 1996), 110.
[12] Schaff, 845.
[13] Cairns, 110-111.
[14] Schaff, 262.
[15] Deimer.
[16] Cairns, 111.
[17] Deimer.
[18] Schaff, 844.
[19] Deimer.
[20] Schaff, 783.
[21] Ibid., 785.
[22] Allan Menzies, *Ante-Nicene Fathers,* vol. 9, 291.
[23] Schaff, 787,
[24] Ibid., 788.
[25] Ibid., 790.
[26] Ibid., 791.
[27] Ibid., 260.
[28] Ibid., 121.
[29] Ibid., 122.
[30] Ibid., 123.
[31] Ibid., 132.
[32] J.M. Carroll, *The Trail of Blood,* (Lexington, Kentucky: Ashland Avenue Baptist Church, 1992), 12
[33] Schaff, 152-163.
[34] Ibid., 187-193.
[35] Ibid., 245-247.
[36] Ibid., 254.
[37] Carroll, 13.

Major Departures from the Christian Faith

The episcopal system of church government took root and grew

The rise of bishops. This system became the germ of the Papacy.

The proliferation of new church offices and officers

The large churches had power, authority and control over the smaller, weaker ones

The embrace of tradition and majority opinion, and not Scripture only, as the final authority for truth and orthodoxy

The concept of the church to mean more than one local congregation

Institutional, ritualistic salvation, which is salvation that is tied to the Lord's Supper and baptism

The introduction of infant baptism

Chapter 9

The Big Wedding

A RADICAL CHANGE IN THE MAKING

Pagan Rome did her best to eradicate Christianity. The government and the people opposed and persecuted Christians in a menagerie of ways. Martyrdom was common. The greatest efforts to erase Christianity from the face of the earth came as the third century gave way to the fourth in what some scholars call "The Great Persecution." [1] The Roman Emperor Diocletian "determined that in his rule he would completely destroy the church, eradicate it. He determined to destroy every building, kill every bishop and make everyone receive a *libelous* or die." [2] Scriptures and other Christian literature were confiscated and burned, the killing of Christians became a sport in the Coliseum, and every effort was made to eliminate Christianity. The worst year was 303; Diocletian determined that there would be no Christians by the end of that year. [3]

The efforts of pagan Rome failed miserably. As bystanders saw Christians dying for their faith, many were greatly convicted. Many realized that they had nothing in their own lives for which they were willing to live and die. People became Christians at a rate higher than the execution rate by the Romans. Diocletian abdicated in 305. He admitted that he was a failure, in large part because he had failed to eradicate the Christians. "There were more Christians when he abdicated than when he started his reign." [4]

Change was on the horizon, change that had a dramatic and profound impact on Christianity. The Roman government was about to make a 180 degree turn in its stance toward Christianity. What it could not eradicate, it would embrace. It would merge with Christianity in a mighty effort to strengthen the empire and unite government and religion as one central authority. In the early stages of the union that was soon formed, the Roman Emperor viewed himself as the head of the new union; over time headship changed back and forth from the emperor to the head of the church in Rome. At times the head of the government exercised ultimate domination over the church. At other times the head of the church exercised ultimate domination over the government.

The union of Christianity and the Roman state appears to have been a matter of expediency on the part of Rome, not a true embrace of the fundamental, apostolic elements of the Christian faith. The Roman government was fragmented and weak. For three centuries Christianity had proven to be a high profile and formidable force which Rome could not eliminate. Many strongly believe that the charismatic Roman emperor Constantine made Christianity the official state religion of Rome because of the enormous political benefits that accrued from such a union. Constantine "realized that if the state could not wipe out Christianity by force, it might make use of the church as an ally to save classical culture." [5]

CONSTANTINE (c. 274-337) [6]

It is impossible to grasp Christianity since biblical days apart from a working knowledge of Constantine. He was the illegitimate son of a pagan military leader named Constantius and his wife Helena. Helena professed Christ as her personal Savior. [7] In 285, Diocletian reorganized the Roman Empire under the leadership of a team of four emperors with himself as chief. Diocletian dominated the eastern part of the empire, and Maximian dominated the western part. Under each was a junior emperor: Galerius under Diocletian and Constantius under Maximian. [8] Galerius was a strong and ambitious military man who succeeded in forcing the abdications (to resign from being emperor) of both Diocletian and Maximian in 305. After being held hostage by Galerius for a while, Constantine escaped and joined his father in the far western end of the empire. At the death of Constantine's father, his troops proclaimed Constantine as their head. [9] Meanwhile Maximian's son, Maxentius, came to power and took the city of Rome. Lesser strong men seized pockets of power in given places in the empire; however, Constantine and Maxentius were the two main western powers, and a showdown between these two became imminent. Constantine crossed the Alps with his army and marched on Rome, the capital of Maxentius. In 312, they met in the famous battle on the Milvian Bridge. As Maxentius fought, he fell from the bridge into the Tiber River and drowned. His army was defeated, and Constantine became the dominant power in the western part of the empire. [10]

Before the battle at the Milvian Bridge, it seemed that Constantine's enemies were about to overwhelm him. He is said to have had a vision of a cross in the sky and heard a voice saying, *in this sign conquer.* [11] In his vision, Constantine saw a Latin *kai* which looks like an English "P" and a Latin *rho* which looks like an English "X." These are the first two letters in the Greek word for Christ. Constantine took this to be a vision from the Christian God. He interpreted the vision to mean that if he allied himself with the Christian God rather than remain an opponent, he'd be victorious. His soldiers placed the Px emblem on their shields and went to battle as a *Christian army.* Constantine won and proclaimed Christianity to be his faith. [12]

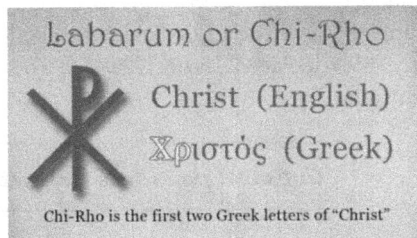

Labarum or Chi-Rho
Christ (English)
Χριστός (Greek)
Chi-Rho is the first two Greek letters of "Christ"

Only God knows the heart; however, many aspects of Constantine's life after his open embrace of Christianity contradict his profession. He delayed baptism until shortly before his death and kept the pagan title of *Pontifex Maximus,* chief priest of the pagan state religion. [13] He continued to worship the Unconquered Sun [14] and supported most of the heresies that had invaded Christianity by this time, including the belief that baptism saves. He neither renounced the false gods of the Roman pantheon nor the mystery pagan gods. [15] "It is likely that Constantine's favoritism to the church was a matter of expediency." [16]

THE EDICT OF MILAN

By the time Constantine established himself as the undisputed leader in the western sector of the empire, Licinius had become sole ruler in the eastern sector. In 313, these two met in Milan, Italy and signed a document granting freedom of religion to all. This is the famous Edict of Milan. "During the next few years Constantine issued edicts that brought about the restoration of confiscated property to the church, the subsidization of the church by the state, the exemption of clergy from public service, a ban on soothsaying, and the setting apart of the 'Day of the Sun' (Sunday) as a day of rest and worship." [17] Christians had kept Sunday as a day of worship since the time of Christ.

THE MARRIAGE OF THE CHURCH TO THE STATE

Licinius was by no means a Christian, but he yielded to the more powerful Constantine. These two strongmen were headed to a fight for ultimate supremacy. That fight came in 323. Constantine won, became sole ruler of the Roman Empire and promptly made Christianity the preferred or state religion of the empire. In what is called *Caesar o papacy* (state rule of the church) Constantine placed himself over the church but refused to be subject or submitted to it. He declared himself to be the chief bishop or ruler of the church. [18]

Caesar o papacy **is the state rule of the church**

Remember the date! A.D. 323! The marriage of the church to the state was one of the darkest days in the history of Christianity! This marriage was responsible for persecutions of many true Christians. It was a dark day when Jesus died on the cross, but out of that darkness came hope, forgiveness of sins and eternal life.

In the days before 323, pagan Rome persecuted all of Christianity. In the days following 323, "Christian" Rome would persecute true Christians in the name of *Christianity*. In terms of magnitude and cruelty, their persecution would eclipse the persecutions of the pagan Romans. As we have already seen, a great drift from true, apostolic Christianity was already well under way within the ranks of Christendom. Two major sides, both calling themselves true Christians while denouncing the other side, were emerging. The chasm between them would dramatically widen within the next few years. One side would align with and capitalize on the political powers of the state; the other side would not. For generations to come, most historians have focused on the state church and viewed it as the real or true church. The other category of believers would not form one united, centrally controlled *church*; each church would remain autonomous and refuse entangling alliances. In the historical scope of things, these would be largely overlooked, ignored and discounted. In spite of its far departure from the apostolic Christianity of the Scriptures, one side would call itself *orthodox* while accusing and persecuting the other side for being *heretics*. That side would do it with the backing of the power of the state. In spite of her compliance with and faithfulness to the Scriptures, one side would become the distinct underdogs, the troublemakers, the heretics. History would treat this side mostly with scorn. This latter group viewed itself as true Christians and knew that the state church deserted Bible truth and practice. Later generations, including our own, would view the state church as mainstream Christianity. They would also view the latter churches as either non-existent, radicals or of almost no consequence or importance. Thankfully God has a far different standard of judgment, and His is the standard that counts.

> **A.D. 323 is the year the state married the church**

THE COUNCIL OF NICEA

In the early years of Christianity, the division between churches adhering closely to the apostolic model and those departing from the faith in favor of tradition was not always clear and distinct. There was a predisposition toward tolerance, unity and fellowship within the ranks of Christianity. It took time and lots of provocation for brethren and churches to break fellowship. Then as now, Christians and churches wanted to extend the benefit of the doubt to other Christians and churches. The fact that sides had not yet polarized and made clean breaks with each other does not necessarily mean they were in agreement.

That was surely the case when Constantine wed the state to Christianity, which he viewed as one church. Not all pastors and churches embraced the move. They welcomed the end of state-approved, pagan persecution, but it is doubtful that they comprehended the ramifications of a state-church. For a while, efforts toward peace and cooperation were made by those who disagreed with the escalating heretical beliefs and practices of those who embraced the state-church.

This was evidenced when Constantine soon called a council of pastors and church leaders to address a schism within the ranks of Christianity. The council met at Nicea in the early summer of 325. Two well-known leaders in the church in Alexandria, Egypt headed a controversy over the deity of Christ. Arius said that Jesus was not the real God of the Bible. He argued that Jesus was a lesser god. He denied the Trinity and claimed Jesus was an offspring of God in the same sense that a child is an offspring of a parent. He argued that Jesus was not eternal. Athanasius was a deacon in the church at Alexandria, Egypt (later a pastor) who opposed Arius. The controversy spread throughout many of the churches in the empire and Christians began to take sides. Constantine was quite disturbed by the schism and called the Council of Nicea to resolve the matter. In addition to 318 bishops or pastors at this conference, there were hundreds of deacons and other church officers plus thousands of spectators. Most of them were maimed with broken limbs, deep scars and bodies injured from persecution. [19] Constantine "presided over the first session and paid all the costs. For the first time the church found itself dominated by the political leadership of the head of the state. The perennial problem of the relationship between church and state emerged clearly here, but the bishops were too busy dealing with theological heresy to think of that particular problem." [20] Many things were agreed, including the date of Easter, although the main affirmation was the Trinity and the deity of Jesus Christ.

Many councils have followed the one at Nicea in 325. Most of them have been called and organized by the state church. Those churches not aligned with the state church ceased to participate.

Do not assume that agreements made at the Council of Nicea or later councils were accepted by and reflect the thinking of all pastors and churches. Furthermore, do not imagine that all pastors and churches that rejected the state-church union also rejected everything believed by the state church and agreed at the councils. The fact is that sometimes the state church was right in its stance and got it right at those councils. Such was surely the case at the Council of Nicea where the Trinity and the deity of Christ were clearly affirmed. Many Christians, who have never agreed with or been a part of a state church, embrace this theology. In fact, this is the scriptural position on the issue. This position was true long before Constantine wed the church to the state and centuries before the Council of Nicea. In our next chapter we shall turn our attention to some of those early pastors and churches which refused to be a part of the big wedding of the church to the state.

---

[1] Justo L. Gonzalez, *The Story of Christianity,* vol. 1, (San Francisco: HarperCollins Publishers, 1984), 102.

[2] Carl Deimer, Professor, *History of Christianity I*, Video Lecture 6, Liberty University DLP, 2004.

[3] Ibid.

[4] Ibid.

[5] Earle E. Cairns, *Christianity Through the Centuries: A History of the Christian Church*, 3rd ed., (Grand Rapids, Michigan: Zondervan, 1996), 119.

[6] Deimer, Lecture 12.

[7] Ibid.

[8] Gonzalez, 102.

[9] Ibid., 104-105.

[10] Ibid., 106-107.

[11] Cairns, 119.

[12] Deimer, Lecture 12.

[13] Cairns, 119.

[14] Gonzalez, 107.

[15] Deimer, Lecture 10.

[16] Cairns, 119.

[17] Ibid., 119.

[18] Deimer, Lecture 12.

[19] Ibid.

[20] Cairns, 126.

The Marriage of Church and State

Year	
285	Diocletian reorganized the Roman Empire under the leadership of a team of four emperors with himself as chief
303	The Great Persecution - Roman Emperor Diocletian decided to eradicate the church and all Christians in this year
305	Diocletian and Maximian abdicated. This was forced by Galerius, who was a strong and ambitious military man.
312	The Battle of Milvian Bridge - Constantine and Maxentius fought at the Milvian Bridge in Rome. Constantine won and Maxentius drowned.
313	Edict of Milan - Constantine (leader of the western sector of the Roman Empire) and Licinius (eastern sector leader) met in Milan, Italy and signed a document granting freedom of religion to all
323	Constantine became sole ruler of the Roman Empire and promptly made Christianity the preferred or state religion of the empire
325	The Council of Nicea affirmed the Trinity and the deity of Jesus Christ

The History of Churches

Chapter 10

Not Everybody Jumped on the Bandwagon

A SPLIT ON THE HORIZON

Long before the big Roman wedding of church to state, major tensions were growing within the ranks of Christendom. As some churches (the bigger, more prestigious ones) moved away from Scripture and apostolic practice, others stayed true. They rejected the growing acceptance of tradition over Scripture, the move away from the New Testament idea of bishop and church government, the shift from salvation by grace through faith in Jesus Christ to baptismal regeneration and institutional salvation, infant baptism and other anti-biblical beliefs and practices. As does the Bible, they stood firm on the separateness and independence of the churches, the subordinate character of church leaders (bishops and others), salvation exclusively by personal faith in Jesus Christ and the baptism of believers only. [1] Tensions mounted as false concepts became stronger and more widely accepted by many preachers and in many churches. Many pastors and churches remained true to biblical Christianity and heeded the warning of Jude. *"Beloved, when I gave all diligence to write unto you of the common salvation, it was needful for me to write unto you, and exhort you that ye should earnestly contend for the faith which was once delivered unto the saints. For there are certain men crept in unawares, who were before of old ordained to this condemnation, ungodly men, turning the grace of our God into lasciviousness, and denying the only Lord God, and our Lord Jesus Christ,"* **Jude 3-4**. They resisted the heretical drift and distanced themselves.

As previously indicated many of them did so with reluctance and parted company only after efforts to turn the drifters. Those who embrace the Scriptures seek peace and harmony within the ranks of Christendom, not division. Paul expressed this benchmark idea of Christianity when he said, *"if any man seem to be contentious, we have no such custom, neither the churches of God,"* **1 Corinthians 11:16**.

Even so, heresy strengthened and proliferated. A split in the ranks of Christendom became inevitable. The marriage of the church to the state merely galvanized and hastened it. Over time churches true to the Scriptures and apostolic practices would disassociate themselves either formally or informally from those that were not.

UNDERSTANDING *"ORTHODOXY"*

So often those who are bigger and stronger subjugate and rule their peers. That does not make them right, even though they frequently declare they are. Unfortunately history often takes their side. That happened in the early years of Christianity and it found tremendous acceleration with the union of the Roman state to those churches that departed from the Scriptures and apostolic practices.

To many minds *orthodoxy* is a term that would properly apply to those who believe and adhere to the Scriptures. Webster defines orthodox as "keeping to the usual or fixed beliefs, customs, etc., especially in religion." [2] As many churches departed from scriptural doctrine and practice, they also grew larger and stronger. They exercised growing control both within and among churches. They began to think in terms of *Church*, not *churches*. Synods and councils were periodically held to determine *the church's* position on given issues. (This is evidenced by the Council of Nicea and Constantine's belief that the church was one, not many.) Not all pastors and churches held this view.

In the minds of those growing in power and clout, the beliefs and positions taken by the stronger churches became orthodoxy. For those in power, orthodoxy was no longer viewed as what the Scriptures said; it was viewed as what the church said it was. Once the church wed the state, the church had the power of the Roman State to enforce its positions. Those who differed quickly found themselves in grave peril.

116

Once this concept was fully in place the state church determined what was orthodox and what was heretical. This state church also determined who was orthodox and who was a heretic. Church tradition instead of Scripture became the rule of faith and practice. This brand of *Christianity* was no longer governed by the Scriptures. Tradition ruled, not the word of God. This element of *Christianity* increasingly came into power, and *Christianity* became evolutionary and governed by the thinking of men. It was no longer fixed and governed by God. ³ Pandora's Box was now opened. As we shall later see, this development became a mighty means of control and oppression. It was used to persecute and kill millions who stayed true to *the faith which was once delivered unto the saints*. Yes! There were millions who did not embrace this brand of *Christianity* but who remained true to the Scriptures.

INESCAPABLE TRUTHS AND RAMIFICATIONS

If you listen to the claims of the *established church* or to many authorities on the history of Christianity, you will get the idea that the churches moving away from the Bible were the real church. They would have you think that those who did not agree with and join the emerging movement of churches either did not exist or were not bona-fide, legitimate, scripturally oriented Christians. It is therefore important to establish certain realities about the existence of these who did not drift and who did not join the state church.

- **Churches that remained true to the core doctrine and practices of Jesus and the apostles have existed continuously from the church in Jerusalem until the present.** Jesus promised the perpetuity of the institution which He personally established. He promised that it would continue until His return. *"And I say also unto thee, That thou art Peter, and upon this rock I will build my church; and the gates of hell shall not prevail against it,"* **Matthew 16:18**. If we had zero historical proof that it has existed from then until now (we do have proof), based upon the integrity of the word of Jesus Christ who was and is God, we would still know that it has. Based on Jesus' promise, "there must be, in every age, a group teaching and practicing New Testament standards." ⁴

117

Furthermore Paul said, *"Unto him be glory in the church by Christ Jesus throughout all ages, world without end. Amen,"* **Ephesians 3:21**. That verse guarantees the perpetuity of the church *"throughout all ages."* From the day Jesus established the institution that He called *my church* and until He returns, there has been and always will be a church after the order of the one He personally established.

Because a given church cannot link its mother church to its grandmother churches all the way back to the church in Jerusalem, many liberals and skeptics ridicule and scorn the idea of church perpetuity. The fact is that it is not necessary for any person to trace his ancestry back to Adam to prove that he is a descendant of Adam. Likewise no church espousing the core doctrine and practices of Jesus and the apostles need prove its legitimacy historically.

- **Church legitimacy is not in the name; legitimacy is in the beliefs and practices of a church.** Many current Baptist churches embrace the core teachings and practices of Jesus and the apostles; however, between Jesus Christ and the present, multitudes of churches existed who embraced these same core teachings and practices, but many of them were not called *Baptist*. Churches that have remained true to the core teachings and practices of Jesus Christ and His apostles have existed continuously from Christ to the present, but they have been called and identified by many, many names such as Montanists, Paulicians, Albigenses, Cathari and Anabaptists. As this study progresses we will identify many of these churches and document their existence.

As we move through the centuries it is important to keep in mind that we are looking at the same stream of people, one continuous line from Christ to the present. Often they were in widely separated geographical areas and not aware of others of their kind. They went by different names and were not in agreement on every detail, but they all held to the core beliefs of first-century Christianity.

Many modern Baptists have become over-infatuated with the name *Baptist*. In too many cases, any church going by the name *Baptist* is accepted as legitimate even when its beliefs and practices are far from those of Jesus and the apostles. On the other hand, any church that does not go by the name *Baptist* is rejected as illegitimate even though its beliefs and practices are in basic harmony with those of Jesus and the apostles. Such a stance is clearly out of line with the Bible which staunchly insists on truth in practice, not merely the pretense of an empty name or title.

There were churches throughout history (and some currently exist) that have believed and acted like the ones in the New Testament. No matter what they were (or are) called, they are true churches of Jesus Christ. Conversely, there were churches throughout history (many currently exist) that did not believe or act like the ones in the New Testament. Regardless of their names, they are not true churches of Jesus Christ. "If so-called Baptist churches today are not acting or believing like New Testament Baptist churches, they are no more Baptist churches than any other denomination that came out of the Reformation." [5] (Let it be duly noted that the churches in the New Testament were Baptist in practice, not in name.) The opposite end of that equation is equally true: a church by another name that believes and behaves like churches in the New Testament is legitimate. Legitimacy is in essence, not labeling; in beliefs and practices, not empty pretense.

A New Testament church is not determined by the name

- **Only those connected to the line of churches which have embraced the teachings and practices of Jesus and His apostles are true, legitimate New Testament churches.** Jesus' promise of perpetuity "removes all license for some group to be started in later years, having devised their own set of doctrinal standards. Put clearly and simply, this *demands perpetuity* for a group that carries out that commission according to the standards set forth in the New Testament writings. It cannot sputter and start again from century to century; it must be here always 'throughout all ages,' and 'unto the end of the age.'" [6]

Churches and denominations have proliferated since the Protestant Reformation and particularly in recent years. Rather than connect with the line that extends back to Christ and His church in Jerusalem, most of them have established new doctrine, creeds and practices. Many were established by a man or woman many years removed from Jesus Christ and their doctrinal ancestry is directly traceable to that person. Any group like that cannot be considered legitimate. All legitimate churches have a continuous historical doctrinal connection to Jesus Christ.

- **There is no church or group of churches in any age, beginning with the church in Jerusalem to the present, that were always right on everything at all times.** Even the church in Jerusalem soon developed internal trouble, **Acts 6.** Each of the seven churches of Asia had flaws, **Revelation 2-3,** including doctrine, **Revelation 2:14,** and practices, **Revelation 2:20.** The church at Corinth was wrong on the understanding and practice of spiritual gifts, especially tongues, **1 Corinthians 12-14.**

Many people condemn and totally reject New Testament churches because they see errors in their beliefs and practices, and because they did not embrace tradition over Scripture. They argue that impure churches could not constitute the line of true churches from Christ to the present. Such a stance presents serious challenges:

o If Jesus was right in His promise about the perpetuity of the church He established, then:

- Either the churches that deserted Scripture in favor of tradition and merged with the state are the true churches of Jesus Christ. These constitute the true line.

- Or the churches that stayed with Scripture and refused to merge with the state are the true churches of Jesus Christ. These constitute the true line.

- One cannot have it both ways. "There is no other way to come through these dark ages. We either accept identity with these persecuted peoples, or else declare that the church became hopelessly corrupted, and the Lord could not protect it against the 'gates of hell.'" [7]

o If impurities in a church which embraces the core doctrine and practices of Jesus Christ and the apostles disqualify that church from being a church that Jesus calls His own, how much more would the wholesale desertion of the beliefs and practices of Jesus Christ and the apostles disqualify it as a church that Jesus calls His own? Those who reject the churches that did not align with the Roman state church, which eventually became the Catholic Church, have a problem. They reject the churches that did not join the state church because they were less than perfect, in favor of a state church that became the epitome of false doctrines, practices and corruption. In essence, those who take such a stance are saying Jesus was wrong and there has not been an unbroken line of true churches back to the one He established in Jerusalem.

o If the Roman state church, which ultimately became the Catholic Church, constitutes the true line of churches but went so far astray as to necessitate a Protestant Revolution, then the line of perpetuity was broken and Jesus was wrong in His promise.

o If the Catholic Church constitutes the true line of churches, then all who broke from her, including all Protestants and their children churches, are no longer a part of the unbroken line and are not true churches.

o If Baptists are Protestants, then Baptists are not in the line or stream of true churches that date back to Christ and thus they are not true churches.

o If the churches that stayed true to the Scriptures did not merge with the state were true churches and constitute the unbroken line back to Christ, then all churches that are not a part of the doctrine and practices of that line are not true churches.

The fact is that a church does not have to be perfect and correct on every point for God to consider it true, legitimate and His church. That is evidenced in each of the churches mentioned above in the New Testament references. Each was less than perfect yet the Bible references each of them as a church. It seems safe to believe that when God calls a church a *church*, it is. God did warn the church in Ephesus that under certain circumstances He would *"remove thy candlestick,"* **Revelation 2:5**. A church can cease to be a church even though it might still call itself a church. Just what would provoke God to no longer recognize a church as one of His is not clearly enunciated in Scripture; however, it can happen. Paul warned the churches of Galatia that those who pervert the gospel message of Christ as clearly set forth in Scripture are to be *"accursed,"* **Galatians 1:6-9**. It is obvious that no church that fails to preach the gospel as defined in Scripture can constitute a legitimate church.

There are core scriptural teachings (listed below). By no means do these constitute all that is taught in the Scriptures. A church may be off base on many points of doctrine and practice, although it is obvious that God will consider that church His as long as it embraces core scriptural teachings (possibly not even all of them). One thing is very certain, a church must be true to the gospel to remain a church of Jesus Christ. The gospel embodies the person and work of Jesus Christ.

- **Historically multitudes of individuals and churches formerly connected to a false church have seen the error of their ways and taken steps necessary to become a part of the continuous line of churches that connect to the one Jesus established**. People like Paul who had a false concept of God have seen the error of their beliefs and practices and turned to the truths set forth in the Scriptures. Vast numbers of Catholic priests have left the false beliefs and practices which they formerly embraced and joined themselves to that unbroken line of churches which stayed true to New Testament doctrine and practices. Many who have entered the unbroken line were formerly pastors and leaders of false churches. In numerous cases they led the church where they served to the truth and whole churches deserted their former doctrines and practices to join the line of true churches. As coming studies will show, the outward testimony of such radical change has been baptism. Those who awakened to the truth have repeatedly realized that baptism must (1) follow (never precede) personal faith in Christ, (2) be by immersion and (3) be administered by a proper authority. Those who administer baptism to people who were previously sprinkled or immersed by a church of beliefs and practices inconsistent with the New Testament model have been called Anabaptists (meaning re-baptizers) for many centuries. Hence through the centuries the name *Baptist* has been the most common name associated with that continuous line of churches that stayed true to the doctrine and practices of Jesus and the apostles.

To say that a person or church is not legitimate because of prior affiliation with a false church is without foundation or merit. To be in the legitimate line, a church need not come from a specific church which came from a specific church all the way back to Jerusalem; however, somewhere along the line it or its ancestors must have broken with the churches of false beliefs and practices and joined the stream of churches that have stayed true to the New Testament. In summary the way to do that is through open repentance and scriptural baptism. Remember that the stream that dates back to Christ is a doctrinal stream, not a succession of one specific church to another.

- **It is impossible to be neutral on the issue of true, legitimate churches.** "One thing needs to be made very clear just here. Either these groups that were referred to as 'heretics' for approximately 1,200 years before the Reformation were indeed true churches, or else we are forced to accept the state church, which became the harlot of Rome seeking to enforce her brand of orthodoxy by the sword, as the true body." [8]

CORE SCRIPTURAL TEACHINGS

Already in this book it has been affirmed that there is a core of scriptural teachings which true churches have embraced throughout the centuries since Jesus Christ established that first church in Jerusalem, Israel. These beliefs must be repeated to insure a continuous line of true churches to the present. Not every church bearing a given name embraced every core teaching. In fact, groups of individuals or churches bearing the name of a generally sound group of churches might reject every core teaching of that group. That should neither come as a great surprise, nor should the entire group be condemned because of the mistakes or heresies of one or a few. Today there is a chasm separating the beliefs and practices of many groups including Baptists. It is the worst kind of discrimination to brand the whole group because a few are out of step. Then as now, the beliefs and practices of a few with a particular name do not necessarily represent the beliefs and practices all bearing that name. This day there are Baptists that run a wide spectrum of beliefs and practices. What Baptists are as a whole cannot accurately be determined by what one or a few Baptist persons or churches believe and practice. For example, the fact that a few Baptists have female pastors and deacons does not prove that Baptists as a whole do. Among almost every group that we will soon examine, there were some who gave the name a black eye. This does not justify writing off the entire group any more than one corrupt and immoral person with your name makes you corrupt and immoral.

Here is a list of core scriptural teachings which have been embraced by a continuous line of churches as a whole dating back to Jesus Christ. [9]

- Jesus Christ personally founded this organization called a church.

- Jesus Christ is God and the head of the church. True churches have always believed in the deity of Christ.

- The church has two kinds of permanent offices: pastors and deacons.

- The government of the church is congregational.

- In congregational government and discipline, all churches are to be entirely separate and independent of each other.

- In congregational government and discipline, all churches are to be entirely separate and independent of the state. True churches have always opposed a state church.

- The church is to keep the ordinances of baptism and the Lord's Supper and to assemble on Sunday.

- Salvation is exclusively by grace through personal faith in Jesus Christ alone.

- Only saved persons are to be baptized. This necessitates the re-baptism of people who were *baptized* before they were saved.

- Only saved persons can be members of a church. This precludes infant baptism.

- Every believer is of equal worth to God and in the church there is to be no ecclesiastical hierarchy. This is belief in the priesthood of every believer.

- The Scriptures and only the Scriptures are inspired of God.

- The Scriptures are the final rule of faith and practice for believers and the church.

There are many, many other beliefs and practices set forth in the New Testament. However these constitute a core of distinguishing beliefs and practices. Adherence to these precludes most of the beliefs and practices of the group of churches that deserted Scripture for tradition and united with the Roman government as a church state. An irreconcilable breach formed and grew between the state church and those churches that embraced these beliefs and practices. With the backing and power of the Roman state, that group of churches grew powerful and soon saw itself as one church. Soon it began to oppress, persecute and seek to destroy every church and individual that did not align with it. For true Christians and churches the days ahead were bleak indeed!

---

[1] J.M. Carroll, *The Trail of Blood,* (Lexington, Kentucky: Ashland Avenue Baptist Church, 1992), 14.

[2] *Webster's New World Dictionary with Student Handbook: Young People's Edition*, s.v. "orthodox," (Nashville, Tennessee: The World Publishing Company, 1973), 490.

[3] Carl Deimer, Professor, *History of Christianity I*, Video Lecture 18, Liberty University DLP, 2004.

[4] I.K. Cross, *The Battle for Baptist History,* (Columbus, Georgia: Brentwood Christian Press, 1990), 29.

[5] Ibid., 33.

[6] Ibid., 29.

[7] Ibid., 42.

[8] Ibid., 42.

[9] The following points have been loosely adapted from J.M. Carroll, *The Trail of Blood*, 8-9.

Inescapable Truths and Ramifications

Continuous Existence ~ Churches that remained true to the core doctrine and practices of Jesus and the apostles have existed continuously from the church in Jerusalem until the present.

Legitimacy in Beliefs ~ Church legitimacy is not in the name; legitimacy is in the beliefs and practices of a church.

Embracing Jesus' Teachings ~ Only those connected to the line of churches which have embraced the teachings and practices of Jesus and His apostles are true, legitimate New Testament churches.

Not Always Right ~ There is no church or group of churches in any age, beginning with the church in Jerusalem to the present, that were always right on everything at all times.

Repentance ~ Historically, multitudes of individuals and churches formerly connected to a false church have seen the error of their ways and taken steps necessary to become a part of the continuous line of churches that connect to the one Jesus established.

Cannot be Neutral ~ It is impossible to be neutral on the issue of true, legitimate churches.

Core Scriptural Teachings

The Founder - Jesus Christ personally founded this organization called a church.

Head of the Church - Jesus Christ is God and the head of the church. True churches have always believed in the deity of Christ.

Permanent Offices - The church has two kinds of permanent offices: pastors and deacons.

Government - The government of the church is congregational.

Separation Between Churches - In congregational government and discipline, all churches are to be entirely separate and independent of each other.

Separation of Church and State - In congregational government and discipline, all churches are to be entirely separate and independent of the state. True churches have always opposed a state church.

Ordinances - The church is to keep the ordinances of baptism and the Lord's Supper and to assemble on Sunday.

The History of Churches

127

Core Scriptural Teachings

Saved by Grace ~ Salvation is exclusively by grace through personal faith in Jesus Christ alone.

Baptism ~ Only saved persons are to be baptized. This necessitates the rebaptism of people who were "baptized" before they were saved.

Membership by Salvation ~ Only saved persons can be members of a church. This precludes infant baptism.

Equal Worth of Believers ~ Every believer is of equal worth to God and in the church there is to be no ecclesiastical hierarchy. This is belief in the priesthood of every believer.

The Inspired Word ~ The Scriptures and only the Scriptures are inspired of God.

The Final Word ~ The Scriptures are the final rule of faith and practice for believers and the church.

The History of Churches

Chapter 11

The True Line of Churches Separates from the Corrupt Line

The prophet Amos asked, *"Can two walk together, except they be agreed,"* **Amos 3:3**? The answer to this rhetorical question is a resounding *No*. A split was inevitable with the move by many churches from Scripture towards tradition as their authority for faith and practice. Those who held to the Scriptures and those who left them could not walk together. A growing fault-line within Christendom was just under the surface. It had been there for many years. Paul spoke of this fracture. *"For I know this, that after my departing shall grievous wolves enter in among you, not sparing the flock. Also of your own selves shall men arise, speaking perverse things, to draw away disciples after them,"* **Acts 20:29-30**. By the time Constantine wed the church and the Roman state in 323, the breach between churches adhering to Scripture and those leaning toward tradition was great. The wedding of church and state was the catalyst that soon resulted in open fractures.

Because many churches stayed true to New Testament beliefs and practices, many modern historians view them as *heretics*. They disassociated themselves with those churches that deserted the Scriptures in favor of tradition and which married the state. These churches were not heretics. It was the traditionalists who departed from the Scriptures. Any reasonable person must admit that the

129

original main line of Christianity was of the apostolic variety as set forth in the New Testament. The splinter groups are those who departed from this model, not the ones who stayed true. The churches that married the state moved away from Scripture and became increasingly corrupt. Over the centuries a variety of others also became corrupt. It is important to keep in focus who left whom.

PREFACE TO THE HISTORY OF THOSE WHO STAYED TRUE TO NEW TESTAMENT DOCTRINE AND PRACTICE

It didn't take long for those churches that refused to become a part of the Roman state church to lose favor with both the political and the state church leaders of Rome. Constantine wanted to use Christianity as the cement of his empire. [1] He dreamed of restoring the ancient glory of the Empire and "believed that it could best be achieved on the basis of Christianity." [2] Naturally, it served his purposes to have all of the churches in his fold. He was not pleased when there was division in Christendom. The Council of Nicea was Constantine's direct effort to end controversy and unite all churches under his state leadership. [3] The breach between apostate churches and those true to New Testament teachings was far deeper than Constantine realized. The Council of Nicea did not bring churches committed to New Testament doctrine and practice into his fold. "Let it be definitely remembered that when Constantine made his call for the council, there were very many of the Christians (Baptists) and of the churches, which declined to respond. They wanted no marriage with the state, and no centralized religious government, and no higher ecclesiastical government of any kind, than the individual church." [4]

Most modern historians depict these New Testament believers and churches as heretics, corrupt and illegitimate. If that is true, then those churches that deserted the Scriptures in favor of tradition constitute the true line of Christianity dating back to Jesus Christ. There is no escaping this conclusion; however this is not a valid conclusion. Men are not heretics because they embrace and uphold the teachings of Jesus Christ and His apostles as set forth in the New Testament. As we shall see, there has been an unbroken line of true New Testament believers and churches dating back to Christ.

The existence of these true churches has been documented in historical records for many centuries. Because most of the people in these churches were poor and illiterate, they did not write historical records. Furthermore, what was written was routinely burned or destroyed by the state church that opposed and persecuted them. Most of the records of these true believers and churches come from their oppressors; however, some in this line did leave records. As they were being tortured, maimed and slaughtered by the millions, charges against them were being recorded. They were persecuted, often to death, because they believed in the Scriptures as the sole authority for faith and practice; because they believed that salvation is exclusively by grace through faith in Jesus Christ, not through institutional rituals; because they rejected infant baptism; because they re-baptized converts who had been baptized by the state church before they were saved and for other such scriptural beliefs. The charges of their adversaries identify these people as existing and being in the line of believers and churches that stayed true to New Testament faith and practice from Jesus until the present.

Extensive histories cataloguing their existence, beliefs and practices have been written, particularly in the eighteenth and nineteenth centuries. Men such as J.M. Cramp (*Baptist History*, 1856-58), D.B. Ray (*The Baptist Succession*, 1870), J.R. Graves (*Old Landmarkism*, 1880), William Cathcart (*The Baptist Encyclopadia*, 1883), Thomas Armitage (*History of the Baptists*, 1887), W.A. Jarrel (*Baptist Church Perpetuity or History*, 1894), John T. Christian (*A History of the Baptists*, 1922), G.H. Orchard (*A Concise History of Baptists*, 1938) and J.M. Carroll (*The Trail of Blood*, 1931) are just a few of those who documented the existence, faith and practice of those who stayed true to first-century Christianity. They were sympathetic to this line of believers and churches, but there were also many who were not sympathetic to them but who none-the-less verified their existence, beliefs and practices. Among these were men such as John Lawrence Mosheim (*An Ecclesiastical History, Ancient and Modern*, 1821), Augustus Neander (*General History of the Christian Religion and Church*, 1851), Edward Gibbon (*The Decline and Fall of the Roman Empire*, 1899) and Philip Schaff (*History of the Christian Church*, 1910). Be assured that a multitude of other sources abound.

In the twentieth century, a new breed of historians emerged. This new breed was and is bent on denying and discrediting all previous histories that give credibility to the line of churches that have through the centuries stayed true to first-century Christianity. They do it in the name of scientific scholarship. W. Morgan Patterson was one of the leading proponents of this new type of history. He wrote that those historians of previous years did not exercise an "application of objective research and accuracy." He charged them with "undue dependence upon secondary sources (and its usual concomitant lack of primary sources)." [5] Patterson and his kind accuse prior historians of being unscientific. "All the records of these godly men, some of whom spent the greater part of their ministerial lives searching through dusty libraries for the facts they recorded, were summarily set aside as being 'unscientific.'" [6]

It should surprise no one that those great historians who traced the true line for so many centuries did not quote more *primary* sources. The state church made as sure as it could that there were no *primary* sources. They destroyed them and then wrote accounts of their own making these Bible believers look as bad as possible. However, their own accounts validate the existence and the positions of these Christians. Observing one's hand in front of his face may not be *scientific proof*, but for reasonable people it is proof enough. Likewise, the records of those who persecuted the people who believed and practiced first century Christianity are proof enough. "For Caesar's *Gallic War* (composed between 59 BC – AD 17) there are several extant MSS, but only nine or ten are good, and the oldest is some 900 years later than Caesar's day." [7] It is strange that the new breed of historians have no problem accepting this writing about Caesar. They do not reject it as *unscientific* because of a shortage of *primary sources*. The same argument can be made about many other old but widely accepted documents. The new breed of historians also cite *a priori* reasoning (conclusions not supported by facts) as justification for rejecting the research of past scholars who wrote histories on the line of churches that refused to align with Rome. For Bible-believing Christians, Jesus' promise that churches like the one He established in Jerusalem would continue until His return is sufficient reason to pre-suppose that it did and will continue. When we look at history, we expect to find historical evidence supporting Jesus' claim. The fact that Jesus made the promise, and we anticipate finding historical proof to validate the promise, does not make the evidence untrue, invalid or unfit for historical claims. Even so, the positions taken in this book are highly discounted and rejected because of the scholastic reasons just cited.

THE MONTANISTS

One of the earliest groups of churches to make a major stand against the growing departure from first century Christianity was the Montanists. (Do not assume that these were necessarily the first or the only churches in dissent, or that purity was the only issue involved. The broad popularity of the Montanists is indicative of wide-spread discontent over the departure of so many pastors and churches from first century Christianity.)

Montanus "was a Phrygian, who arose about the year A. D. 156." [8] Montanus and those who followed him became increasingly disillusioned with the carnality that more and more pervaded Christendom. "Montanism was not, originally, a departure from the faith." [9] "It was not a new form of Christianity: it was a recovery of the old, the primitive church set over against the obvious corruptions of the current Christianity." [10]

Montanists held very firmly to the traditional rule of faith. They believed in salvation by a personal faith in Jesus Christ and opposed infant baptism. Montanists also strongly emphasized the universal priesthood of all Christians, and thus rejected the episcopate (a church hierarchy above the common people) that was growing in many churches. They were also strong believers in the coming Millennial Kingdom. They expected Christ to return and set up His kingdom at any time. Their emphasis on earthly, material things was minimal. They also emphasized purity of life. They stressed a holy lifestyle in God's people. Long before Constantine, the Montanists were adamantly opposed to external government over a given church. That would include no governmental control over a church and no control by one church over another. In conformity with their long-standing stance, they refused to be a part of Constantine's church-state marriage. [11] "The

Montanists were deeply rooted in the faith, and their opponents admitted that they received the entire Scriptures of the Old and the New Testaments, and they were sound in their views of the Father, and of the Son, and of the Holy Spirit." [12]

Like churches of every age, Montanism was not without its weaknesses. Montanus "sought a forced continuance of the MIRACULOUS GIFTS of the apostolic church." [13] This included "the continuance of prophecy" and "ecstatic oracular utterances." [14] They were fanatically ascetic and stern in church discipline. "They insisted that those who had 'lapsed' from the true faith should be rebaptized, because they had denied Christ and ought to be baptized anew. On this account they were termed 'Anabaptists.'" [15]

Montanism found extensive sympathy throughout the empire, especially in North Africa. The Montanists continued in Africa into the sixth century. They also "had many adherents in Phrygia, Galatia, Cappadocia, Cilicia and in Constantinople." [16] "Montanism continued for centuries, and finally became known under other names." [17] Tertullian became a Montanist and championed many Montanist positions. [18]

The churches that drifted ever farther from first century Christianity vigorously opposed the Montanists. They were condemned by many councils. [19] Like other groups of churches that opposed the departure from first century Christianity, the Montanists became *heretics* and created corrupt churches according to those growing in power. They became the objects of scorn and persecution. Once the actual corrupt churches wed the Roman state and had the power of the state behind them, they increasingly made war on all who did not join them. This included the Montanists, who over time also drifted from their roots.

THE NOVATIANS

It should be kept in mind that Christians were under severe persecution prior to the Edict of Milan in 313. Multitudes were martyred. In the face of such duress many Christians fled, lapsed and even recanted. In about 250, a schism broke out in Carthage over the election of Cyprian as the bishop. Cyprian viewed the churches as one, not many. He also believed that the pastorate of the church in Rome was traceable to Peter. He further laid the groundwork for transubstantiation by teaching that clergymen are sacrificial priests who offer Christ's body and blood in the Communion service. [20] Cyprian met opposition in Novatus, a church leader of questionable character and spirit. [21] Novatus' opposition was mainly to Cyprian's re-instatement after having fled persecution; however, his opposition was not limited to one issue. Many times those who oppose are waiting for an excuse, a peg on which to hang a hat, a catalyst. Cyprian fled in the face of persecution shortly after he was elected bishop. When he attempted to return, the schism turned into a split that centered on whether or not those who lapsed in the face of persecution should be re-admitted to the church. Cyprian was brought into question by the church in Rome.

Cornelius, the bishop of Rome, favored re-admission of those who lapsed. Novatian was a preacher in the Roman church who was at odds with Bishop Cornelius. [22] Novatian thought Cornelius was elected under false pretenses, so he quickly summoned a few bishops to make him bishop of Rome. Cornelius called a council about this hurried election. Sixty bishops attended the council and Novatian was excommunicated. [23] The schism spread. Many of the Montanists flooded to Novatian. [24] Though the initial Novatian schism was over purity and re-admission to the church, many of the Novatians embraced the New Testament doctrine and practices of the Montanists. Because of the severe persecutions the Novatians faced, they were forced into hiding; however, they continued to flourish for many centuries. They were called by a variety of names, including Cathari which means pure. They were also called Anabaptists because they baptized those who came to them from false churches. [25]

Cathari means pure

THE DONATISTS

Donatism developed toward the end of the third century and came to maturity soon after the turn of the fourth century. Like

Novatianism, it too was rooted in the controversy over church discipline and martyrdom. In 311 Caecilian was elected bishop of Carthage. A movement earlier originated by a man named Donatus rejected Caecilian and had him deposed and replaced by Majorinus. When Majorinus died two years later, a second man named Donatus took his place. This Donatus was a gifted man of great charisma, and it is from him that the movement took its name. [26] "The bishops of Rome and of several other important cities declared that Caecilian was the true bishop of Carthage, and that Majorinus and Donatus were usurpers." [27] Without success, the Donatists attempted to get Constantine's approval. Constantine not only refused to take their side, but he warned them to stop the schism or face severe penalties. [28]

The Donatists rejected infant baptism and were congregational in their form of government. Great effort has been made to discredit the Donatists. Just as today among Baptists there is great diversity, and some Baptists have departed the faith, likewise there were Donatists who went astray. This does not make all Donatists corrupt. For several centuries the Donatists claimed they alone constituted the pure church. In doctrine and practices, the mainline Donatists were Anabaptists and a part of that line of true churches that extends back to Jesus Christ. [29]

SUMMARY STATEMENT

As a growing number of churches moved farther and farther from first century Christianity, some withdrew and became hermits. "Others simply declared that the church at large had been corrupted, and that they were the true church ... There were many Christians who remained firm in their faith, and as a result suffered imprisonment, torture and even death." [30] The ones mentioned here are not all who stayed true; they are specific, documentable examples of those who did. These faithful Christians and churches continued by various names and in many locations through the centuries to come. As we progress through this book, we will identify many of them. To properly grasp and appreciate the situation in which these true churches found themselves, it will also be necessary to follow the development and history of the Roman state church that eventually became the Catholic Church.

[1] Carl Deimer, Professor, *History of Christianity I,* Video Lecture 12, Liberty University DLP, 2004.

[2] Justo L. Gonzalez, *The Story of Christianity,* vol. 1, (San Francisco: HarperCollins Publishers, 1984), 118.

[3] Deimer.

[4] J.M. Carroll, *The Trail of Blood,* (Lexington, Kentucky: Ashland Avenue Baptist Church, 1992), 16.

[5] Morgan W. Patterson, *Baptist Successionism: A Critical View,* (Valley Forge, Pennsylvania: Judson Press, 1969), 23.

[6] I.K. Cross, *The Battle for Baptist History,* (Columbus, Georgia: Brentwood Christian Press, 1990), 119.

[7] F.F. Bruce, *The New Testament Documents: Are They Reliable?* (Downers Grove, Illinois: InterVarsity Press, 1981), 11.

[8] John T. Christian, *A History of the Baptists,* vol. 1, (Texarkana, Ark.-Tex.: Bogard Press, 1922), 43.

[9] Philip Schaff, *History of the Christian Church,* vol. 2, (Peabody, Massachusetts: Hendrickson Publishers, 2002), 417.

[10] Christian, 43.

[11] Schaff, 421-427.

[12] Christian, 43-44.

[13] Schaff, 423.

[14] Ibid.

[15] Christian, 43.

[16] Schaff, 421.

[17] Christian, 44.

[18] Schaff, 420.

[19] Deimer, Lecture 8.

[20] Earle E. Cairns, *Christianity Through the Centuries: A History of the Christian Church,* 3rd ed., (Grand Rapids, Michigan: Zondervan, 1996), 110.

[21] Schaff, 194.

[22] Gonzalez, 88-90.

[23] Schaff, 196-197.

[24] Deimer.

[25] Christian, 44-45.

[26] Schaff, vol. 3, 360-361.

[27] Gonzalez, 152.

[28] Deimer.

[29] Christian, 45-47.

[30] Gonzalez, 151-152.

Books About the True Churches

These extensive histories of true churches catalog their existence, beliefs and practices.

Year		
1856-58	J.M. Cramp	*Baptist History*
1870	D.B. Ray	*The Baptist Succession*
1880	J.R. Graves	*Old Landmarkism*
1883	William Cathcart	*The Baptist Encyclopadia*
1887	Thomas Armitage	*History of the Baptists*
1894	W.A. Jarrel	*Baptist Church Perpetuity or History*
1922	John T. Christian	*A History of the Baptists*
1931	J.M. Carroll	*The Trail of Blood*
1938	G.H. Orchard	*A Concise History of Baptists*

These books verify the existence, beliefs and practices of the true churches.

1821	John Lawrence Mosheim	*An Ecclesiastical History, Ancient and Modern*
1851	Augustus Neander	*General History of the Christian Religion and Church*
1899	Edward Gibbon	*The Decline and Fall of the Roman Empire*
1910	Philip Schaff	*History of the Christian Church*

The History of Churches

Montanists (A.D. 156)

Their Stance:

Held very firmly to the traditional rule of faith

Believed in salvation by a personal faith in Jesus Christ

Opposed infant baptism

Strongly emphasized the universal priesthood of all Christians

Rejected the episcopate and hierarchy that was growing in
many churches

Strong believers in the coming Millennial Kingdom

Minimal emphasis on earthly, material things

Emphasized purity of life

Stressed a holy lifestyle in God's people

Adamantly opposed to external government over a given church

The History of Churches

Montanists (A.D. 156)

Their Weaknesses:

They wanted to continue the miraculous gifts from the apostolic church

This included the continuation of prophecy and divinely inspired utterances

They were fanatically ascetic and stern in church discipline

True believers who are properly baptized can backslide; and under persecution, even deny the faith as did Simon Peter. Backsliders need to confess this sin unto God, but they do not need rebaptism. The weakness of the Montanists was their insistence that those who denied Christ had "lapsed" from the true faith should be rebaptized (baptized anew).

Chapter 12

Evil Strengthens Its Grip

Understanding and appreciating true Christians and churches requires knowledge of the false Christians and churches. The true Christians and churches attempted, with much diligence, to stay true to first century Christianity. The false Christians and churches claimed to be the main line of Christianity, but supplanted the Scriptures in favor of their own ideas or traditions. Therefore, as this book moves chronologically forward, attention will be given to the true and to the false. Both groups claimed to be the true Christians. The false group grew stronger and stronger and sought total control. More and more this group saw itself as one church, not many. This group targeted all who refused to agree with, support and join their ranks. Those who refused were branded as heretics. The established state church grew stronger and sought to eliminate them by whatever means necessary, and to do so with state power. The predator and prey connection developed; for hundreds of years it became impossible to understand one without the other.

THE RISE OF THE CATHOLIC CHURCH

Prior to Constantine, the church in Rome had risen in prestige, influence and power. That rise accelerated when he came to power. By the early 13th century, the false church headquartered at Rome dominated the western world and much of the east. Though there was no true pope prior to 600,[1] groundwork was established which would facilitate the development and growth of

141

a church organization that would dominate much of the world for many centuries. Since this organization aggressively persecuted true Christians and churches, it is important to understand how it formed and grew.

CONSTANTINE

Constantine saw Christianity as a valuable tool with the potential of uniting a mighty religious force with the power of the state. When he professed that he had become a Christian and threw the support of the Roman state behind Christianity by uniting the Christian church with the Roman state, the state church had instant authority and power. When Constantine became sole ruler in 323, he immediately made Christianity the preferred religion of the Empire and declared himself to be the chief bishop. [2] At that time Constantine resided in Rome. Location obviously dictated that his communications and dealings with church people were primarily with the pastor and officials of the Church in Rome. The pastor in Rome, generally called the bishop of Rome, became a key person in Constantine's efforts to control the vast numbers of churches throughout the empire, all of which he viewed as one. Politics demanded unified support from the churches, and that required an open line of communication. The pastor in Rome was the most readily-accessible and renowned of all church leaders. Naturally, the prestige and clout he gained because of his access to and influence upon the emperor was enormous.

> **Constantine had instant authority and power as the chief bishop of Christianity**

STRONG AND CHARISMATIC PASTORS IN ROME

Anicetus (c. 157 - c. 168) [3]

Even before Constantine, pastors in Rome rose in prestige and power. Rome was the capital and chief city in the empire. The church there grew and reproduced. Several pastors of the church in Rome established precedents with enormous ramifications. One of those men was Anicetus, who gained the status of monarchical bishop (one who is over several *presbyters* or pastors). By this time there were several congregations in Rome. In light of the growing corrupt ecclesiology (theology regarding the church) of that day, the big church in Rome did not view the smaller churches as separate, autonomous congregations. Instead they were viewed merely as extensions of one Roman church. This concept was imitated throughout the empire. The biblical concept of local, autonomous bodies was disappearing from mainline thinking.

The assumption of power over other churches by pastors in Rome was asserting itself. In 190, Victor was bishop of Rome. Because he opposed Polycrates of Ephesus, Victor excommunicated the churches of Asia. [4] Bigger churches sought to dominate smaller churches.

A monarchical bishop is a bishop over several pastors

Innocent (402-417) [5]

Another notable pastor or bishop of the church in Rome was Innocent. He is the first bishop of Rome to make the claim that Peter had a tradition and that he was in it. Without proof or evidence, Innocent created a list of pastors of the church in Rome whom he claimed had direct succession and authority from Simon Peter. This line is called the *Petrine Tradition* and is claimed to the present as a mainstay of the Catholic Church and their pope. This is the ace *evidence* of the Catholics for their claim that they are the true church and that the pope is the supreme head of all Christendom.

In the Pelagian controversy which shook Christianity during Innocent's time, both Pelagius and five of the more influential bishops of North Africa sent letters to Innocent for his opinion. "He commended the Africans for having addressed themselves to the church of St. Peter, before which it was seemly that all the affairs of Christendom should be brought." [6] It is obvious that the hand of the Roman Church was growing stronger.

The *Petrine Tradition* is a list of pastors of the Church in Rome that supposedly had direct succession and authority from Simon Peter

---

Leo I (440-461) [7]

Leo I capitalized on the claim that the pastors of the Church in Rome were in a line of direct succession to Simon Peter. He cited Scriptures to support his claim including **Matthew 16:18-19, Luke 22:31-32** and **John 21:15-18**. [8] Even though there are no valid hermeneutical reasons for doing so, Leo I claimed that these passages teach that the church was built on Peter. He surmised that Peter was thus the head of all Christendom, and that every following pastor of the church in Rome occupies that role and status.

Leo I had "an ability, a boldness, and an unction displayed by none of his predecessors, and by few of his successors." [9] When corruption and immorality threatened to destroy the state church, a council of over 700 bishops was convened at Chalcedon (near Constantinople). On October 10, 451 the *Epistola Dogmatica*, Leo's rulings on the issues at hand was read to the assembly. "That is the faith of the Fathers! That is the faith of the apostles! So we all believe! So the orthodox believe! Anathema to him who believes otherwise! Through Leo, Peter has thus spoken. Even so did Cyril teach! That is the true faith." [10] It is clear that the voice of the pastor of the Church in Rome was rising in primacy above all other voices. It is also clear that state-church pastors throughout the empire were thinking in terms of one church, not many. They also viewed what the state-church taught to be the truth and orthodoxy. All who believed otherwise were cursed. Furthermore what the church (no longer churches) as a whole believed was best expressed by the bishop of Rome whose voice carried the most authority. Leo's position was clear: when he spoke, Peter had spoken. Amazingly, the multitude of bishops at Chalcedon was cheering when he said it. It is not difficult to see where the Donatists, Novatians and others, who never became a part of the state-church and who rejected such anti-scriptural doctrine, stood.

Gregory I (590-604) [11]

Gregory I was one of several pastors of the church in Rome who made political and military alliances with the new political powers that emerged as Roman political rule became weaker. During

Gregory's reign, for the first time the church ran the state rather than the state running the church as in the days of Constantine. "To me this makes him justifiably the first pope because he did that which, it seems to me, is essential to the core of the institution of the Roman Catholic papacy; that is the union of church and state." [12]

Because of his enormous power and his position that all who did not support his beliefs and practices were rebellious heretics, it is understandable that Christians and churches that did not submit to Gregory's power and positions were rejected and rigorously persecuted.

It can be safely said that by this time the Catholic Church had come into existence and that it had risen to a position of great power.

THE GEOGRAPHICAL POSITION OF ROME

The leaders of many churches in the Roman Empire were vying for the position of supremacy. Those in Jerusalem contended that the Jerusalem Church and her pastor should have supreme authority and the chief, ruling voice over *the church* because it was the first church to ever exist. Those in Antioch sought supremacy because of Paul and the reputation of this church as a missionary center. A powerful and influential school had sprung up at Alexandria. Ephesus also desired supremacy as did Constantinople.

One of the great reasons why Rome ultimately prevailed was her location. The instant Constantine became emperor, the bishop of Rome became the most important, powerful and influential bishop in the entire empire. The capital was there and the emperor considered the voice of the bishop of Rome to be the voice of the church as a whole. Furthermore, when the emperor told the bishop of Rome something, he considered the entire *church* told. With Constantine in power, the pastor of the church in Rome had the might of the state behind him. The big struggle among churches for supremacy had been in progress for decades; with the marriage of the church and the state, the competition ended. Rome was supreme among the churches that accepted the idea of a universal church and the state-church concept.

THE MOVE OF THE CAPITAL TO CONSTANTINOPLE

At first it may seem strange to say that the move of the capital from Rome to Constantinople greatly strengthened the hand of the bishop of Rome, but it did.

Constantine "clashed with the interests of the Roman Senate." [13] Furthermore the Germans and other barbaric groups were putting significant pressure on his northern borders. The move to Byzantium relocated his capital from the edge of his kingdom nearer to its center. [14] In 330, Constantine moved his capital from the city of Rome to Byzantium and renamed the new city "Constantinople" which means "city of Constantine." [15] Because of its proximity to the Bosporus, through which all shipping between the Black and Mediterranean Seas passed, Constantinople was a very strategic location.

By this time the bishop of Rome was respected as the best and chief bishop of the empire. As long as Constantine lived in Rome, he had his thumb on the bishop; however, that changed dramatically when Constantine moved so far away. With the tremendous authority he had achieved, the bishop of Rome suddenly had the power to do whatever he pleased. By default he became the head of politics in Rome as well as the head of the church. When Constantine moved out, German rulers moved in and the charismatic bishops of the church in Rome began to make deals with them. At this point the church began to dictate to the state; not to the old Roman state, but to the newly emerging Germanic and French states. From their distant eastern location in Constantinople there was little that the feuding, weakening Roman emperors could do about the growing Roman Church power base in Rome. The Roman bishop quickly became the top person in the west. [16]

DOCTRINAL CONTROVERSIES

Long before Constantine, doctrinal controversies raged within the ranks of Christendom. Many of them were over the deity of Christ.

The Arian Controversy

Arius argued that Jesus was different and not equal with God the Father. Arius said Jesus was created and not eternal. Athanasius of Alexandria argued that Jesus Christ was identical to the father in substance. Christians throughout the empire took sides. Eusebius, who was close to Constantine and who is often called the father of church history, offered a compromise. He said Jesus is similar to the Father.

Athanasius prevailed. At the Council of Nicea the majority voted unanimously that Christ was "the same substance, the same essence, co-eternal with the Father, distinct from the Father only in person." [17]

The bishop of Rome was on the winning side; his hand was strengthened.

The Nestorian Controversy

This controversy was over how Jesus could be both fully God and fully man. The Greek term <u>theotokos</u> was confusing to many. <u>Theos</u> is the word for "God" and <u>tokos</u> is the word for "bearer". The controversy was over whether or not Mary was the God-bearer. The debate spread throughout the empire.

In 451 Leo I, who was the bishop of Rome, sent a letter to the Council of Chalcedon. He stated that "Christ has two natures, without confusion, without change, without division, without separation." [18] This is generally known as the hypostatic union.

Again the bishop of Rome ranked high in authority. The fact that his position prevailed increased his prestige.

The Pelagian Controversy

Pelagius argued that men have freedom of choice and that they are responsible to God to make good decisions. Pelagius ignored original sin and said sin is solely by choice. One ramification of this view is that if they chose to do so, people (including children) could live sin-free lives. In so-doing they would never die.

Augustine headed the opposing side in this controversy. He argued for original sin and against man's free will. Augustine strongly advocated the doctrines of sovereign grace which were later enunciated by John Calvin. He also took the position that children should be baptized to wash away the tint of original sin. Baptism was thus viewed as a sacrament which was necessary to the washing away of sins. This obviously fit the developing institutional salvation theology of the state church.

The Iconoclastic Controversy

The issue in this controversy had to do with when an icon becomes an idol. The western Catholics, who gravitated toward Rome, took the position that a full figure of an image is only an icon, not an idol. The eastern Catholics, who gravitated toward Constantinople, took the position that full figures are idols but that flat surface figures are icons.

Western churches were full of full-figure images as well as flat-figures. The Iconoclasts wanted to destroy icons. Many of them did so rather dramatically with axes and hammers, and with the support of their church and political leaders. The controversy sharply divided eastern and western state churches. One man suggested that "if you can with two fingers pull the images off the wall," you should destroy them. [19]

EAST VERSUS WEST

In many ways state-church Christianity was becoming sharply divided between the east and the west. Many of the controversies pitted the two sides against each other. The move of the capital divided the state church of the empire into two camps, the west headquartered at Rome and the east headquartered at Constantinople. The gradual alignment of the empire into two political entities further exacerbated the division. While the eastern churches continued to find themselves under the control of the emperors of the old Roman Empire, the western churches found themselves increasingly under the power of the bishop of Rome. As we shall see in chapters that are just ahead, major events were on the horizon which would dramatically impact the overall political and state-church picture.

Though the churches that continued to practice first-century Christianity were impacted and influenced to some degree by all these developments, for the most part they were neither involved in the controversies, nor drawn under the control of the bishop of Rome. As detached as they tried to be, they could not stay out of harm's way. The establishment churches actively sought after and persecuted them.

---

[1] Gregory I was the first bishop of the Roman Church to successfully subjugate state authorities both politically and militarily. Until this position of power was achieved, the term *pope* could not be legitimately used in reference to the chief official of the Roman Catholic Church; however, reference to the bishop of Rome as the pope occurred long before A.D. 600.

[2] Carl Deimer, Professor, *History of Christianity I,* Video Lecture 12, Liberty University DLP, 2004.

[3] *Wikipedia,* (en.wikipedia.org/wiki/Pope_Anicetus).

[4] Earle E. Cairns, *Christianity Through the Centuries: A History of the Christian Church,* 3rd ed., (Grand Rapids, Michigan: Zondervan, 1996), 101.

[5] Deimer.

[6] Philip Schaff, *History of the Christian Church,* vol. 3, (Peabody, Massachusetts: Hendrickson Publishers, 2002), 797.

[7] Ibid., 740.

[8] Deimer.

[9] Schaff, 740.

[10] Ibid., 744.

[11] Ibid., 328.

[12] Deimer.

[13] Justo L. Gonzalez, *The Story of Christianity,* vol. 1, (San Francisco: HarperCollins Publishers, 1984), 118.

[14] Deimer.

[15] Gonzalez.

[16] Deimer.

[17] Ibid., Lecture 13.

[18] Ibid.

[19] Ibid.

Strong and Charismatic Pastors in Rome

Anicetus (157-168)

He gained the status of monarchical bishop (one who is over several presbyters).
The corrupt ecclesiology of one big church started to grow.

Innocent (402-417)

He created a list of pastors (called the *Petrine Tradition*) whom he claimed had direct succession and authority from Simon Peter. This list is used to claim that the pope is the supreme head of all Christendom.

Leo I (440-461)

He cited scriptures that claimed that the church is built on Peter, which led to his surmise that Peter was the head of all Christendom.

Gregory I (590-604)

He made political and military alliances. During his reign, the church ran the state.

Doctrinal Controversies

Arian Controversy

Arius argued that Jesus was different and not equal with God the Father. Arius said Jesus was created and not eternal. The Council of Nicea voted unanimously that Jesus Christ was identical to the father in substance.

Nestorian Controversy

This controversy was over how Jesus could be both fully God and fully man. Leo I, the bishop of Rome, sent a letter to the Council of Chalcedon stating that Jesus Christ had both human and divine natures (called a hypostatic union).

Pelagian Controversy

Pelagius argued that men have freedom of choice and that they are responsible to God to make good decisions. He said that sin is by choice. Augustine headed the opposing side and argued for original sin and against man's free will.

Iconoclastic Controversy

This had to do with when an icon becomes an idol. The western Catholics took the position that a full figure is only an icon, not an idol. The eastern Catholics took the position that full figures are idols, but that flat surface figures are icons.

The History of Churches

Chapter 13

The Growth and Tyranny of the Catholic Church

The formation and development of one, world-dominating church would seem to be the fantasy of a wild imagination. Visualize many churches in one city and multitudes of other churches in other cities. The idea that most of the churches in a given city would submit themselves to the headship and domination of one church and one pastor in one city is unfathomable, yet it happened in Rome, Italy. Furthermore, over the years, that dominating church in Rome succeeded in bringing multitudes of churches throughout the empire and world under its headship, domination and authority. That it ever happened is a most astounding phenomenon. As unlikely as it may seem, it did happen and that dominating church is now called the Catholic Church.

Many factors contributed to the rise and growth of Catholicism. We have considered (1) Constantine, (2) a series of strong and imaginative bishops in Rome, (3) the geographical position of Rome, (4) the move of the capital of the Roman Empire to Constantinople and (5) a series of doctrinal controversies in which the bishop of Rome was always on the winning side. These were major contributors; they were not all. Other factors should be considered.

THE NEW POLITICAL LANDSCAPE

We have already considered how the move of the capital from Rome to Constantinople greatly strengthened the hand of the bishop of Rome. He became the chief political and top religious figure in the west. At the same time the power of the Roman emperor began to diminish, especially in the west. The government became increasingly divided, inept and weak. Distance and weakness made it impossible for Roman emperors to adequately govern and defend the far reaches of the empire, particularly in the west. At the same time strong political and military forces were developing north of the western parts of the empire.

When Constantine moved, the Roman bishops accomplished the remarkable feat of being able to maintain their theology, their churches and their positions. They did so mainly by transferring their allegiance from the old Roman Empire to the new Germanic political powers that came upon them. [1]

The New Political and Military Players

As far back as the second century, large migrations of people from the territory east and north of the Rhine and Danube Rivers were moving southward into northern Europe. The barbaric Teutonic people of Germanic origin who lived there began to feel the pressure of the Huns, Mongols and other invaders. They moved southward and westward. The Roman emperors were forced to keep large numbers of troops on their northern borders to keep out these Germanic people. By the fourth century, it was a generally accepted conclusion that these invaders would eventually take control of the western empire. This is one of the reasons Constantine moved his capital from Rome to Constantinople in the eastern part of the empire. [2]

These marauding barbarians consisted of several groups, but they were not united. The better known of them were the Vandals, the Franks, the Lombards, the Goths, the Burgundians and the Anglo-Saxons. The Visigoths (western Goths) came first; they finally settled in Spain. The Visigoths were followed by the Vandals who made their way to North Africa. They made havoc of many of the

Christian communities located there. The Ostrogoths (eastern Goths) followed and took control of the bankrupt Roman government. The Lombards, Burgundians and Franks moved into what is now modern France, and the Anglo-Saxons settled in England. [3]

After the Arian controversy, many people still embraced the false doctrine of Arius. It should be remembered that Arius taught that Jesus was not of the same substance or essence as the Father. He taught that Jesus was a lesser god who was not all-powerful or eternal. Many who embraced this false doctrine continued to spread it with missionary zeal, particularly in the east. Before they invaded the west, most of the barbaric Teutonic people had been converted to this brand of Christianity; however, they were not strong in their beliefs. The main missionary to the Goths was Ulfilas who "rejected Christ as a secondary God and the Holy Spirit merely as a sanctifying power." [4] Because their Arian Christianity was weak and due to their desire to adopt the more civilized and affluent lifestyle of the Romans whom they were conquering, most of these barbaric people were ready to convert to the western-style Christianity of the bishops of Rome. This western-style Christianity was widely known as Nicene Christianity. By this point in time institutional Christianity based on sacraments and rituals prevailed. For example, in the fifth century a Frankish king named Clovis faced a crucial battle the next day. He vowed that if he won the battle he would desert Arianism and become a Nicene Christian. He won. Not only did he convert, he determined that his whole army would become Christian. He lined up all of his soldiers by a river and selected a priest to baptize them. To accomplish this, the priest cut a large branch from a tree. As Clovis' troops marched by, the priest dipped the branch into the river and flung the water over them while repeating the words "I baptize you in the name of the Father, the Son and the Holy Spirit." Supposedly the whole army became Christian in a day. [5] No one who stays true to the Scriptures could accept this as true conversion; however, it is typical of the way the state church that became the Catholic Church made converts. According to their theology and practice, salvation came through the church by the sacraments, not through a personal relationship with Jesus Christ by faith.

Long before, the churches that identified with the church in Rome had lost their personal connection to Jesus Christ. They taught that salvation came through identification with the church by baptism and communion. Therefore it was easy for masses to go through those rituals and become "Christians." From a biblical standpoint it is certain that one becomes a Christian because of putting his or her personal faith in Jesus Christ in view of His death, burial and resurrection.

Nicene Christianity accepts the deity of Christ

Converting the Conquerors

Constantine was right. The invaders did reach Rome. Under the leadership of Aleric the Visigoths took Rome in 410. [6] The bishops of the church in Rome were opportunists. They had no real principles or allegiances; they were ready to go with whomever could offer them the most power. At this point that was obviously the new conquerors, not the weak and distant Roman rulers in Constantinople. The chief political and religious leader with whom the conquering invaders must bargain was the bishop of Rome. Rather than resist the new conquerors, the bishops repeatedly convinced these winners that the allegiance of the Christian church was not to old Rome. To the contrary, they promised to work with the new conquerors. In exchange for the conversion of the invaders to Nicene (western) Christianity, the bishops of Rome would bring them the support of the people. Masses of people and whole people groups throughout the western empire converted to the Roman Church's brand of Christianity. [7] Of course, the bishop of Rome was already the head of the church. Now the church was directing the state. Amazingly, the new conquerors agreed and moved in as converts and supporters of the bishops in Rome. This was not the case in every location throughout the western empire, but it was the case in the vast majority of locations.

The Continuation of the Church-State Relationship

The bishops of Rome had already tasted the power that goes with a church-state relationship. For them there was no turning back. If the old Roman state was dying, the church must marry the new state. Regardless of who was in power these rulers would see to it that their brand of Christianity would always be the official and only religion allowed within the state. If necessary, all others would be persecuted, even to death. The massive wave of persecution and martyrdom that proliferated during this time is testimony to a steady stream of people which never became a part of the state church. They never embraced the theology that continually moved farther and farther from the Bible. This was hundreds of years prior to the Protestant Reformation.

The union of the bishop of Rome with the Franks illustrates the determination of the Roman bishops to insure their position and power. In 751 Roman Bishop Zacharias deposed the unpopular Childeric III, king of the Franks, and crowned Pepin (the Short) in his stead. [8] This recognition was a big honor to the Franks, but it also enhanced the prestige and power of the bishop of Rome. He was now seen as in a position to make kings. [9] In return for being made king, Pepin gave the bishop the large Italian territory called the Papal States. Now the bishop of Rome was not only the head of the church, he was also ruler over a large territory, about one fifth of modern Italy. [10]

From the time of Pepin, "the alliance between the Franks and the popes grew closer, until Pope Leo III crowned Charlemagne emperor of the West on Christmas Day, A.D. 800." [11]

MONASTICISM

Strangely enough, monasticism sprang up as the Catholic Church took shape and developed. As time passed, monasticism played right into the hands of the bishop of Rome, who could be rightly called the pope after the time of Gregory I.

Monasticism is the practice of giving up worldly pleasures in order to focus on religious pursuits. At the beginning of the movement they separated themselves from the evils they perceived and those who practiced such evils. Over time many retreated to caves, deserts and other remote places. Later individuals congregated into societies of like-minded people. Monasticism came into being for three primary reasons. One was missions. A second reason was lack of persecution against members of the state-church. (They were the ones doing the persecuting.) The third reason for monasticism was worldliness in the state-church. [12] There were many who were zealous to extend the gospel to the ends of the earth. To be a missionary, one had to give up most of the comforts of life, including wealth and family. Persecution had resulted in a great measure of purity within Christendom. Corruption proliferated when persecution ceased. Those who entered into a life of monasticism thought that punishing the body purified the soul. Many who viewed the church as becoming corrupt and worldly joined monasteries where they lived fiercely ascetic lifestyles. Monasticism was their answer to corruption, ease and worldliness in the Catholic Church.

Over time, monasticism went through four stages. At first, ascetic practices were carried out by people within the state-church. Later, men began to withdraw to remote places like desert caves, especially in Egypt where they lived the most meager of lifestyles. They were called hermits. In the third stage, those who opposed the corruption, ease and worldliness they saw in the church moved into close proximity to a hermit to whom they looked for leadership. Though they lived separate lives, they cloistered for common exercises. Finally these hermits organized and began to live in monasteries. [13] Monks did all kinds of weird things. One "known as Simon the Stylite (ca. 390-459), after having lived buried up to his neck in the ground for several months, decided to achieve holiness by becoming an ecclesiastical 'pole sitter.' He spent over thirty years on the top of a sixty-foot pillar near Antioch." [14] Some ate grass like cattle, some never bathed and one "wandered naked in the vicinity of Mount Sinai for fifty years." [15]

Pachomius was the first to gather a group of hermits into a communal arrangement called a monastery. [16] Unlike eastern monasticism, western monasticism did not punish the body for the sole purpose of renunciation. It trained monks for missionary and apologetic work. In 529 Benedict founded a monastery just south of Rome. [17] Benedict established the *Rule* for monks. The *Rule*

shaped monasticism for centuries. The main features of the *Rule*
were permanence and obedience. Each monk must remain in his
initial monastery for the rest of his life and the *Rule* must be rigidly
obeyed. That meant obeying the abbot who was the head of the
monastery. The move that strengthened the Catholic Church most
was the placing of the government of each monastery under the
authority of the local governing bishop. [18] This tied monasticism
to the Catholic Church and contributed greatly to the rise of the
papacy. By this act, groundwork was laid for full control of all
monasteries by the pope or bishop of Rome.

Monasteries tend to become lax and worldly over time. By the
arrival of the 10th century, monasticism had largely become
wealthy, immoral and corrupt. In 909, Duke William III of
Aquitaine established a monastery at his favorite hunting grounds
in Cluny, France and appointed a steadfast monk named Berno in
an effort to reform monasticism. Duke William deeded the
monastery and the lands around it to "Saints Peter and Paul." [19]
This placed the new monastery and monastic community under the
direct jurisdiction and protection of the pope or bishop of Rome.
Before long there appeared an entire network of second Clunys or
monasteries under the direct jurisdiction under the pope. This
reform effort was the first to open the door to women's monastic
communities.

In time, all monasticism followed the leadership of Cluny and was
brought under the direct control of the bishop of Rome. Now the
bishop of Rome had personal and full control of monasteries
across Western Europe and Britain. With thousands of monks
now under his command, the bishop of Rome had an army to use
as he saw fit. Many of them went forth as missionaries.
Multitudes served as military men, especially in the coming
Crusades. They raised money, persecuted non-Catholics and did
whatever the pope desired. The power of the bishop of Rome was
becoming enormous.

> **The main features of the Benedictine *Rule*
> are permanence and obedience**

THE CATHOLIC CHURCH AT THE
END OF THE SIXTH CENTURY

A glance at the power of the bishop of Rome as the seventh century dawned can help with perspective. The bishop at that time was Gregory I. He was the bishop of Rome from 590 until 604. The following is a list of practices initiated by Gregory. Though he was not able to enforce all of these, they later became standard and universal throughout the Catholic Church.

- Gregory created the Gregorian chant.

- Gregory permanently established the sacramental system. Later it was refined to include seven sacraments, but Gregory established it as a system.

- Gregory instituted celibacy in the clergy.

- Gregory established that one must have the consent of the Roman bishop in order to be ordained as a bishop.

- Gregory made sacramentalism the official way of the Catholic Church. [20]

The policies that Gregory established gave more power to the state-church. The state-church gained more power by switching political allegiances when the Germanic people took over most of Europe. The power of the Roman state church increased because most of the invading people converted from Arian Christianity to Nicene Christianity. The church thus had influence over a larger number of people. The introduction of monasticism allowed more people to join the state-church in a safe way. Some of the land that the monasteries were built on was donated to the church, so their power and wealth grew even more. The state-church had come of age. Even though much of its doctrine and many of practices did not agree with the core teachings of Jesus Christ and His apostles, the state church now had the power it needed to enforce the idea that it was the only true church.

Even though the state-church had power and wealth, there were still those who believed in and practiced first-century Christianity. Their names varied over time. When their doctrine and practices are examined, it becomes apparent that through the centuries there were always those who embraced and practiced the basic, core teachings of Jesus Christ and His apostles.

[1] Carl Deimer, Professor, *History of Christianity I,* Video Lecture 15, Liberty University DLP, 2004.

[2] Ibid.

[3] Earle E. Cairns, *Christianity Through the Centuries: A History of the Christian Church,* 3rd ed., (Grand Rapids, Michigan: Zondervan, 1996), 121.

[4] Philip Schaff, *History of the Christian Church,* vol. 4, (Peabody, Massachusetts: Hendrickson Publishers, 2002), 78.

[5] Deimer.

[6] Justo L. Gonzalez, *The Story of Christianity,* vol. 1, (San Francisco: HarperCollins Publishers, 1984), 232.

[7] Schaff, 78-80.

[8] Gonzalez, 248.

[9] Deimer, Lecture 16.

[10] Ibid.

[11] Gonzalez.

[12] Deimer, Lecture 15.

[13] Cairns, 145.

[14] Ibid, 146.

[15] Ibid.

[16] Deimer.

[17] Ibid.

[18] Gonzalez, 239.

[19] Ibid., 278.

[20] Deimer.

Monasticism

Monasticism is the practice of giving up worldly pleasures in order to focus on religious pursuits.

Monasticism came into being for three primary reasons

1. Missions
2. A lack of persecution against members of the state-church
3. Worldliness in the state-church

Monasticism went through four stages

1. Ascetic practices were carried out by people within the state-church
2. Later, men began to withdraw to remote places like desert caves where they lived the most meager of lifestyles. They were called hermits.
3. Those who opposed the corruption, ease and worldliness they saw in the church moved into close proximity to a hermit to whom they looked for leadership
4. These hermits organized and began to live in monasteries

The *Rule*

In 529, Benedict established the *Rule* for monks, which featured permanence and obedience. Each monk must remain in his initial monastery for the rest of his life, and the *Rule* must be rigidly obeyed

The History of Churches

161

Chapter 14

Staying True in the Face of Enormous Oppression

We have met the Montanists, the Novatians and the Donatists. These Christians all had flaws, but their tenacious commitment to the "absolute and unconditional authority of the New Testament as the sole rule of faith and practice in religious matters" gave them "a powerful preventative to error and a specific corrective" when there was an aberration from the truth. [1] Do not imagine that these Christians were the only ones who rejected the way of Rome and the widespread departure from first-century, New Testament Christianity. Across the Roman Empire, east, west, north and south there were multitudes of unaffiliated believers and churches that were true to *"the faith which was once delivered unto the saints,"* **Jude 3**.

OBSCURE RECORDS

More should be said about the records of those Christians and churches that refused to depart from the scriptural pattern. A few of their own records have survived but not many. As J.M. Carroll summarized, their existence is mainly a *Trail of Blood.* An explanation given by John T. Christian in the preface of his history of these people captures the situation quite well. "We are far removed from many of the circumstances under survey: the representations of the Baptists were often made by enemies who did not scruple, when such a course suited their purpose, to blacken character; and hence the testimony from such sources must be received with discrimination and much allowance made for many statements; in some instances vigilant and sustained attempts were made to destroy every document relating to these people; the material that remains is scattered through many libraries and archives, in many lands and not always readily accessible; often, on account of persecutions, the Baptists were far more interested in hiding than they were in giving an account of themselves or their whereabouts; they were scattered through many countries, in city and cave, as they could find a place of concealment; and frequently they were called by different names by their enemies, which is confusing." [2]

It should be obvious to every observer that the coverage of the study in progress is not comprehensive. Serious students could and should conduct much deeper studies at many junctures. For example, a whole course could easily be taught on the Montanists. The Donatist movement was huge and lasted for centuries. David Benedict wrote a large book on the Donatists. [3] Do not think that the Paulicians, the Albigenses or dozens of others that could be named were small splinter groups. There were millions of these people, and they were scattered across Eastern and Western Europe, North Africa, the British Isles and wherever Christianity went. Furthermore, the brief looks we are taking in this book often cover several centuries. Faithful communities of Christians and churches that remained true to the faith on the core issues flourished in the Piedmont Valley of France for well over a thousand years. There is no way that we could completely cover their history by a few brief mentions in a book like this. These facts are mentioned so that you may realize that you are seeing only the small tip of a huge, huge iceberg. The idea that only a small group of heretics did not join the Roman Church movement and embrace their doctrine is far, far from the truth. Evidence to the contrary is overwhelming and that evidence can readily be accessed. [4]

SOME OF THOSE WHO STAYED FAITHFUL
TO CORE SCRIPTURAL POSITIONS

Keep in mind that no Christian group can be said to have been without biblical shortcomings. (Such is still the case.) Even with their weaknesses the vast, vast majority of these *dissidents* insisted on the authority of the Scriptures, the deity of Christ, salvation by a personal relationship with Jesus Christ, the baptism of believers only, a pure church separate from the state, congregational and autonomous church government and holy living by believers.

The Montanists gave way to the Novatians who blended into the Donatists. We have seen that groups differed slightly on various issues, but when it came to most of the core beliefs, those who refused to desert Scripture in favor of tradition were in agreement. They were in essence the same people.

It should not be difficult for a reasonable thinker to put the picture into perspective. The people who stood with the Scriptures and first-century Christianity were often separated from each other by vast geographical distances in an age where long-distance communication was slow and often non-existent. Wild animals, bandits and a lack of lodging and transportation made travel hazardous. As the state-church grew and the Roman Church matured, those Christians and churches that were not a part of the establishment were hunted, persecuted and killed as though they were criminals and a threat to the world. This usually made caution and secrecy necessary for survival. It is not difficult to see why many of these Christians and churches were not aware of others who believed essentially the same as they did. These believers and churches often assumed the name of the area where they lived. This was true of the Albigenses who lived in and around Albi, France. The Montanists and Donatists assumed the name of one of their strong leaders. That these early believers didn't go by one common name such as Baptist should not come as a surprise to anyone. The rope that tied them together as one people, regardless of the name or location, was their common doctrine: the authority of the Scriptures, the deity of Christ, the necessity of personal regeneration by grace through faith in Christ alone, no church state, the autonomy of each church, the purity of church and private life and liberty of conscience and expression. Doctrine and practice are the common bonds that transcend the centuries. This is the unbroken line from the church that Jesus personally established in Jerusalem, Israel to the present. They were here and they were there, they were called this or that, but they were always somewhere.

The most common denominator among them was their practice of baptizing believers only. Within their own ranks a person had to be mature enough to make a personal decision of faith in Christ before baptism. There was thus no baby baptism. If they received anyone who had been baptized either as a baby or before he was saved, they re-baptized that person. Furthermore, when someone came to them from the state or other false church, they re-baptized that person. They did not believe that a false church had the authority to baptize and thus concluded that such ones had never been scripturally baptized. It was Christ before the church and blood before water. It is not difficult to see why these believers and churches were quickly dubbed Anabaptists.

> **The common denominator was the baptism of believers only**

GENERAL NAMES

Usually specific groups of believers and churches were known by more than one name. There were general umbrella names used to denote a large number of churches with similarities. There were also specific names used to denote groups of churches with similar beliefs and practices especially those living within specific geographical areas.

This will not be difficult to understand when compared to current Christianity. For example, the name Baptist encompasses a very broad spectrum of churches. Under that umbrella name there are Southern Baptists, the General Association of Regular Baptists, unaffiliated Baptists and Baptists who compose the Baptist Bible Fellowship. There are many others. Within each of these groups there are many specific congregations. Through the centuries the same churches and groups of believers have gone by several different names. Do not assume that a different name automatically means a totally different group of people with radically different beliefs and practices. Sometimes that assumption may be correct; many times it is not.

For the early time-period covered in this chapter, two of the more common general names for those who embraced and practiced first-century Christianity and who never became a part of the state church are *the Cathari* and *the Anabaptists*.

The Cathari

The name *Cathari* means pure. A common characteristic of many of those who maintained first-century Christianity was purity of life. Reinerius Saccho, who was a Cathari before becoming a Catholic inquisitor, made these accusations against those whom he once embraced. "Heretics are distinguished by their manners and their words, for they are sedate and modest in their manners. They have no pride in clothes, for they wear such as are neither costly nor mean. They do not carry on business in order to avoid falsehoods, oaths, and frauds, but only live by labor as workmen. Their teachers also are shoemakers and weavers. They do not multiply riches, but are content with what is necessary, and they are chaste, especially the Leonists. They are also temperate in meat and drink. They do not go to taverns, dances, or other vanities." [5]

Until fairly recently in Christianity, names did not seem to greatly matter with most Christians and churches. Christians through the centuries have been far more interested in what a man or church believed and practiced than in the name. Once Christian groups with differing names realized they stood on the same truths, they commonly accepted each other.

Cathari is a name given through the ages to many groups who dissented with the Roman Church. That name does not mean they were all in full agreement on doctrine and practice; it does mean that they had a reputation of purity. Do not be confused when you hear Novatians, Paulicians, Albigenses and other groups that refused the Roman direction also called *Cathari*.

The Anabaptists

Anabaptist was also a name widely used to denote dissenting believers and churches. The name was rarely self-applied; it was given by their enemies to those who re-baptized others who came from false churches or who were baptized before they were saved.

As the word *Christian* was originally used in scorn of those who were copycats of Christ, **Acts 11:26**, likewise *Anabaptist* was a name of hostility against Christians and churches true to New Testament teachings on baptism. The Montanists were firm on "the re-baptism of those coming from heretical societies, and an extremely pure church discipline." [6] The Novatians insisted on strict church discipline and "required those coming from communions practicing such loose discipline to be re-baptized." [7] The Donatists likewise re-baptized those coming from the state churches. [8] The practice of re-baptizing by those who rejected the Roman direction was almost universal. Regardless of their specific and local names they were generally viewed and identified under the broad umbrella name *Anabaptist*. For example, the Albigenses and the Paulicians were also known as Anabaptists.

> **Anabaptist means to re-baptize**

SPECIFIC NAMES

It is now time to take a specific and closer look at some of those believers and churches that held to first-century Christianity even while the state church developed into the Roman Catholic Church.

The Paulicians

Most of the information on the Paulicians comes from two main sources. First there were two Greek writers who wrote very maliciously against the Paulicians. The second is an Armenian source discovered and translated by Fred C. Conybeare of Oxford University. This is an old book by the Paulicians called *Key of Truth*. [9] The Paulician churches originated in the first century in the area of Armenia and "spread in the Taurus mountains as far as Ararat." [10] Constantine (not to be confused with the Roman Emperor, Constantine) greatly advanced this sect of believers in the mid-seventh century.

They have been falsely maligned as being Manichaean [11], but they were not. They rejected tradition and held to the Scriptures. They also rejected the relics and images of the Catholics and held to

167

baptism and the Lord's Supper as the only two ordinances of the church. They baptized only adults, and the Lord's Supper was restricted to believers. [12] They were believers in the Trinity and knew no other mediator than Jesus Christ. [13] Dr. I.K. Cross lists ten distinctive marks of the Paulicians.

- They held tenaciously to the sacred writings.

- They were especially concerned with the writings of the apostle Paul and determined to build their churches upon his teachings. Their ministers tried to follow his footsteps to the extent that they as his followers adopted the name as their own.

- They totally rejected all relics and image worship.

- They demanded a genuine experience of salvation before admitting any for baptism. This is what is commonly called 'believer's baptism.'

- Their churches were independent and self-governing.

- They accepted only baptism and the Lord's Supper as ordinances of the church and baptized by dipping or immersion.

- They re-baptized those who came to them from other communions, thus identifying them in the eyes of their enemies as Anabaptists.

- They believed they were in succession from the churches of the New Testament.

- They believed and practiced purity of church discipline, causing them to be called Cathari.

- From New Testament days they brought their faith across Europe and into the Reformation which was a rejection of the state church and its doctrine. The Reformation led to many other new church movements. [14]

The Paulicians were mercilessly hunted and violently persecuted by the state church. They were able to migrate across Europe, where they found solace and became deeply planted with the Albigenses. [15] The pure lifestyle of the Paulicians won them respect among the

Arabs, who called them Sabians (an Arabic word meaning Baptists). "They literally filled with their members Syria, Palestine, and Babylonia." [16] The immoral Empress Theodora "instituted a persecution in which one hundred thousand Paulicians in Grecian Armenia are said to have lost their lives." [17] Under severe persecution they took refuge among the Arabs where they were tolerated. The Arabs recognized them to be different from the Roman state church. In the ninth century some of the Paulicians re-established themselves in Armenia and sent a host of missionaries who won converts and established churches among the Slavonic tribes of Bulgaria, Bosnia and Serbia. [18]

"They are the Paulicians of Armenia, the Bogomil sect round Moscow whose members call themselves Christ's, the adult Baptists (those who practice adult baptism) among the Syrians of the upper Tigris valley, and perhaps, though not so certainly, the popelikans, the Mennonites, and the great Baptist communities of Europe." [19] They were known as Bogomilians in the Balkans where they were sometimes called Acephali meaning *headless* because they had no distinct order of clergy, or presiding person in their assemblies. In France they were called Bulgarians, Publicans and boni homines meaning *good men*. Many of them clustered around Milan, Italy where they were called Paterini and Cathari. [20] They were Anabaptists in practice. The name Paulicians came from the apostle Paul. [21]

The Albigenses

The Alps, particularly the French Alps, became a refuge for many groups of Christians and churches that remained faithful to the doctrine and practice of first-century Christianity. It seems that God prepared a hiding-place that acted somewhat as a fortress for the preservation of His people. The state church which developed into the Catholic Church hunted and sought to eradicate them. They even launched crusades against them. God used the rugged Alps to preserve them. There were other reasonably safe havens, but the Alps proved to be the greatest place of safety for the faithful.

Some historians contend that the Albigenses came from the Paulicians, although there is substantial evidence that communities of churches that practiced first-century Christianity existed in the valleys of France from the earliest ages of Christianity. When the Paulicians arrived, "they spread rapidly through Southern France and the little city of Albi, in the district of Albigeois, became the center of the party." [22] From this location the Albigenses gained their name. They too were known by many names: Cathari, Paterines, Publicans, Paulicians, Good Men, Bogomiles and others. [23] These people were so numerous and existed for so many hundreds of years that this brief discussion cannot possibly do them justice.

The Albigenses and Paulicians were in essential agreement; over time they became one people. They are well-known for their rejection of infant baptism and their purity of life. Their godly lifestyles gained for them the respect of many who joined their ranks. This upset the Catholics, who condemned them and launched crusades and war against them. In the second crusade, Braziers, with a population of approximately 40,000, fell. "When Simon de Monfort, Earl of Leichester, asked the Abbot of Ceteaux, the papal legate, what he was to do with the inhabitants, the legate answered: 'Kill them all. God knows His own.' In this manner the war was carried on for twenty years. Town after town was taken, pillaged, burnt. Nothing was left but a smoking waste." [24]

The Waldenses

The Waldenses blended with the Albigenses to become essentially the same people. Dr. Cross quotes historian William Jones as saying of the Waldenses, "they existed at least 500 years before Peter Waldo." [25] Waldo was from Lyon, France in the closing decades of the twelfth century. Waldo was also known as Waldensis. With the coming of Waldo this long-existing group was energized and assumed his name. [26]

Peter Waldo was a rich man who obtained a copy of the Scriptures, which he embraced and began to practice. He soon had a following. He also gained the attention of the Roman Catholic hierarchy who forbade him to preach. When he refused, he was expelled from Lyons. He and his followers, along with their families, set out as missionaries clad in woolen garments and wooden shoes. They penetrated Switzerland and Northern Italy. They were met with hearty response, and their numbers multiplied into the thousands. Their primary stronghold became the slopes of the Cottian Alps and East Piedmont, West Provence and Dauphiny. [27]

Here is a list of some of their more prominent beliefs.

- They believed in the universal priesthood of the believer.

- They believed they were distinguished by their great knowledge of the Bible. It was said that a man or woman could rarely be found who could not repeat the entire New Testament in the vernacular language.

- They believed in great piety. They rejected oaths, falsehood and fraud.

- They were hard workers and did not believe in amassing wealth.

- They were very evangelistic. They particularly spread the gospel and made converts through trade.

- They believed the Scriptures alone were the source and authority for faith and practice.

- They believed forgiveness comes exclusively from God through the mediation of Christ, and not through a priest or church.

- They believed salvation comes through grace through faith in Jesus Christ. [28]

The Waldenses were very much like their brethren in other valleys in the Alps; and like their brothers in faith and practice, they were hated, hunted and persecuted by the Catholics.

OBSERVATIONS

Do not imagine that the groups briefly mentioned here constitute all Christians and churches that from Christ forward practiced New Testament Christianity. To assume that would be a gross misconception. True churches existed from the eastern end of Europe to the British Isles and across North Africa. In every age they existed in large numbers.

Like all true churches today, they had weaknesses and did not all agree on every point, but for the most part they were together on the core issues. Here and there churches would completely depart from the faith and practice of the New Testament but continue to use the name of true churches. These renegade churches gave the true churches a bad name. These are the ones many modern historians tend to highlight as being indicative of the Cathari, Paulicians, Albigenses and other legitimate groups. To do so is historical dishonesty. The vast majority of these groups embraced core Christian beliefs and practices.

Furthermore, all that a group with a certain name believed at one point in time may not be indicative of those who bore that name 100 miles away or 100 years later. It is deceptive and discriminatory to condemn everyone within a group because of the beliefs and practices of a few within that group. Unfortunately the condemnation of all because of the shortcomings of a few has been the widespread practice of many modern historians, particularly when it serves their biased purposes to do so. When conditions caused those early Christians who embraced New Testament doctrine and practice to adopt a new name, their doctrine and practice did not change. Consequently a name change was not a deterrent to the fellowship of believers with different names. Their fellowship centered around the core teachings of Jesus Christ, not on the name.

Please keep in mind that the scope of the people covered in this lesson covers about 1,600 years. It must be emphasized that a book as short as this one cannot possibly be in-depth. It is hoped that the evidence and information submitted here are sufficient to prove that an unbroken line of true churches has continued from Jesus to the present. Later in this book we will visit many of these churches again in greater detail.

What they believed, not their name, made the difference

---

[1] John T. Christian, *A History of the Baptists*, vol. 1, (Texarkana, Ark.-Tex.: Bogard Press, 1922), 4.

[2] Ibid., 3.

[3] David Benedict, *History of the Donatists*, (Paris, Arkansas: The Baptist Standard Bearer, Inc., 1875.)

[4] I strongly recommend *The Baptist History Collection* available from Baptist Standard Bearer, Inc. at www.standardbearer.org.

[5] William Cathcart, *Baptist Encyclopaedia*, vol. 1, (Paris, Arkansas: The Baptist Standard Bearer, Inc., 1887), 51-52.

[6] I.K. Cross, *The Battle for Baptist History,* (Columbus, Georgia: Brentwood Christian Press, 1990), 90.

[7] Ibid., 93.

[8] Ibid., 97.

[9] Christian, 48-49.

[10] Ibid., 49.

[11] Manichaenism is a compound of dualistic, pantheistic, Gnostic and ascetic elements. It was derived from Persian Zoroastrism and emphasized light and darkness as the two great forces of nature. While accepting the power of nature this religious system rejected the incarnation, the humanity and the resurrection of Christ. The Old Testament was completely rejected as was most of the New Testament. The authority for advocates of this system were the writings of Mani.

[12] George Herbert Orchard, *A Concise History of Baptists,* CD Rom, version 1, (Paris, Arkansas: The Baptist Standard Bearer, Inc., 2005), 91.

[13] Ibid.

[14] Cross, 104.

[15] Cross, 100-101.

[16] Christian, 50-51.

[17] Ibid., 51.

[18] Ibid.

[19] Ibid., 53.

[20] Orchard, 91.

[21] Christian, 50.

[22] Ibid., 60.

[23] Cathcart, 18.

[24] Christian, 63.

[25] Cross, 105.

[26] Christian, 69.

[27] Ibid., 70.

[28] Cross, 106-107.

Groups Who Stayed Faithful

Cathari

The name Cathari means pure. Cathari is a name given through the ages to many groups who dissented with the Roman Church. This group had a reputation of purity.

Anabaptists

Anabaptist was also a name widely used to denote dissenting believers and churches. The name was rarely self-applied; it was given by their enemies to those who re-baptized people who came from false churches.

Paulicians

The name Paulicians came from the apostle Paul. They rejected tradition and held to the Scriptures. They also rejected the relics and images of the Catholics and held to baptism and the Lord's Supper as the only two ordinances of the church

Albigenses

The Alps became a refuge for many groups of Christians. This group is well-known for their rejection of infant baptism and their purity of life.

Waldenses

They were distinguished by their great knowledge of the Bible. They were hard workers and very evangelistic. They believed the Scriptures alone were the source and authority for faith and practice. They believed salvation comes through grace through faith in Jesus Christ.

The History of Churches

Chapter 15

The Birth of Islam

As the old Roman Empire grew steadily weaker, a major new dynamic developed which greatly impacted all of Europe, the Middle East and North Africa. Islam leapt upon the scene. By the beginning of the seventh century, the Roman Catholic Church had reached maturity. The church had entrenched itself as the dominate entity in the entire region both politically and religiously. No one, not even the Patriarch in Constantinople, could rival the Bishop of Rome. As the Roman Empire politically disintegrated in strife and division, the bishop in Constantinople (known as the Patriarch), whose power and influence was tied closely to the Roman emperor, grew increasingly weaker. Meanwhile the Bishop of Rome grew stronger, particularly in view of the alliances he made with the invaders and new political powers. These new political powers had no connections with old Rome. They ruled in the West where the old Roman Empire once was. The old Empire survived weakly but only in the East. By virtue of alliances with the new western powers, and as head of the state church, the creative and innovative Roman Church bishops were able to keep the church wed to the state. The state church simply changed lovers: from the old Roman Empire to the emerging new Roman Empire.

As the sixth century ended and the seventh century dawned, the Bishop of Rome was so firmly entrenched in power that he controlled most of Western Europe and North Africa. The Bishop of Rome controlled the churches professing to be Christian that had been planted throughout the entire area, except for the dissenters of whom we have spoken. By this time the state church had become the Roman Catholic Church. Because of the power and dominance of the state church, dissenting individuals and churches (heretics as they were called by the Catholics) were forced to flee and hide. Their haven became the Alps; however, they existed throughout Europe both West and East. Tens of thousands of them were killed by the Catholics.

When the old Roman power faded, the new central political power that developed in its place was the church. The real estate that we know today as France, Germany, Italy, England and other European countries piecemealed into fragments ruled locally by strong war lords. The only recognized central power became the Bishop of Rome, who became known as the pope. He ruled the church and with that came enormous political power. We have already looked at some of the factors that brought him to power: his association with Constantine, the move of the capital to Constantinople, the many doctrinal schisms and his alliances with the new political powers who took control of the West. There were other factors.

As we continue, we will return to the rise of the papacy and see how it became increasingly corrupt and powerful; however, the picture of what happened in the Mediterranean theater cannot be adequately understood apart from the birth and meteoric rise of Islam. We shall therefore open a parenthesis here and speak of Mohammed and Islam. Afterwards we will return to the papacy, to Roman Catholicism and to those faithful men and women of God whom they tried to eradicate. Keep in mind that scattered throughout Europe, the Middle East and North Africa there were tens of thousands of Christians who continued to practice first-century Christianity. Because they believed and practiced local church theology and autonomy, they were not centralized. The Muslims did not see them as adversaries in the same light that they viewed the Catholics. The main suffering and persecution of these true believers came at the hands of the Catholics rather than the Muslims.

MEET MOHAMMED

Mohammed was the founder of a new religion that he called Islam. In Europe it was called Mohammedanism. The date of his birth is uncertain; however, he died on June 7, 632. He was either 63 or 65 years old. [1] This Arabic boy, who was born in or around Mecca to a nomadic caravan family, lived a life of violence and tragedy. In the Arabic culture of that day, women were little more than slaves. Female infanticide was commonly practiced. [2]

His early life was met with a series of tragedies. He was born posthumously (after his father's death). [3] At age four Mohammed was seized with epilepsy. As he grew he had episodes where he lost control; some interpreted these to be ecstatic experiences with God. His mother died when he was six. [4] He was taken by his grandfather who was a wealthy caravan trader; and for three years, he traveled the trade routes. When Mohammed was nine, his grandfather died, and he was taken by his uncle's brother, Abu. [5] Abu was also a trader; and during these years, Mohammed accompanied Mecca traders to Syria and South Arabia. He also learned the ways and language of the Bedouins. It is likely that he was in Egypt and Mesopotamia. [6] As he traveled, Mohammed became familiar with Judaism and Christianity. The Arabs of that era were pagans who worshipped the moon and many other gods. Mohammed became very familiar with all three of these religious systems: Judaism, Christianity and Arabic paganism. [7]

At 25 Mohammed married a rich forty-year-old widow named Khadija who was 15 years his senior. [8] Khadija gave Mohammed three sons and four daughters. All his sons died. [9] Though he was barely able to read or write, Mohammed gained a reputation for great practical wisdom. Some think he could not read or write at all. (This is one of the reasons his followers believe that what he said and wrote were miraculous divine revelations.) [10] In 610, Mohammed had a religious experience in which he claimed the prophet Gabriel appeared and told him to begin a brand new religion. [11] In *The Koran*, sometimes called *The Qur'an*, Mohammed gave four contradictory accounts of this event. In one place he affirmed that Allah personally appeared to him in the form of a man (Surah 53:2-8). [12] In another place he said the Holy Spirit appeared to him (Surah 16:102). In still another place he said angels appeared to him (Surah 15:8). Only at the end does Mohammed say it was Gabriel who appeared to him (Surah 2:97). [13]

For the next 20 years, Mohammed would periodically fall on the ground, foam at the mouth, have seizures and claim he received revelation from Allah. [14] In 619 Khadija died. Mohammed married 12 other women. Of all these women, Mohammed had only one son, and he died in infancy. [15]

> **Epileptic seizures were Mohammed's means of divine revelation**

THE RAPID SPREAD OF ISLAM

Mohammed's new religion was a mixture of Judaism and Christianity into Arabic paganism with its emphasis on moon worship. The new religion contained no truly original elements, although it distorted and perverted the teachings of each of its parent religions. For example, Muslims claim that in pre-Islamic times Allah was the biblical God of the patriarchs and prophets of whom Mohammed is the last. "The hard evidence demonstrates that the god Allah was a pagan deity. In fact, he was the moon god, was married to the sun goddess, and the stars were his daughters . . . The moon god was called Alliah, the god, which was shortened to Allah." [16]

At first Mohammed's new hodgepodge religion was not popular with his peers. Mohammed claimed to be the mouthpiece of God. The rulers of Mecca perceived the claim made by Mohammed was that he should be a dictator or autocrat; he was ridiculed by them. [17] Tensions quickly mounted, and Mohammed was forced to flee from Mecca. The flight which took him to Yathrib, afterwards known as *al-Medina* (Medina meaning *the City*), approximately 250 miles away is called Mohammed's *hejira*. This event "initiated the Mohammedan era, July 16, 622." [18]

In Medina, through trickery and deceit, Mohammed gathered followers whom he formed into a military force. *Islam* means submission, and Mohammed developed the motto: *Islam or the sword.* [19] In Medina Mohammed eliminated all his enemies by force.   He then attacked and conquered Mecca, where he established the Muslim temple called *Kaaba*. Mecca then became the center of Islam.   Mohammed had successfully welded a great number of the Arabic people into a theocracy with his religion dominating the military.   From Mecca Mohammed began to plan world conquest. [20] His death in 632 interrupted his plans, but his followers assumed his plans with passion.

Mohammed's death was followed by 100 years of world conquest by the Muslims. Jerusalem and Caesarea fell in 638. The eastern half of Asia Minor (currently Turkey) fell later that year. The resistance the invaders found at Constantinople shifted their march to North Africa. In 642, they defeated Alexandria and conquered all of Egypt. All of Mesopotamia and Persia fell in 646. Carthage was conquered in 697 and the Muslims entered Spain in 715. Finally, the Muslims (Moors) were defeated by Charles Martel at Tours, France in 732. [21]

Be assured that the Muslim invasion had the full attention of the pope and the Catholic Church. The Muslims had conquered in the East and were at the doorstep of Constantinople. In the west, they were in Spain and at the doorstep of France. The empire of the Catholic Church was threatened on the East, on the West and from the South. The climate that would soon lead to the Crusades was forming.

> **Islam means submission;**
> **Their Motto is "Islam or the sword"**

THE ISLAMIC BELIEF SYSTEM

Keep in mind that what is said here is not in depth. Much of the world has embraced this religious system and thousands upon thousands of pages have been written related to it.   Not all Muslims are in full agreement on all aspects of the Islam Religion. Time has produced three main types of Muslims. There are the *Secularists* who have very little knowledge of Islam's beliefs and practices. Islam is a religion in name only for them. There are also the *Moderates* who know the Koran but who seek to make its teachings relevant to modern life. They are generally tolerant of non-Muslims. They seek peace in spite of the teachings of the Koran. There are also the *Fundamentalists* who seek to apply the extreme verses of the Koran to the letter. [22]   In this book, consideration is given to Islam as originally set forth by Mohammed in the Koran.

Major Doctrinal Positions

* **Islam is monotheistic**

  The key position of Islam is that, "There is no god but Allah and Mohammed is his prophet." [23]   Islam is opposed to all types of polytheism. Allah is an impersonal god who cannot be known. Though the Koran speaks of the love of God, the emphasis is upon judgment, not grace, power or mercy. [24]

  Mohammed denied the Trinity. Though he mentioned the Holy Spirit, he rejected His existence as a person. He also denied that Jesus Christ was deity. In the Koran he wrote, "Wonderful Originator of the heavens and the earth! How could He have a son when He has no consort, and He (Himself) created everything, and He is the Knower of all things" (Surah 6:101).

* **Islam believes in prophets**

  The belief is that God has spoken through 28 prophets. Abraham, Jesus and Mohammed are thought to be among the greatest of the prophets, and Mohammed is thought to be the last and greatest of the prophets. [25]   Mohammed regarded Christ's meekness, gentleness and self-denial as signs of weakness. Islam says Jesus Christ did not die on the cross, and thus cannot be the Redeemer. Mohammed taught, "that God caused someone else who looked like him, probably Judas, to be crucified, and that, instead of being crucified, Jesus was taken up by Allah into heaven." [26]   Mohammed wrote, ". . . they slew him not nor crucified him, but it appeared so unto them . . . they slew him not for certain, but Allah took him unto himself. . ." (Surah 4:157-158).

- ## Islam believes Mohammed was only a prophet, not god

Mohammed saw himself as the fulfillment of Jesus' promise that he would send another Comforter. [27]

- ## Islam believes in a final day of judgment

Mohammed taught that at the last day, there will be a time of resurrection and judgment. Those who follow and obey Allah and Mohammed will go to Paradise, a sort of Islamic heaven. Those who oppose Allah and Mohammed will be tortured in hell. [28]

- ## Islam believes in salvation by works

Mohammed taught that salvation comes by submitting to Allah and doing good works. The good works include the daily reciting of the *Shahadah,* which says, "There is one god; his name is Allah; and Mohammed is his prophet." [29] Good works also include the giving of alms and praying five times daily toward Mecca; however, salvation is a sort of fatalism. One can be saved only because Allah decides to save him. Allah being sovereign saves who he will. There is no assurance of salvation except for those who die in *Jihad* or "holy war." The Koran indicates that God will be inclined to save all of these. "And if you are slain in the way of Allah or you die, certainly forgiveness from Allah and mercy is better than what they amass. And if indeed you die or you are slain, certainly to Allah shall you be gathered together" (Surah 3:157-158). "Surely Allah has bought of the believers their persons and their property for this, that they shall have the garden; they fight in Allah's way, so they slay and are slain; a promise which is binding on Him in the Taurat and the Injeel and the Quran; and who is more faithful to his covenant than Allah" (Surah 9:111).

According to Mohammed, at the end of life there is a long bridge and one must cross it to inherit eternal life. The bridge is long and narrow, and it is difficult to maintain balance on this bridge; but one must get across it to have eternal life. Those who Allah has not selected will fall off the bridge into the pits of hell; the elect will make it across. For those who make it across, unlimited sensuous delight awaits. There is a pool of wine that does not intoxicate. According to this religious system, heaven is mostly for males; however, there are sufficient earthly women there to fulfill all of the sexual lusts of the men who go there. Furthermore these women, who are called *Hurs,* are virgins. [30] This claim is made in the Koran, Surah 52:17-20, 22.

- **Islam's holiest book is the Koran**

  Koran means "the recitation." It is made up largely from the Old Testament; however, New Testament ideas are also included. "It is claimed that it was dictated to Mohammed by the angel Gabriel between 610 and his death in 632." [31] It is hard to understand how this could be the case, since Mohammed could barely, if at all, read or write.

  Muslims also believe the books of Moses (the Torah), the Psalms of David (the Zabur) and the Gospel of Jesus Christ (the Injil) are inspired; however, they believe these books have been corrupted by Jews and Christians. They also believe the Koran supersedes the other holy books. [32]

  Muslims believe Mohammed was caught up by Gabriel at the Temple Mount in Jerusalem and given the Koran. While caught up Mohammed supposedly left his horse *Barack* (meaning *lightning*) there. Without evidence to substantiate their claim, they teach that it was Ishmael, not Isaac, who was offered on the big rock on the Temple Mount. The Mosque of Omar currently houses this spot which is under the control of the Islamic Palestinians. This also accounts for why Jerusalem, and especially the Temple Mount, is so important and sacred to the Muslims.

Koran means the recitation

The Five Main Articles of Faith in Islam

- **Belief in Allah as the one true god**

- **Belief in angels as the instruments of god's will**

- **Belief in the four inspired books:**

  o The Torah (books of Moses)

  o The Zabur (Psalms of David)

  o The Injil (the Gospel of Christ)

  o The Koran which is the final and most complete revelation of God.

- **Belief in the 28 prophets of Allah of whom Mohammed is the last**

- **Belief in the final day of judgment** [33]

Five Rules of Conduct Which Are Binding Upon Muslims

"Western people have a difficult time comprehending Islam because they fail to understand that it is a form of cultural imperialism in which the religion and culture of seventh-century Arabia have been raised to the status of divine law." [34] The goal of Islam is a one-world Islamic state. [35] Muslims are to fight non-Muslims until all other religions are exterminated, and Islam is the only religion in the world. "And fight with them until there is no persecution, and religion should be only for Allah, but if they desist, then there should be no hostility except against the oppressors" (Surah 2:193). "Fundamentalists look at Jews and Christians and all non-Muslims as infidels who must be killed because they have no value as human beings and must be exterminated from the face of the earth." [36] The following five rules of conduct, which are binding upon Muslims, foster this age-old cultural and religious Islamic vision.

- **The reciting of the *Shahadah* or Islamic motto.**

- **Daily prayers toward Mecca.** Five times a day Muslims kneel with their foreheads touching the ground while reciting ritualistic prayers. Mosques worldwide all face Mecca.

- **Almsgiving.** Charity is an institutionalized tax in most Muslim countries.

- **Fasting during the month of Ramadan.** During this month,

Muslims are forbidden to eat or drink between sunrise and sunset. This is not a true fast and Muslims routinely abuse it by hearty eating and drinking at night.

- **A pilgrimage to Mecca.** In order to facilitate his salvation, every Muslim must attempt to make a trip to Mecca once in his lifetime. Once there he is to walk seven times around the Kaaba (temple) which holds a black rock. If possible, he is to kiss the rock which Muslims believe was carried to earth by Gabriel. [37]

Western people who are not knowledgeable of the Koran also find it difficult to believe that Islam is a religion of hatred and violence. Mohammed urged Muslims to fight for the cause of Allah. "O prophet! urge the believers to war; if there are twenty patient ones of you they shall overcome two hundred, and if there are a hundred of you they shall overcome a thousand of those who disbelieve, because they are a people who do not understand" (Surah 8:65). "Fighting [*Jihad*] is enjoined on you, and it is an object of dislike to you; and it may be that you dislike a thing while it is good for you, and it may be that you love a thing which is evil for you, and Allah knows, while you do not know" (Surah 2:216). *Jihad*, which means "holy war" in Allah's cause, is the word used in this verse of the Koran. [38] The Koran commands Muslims to fight Jews and Christians (Surah 9:29) and not to befriend them (Surah 5:51).

The Koran commands Muslims to fight Jews and Christians

A FORCE THAT COULD NOT BE IGNORED

Islam burst on the scene with a violence and goal of world conquest that could not be ignored. The goal of Islam has never changed and is currently closer to attainment than it has ever been. At the time of Mohammed and his immediate followers, the Catholic Church had seized power from one end of the Mediterranean Sea to the other. The Catholic Church was the dominating force from Mesopotamia to England and from North Africa to the North Sea. The scene dramatically changed with the birth and explosion of Islam. The pope and his multitudes were in peril of losing their empire. War was eminent and the coming Crusades would be a time of war.

Those who continued to practice first-century Christianity were not a clear and united target for the Muslims. They were scattered throughout the Empire in small villages and remote places. Many of them were in the Alps and not easily accessible. Caution and hiding was their common practice because of the severe persecution they faced from the Catholic Church. The Muslims did not view most of them in the same light that they viewed the Catholics. Particularly at the eastern end of the Mediterranean World, Arabs saw the persecution that dissenters endured at the hands of the Catholics. In many cases Arabs actually befriended them and offered sanctuary. Furthermore, when Islam was born, not all Arabs joined the movement; it was many years before their stance against Christians and Jews became united. It should also be kept in mind that the Muslim invasion was halted at both ends of Europe; however, even those not directly impacted by Islam could not and did not ignore the fact that they were in harm's way.

Islam's goal is world conquest

[1] David Samuel Margoliouth, *Encyclopaedia Britannica*, vol. 15, s.v. "Mohammed or Muhammad or Mahomet," (Chicago: William Benton, Publishers: 1960), 646.

[2] Carl Deimer, Professor, *History of Christianity I*, Video Lecture 17, Liberty University DLP, 2004.

[3] Margoliouth.

[4] Deimer.

[5] Ibid.

[6] Margoliouth.

[7] Deimer.

[8] Margoliouth.

[9] Deimer.

[10] Margoliouth.

[11] Deimer.

[12] Surah is the Koran word for chapter.

[13] All references to *The Koran* in this course are to the translation by M.H. Shakir, *The Koran,* (Elmhurst, New York: Tahrike Tarsile Qur'an, Inc., 2005).

[14] Deimer.

[15] Ibid.

[16] Sheldon Smith, 2002, "Islam: A Raging Storm," *The Sword of the Lord*, 1 February, 3rd in a series.

[17] Margoliouth, 647.

[18] Ibid.

[19] Deimer.

[20] Ibid.

[21] Ibid.

[22] Labib Mikhail, 2002, "Understanding Islam," *The Jerusalem Connection*, March.

[23] Deimer.

[24] Smith.

[25] Ibid.

[26] Jim Vineyard, 2002, "What We As Born-Again Christians Should Know About the Religion of Islam," *Fundamental Baptist World Missions*, January.

[27] Deimer.

[28] Smith.

[29] Ibid.

[30] Deimer.

[31] Ibid.

[32] Smith.

[33] Vineyard.

[34] Robert Morey, *The Islamic Invasion: Confronting the World's Fastest Growing Religion*, (Las Vegas, Nevada: Christian Scholars Press, 1992), 19.

[35] DVD video, *Islam: Religion of Peace?*, (Fort Lauderdale, Florida: Coral Ridge Ministries).

[36] Mikhail.

[37] Smith.

[38] Mikhail.

Major Doctrinal Positions of Islam

Monotheistic

The key position of Islam is that Allah is the only god and Mohammed serves as his prophet.

Belief in Prophets

The belief is that God has spoken through 28 prophets. Abraham, Jesus and Mohammed are thought to be among the greatest of the prophets, and Mohammed is thought to be the last and greatest of the prophets.

Mohammed Was Only a Prophet, Not God

Mohammed saw himself as the fulfillment of Jesus' promise that he would send another Comforter.

Final Day of Judgment

Those who follow and obey Allah and Mohammed will go to Paradise, a sort of Islamic heaven. Those who oppose Allah and Mohammed will be tortured in hell

Salvation By Works

Mohammed taught that salvation comes by submitting to Allah and doing good works.

Holiest Book Is the Koran

Koran means the recitation. It is made up largely from the Old Testament; however, New Testament ideas are also included

The History of Churches

Five Rules of Conduct for Muslims

Reciting of the *Shahadah* or Islamic Motto

The *Shahadah* says, "There is one god; his name is Allah; and Mohammed is his prophet."

Daily Prayers Toward Mecca

Five times a day Muslims kneel with their foreheads touching the ground while reciting ritualistic prayers. Mosques worldwide all face Mecca.

Almsgiving

Charity is an institutionalized tax in most Muslim countries.

Fasting During the Month of Ramadan

During this month, Muslims are forbidden to eat or drink between sunrise and sunset.

A Pilgrimage to Mecca

In order to facilitate his salvation, every Muslim must attempt to make a trip to Mecca once in his lifetime.

Chapter 16

Ramifications of a State Church Plus the Big Catholic Split

We have looked at seven centuries of major developments which came about as a direct result of Christianity. From a practical standpoint the marriage of the church to the state laid the groundwork for domination, corruption, abuse of power and persecution on a scale unparalleled in the history of mankind. "Since that time the church and the state, though frequently jarring, have remained united in Europe, either on the hierarchical basis, with the temporal power under the tutelage of the spiritual, or on the *caesaro-papal*, with the spiritual power merged in the temporal ... The church could now act upon the state; but so could the state act upon the church ..." [1] The *church* which the Roman state married was that alliance of churches which, by the time of the marriage, had greatly departed from the doctrine and practices of first-century, New Testament Christianity. With the new-found authority and power of the state behind her, this corrupt church grew very fast. It was the desire of Emperor Constantine and most of his followers to have all Christendom united in this *one church*. This perfectly suited the ambitions and purposes of the leaders of both state and church. They were hungry for power and control. They took advantage of every opportunity and means to strengthen their position. In the ensuing struggle for domination and supremacy, the church in Rome ultimately prevailed. Eventually this state church became the Roman Catholic Church. For many centuries, this church dominated Europe, North Africa and much of the Middle East.

PRACTICAL RAMIFICATIONS
OF THE STATE-CHURCH

Jesus taught that political power and religious power are not one and the same. He said, *"Render therefore unto Caesar the things which are Caesar's; and unto God the things that are God's,"* **Matthew 22:21**. Like wheat and tares growing together in the same field, Jesus spoke of saved and lost people living side by side within the same society. *"Let both grow together until the harvest,"* **Matthew 13:30**. He taught that saved people live in the world but they are of His spiritual kingdom, **John 15:18-19**. The political and spiritual realms coexist, but they are separate entities. Society is composite, not monolithic. It is made up of two separate components: a spiritual realm and a political realm. The biblical stance is that New Testament Christians living in any nation or society are first and foremost Christians according to the Bible order. They are law-abiding citizens who seek loyalty to their political government; but their allegiance is first to God, then to the state. When pitted against the teachings of Scripture, they must obey God, *"We ought to obey God rather than men,"* **Acts 5:29**.

Whether Christian or otherwise, the state church concept defies and contradicts this biblical position. Such states see society as monolithic rather than composite. [2] Religion and the state are seen as one. When governments of this type conquer territory, the people within the territory are expected to embrace the state religion. Failure to do so is considered to be disloyalty and defiance of the state. In such societies there is no room for a church or religion outside that of the state. Typically as state churches and religions grow stronger, they impose their theology and practices upon the citizens of the state by force. They decide what is orthodox and acceptable and brand as heretics all who do not conform to their ideas. These *heretics* then become enemies of the church and state and are to be persecuted into compliance or exterminated. Such was the case when Christianity became the state religion of Rome. Emperor Theodosius stated it quite bluntly, "All peoples over whom our rule extends shall live in that religion which was revealed to St. Peter . . . We give orders that all these are to adopt the name 'Catholic Christians'; the rest we shall let pass for fools and they will not have to bear the reproach of being called heretics. They must come first under the wrath of God and then also under ours." [3] A large number of current Muslim states provide classic illustrations of this reality. There is no freedom of religion. With Islam it is submit. To fail is to face harsh persecution and possibly death.

No sooner had the corrupt *Christian Church* married the state than efforts to coerce all Christians and churches to join her began. She quickly negotiated state laws that mandated membership and full allegiance to her and made refusal a crime. Church officials and state authorities were deputized to enforce the laws.

Beginning with Constantine, Roman emperors began to pass new laws, many of which were good: the abolition of crucifixion, the prohibition of gladiatorial games and the discouragement of infanticide. [4] Over time, two great collections of legal codes became the central law of the land: the Theodosian (429-438) [5] and the Justinian Codes (527-534) [6]. As good as many of these laws were, they were "limited ... exclusively to the catholic or orthodox church." [7] However these laws, which grew out of the state church, did not provide universal coverage and protection for all citizens; those multitudes of Christians and churches throughout the empire that refused the theology and practices of the state church had no protection. To the contrary, every imaginable means of oppression was exercised against them with a cruelty that would not be suspected of even the most barbaric savage; however, the Catholics did it in the name of God with the power of the state. "The heretical and schismatic sects without distinction, excepting the Arians during their brief ascendency under Arian emperors, were now worse off than they had been before, and were forbidden the free exercise of their worship even under Constantine upon pain of fines and confiscation, and from the time of Theodosius and Justinian upon pain of death." [8] Equal religious protection to all Christian parties was a totally foreign concept to all of the Byzantine emperors and to every pope.

State churches impose their theology and practices by force

191

To better understand the practical impact of the church-state union upon the day-to-day existence of citizens of the empire, both east and west, it is helpful to consider some of the laws that emerged over the years. [9]

The Exemption of the Clergy from Most Public Burdens

State-church priests, bishops and other officials were exempted from military service, most taxes, low manual labor and other public services. These privileges were first granted by Constantine to the state-church clergy in North Africa in 313 and extended by him throughout the empire in 319.

The Enrichment and Endowment of the State Church

Beginning with Constantine and strengthening over the years, churches were given property and buildings, including those confiscated from pagans and heretics. The state church began to amass great property and wealth, including sites in the Holy Land. Rich people began to give to the church and the church began to inherit much land and money. Soon the state church, which was rapidly becoming the Catholic Church, became very rich.

State-Church Support of the Clergy

The state church began to financially support the clergy. The New Testament method of pastoral support is the tithes and offerings of the people. Before Constantine the clergy had been totally dependent upon the tithes and offerings of the people. Now they received a fixed income from church funds and from the imperial and municipal treasuries.

Voluntary support of the church vanished. People were compelled to tithe.

The State Church Assumed Legal Jurisdiction over the People

As early as Constantine the church became the court system. The people were to take their spiritual matters (and later many civil and even criminal matters) before the church courts rather than to non-church tribunals. Church tribunals now had the force of law; and in spiritual matters, no appeal could be taken from them to the civil courts. The judgments of the priests were regarded as the judgments of Christ himself.

It is easy to see the difficult situation of those who rejected the corrupt state-church with its system of institutional salvation. When they were brought to trial for their refusal to support the corrupt church, they were tried by and subjected to the jurisdiction of the very ones whom they rejected. There was no impartiality and justice in the system.

The Episcopal Right of Intercession

The right to intercede for criminals, rebels and other accused persons became the right of priests. Very often this resulted in obstructed justice. These Catholic priests were unlikely to advocate the cause of anyone considered a heretic by the state church.

The Right of Asylum in Churches

Anyone who mistreated an unarmed fugitive in a church was subject to the penalty of death. In a church, a slave could find refuge from the rage of a master, a debtor could find refuge from the persecution of a creditor, conquered people could find safety from the swords of their conquerors and women and virgins could find safety from profligates (those with immoral intentions).

Of course, this protection did not apply to those who rejected the state church.

The Observance of Sunday and Other Festivals of the Church Was Made Obligatory

With the passing of time all citizens in the empire were expected to go to church on Sundays. Fines were often imposed upon those who failed. Many activities conflicting with church attendance on Sundays were prohibited.

SUMMARY

Even from this very brief listing of legal developments within the empire, it is not difficult to see that the state church began to exercise enormous influence and control over the day-to-day lives of the people. Over the years a multitude of detailed laws and edicts required the people to embrace the state-church system. Specific rituals, prohibitions and activities were mandated regarding behavior on Sundays; religious festivals throughout the year (Christmas, Easter, Pentecost, etc.); the worship and exaltation of Mary; the worship of saints; the worship of martyrs; the worship of relics; processions and pilgrimages; sacraments; baptism and the list goes on. [10] "The Church and State quickly became closely associated, and it was not long before the power of the State was at the disposal of those who had the lead of the Church, to enforce their decisions." [11]

Hopefully a picture is emerging in your mind. The church state made it extremely difficult for all who stayed true to the Scriptures and to first-century Christianity. Whether in the East or in the West, officials of the church and the state made the laws that governed the people. State and church officials were in fundamental agreement, and they had the power to enforce the laws they made. This was not a time of democracy, and there were no checks and balances. For those who lined up with the official church of the state, all went well. For those who stayed true to God and His Word, life was extremely hard. When they didn't baptize their babies, they were guilty of a crime. If they did not attend a state church on Sunday, they broke the law. If they told their son or a neighbor that salvation is exclusively by grace through faith in Jesus Christ, they were guilty of heresy and were likely to be burned at the stake.

They were officially viewed as heretics and criminals. They were considered to be enemies of God and the state. With passion and zeal they were hunted and prosecuted by the official church and government. They were tried and judged by laws which the corrupt church and state had made; and because they were not members of the state church, they had no protection under the law. The courts that tried them were state church courts and their prosecutors, their defenders and their judges were all state church agents. There was no impartiality, no justice and no mercy. The deck was always stacked against them. To survive, they had to live as fugitives. It is no wonder that they often retreated to gorges, canyons and the ruggedness of the highest mountains and made their abodes in places where it was hard for their oppressors to find them.

Life was extremely hard for those who stayed true to God and His Word

---

BYZANTIUM

For reasons previously discussed, the Church in Rome grew ever stronger; however, the elevation of tradition over Scripture by her leaders produced major departures from New Testament Christianity on multiple fronts. Eastern churches were slower in their departures, but they got there. Early in the fourth century Papa ben Aggai federated many of the churches in Persia, Syria and Mesopotamia under his rule as bishop of Seleucia-Ctesiphon, the capital city. By 498 this bishop was called the *Patriarch*. Over time, the East accepted five Patriarchs as head of their church: Rome, Constantinople, Alexandria, Antioch and Jerusalem. Later the bishop of Moscow was made a patriarch, and Rome was dropped. For eastern Catholics, the Patriarchs are the church's head; they reject the idea that the pope of Rome is exclusive head of the church. The pope is accepted as sole ruler among the Catholic churches in the west. [12]

With Constantine's move of the capital of the Roman Empire to Constantinople, two major centers emerged in the state church: one in Rome, another in Constantinople. Although Rome grew much stronger and dominated Catholicism for centuries to the present, do not assume that eastern Catholicism was small and insignificant. Though the two centers of Catholicism became increasingly independent and hostile toward each other, the vast majority of their beliefs and customs remained the same. Eastern and western Catholics were in fundamental agreement on the authority of ecclesiastical tradition as a joint rule of faith with the holy Scriptures, the worship of the Virgin Mary and saints, justification by faith plus good works, the seven sacraments, baptismal regeneration and the necessity of water baptism for salvation, transubstantiation, the sacrifice of the mass for the living and the dead, priestly absolution by divine authority, an episcopate hierarchy and a vast number of rites and ceremonies. Both also embraced a doctrine of purgatory. The two disagreed on the Holy Spirit with the East saying He proceeds from the Father only, while the West taught that He proceeds from the Father and the Son. The East denied the universal authority and infallibility of the pope and the Immaculate Conception of the Virgin Mary (Mariolatry is abundantly practiced). Easterners allow the marriage of their lower clergy, laymen to receive consecrated bread dipped in wine, infant communion, the use of leaven bread in their Eucharist and the use of dairy products in lent; Western Catholics differ on these and many other lesser points. [13]

For a period of several hundred years the laws of the Empire which governed the day-to-day lives of the citizens were enforced much more rigorously in the east than in the west. Constantinople (Byzantium) became the glitzy headquarters of a far-reaching, militant Christian empire which took great pride in pomp, ceremony and grandeur. With fanatical zeal, eastern leaders determined to impose their ideas of Christianity upon the people down to the finest points. Roman emperors following Constantine resided at the new capital of Constantinople. They continued to rule the eastern part of the later Roman Empire and they were very wealthy. Byzantium was re-named Constantinople, and the empire flourished from 395 until 1435. [14]

As the church and state became merged into one, it determined to make Byzantium (Constantinople) a showplace of wealth and extravaganza. These emperors bore themselves as gods upon earth and called their laws, edicts and palaces *divine*. Byzantium was Christianity's apex of empty pretense. "The Christianity of the Byzantine court lived in the atmosphere of intrigue, dissimulation, and flattery." [15] The extravaganza, excess and vanity of state and church rulers are difficult to comprehend. The household of ruler Constantius is said to have "embraced no less than a thousand barbers, a thousand cup bearers, a thousand cooks, and so many eunuchs, that they could be compared only to the insects of a summer day." [16] Byzantium became a showplace. Though

Christianity was forced and mechanical, it was full of glamour. The buildings were grand, artwork with beautiful mosaics abounded, pomp and ceremony ruled and the impact of this Byzantine Empire remains today in such far-away places as Israel, Jordan, Turkey and Russia.

Byzantium was Christianity's apex of empty pretence

THE BIG SPLIT

Though they were almost identical twins in doctrine and practice, tensions between the East and the West continued to mount. The Arian, Nestorian, Pelagian and Iconoclastic controversies had all driven deep wedges. Both sides thought they were right and that they were the real, true church and that the other side was not. Jealousies, ambitions and pride abounded. On December 25, 800 Charlemagne came to power. He did not want the power in the East to threaten or influence him. The Eastern patriarchs began to claim that Rome was heretical in doctrine and practice. Trouble continued to brew. The Muslims threatened in the East and the West was facing a German invasion. Both sides were occupied in resisting these powers and needed the other. Even though internally they had been fatally fractured for 250 years, they were able to formally and officially remain one state church.

The rift between the Eastern and Western Catholics came to a head in 1054. The patriarch of Constantinople (Byzantium) was Michael Cerularius. He actually sought an occasion when he might separate from the West. He was opposed to Leo IX who was pope in Rome from 1049 to 1054. In July of 1054 Cerularius refused to receive a papal representative who was sent to his court by Leo. When he refused, Leo formally excommunicated Cerularius. Excommunication literally means consigning the excommunicated to hell. On July 16, 1054, Cerularius in turn laid a formal bull [17] upon the high altar of St. Sophia's Church in Constantinople, formally consigning Pope Leo IX to hell. At the same time in Rome, Pope Leo IX was placing a formal bull of excommunication of Cerularius upon the high altar of St. Peter's Basilica in Rome, consigning Patriarch Cerularius to hell. [18]

197

Thus what is commonly known as the Eastern Orthodox Catholic Church was formed. The formal name of this church is Holy Oriental Orthodox Apostolic Church. Over the years this church faced many pressures. It has reorganized and now has three main divisions: The Orthodox Church in Turkey, the State Church of Russia and The Church of the Kingdom of Greece. [19]

---

[1] Philip Schaff, *History of the Christian Church,* vol. 3, (Peabody, Massachusetts: Hendrickson Publishers, 2002), 91.

[2] Leonard Verduin, *The Reformers and Their Stepchildren,* (Grand Rapids, Michigan: William B. Eerdmans Publishing Company, 1964), 23.

[3] Ibid., 34.

[4] Schaff, 108.

[5] Ibid., 110.

[6] Ibid.

[7] Ibid., 95.

[8] Ibid., 95-96.

[9] The following list is adapted from Philip Schaff's *History of the Christian Church,* vol. 3, pages 96-106.

[10] I recommend the reading of Schaff's *History of the Christian Church,* vol. 3, chapter VII.

[11] E.H. Broadbent, *The Pilgrim Church,* (Grand Rapids, Michigan: GOSPEL FOLIO PRESS, 1999), 43.

[12] Ibid., 90-91.

[13] Schaff, vol. 4, 306-309.

[14] *Webster's New World Dictionary with Student Handbook: Young People's Edition,* s.v. "Byzantium," (Nashville, Tennessee: The World Publishing Company, 1973), 98.

[15] Schaff, vol. 3, 130.

[16] Ibid., 129.

[17] A *bull* is an official public proclamation by a pope or patriarch. It is named after the lead seal (bulla) which was attached to the end in order to authenticate it. It is understood that the authority of the church and of God are behind the proclamation.

[18] Carl Deimer, Professor, *History of Christianity I,* Video lecture 18, Liberty University DLP, 2004.

[19] Schaff, vol. 4, 309.

Ramifications of the State-Church

The Exemption of the Clergy from Most Public Burdens

State-church priests, bishops and other officials were exempted from military service, most taxes, low manual labor and other public services.

The Enrichment and Endowment of the State Church

Over the years, churches were given property and buildings, including those confiscated from pagans and heretics. The state church began to amass great property and wealth.

State-Church Support of the Clergy

The state church financially supported the clergy with a fixed income from their treasuries.

The State Church Assumed Legal Jurisdiction over the People

Church tribunals now had the force of law; and in spiritual matters, no appeal could be taken from them. The judgments of the priest were regarded as the judgments of Christ himself

The Episcopal Right of Intercession

The right to intercede for criminals and rebels became the right of priests.

The Right of Asylum in Churches

Anyone who mistreated an unarmed fugitive in a church was subject to the penalty of death.

The Observance of Sunday and Other Church Festivals Were Made Obligatory

All citizens in the empire were expected to go to church on Sundays. Fines were often imposed upon those who failed

The History of Churches

Eastern vs. Western Catholics

They both agreed with these beliefs

The authority of ecclesiastical tradition as a joint rule of faith with the Scriptures

The worship of the Virgin Mary and saints

Justification by faith and good works

The seven sacraments

Baptismal regeneration

Water baptism for salvation

Transubstantiation

The sacrifice of the mass for the living and the dead

Priestly absolution by divine authority

An episcopal hierarchy

A vast number of rites and ceremonies

A doctrine of purgatory

The Western Catholics disagreed with these Eastern Catholic beliefs

The Holy Spirit proceeds from the Father only

Denies the universal authority and infallibility of the pope

Denies the Immaculate Conception of the Virgin Mary

Allows the marriage of their lower clergy

Laymen can receive consecrated bread dipped in wine

Infant communion

The use of leaven bread in their Eucharist

The use of dairy products in lent

Chapter 17

The Consolidation of Papal Power

To adequately grasp the dire plight faced by those believers who from the first century to the present remained true to New Testament Christianity, it is important to understand the Roman Catholic Church, her pope and the enormous power and ruthless control that this entity gained. In this chapter we will look at the rise of the Roman Catholic Church and the papacy. We will further see how the papacy gained such power and domination.

We have seen how that for five centuries the bishops in Rome and Constantinople fostered the idea of one universal church in contrast to the New Testament concept of local churches. Individual churches across the empire were increasingly viewed as small parts of one big, universal church made up of individual churches collectively. Individual churches were not thought to be autonomous; they were merely parts of the universal church and as such were to be ruled by bishops or episcopates. Many churches across the Roman Empire began to accept ecclesiastical tradition as equal to or above the authority of Scripture. The church in Rome grew in prestige and influence because of the location of the church and the connection of the pastors to early Roman emperors. Many of the charismatic pastors or bishops exploited every opportunity to make the church in Rome dominant among all the churches. They negotiated political agreements with the new Germanic conquerors and claimed that they had a right to rule over all others due to their direct connection to Peter, whom they claimed to be the first pope. Their tradition allowed them to develop the theology that salvation is in and through the church by sacraments such as baptism and the Lord's Supper. They also reasoned that, to be valid, the sacraments must be administered by a priest of the church and that one could become a priest only by the authority of the bishop in Rome. Over time they reached the conclusion that since salvation was in the church, the church could grant, deny or withdraw salvation from anyone.

It is easy to see how the Roman Catholic system was conceived and developed. Before the seventh century, it was not yet fully formed and could not rightfully be called *the Roman Catholic Church* any more than a tadpole can be called a frog or an egg can be called a chicken; however, groundwork was being laid. By 600 the Catholic Church was in place and had reached maturity. We will now give attention to how the Roman Catholic Church achieved such phenomenal power and control. This will provide great insight into the plight of those who refused to be a part of the Roman Catholic Church, for it was totally outside the church leaders' thinking to allow even one person to exist who did not fully embrace and support their doctrines and practices. As the church grew in power, the church leaders became ever more determined to either force every person into their fold or kill him.

Keep in mind that these conditions did not happen instantly or even quickly. No war between nations and no governmental coup resulting in a new ruler and radical change in society brought about Catholicism. The move from New Testament Christianity to the existence of the Catholic Church and its enormous corruption, power and control over society was slow, subtle and gradual over hundreds of years. The move away from New Testament Christianity started before the end of the first century, but the greatest boost for this corrupt church came early in the fourth century when the church married the state. The church became mature when the papacy was fully entrenched at the beginning of the seventh century, but its zenith of power was not reached until the middle of the eleventh century. Through all of those years this false church was developing and becoming ever more dominate both in religion and in politics. As the church's power and control grew, it became increasingly corrupt, degenerate, immoral, oppressive and cruel.

GREGORY I

Mention has been made of the vacuum of political leadership which was created in Rome when Constantine moved the capital of the empire to Constantinople. The bishops of the Church in Rome were not timid. While keeping their religious power, they immediately stepped forward and assumed political power as well. Alliances with invaders continued for several centuries.

Among those early invaders were the Franks. One of their kings was Clovis who ruled from 481 until his death in 511. He too faced a decisive battle and vowed to convert to Nicene Christianity, if he won. When he won, he decided that his entire army would become Christians. He accomplished this by placing a priest in a tree by a river. As Clovis' troops marched by, the priest dipped a large branch from the tree into the river and sprinkled water over the troops while repeating, "I baptize you in the name of the Father, the Son and the Holy Spirit." [1] This reveals the nature of the state church. It is obvious that a personal faith in Christ and relationship with Him in view of His death, burial and resurrection was not a prerequisite to becoming a member of the corrupt state church. It is no wonder that there were multitudes of believers (the state church called them *heretics* and modern, revisionist historians call them *dissenters* and even *protestants*) who rejected this invalid baptism and re-baptized these people when they truly trusted Christ. Because of Clovis' supposed conversion to Christianity, the Catholics call him the oldest son of the church and with him begins the history of the French nation. [2]

Gregory I, who is also called Gregory the Great, was the bishop of Rome from September 3, 590 to March 12, 604. For years the bishops of Rome consistently had great ambitions, especially the spread of Christianity and an independent hierarchy. At that time the savage Lombards were ravaging Europe, which included Rome. Though he was often bed-ridden and in great pain due to gout, Gregory I was exceedingly energetic and succeeded in converting the Lombards to his brand of Christianity. [3] Because of his success in uniting the German political powers into a theocracy with the Roman ecclesiastical power, he is regarded by many as the first true pope. [4] Gregory I was also the father of several other practices which ultimately became standard in the Catholic Church. He created the Gregorian chant, made the sacramental system an official and permanent part of Catholicism, established celibacy in the clergy and made the consent of the Roman bishop necessary for anyone to be ordained as a bishop. [5] Few have established and strengthened the authority of the papal chair like this man. He established the universal episcopacy of the Latin Catholic Church; however, he did not claim jurisdiction over the Eastern Catholic churches. [6]

Gregory I was the first pope

THE EXPANSION OF THE PAPACY

The papacy expanded greatly from the time of Gregory I until 1054, at which time the Eastern and Western Catholics split. Here are some of the reasons why.

Political and Military Alliances

The Roman Catholic Church is characterized by union with the state. The pope always thought the church should dominate the state; however, the state usually wanted the church to foster the state's purposes. Two cases serve to illustrate this on-going struggle between church and state for dominance.

- **Pepin the Short**

  In 751 Pope Zacharias [7] crowned Pepin as king of the Franks. This move played strongly to the ego of Pepin while it greatly enhanced the prestige of the pope (bishop of Rome). Pepin was already the ruler of the Franks; however, the title of king inflated his ego. After this the pope was seen as having the power to make kings. In return for the pope's favor toward him, Pepin gave Zacharias a large territory called the Papal States. This territory constituted about one-fifth of modern Italy. After this the pope was not only the bishop of Rome, he was also the undisputed ruler over a large territory. [8] Clearly the church and the state were fully embraced.

- **Charlemagne**

  On December 25, 800, Pope Leo III crowned Charles the Great as "The Holy Roman Emperor." [9] A king is thought to be over one nation or people group; an emperor is over many. Charlemagne could not unite all of the people in his domain. He had no connection with the Roman Empire of former days, the remnants of which continued in the East. Furthermore Charlemagne was not a holy ruler, and there was nothing holy about his domain; however, as he conquered, he brought his subjects under the influence of the church in Rome and under the power of the pope, who dominated the area. The pope had made Charlemagne ruler and exercised extensive domination over him. The power of the papacy was growing.

The pope was seen as having the power to make kings

Forged Documents

Many of the popes were deliberate liars and deceivers. Some of their deceptive efforts to enhance the papacy have been exposed.

- ### The Donation of Constantine

  One such document claimed that when Constantine moved his capital from Rome to Constantinople in 330, he granted the bishop of Rome secular authority over Rome and its environs. In the sixteenth century, a Catholic named Lorenzo Valla found that this was a fake document. Evidence proved that the document supposedly granting secular authority to the bishop by Constantine was actually from the eighth century; however, Valla hid his findings, and the truth was not revealed until 100 years later by Protestants. In spite of the fact that Pope Zacharias knew that the document was forged, he nonetheless used it as a claim to political and secular power. [10]

  The deliberate dishonesty of Catholics through the centuries is shocking. To large numbers of them, truth and honesty appeared to be totally unimportant. The end has been repeatedly used to justify the means. Whether to seize land and power, to maintain their positions, to gain money or to eliminate those who disagree or oppose them, any evil, however cruel and dishonest, has been acceptable.

205

- ## The Pseudo-Isidorian Decretals

The Pseudo-Isidorian Decretals is a series of illegitimate, forged church documents, laws and creeds. These documents found their way into the collection of a man named Isidor. They were discovered to be false during the eighteenth century. Even though they were false documents, there is reason to believe that they have been used by the popes for their gain. Both the false document from Constantine and the Pseudo-Isidorian Decretals appear to have been used by Zacharias to get the Papal States from Pepin. [11]

Feudalism

When Charlemagne died, his whole dominion fell into the hands of his many sons. None of them could prevail over the others and anarchy grew. In the absence of central authority, all of Europe broke down into small independent, feudalistic kingdoms. Each depended upon the strength of its leader, who was monarch over his domain. There were shifts of power with the passing of time. Some lords placed parcels of their land in the hands of vassals in return for help in war and for other services. The land was worked by serfs or peasants. [12]

This system of political rule was one of endless rivalries, feudal wars and power struggles. There were many similarities between feudal kingdoms. Each feudal lord controlled land and border disputes were constant. Each king had a castle surrounded by a moat (sometimes two) with a drawbridge leading to a road. On both sides of the road were dirt-floor huts where the serfs or peasants lived. At the end of the road opposite from the castle, there was customarily a Catholic Church where a priest lived.

In this system, there were only two classes. The upper class consisted of the rich who lived in the castle: the lord or king and his family who were the aristocrats or nobility, the knights who were mainly warriors, and the Leudes, who were the servants of the upper class. The priests and other officers of the church were also upper class. All others constituted the lower class. These lived in huts and in the woods outside the castle. They had very little and their lives meant almost nothing to the upper class.

These peasants were treated in the worst possible ways. To the aristocracy (upper class) killing a peasant was like killing a wild animal. On hunting excursions in the cold European winters, records tell how feudal lords would sometimes have their servants cut open the stomach of a peasant in order that the lord might warm his feet in the cavity. [13] The feudal system was enormously wicked and cruel.

In the feudal system, there was no middle class and almost no possibility for upward social movement. Those who were born serfs could not escape their social strata. For them there was no educational system. No jobs were available. They were locked into poverty for life and from generation to generation. The one place of possibility was the Catholic Church. If a peasant boy could gain favor with the local priest, he could potentially move upwards in the Catholic Church hierarchy. It is not difficult to see why so many peasant boys were attracted to the Church. (Until much later there was no place for peasant girls.)

The kings and vassals were almost all Catholic. Do not misunderstand. In many places in Europe, from the Balkan states and Russia to England and Wales, there were people who were not under a feudal lord. In many cases they lived in mountainous areas where they could hide in relative safety. They had their own villages and communities. The land where they lived was usually claimed by a feudal lord, but many lords did not have the strength to fully control the territory they claimed. Even in this desperately wicked and dangerous environment, true, first-century, New Testament Christianity prevailed and even flourished in many locations.

During this time the state church, which with time became the Catholic Church, dominated Europe with a heavy and ironclad hand; and from Constantine forward, that grip continually tightened. Long before Charlemagne, the feudal system was emerging. With his death, it was the political system of mainstream Europe, and it played directly into the hands of the papacy and the Roman Catholic Church. With no central political leadership in Europe and little sense of nationality, the pope became the one generally recognized figure of central prestige and power. The pope (the bishop of Rome) emerged as the most powerful bishop among all the bishops. He had tremendous power and influence with the new Germanic powers that ruled Western Europe. He single-handedly ruled a large land area and had fabulous wealth. The vast majority of the feudal lords were Catholic and supported the pope. This greatly added to the pope's power and influence. The false doctrine that salvation was in the hands of the Church was commonly accepted; and as we shall later see in greater detail, the pope had the power to excommunicate. Excommunication meant damnation to hell. The pope had great power over feudal kings, lords and vassals. In their minds the pope (the bishop of Rome) had the power to damn them to hell, plus the power to summon other kings, lords and vassals to military action against any one of them who stepped out of line and gained his disfavor.

> **The pope had great power over feudal kings, lords and vassals**

Internal Developments in the State Church

- **Standardized Worship**

  Over the years the state church worked to standardize worship throughout its domain. With the Gregorian chant, music became the same regardless of location. The central feature of worship became the Mass. Western theology became universal and worship practices were the same in all of these churches. Latin became the standard language of the Church. Whether a person spoke Spanish, German or Italian, whenever he went to church, the worship he heard was in Latin. The vast majority of the people did not understand Latin. That mattered not, for salvation was in ritual and form, not in a personal, heart knowledge of God and His truths.

- **Doctrinal Controversies**

  The doctrinal controversies previously discussed (and others) intensified between the East and the West. Eventually the pope excommunicated the patriarchs of the East. This effectively did away with dissent in the Roman Catholic Church and strengthened the papacy.

GREED AND FINANCIAL EXPLOITATION

A proper grasp of the degradation and corruption of the Roman Catholic Church would not be complete apart from at least a brief look at its greed and financial exploitation. These practices expanded from the rule of Gregory I (about 600) and became dominant and common practice between 1054 and 1215.

Religious financial exploitation is called *Simony* because of Simon, who in Acts 8 thought he could buy the power of the Holy Spirit with money. The Roman Catholic hierarchy took financial advantage of Europe for hundreds of years. The following is a very brief listing of some of the practices the pope succeeded in imposing upon those under his power. [14] As we move through this list, keep in mind that most of these practices relate to priests and other officers within the church hierarchy. The people, both upper and lower classes, were required to tithe and to support with offerings the churches that made up the Catholic system. The peasants (lower class) had almost nothing. They were to give; however, it was the kings, lords and upper class that brought great wealth to the local churches and their officers. As the list will show, by wicked practices the pope siphoned off as much wealth as he possibly could from the local churches. By the following practices, the papacy bled Europe of her wealth and became astoundingly rich at her expense.

Annates

"The requirement that either a bishop or an abbot (head of a monastery) the 1st year's income be given to the pope." Popes controlled and gave these jobs; it was impossible to become a bishop or an abbot apart from confirmation by the pope. "When the bishop went into a bishopric for the first year, the ANNATE meant the pope got his first year's salary." [15]

Collations

Not all areas or bishoprics were of the same size. A small bishopric could be next to a large one. The larger the bishopric, the more the pay! Many bishops wanted larger bishoprics and more pay. Each time the pope put a bishop into a new bishopric, he received that bishop's salary for one year. The move also opened up another bishopric into which the pope moved another bishop, who must pay his first-year salary to the pope. The pope was eager to move bishops into new bishoprics. Each time there was a change of bishops, he made more money. This rotation and shifting of bishops and abbots is called collations.

Commendations

Commendations were the annual tax paid by a bishop or abbot to remain in a particular office. The pope had the power to remove or demote a bishop to a lesser bishopric. Bishops paid to protect themselves from demotion.

Expectancies

Bishoprics were often sold (even before they were vacated) to the highest bidder. For example, when a bishop was sick or getting old, other bishops commonly bid to the pope for his job. The job usually went to the highest bidder; however, in order to make more money, bidding was occasionally repeated.

Reservations

Reservations were the richest and best of the bishoprics. These were reserved for papal use. The pope would send a minor priest to administer the affairs of that area and pay him a small wage. The large income of the prestigious place would go to the pope.

Jus Spoliorum

Jus spoliorum means just spoils. When an officer of the church received money, land or other property, that property was expected to go fully to the Roman Catholic Church at the death of that officer. Since priests could not marry, they had no heirs. Many church officers were given highly valuable assets; at their deaths, all that was theirs went to the Church.

Tithing

Tithing does not refer to the 10% given by the people. When a bishopric had significant land, building or property, it was taxed by the pope. The tithe was really a real estate tax which began as a way to fund the Crusades; however, the tax did not go away after the Crusades.

Dispensations

Dispensations had to do with ecclesiastical violations. When someone of wealth broke the rules, the pope would commonly threaten to excommunicate him to hell. If that offender paid enough money to the pope, he could be excused.

Indulgences

The Roman Catholic Church developed the unbiblical idea of Purgatory. It is the idea that one does not go directly to heaven at death. It says all of the sins of the sinner may not be yet forgiven by Christ. Depending on the number and severity of these unforgiven sins, one might have to spend few or many years in Purgatory. Popes and priests could increase one's time in Purgatory, and often did so to people of means such as kings, lords and vassals.

No one was sure how much time any individual might have to spend in Purgatory. An indulgence was simply a paper with a place for a person's name, the amount of money he was contributing to the Church and how many years were being taken off his time in Purgatory. Naturally the more money one gave to the Church, the more years a pope or priest would take off his time in Purgatory.

The abuse of indulgences became rampant and a two-edged sword. The Roman Catholic Church used its power to increase one's time in Purgatory. It also used the sale of indulgences to shorten that time and extract large sums of money. The Church even told people that if they bought too many credits for their time in Purgatory, those credits could go into a *Treasury of Merit* to apply to whomever the purchaser might choose. On the other hand some people of wealth bought indulgences to obtain forgiveness for future sins. This supposedly gave them perfect liberty do whatever they pleased, however wicked.

Over time the sale of indulgences became one of the Roman Catholic Church's most hated practices.

> **Religious financial exploitation is called Simony**

The state church of Constantine became the Roman Catholic Church. It took a while for that church to develop and get there, but it did. The Catholic Church became increasingly dominant and oppressive. As we shall soon see, it invented and employed many diabolical means to destroy all who refused to join and support the church; however, it could not and did not fully succeed. Despite the church's best efforts, it could not eradicate true Christians and churches.

---

[1] Carl Deimer, Professor, *History of Christianity I,* Video Lecture 15, Liberty University DLP, 2004.

[2] Philip Schaff, *History of the Christian Church,* vol. 4, (Peabody, Massachusetts: Hendrickson Publishers, 2002), 80-81.

[3] Ibid., 211-216.

[4] Deimer.

[5] Ibid.

[6] Schaff, 218-219.

[7] Ibid., 205.

[8] Deimer, Lecture 16.

[9] Ibid.

[10] Ibid.

[11] Ibid.

[12] *Webster's New World Dictionary with Student Handbook: Young People's Edition,* s.v. "feudal," (Nashville, Tennessee: The World Publishing Company, 1973), 263.

[13] Deimer.

[14] This list is adapted from Video Lecture 23 by Carl Deimer.

[15] Deimer, class notebook, Lesson 23, 3.

Expansion of the Papacy

Here are some of the reasons why the papacy expanded between the time of Gregory I until 1054.

Political and Military Alliances

Pepin the Short

In 751 Pope Zacharias crowned Pepin as king of the Franks. After this, the pope was seen as having the power to make kings. In return for the pope's favor toward him, Pepin gave Zacharias a large territory called the Papal States. This territory constituted about one-fifth of modern Italy.

Charlemagne

On December 25, 800, Pope Leo III crowned Charles the Great as "The Holy Roman Emperor." As he conquered, he brought his subjects under the influence of the church in Rome and under the power of the pope, who dominated the area. The pope had made Charlemagne ruler and exercised extensive domination of him.

Forged Documents

The Donation of Constantine

This document claimed that when Constantine moved his capital from Rome to Constantinople in 330, he granted the bishop of Rome secular authority over Rome and its environs. A Catholic named Lorenzo Valla found that this was a fake document. Pope Zacharias knew that the document was forged, so he used it as a claim to political and secular power.

The Pseudo-Isidorian Decretals

This is a series of illegitimate, forged church documents, laws and creeds. They were discovered to be false during the eighteenth century. These documents appear to have been used by Zacharias to get the Papal States from Pepin.

The History of Churches

Expansion of the Papacy

Feudalism

In the absence of central authority, all of Europe broke down into small independent, feudalistic kingdoms. Each depended upon the strength of its leader, who was an absolute monarch over his fiefdom (domain). Some lords placed parcels of their land in the hands of vassals in return for help in war and for other services.

The kings and vassals were almost all Catholic. With the death of Charlemagne, feudalism became the political system of mainstream Europe. With no central political leadership in Europe, the pope became the one generally recognized figure of central prestige and power.

The pope had great power over feudal kings, lords and vassals. In their minds, the pope (the bishop of Rome) had the power to damn them to hell, plus the power to summon other kings, lords and vassals to military action against any one of them who stepped out of line and gained his disfavor.

Internal Developments in the State Church

Standardized Worship

The state church worked to standardize worship throughout its domain. The central feature of worship became the Mass. Western theology became universal and Latin became the standard language of the Church.

Doctrinal Controversies

The pope excommunicated the patriarchs of the East, which effectively removed dissent in the Church and strengthened the papacy.

Greed and Financial Exploitation

Religious financial exploitation is called Simony because of Simon, who in Acts 8 thought he could buy the power of the Holy Spirit with money. This is a brief list of some of the practices that the pope imposed on the Church.

Annates – the first year's income of all bishops and abbots must be given to the pope.

Collations – the rotation and shifting of bishops and abbots to new bishoprics. This would give his first-year's salary to the pope, so the pope made money with this practice.

Commendations – the annual tax paid by a bishop or abbot to remain in a particular office.

Expectancies – paying the pope money to get a job at a bishopric. The job usually goes to the highest bidder.

Reservations – the richest and best of the bishoprics. These were reserved for papal use.

Jus Spoliorum – means just spoils. When an officer of the Church dies, his property is given to the Church.

Tithing – a real estate tax on any significant land, building or property in a bishopric.

Dispensations – paying the pope money to excuse someone when they broke the rules.

Indulgences – paying money to reduce your time in Purgatory for unforgiven sins.

Chapter 18

Crush the Opposition

Most people have no idea of how horribly corrupt, wicked and cruel the church that developed in Rome became. To this day multitudes are in ignorance and blindness to truth. Some refuse to acquaint themselves with the facts and face the truth. The false church in Rome opportunistically committed spiritual adultery with lovers which paid it the highest price in terms of power and riches. The state church which ultimately became the Roman Catholic Church is the mother of harlots described in Revelation 17. The blood of millions who have perished at her hands cries out against her.

We have seen that the state church was intolerant. Every person who rejected its doctrine and practices and who refused to join the church was considered to be a heretic deserving of death. Its practice was *conversion by the sword;* it was either embrace the false doctrine or die. The goal was the elimination of all opposition. Yes, "all opposition!" This chapter is designed to show some (not all) of the tools used by the Church of Rome to accomplish its macabre goal.

POPE GREGORY VII

The mention of a despot such as Gregory VII is made only to connect the story line and help the reader grasp the climate that prevailed against those who believed and practiced first-century

216

Christianity. He was born to a peasant goat herder and named Hildebrand. [1] He was appointed a Cardinal in 1049 and controlled papal politics through five popes until 1073 when he became pope. [2] He was frail but fiery, consumed with lust for power and absolute control. While claiming to be unworthy of such high office, he was ruthless and arrogant. This is the man who claimed he was the Vicar of Christ, [3] a claim embraced by all following popes. He was determined to establish the absolute supremacy of the papacy at any cost.

The Three Primary Goals of Gregory VII

- **Eliminate internal opposition**

  He was determined to destroy all priests, bishops, monks, lay people or anyone in the Roman Catholic Church who might oppose papal domination.

- **Eliminate external opposition**

  He was determined to destroy all kings, princes or other secular rulers who might oppose the papacy. He accomplished this goal by forming *the College of Cardinals*. Before his time, lay people had a voice in selecting bishops, priests and popes. Large and rich landowners had a powerful say about who was elected bishop in their areas. Gregory VII eliminated this secular influence by deciding that only the pope could select bishops, only bishops could select priests, only priests could select presbyters and only presbyters could select deacons. Furthermore only *the College of Cardinals* could select a pope.

  It is interesting that the Cardinals keep no records; they burn them in a stove. When a pope is being selected and no decision has been made, the smoke is black. White smoke means a new pope has been selected. Chemicals are used to determine the color of the smoke.

- **Gain the support of secular rulers**

  The pope needed the support of secular rulers. Do not assume that the pope sought that support on a strictly voluntary basis. He would use whatever force at his disposal to force secular rulers to submit to and support him. [4]

Gregory VII viewed himself as the supreme head and authority of all Christendom. He believed it to be his right to control *the Church*. Furthermore he saw *the Church* as superior to the state. In a letter to William of England, he compared *the Church* to the sun and *the state* to the moon. He also compared *the Church priesthood* to gold and royalty to lead. To achieve his goals, Gregory VII issued a *papal bull*. The year was 1075. A *papal bull* is an official proclamation by the pope. [5] Gregory's *bull* proclaimed the use of three tools to accomplish his goals.

Gregory VII claimed he was the spokesman for God

The Three Tools of Gregory VII

- **Excommunication**

  By this time the stance of Roman Catholicism had long been that salvation comes from Christ only through the Roman Catholic Church. The Church viewed itself as God's salvation broker. To the Catholic hierarchy, God had placed salvation in the hands of the Catholic Church. Regardless of one's faith and relationship to Christ, the church could give him salvation through baptism and the Lord's Supper. Conversely the church could take away one's salvation. The Catholic stance was simple: if you were a member of the church, you had salvation; it you were not a member of the church, you didn't have salvation.

  Excommunication removed one from membership in the church. That meant his salvation was taken away and he was damned to hell. Excommunication had been practiced by the state church for 700 years before Gregory VII. Bishops who excommunicated people used the foulest of profane language and cussing. This was especially true of bishops and popes. Excommunication also resulted in seizure of property, imprisonment, bodily torture and maiming. [6] Gregory VII formalized excommunication as a tool of the Catholic Church against opposition.

- **Interdict**

  The Interdict was an expansion of excommunication. By the Interdict, a whole community (the innocent and the guilty) could be excommunicated. This gave the pope power to close all of the churches in a particular community or country. Even marriages and funerals were forbidden. "It cast the gloom of a funeral over a country, and made people tremble in expectation of the last judgment." [7] According to Catholic theology when the church doors are shut, there are no sacraments and consequently no salvation. This meant the entire community was cut off from salvation and damned to hell.

  Like excommunication, the Interdict was not new to the Catholics; however, no bishop or pope had used it as a routine tool of the church to force subjection. Gregory VII did.

- **Ban**

  The Ban had already been in effect; Gregory VII solidified and formalized it. It was a direct outgrowth of the state-church connection and found its strength where a local ruler was sympathetic to the Catholic Church. It had to do with individuals who were at odds with the Catholic Church. Once a church official banned a person from the church that person was run out of the territory by the secular authorities. Papal representatives (legates) were sent throughout Europe to sit in palaces. They advised kings and princes and told them who to ban.

By the Interdict, a whole community or nation can be condemned to hell

---

THE TEST CASE OF HENRY IV

During the reign of Gregory VII, Henry IV was the Holy Roman Emperor. He was not inclined to submit fully to Gregory VII, particularly regarding the appointment of bishops. Henry appointed a bishop in northern Italy, but Gregory rejected the appointment. Henry responded by saying that if the bishop he had appointed was not a bishop, then Gregory was not a pope. In turn Gregory excommunicated Henry which damned him to hell. Henry's excommunication also freed all his subjects from obedience to him.

Henry finally decided that this was too much trouble over one bishop. He left his capital and headed toward Rome to ask the pope's forgiveness. Meanwhile the pope left Rome and headed toward Germany to make a test case out of Henry. They met at a castle in Canossa. Gregory arrived first, went into the castle and shut the doors. When King Henry arrived, Pope Gregory made him wait outside barefoot in the snow for three days while begging Gregory for forgiveness. Finally Gregory forgave Henry and restored him to his throne. [8]

The point was made. The pope had backed down a strong king. The tools of control had worked. Secular authority had been brought under the authority of the Roman Catholic Church with her papacy.

ADDITIONAL TEST CASES

This power was later solidified by additional test cases. Henry II was king of England from 1154 to 1189. Alexander III was pope. Henry was in full doctrinal sympathy with the pope, but he did not like the pope's power in England. Henry appointed Thomas à Becket as Archbishop of Canterbury (the highest church office in England). Henry wanted to distance himself from the pope's domination and passed *The Constitutions of Clarendon* which said that any clergyman in England with a problem should take it to the king and not the pope. Pope Alexander threatened to excommunicate Henry II. Powerful nobles and lords in England united against King Henry, rode to his palace and forced him to renounce *The Constitutions of Clarendon.* They were not willing to lose their salvation and go to war with the pope over who had the greatest voice in England.

In 1215 a similar scenario occurred between Pope Innocent III and King John I of England. In every case, the pope prevailed. The kings all buckled and became subject to the popes. The power of the papacy was enormous. The pope was now ruling kings and kingdoms throughout Europe with an iron hand. Gregory VII arrogantly sent edicts and demands to kings and rulers all across Europe. [9] Popes who followed him continued the practice.

Please synthesize this with relationship to those who insisted on the practice of first-century, New Testament Christianity. The pope ruled supreme, and kings and other secular rulers across Europe submitted to him and carried out his wishes. He and the Catholic Church viewed all non-Catholics as heretics worthy of extreme punishment and death. The pope and his hierarchy demanded the extermination of those heretics and the secular authorities were their enforcers. Even those secular rulers who were not in sympathy with the pope were forced to be the pope's persecutors and executors. If they failed, they risked the high likelihood of losing their kingdoms and lives. True Christians, who are often called *dissenters* by modern writers, were in constant peril. It is not difficult to see why they fled to mountains, caves and wherever they might find shelter. The pope ruled the Roman Catholic Church, and the Roman Catholic Church ruled Europe. These popes were bent on absolute control and the crushing and extermination of every person who opposed them. "The history of the centuries which followed Constantine unfolds the growth in worldliness and ambition of the clergy, both of the Eastern and Western Catholic churches, until they claimed entire dominion over the possessions and consciences of mankind, enforcing these claims with a violence and guile that knew no limits." [10]

> **True Christians, often called *dissenters*,
> were in constant peril**

LEGATES

Legates have been mentioned, but it is helpful to better understand who they were and their role in the Catholic Church's efforts to silence all who rejected or opposed it.

Gregory VII instituted a company of strong men to act both as spies and enforcers for the popes. They were appointed by the pope as his personal representatives. As ambassadors of the pope, they carried his power and authority. They took precedence over all others, including bishops and kings. They were dispatched throughout the domain of the Catholic Church to preside at synods and demand the will of the pope. As grounds for these officials, Gregory VII quoted **Luke 10:16**, *"He that heareth you heareth me."* Almost all of the legates were extraordinarily corrupt and self-serving. [11]

From the time of Gregory VII and afterwards, legates became the prime movers against first-century Christians. Wherever these Christians were found to exist the popes sent legates with authority to persecute and destroy them. These legates probed in the communities to learn who and where these *heretics* were. The legates were especially interested in the leaders of these churches and the groups who refused to be a part of the Roman Church. Legates commanded secular authorities to seize their property and to imprison and persecute their leaders and their lay members. In the name of the pope, legates demanded that kings wage war and crusades against those who stayed true to New Testament doctrine and practice. They threatened to remove kings who failed to follow their orders.

For example, beginning in 1168 Culin was king of Bosnia for 36 years. Culin had become a Bogomil. (Bogomils were first-century Christians, and they flourished in great numbers in Bosnia.) Pope Alexander III was infuriated and sent legates to Bela III who was king of Hungary to force Culin back into the Catholic Church. Under the threat of attack from Hungary, in 1181 Culin recanted; however, Culin soon returned to his Bogomil faith and led a revival which resulted in at least 10,000 conversions. By this time (1199) Innocent III was pope. He too was furious and demanded the Hungarian king to punish Culin. By this time Culin was too strong for the King of Hungary, who could not enforce the pope's wishes. [12]

Such was the power and efforts of the popes. The legates were their personal enforcers.

THE INQUISITION

In her earlier years even the leaders of the Catholic Church forbad the use of torture and force to gain confessions. That changed. At the fourth Lateran Council in 1215 the Roman Catholic Church established the infamous *ecclesiastico-political* courts of Inquisition. "These courts found torture the most effective means of punishing and exterminating heresy, and invented new forms of refined cruelty worse than those of the persecutors of heathen Rome." [13] In his papal bull, *Ad extirpanda*, Pope Innocent IV "ordered the civil magistrates to extort from all heretics by torture a confession of their own guilt and a betrayal of all their accomplices." [14]

From this point forward the Roman authorities could torture and maim people in the name of God and with the authority of the *Church*. This they did without mercy or restraint. Stories of horror abound. *Fox's Book of Martyrs* is only one of several accounts of the inhumane treatment inflicted by the Roman Catholic Church upon those who refused to embrace and support her. [15]

Initially Dominican and Franciscan monks were sent by the pope to "both enjoin to stir up the Catholic princes and people to root out the abettors of erroneous opinions, and to transmit a regular account of their proceedings to Rome, whence they obtained the name of Inquisitors." [16] These Inquisitors were not bound by ordinary rules or law in their inquiries. "The accused was surprised by a sudden summons, and as a rule imprisoned on suspicion. All the accused were presumed to be guilty, the judge being at the same time the accuser." [17] Almost anyone, regardless of age or character, could be a witness for the prosecution but not for the defense. Witnesses who retracted their hostile evidence were punished as false witnesses. Witnesses who refused to give evidence were considered guilty of heresy. The accused were bound to denounce and disclose all who were partners in their *heresy*. All confessions and dispositions made in the torture chambers were considered true. Since any lawyer defending the accused was also considered guilty of heresy, the accused had no legal defense. There was never a case of acquittal. The accused lost their property. They were tortured and severely abused. Every effort was made to torture them into reporting others who held their beliefs. [18] In a later chapter we shall re-visit the Inquisition, look specifically at some of their tactics and examine cases. It is truly a sordid picture. The pope and his domineering, power-hungry Catholic Church would stop at nothing to impose their will on every person.

The whole idea of the Inquisition was to ferret out and destroy every person who refused total submission to the Catholic Church throughout the entire domain which Roman Catholics viewed as their own. Under the authority and direction of the pope and his regime, Inquisitors fanned out across Europe like bloodhounds. With the passing of time they became increasingly rabid, cruel, savage and inhumane. Their atrocities are stunning. It is difficult to imagine such brutality and debauchery in humans, especially in the name of God. That reality will become especially apparent and shocking when we look at the Spanish Inquisition. Who were their primary targets? The Albigenses, the Waldenses, the Paulicians, the Anabaptist and all others who refused Catholic doctrines and practices!

The Inquisition used torture to extract confessions from heretics

---

PREVIEW

As we progress through this book it should be obvious that the deck was becoming increasingly stacked against all who believed and practiced first-century Christianity. The Catholics were determined to crush them and systematically invented the tools for this purpose. Obviously they failed; however, the trail of blood, suffering and misery is long and repulsive. In our next chapter we will turn our attention to these supposed heretics who were such a thorn in the side of the Catholics. Who were these people? Why would the Catholics invent such sinister and macabre means of torture and go to such great lengths to eradicate them? What were their crimes? Where did they live? Were there many or few? What is their history? We will provide answers to these and other questions.

[1] Philip Schaff, *History of the Christian Church,* vol. 5, (Peabody, Massachusetts: Hendrickson Publishers, 2002), 10.

[2] Carl Deimer, Professor, *History of Christianity I,* Video Lecture 22, Liberty University DLP, 2004.

[3] Schaff, 29

[4] Deimer.

[5] Schaff, 31.

[6] Ibid., vol. 4, 377-378.

[7] Ibid., 379.

[8] Deimer.

[9] Schaff, vol. 5, 32-34.

[10] E.H. Broadbent, *The Pilgrim Church,* (Grand Rapids, Michigan: GOSPEL FOLIO PRESS, 1999), 64.

[11] Schaff, vol. 5, 783-784.

[12] L.P. Brockett, *The Bogomils of Bulgaria and Bosnia; or the Early Protestants of the East,* (Philadelphia: American Baptist Publications Society, 1879. Classic Reprints #43 by Vance Publications, Pensacola, FL., 2001), 63-66.

[13] Schaff, vol. 4, 351.

[14] Ibid.

[15] This book written by John Fox is strongly recommended. There are several editions including those by editors William Byron Forbush and Adam Clarke.

[16] John Fox, *Christian Martyrology,* (London, Paris and New York: Fisher, Son, & Co., 1840), 663.

[17] *Encyclopaedia Britannica,* vol. 12, (Chicago, London, Toronto: William Benton, Publisher, 1960), 378.

[18] Ibid., 379-380.

Pope Gregory VII

Gregory VII was appointed a Cardinal in 1049 and controlled papal politics through five popes. He became pope in 1073.

His three primary goals were:

Eliminate Internal Opposition - He was determined to destroy anyone in the Roman Catholic Church who might oppose papal domination

Eliminate External Opposition - He was determined to destroy all secular rulers who might oppose the papacy. He accomplished this goal by forming *the College of Cardinals*, which is the only entity that can select a pope. He also decided that only the pope could select bishops, only bishops could select priests, only priests could select presbyters and only presbyters could select deacons.

Gain the Support of Secular Rulers - He would use whatever force at his disposal to force secular rulers to submit to and support him.

He viewed himself as the supreme head and authority of all Christendom. He believed it to be his right to control the Church. Furthermore he saw the Church as superior to the state.

Gregory VII claimed he was the Vicar of Christ, a claim embraced by all following popes. He was determined to establish the absolute supremacy of the papacy at any cost.

The History of Churches

Tools of the Catholic Church

In 1075 Gregory VII issued a papal bull, which is an official proclamation by the pope, to proclaim the use of excommunication, interdict, and ban as tools to accomplish his goals.

Excommunication

This means the church can take away one's salvation.

Interdict

As part of the Catholic law, this expanded the church's excommunication power, making it possible for the church to send a whole nation or populace of people to hell

Ban

Also a part of the Catholic law, this gave the church power (enforced by civil authorities) to run an excommunicated person out of the territory and exile him.

Legates

They are appointed by the pope to carry out his wishes. They carried the personal power and authority of a pope and took precedence over all other Catholic authorities.

The Inquisition

In 1215 the Roman Catholic Church instituted courts of Inquisition and gave them the power to hunt and torture heretics. The Inquisitors set up business in either a Dominican or Franciscan monastery, which became both the court and the prison where the crimes against humanity were carried out. It was a crime to oppose the Inquisition and the decisions of the Inquisitors were arbitrary.

The History of Churches

Chapter 19

The Bogomils

THE UNBROKEN LINE

Throughout this book reference has been made to an unbroken line of first-century Christians. With this study we move back in time to look at and follow that line. Claims should be backed with evidence. From what we have already seen, it is glaringly obvious that a great multitude did not agree with those churches which embraced tradition over Scripture and which developed institutional and ritualistic means of salvation mainly through the church by baptism and the Lord's Supper rather than by personal faith in Christ. Even modern historians, who deny the unbroken line, speak repeatedly of these *dissenters*. No honest historian can say that prior to the Protestant Reformation there were never people and churches that stayed true to first-century Christianity. There were multitudes of them all over Europe. "They recurred in wave upon wave of dissent against the medieval sacralist order" [1] When the Reformation erupted, many of them joined it. They thought the reformers were coming to where they had been since Christ. When they saw that there was little difference between the reformers and the Catholics, they broke with the reformers. Even Martin Luther admitted this reality. [2] These Christians after the biblical order never deserted the autonomy of the local church and never banded together with those who saw themselves as *the Church*. They were never a part of the state church. They were first-century Christians with New Testament doctrine and practices, plain and simple. That's all they were or wanted to be.

To them, there was nothing bigger and better than a church true to Christ as set forth in the Scriptures. He was their Master and Father: they rejected all other masters and fathers. As more and more churches departed from the truths of the Bible, embraced doctrine and practice contrary to biblical teachings and banded together to form a powerful organization which they called *the true church*, they began to condemn, reject and persecute those churches and individuals that stayed true to the faith that was once delivered to the saints, **Jude 3**. The false ones called themselves *orthodox* and called true believers and churches *heretics*. Even before Constantine wed the false ones into a state church, those false churches that banded together pressured the ones who didn't. With the formation of a state church, that pressure quickly turned to outright attack and persecution.

Not all of those first-century churches stayed true to God's Word on all points. Just like churches today, they all strayed here and there; however, they stayed true to the core New Testament beliefs and practices which have been repeatedly mentioned in this book. The big anchor points that united them as a common people were the absolute authority of the Scriptures, the deity of Christ, salvation by personal faith in Jesus Christ, salvation before baptism, baptism by immersion, the autonomy of each church, the priesthood of every believer, liberty of conscience and purity in the lives of believers. It must be re-stated that it is not a common name that constitutes an unbroken line from the church Jesus personally established in Jerusalem to the present; it is common doctrine and practice. This unbroken line is "identified by her characteristic features." [3] New Testament Christians throughout the centuries have been far more concerned with beliefs and practices than with names. Names have been important and many true believers have rejected the names imposed upon them by their enemies; but the thing that has bound and united them and enabled them to band together and fellowship as one has been their common adherence to the doctrine and practice of the New Testament, not their names. Some have been over-zealous against backsliders, many have had wild and anti-biblical ideas about the person and ministry of the Holy Spirit, others like those in Thessalonica have misunderstood the Second Coming of Christ, many in the East failed to rightly divide the dualistic concept of good and evil, some went overboard on the sovereignty of God and others made too much of dress codes and made rituals out of certain practices; yet they held true to core beliefs.

Earlier in this book we spoke briefly of the Montanists, the Novatians and the Donatists. Do not assume these were the only ones who refused to go along with the prevailing drift of the day. There were others. "In every century you can find groups who were against the Roman Catholic Church including the whole idea and all for which it stood." [4] "Even in the first three centuries there were numerous bodies of Christians who protested against the growing laxity and worldliness in the Church, and against its departure from the teachings of Scripture." [5] D.B. Ray said, "The true churches throughout the Empire declared non-fellowship with the false churches and false members in the year 251." [6] This was over 60 years before Constantine's formation of a state church and hundreds of years before a fully organized Catholic Church. Already the true churches that were continuing first-century, New Testament doctrine and practice were putting distance between themselves and those who were steadily drifting away from any semblance of true biblical Christianity. "The true histories of these have been obliterated as far as possible. Their writings, sharing the fate of the writers, have been destroyed to the full extent of the power allowed to their persecutors. Not only so, but histories of them have been promulgated by those in whose interest it was to disseminate the worst inventions against them in order to justify their own cruelties. In such accounts they are depicted as heretics, and evil doctrines are ascribed to them which they repudiated. They are called 'sects,' and labels are attached to them which they themselves would not acknowledge." [7] Both the Greek and Roman churches "put the brand of heresy on every sect which dared to deny their dogmas." [8]

The time has come for us to look specifically and more closely at some of these Christians and churches that remained true to the faith in the face of tremendous pressure. We shall see who the Catholics called *heretics* and why they thought them worthy of persecution, torture and death. You will see that they were us; those of us who today believe and practice New Testament Christianity. They are our spiritual ancestors, an unbroken line of ancestors back to the first church of Jesus Christ that ever existed, the one in Jerusalem. Not in name, but in doctrine and practice, they constitute the unbroken line. Dr. J.M. Carroll called it, *The Trail of Blood*. [9] It is not a connection of every church to a mother church; it is a connection of continuous New Testament doctrine and practice in churches in one place or another from Jesus until now.

When you complete this book, do not assume that every church or set of churches in the unbroken line has been considered. They are too numerous for a study of this length. They were all over Europe and beyond; new evidence and proof of their existence continues to surface. In this book we look at only a few of those where the trail is irrefutable and the impact is very great. We will begin with the Bogomils, whose very existence refutes the claims of modern historians who contend that there is no evidence for the existence of churches with Baptist doctrine and practice between the fourth and eleventh centuries.

Common doctrine and practice create the unbroken line

THE BOGOMILS

True Churches from the Start

The New Testament records the dramatic spread of churches, particularly to the north and west of Jerusalem. (See *The Proliferation of Churches* chart in Chapter 1). Paul was greatly used of God to plant many churches, especially around the Aegean Sea. Churches are mentioned in such places as Antioch of Syria (Acts 13), Ephesus (Ephesians), Corinth (Corinthians), Thessalonica (Thessalonians) and Philippi (Philippians). A look at regions mentioned in association with the gospel before the end of the New Testament gives at least a partial understanding of the broad extent of Christianity's spread. Peter mentioned *"Pontus, Galatia, Cappadocia, Asia, and Bithynia,"* **1 Peter 1:1**. Paul spread the gospel through *"Syria and Cilicia,"* **Acts 15:41** and testified that he had preached the gospel all the way *"from Jerusalem, and round about unto Illyricum,"* **Romans 15:19**. Illyricum includes Dalmatia. Paul and Silas preached through Phrygia and into Mysia, **Acts 16:6-7**. *"Italy"* is named, **Hebrews 13:24**, and Paul mentioned *"the regions* *beyond*" those already named, **2 Corinthians 10:16**. **Acts 20:1-2** mention both "*Macedonia*" and "*Greece*" and 2 Corinthians and ten other references speak of "*Achaia.*" Mark and Barnabas ministered on "*Cyprus,*" **Acts 15:39**.

Note the location of Thessalonica, Philippi and Berea. Christianity flourished in these areas; Paul wrote letters to the churches of Philippi and Thessalonica. He specifically mentioned "*the churches of Macedonia,*" **2 Corinthians 8:1**. By A.D. 55 when he wrote 2 Corinthians, there were obviously several churches in that area. Maps of the time quickly show that for the first three centuries, Christian churches flourished in the area which later became known as the Balkan States. The Balkan States include Albania, Bosnia, Herzegovina, Bulgaria, Croatia, Greece, Macedonia, Romania, Serbia, Montenegro (Yugoslavia), Slovenia and Turkey. The history of that area demonstrates "that there were churches of faithful witnesses of Christ who had never paid their homage or given their allegiance to the anti-Christian churches of Constantinople or Rome." [10] There is no evidence that every church in that area accepted tradition over Scripture, departed from New Testament teachings and adopted the false doctrine and practice of salvation through the church and its rituals. When a look is taken at the Slavic people at the beginning of the fourth century, multitudes of them were still preaching salvation by grace through faith in Jesus Christ and baptism by immersion only after salvation. They were not a part of the new state church. The unbroken line of first-century, New Testament Christians had prevailed for 300 years in that part of the world. Furthermore it continued in the years to come.

Early Paulicians

Bogomils is the name given over time to descendents who remained true to the faith of their first-century, New Testament ancestors in Bosnia, Bulgaria and Armenia. "I have found, often in unexpected quarters, the most conclusive evidence that these sects were all, during their earlier history, Baptists, not only in their views on the subjects of baptism and the Lord's Supper, but in their opposition to Paedobaptism, to a church hierarchy, and to any worship of the Virgin Mary or the saints, and in their adherence to church independence and freedom of conscience in religious worship." [11]   During the first three centuries, these were among others in the Roman Empire who protested against the growing laxity and worldliness in churches and the general trend of departure from the teachings of Scripture.   The alliance of false churches accused them of being Manichaeans, a charge that is unjustified and which these true believers staunchly rejected.   As the Greek, Latin and Armenian churches became increasingly godless, these true churches "denied them the title of churches, declaring that they forfeited it by their union with the State, by introduction of unbelievers into their circles through the system of infant baptism, by their giving the Lord's Supper to unbelievers, and by various other evils they had introduced." [12]

"The name Paulician was frequently given to these churches" [13] and they wore that name for nine centuries.   Modern skeptics and critics commonly claim that the Paulicians originated with Paul of Samosata who became bishop of Antioch toward the end of the third century.   This unscrupulous, conceited, self-glorifying man taught that Christ was not divine but merely a good man. [14]   The fact is that the faithful, first-century Christians of the Bosnia-Bulgaria area were called Paulicians apart from any connection to Paul of Samosata.   Even the outstanding historian Philip Schaff, who was not a proponent of the perpetuity of New Testament Christianity through the ages but who was quite honest and objective in most of his claims, said their name probably derived "from their preference for St. Paul, whom they placed highest among the Apostles." [15]   That is a natural conclusion to be drawn from the fact that Paul was the apostle who chiefly evangelized this area.   *Cathari* means "the pure" and because of their pure lifestyles they were sometimes called *Cathari;* however, *Bogomil* is the name by which they ultimately became best identified.   The name *"Bogomil* is thought to be derived from the Bulgarian *Bog z'milui,* signifying 'God have mercy.'" [16]   They were derogatorily discredited as being Massalians and Euchites by their enemies, but the Bogomils rejected the charges.   They even dropped the name *Cathari* and simply called themselves *Christians.* [17]

Paulicians was the original name that was given to the Bogomils

---

Bosnia, Bulgaria and Armenia

Remember that in their early years the Bogomils were known as Paulicians. There were two sects of these believers, one in Bulgaria and another in Bosnia. Though both adhered to New Testament Christianity, the Bulgarians were (for a while) somewhat influenced by the dualistic, *two-equal-divinities* ideas of the Manichaeans. Their enemies seem to have greatly exaggerated claims against them. It should be kept in mind that these believers had only a few manuscript copies of the four Gospels and later a few other books of the New Testament. As more accessibility to the completed Word of God reached them, their theology became increasingly sound.[18] Even with their weaknesses, the Bulgarian believers were true to salvation by grace through faith in Christ and baptism by immersion after salvation. [19] The later Bosnian Paulicians, who were also called Bogomils, had more access to the completed Word of God and were a sounder sect.

It should be noted that these early Paulicians were not confined to Bulgaria and Bosnia; from the beginning of Paul's ministry, they multiplied throughout the region. The Paulicians were "very numerous among the Armenians and the inhabitants of the Caucasus region." [20] These Armenian Paulicians are the ones who, under severe persecution by the state church, began a migration to Bulgaria and Bosnia. Hence, over time the Paulician movement took on a very Slavonic identification. Bulgaria had become an independent state and extensive empire. Furthermore on the west and north-west of Bulgaria, three other independent Slavonic states were rising in prominence. All of these new Slavonic states resisted the inroads of the Greek emperors and their Eastern, Greek Church. [21] The climate in this part of the world was a favorable place of shelter for the Armenian Paulicians who were facing persecution. They came here by the hundreds.

Paulician Evangelism

One of the greatest doctrinal positions of the New Testament is evangelism. Every believer is to reproduce himself in the life of another; every Christian is to win others to Christ. Jesus said, *"Go ye therefore, and teach all nations, baptizing them in the name of the Father, and of the Son, and of the Holy Ghost: Teaching them to observe all things whatsoever I have commanded you: and, lo, I am with you alway, even unto the end of the world. Amen,"* **Matthew 28:19-20**. The Paulicians took that as a literal command and promise. Within a few years Bulgaria, Bosnia and the Slavonic people as a whole were teeming with people who practiced first-century, New Testament Christianity. Over the years many of their leaders (Slavonic kings were called *bans*) were converted and became Paulicians, who were increasingly being called *Cathari* and *Bogomils*.

The result over the years was enormous political struggles. The Catholics were by no means willing to concede religious liberty or tolerance to anyone. The Eastern Catholics headquartered at Constantinople exercised every merciless, cruel, under-handed and heavy-handed force at their disposal to destroy and eradicate these uncompromising believers and churches. For hundreds of years, primarily between the fourth and twelfth centuries, the struggle went back and forth. When the Catholics were able to seize power in Bulgaria, Bosnia or one of the other countries, they would orchestrate persecution against the Bogomils and seek to destroy them. The Hungarian kings were usually loyal to Catholicism and were often commanded by one of the Eastern Patriarchs to attack and punish the Bulgarians or Bosnians. Many times the Bogomils were forced to form an army of resistance and fight back. This was especially true when their king (*ban*) was also a Bogomil. For centuries, turmoil, fighting and opposition continued against these New Testament Christians who were never a part of the corrupt, false organized church. Ultimately the false church prevailed. Additionally, the faithful Christians of this region were betrayed by the Muslims, who had at first given them shelter and a measure of protection. They became the victims of cruel, evil politics. Even though thousands upon thousands of these true saints of God were horribly persecuted and laid down their lives for the cause of Christ, they never ceased to exist. Be assured that what is being said here is but a feeble summary of a wealth of documentable evidence. [22] The reader is reminded that the nature of this book does not permit comprehensive, in-depth examinations of all of the evidence. The book is intended as a faithful report and summary that is sufficient to offer considerable insight and prove the point that there is an unbroken line of New Testament churches from Jesus to the present. They stayed true to New Testament doctrine and practice.

The true saints never ceased to exist

Bogomil Evangelism

The Bogomils, as they were becoming commonly known, not only evangelized their own people locally, they also sent missionaries abroad. The membership of Bogomil churches was divided into two classes. There was no hierarchy; all were seen before God on equal footing; however, there were differing roles. The *Credentes* were regular believers and the *Perfecti* were the leaders, mainly pastors, missionaries and women who assisted them. Among other good works, the women set up places of medical help. By 1240, Bogomilian doctrines had spread over all Europe and the number of believers (*Credentes*) was said by Reinero Sacconi, a Bogomil turned Inquisitor, to have been between two and one-half and three million. The *Perfecti,* which at that time numbered about four thousand, were dependent upon the financial support of the *Credentes* and were sent forth as missionaries by twos. [23]

The Bulgarian *Perfecti* moved across Europe making converts as they went. Some came to an area in the Alps near Albi, France. Due to the location, Bogomil converts in that area became known as Albigenses. They too were evangelistic and became very numerous around Milan, Italy. The Albigenses are the spiritual descendents of the Bulgarian Bogomils. They are the fruit of missionary zeal. Bulgarian *Perfecti* also did extensive missionary work in Croatia, Wallachia, Moldavia and in provinces which are in southern Russia. [24]

The Bosnian Bogomils were also very evangelistic and sent missionaries throughout Europe. They particularly went into Lombardy and the South of France. They also went into Spain, into Bohemia, into the Lower Rhine, into Flounders and into England. The Waldensian congregations are their descendents and are in part the result of their missionary work. The Bogomil turncoat Sacconi said Bogomil churches "were scattered throughout all the countries of Europe, and extended in an unbroken zone from the Black Sea to the Atlantic and from the Mediterranean to the Baltic." [25] A host of eminent scholars of the past have spent lifetimes collecting facts on this subject and have concluded that the Waldenses, the Bohemians, the Moravians, the Henricians of Toulouse, the Patarenes of Dalmatia and Italy, the Petrobrussians, the Bulgars and the Catharists of Spain all came from a common source, the Bogomils of Bulgaria and Bosnia. [26]

Catholic Backlash

After the fall of Constantinople, Roman popes became more powerful and blood-thirsty. The Bogomils were making inroads into their turf. Their response was wholesale efforts to destroy the Bogomils. At the request of the pope, the King of Hungary entered Bosnia in 1222 and used the sword in an effort to purge the Bogomils from Bosnia. The Bogomils remained and in 1238 Pope Gregory IX orchestrated a second crusade against Bosnian Bogomils. There were additional crusades and Inquisitors were sent to hunt and destroy Bosnian Bogomils. [27] Eventually most of the Bogomils were destroyed in Slavonic countries; but not all, and not before these devotees to New Testament Christianity had reproduced themselves abroad.

In our next chapter we will follow the unbroken line with a look at some of the descendants of the Bogomils.

---

[1] Leonard Verduin, *The Reformers and Their Stepchildren,* (Grand Rapids, Michigan: William B. Eerdmans Publishing Company, 1964), 33.

[2] Ibid., 18.

[3] D.B. Ray, *Baptist Succession: A Hand-book of Baptist History,* (Parsons, Kansas: Foley Railway Printing Company, 1912), 33.

[4] Carl Deimer, Professor, *History of Christianity II,* Video Lecture 3, Liberty University DLP, 2004.

[5] E.H. Broadbent, *The Pilgrim Church,* (Grand Rapids, Michigan: GOSPEL FOLIO PRESS, 1999), 64.

[6] Ray, 38.

[7] Broadbent.

[8] L.P. Brockett, *The Bogomils of Bulgaria and Bosnia; or the Early Protestants of the East,* (Philadelphia: American Baptist Publications Society, 1879. Classic Reprints #43 by Vance Publications, Pensacola, FL., 2001), 9.

[9] J.M. Carroll, *The Trail of Blood*, (Lexington, Kentucky: Ashland Avenue Baptist Church, 1992).

[10] Brockett, 8.

[11] Ibid., 11-12.
[12] Broadbent, 64-65.
[13] Ibid., 66.
[14] Earle E. Cairns, *Christianity Through the Centuries: A History of the Christian Church*, 3rd ed., (Grand Rapids, Michigan: Zondervan, 1996), 100.
[15] Philip Schaff, *History of the Christian Church*, vol. 4, (Peabody, Massachusetts: Hendrickson Publishers, 2002), 574.
[16] Brockett, 29.
[17] Ibid., 30.
[18] Ibid., 22.
[19] Ibid., 17-19.
[20] Ibid., 23.
[21] Ibid., 28-29.
[22] The book by Dr. Brockett from which this summary is taken is highly recommended. Publication information is cited in footnote 8.
[23] Brockett, 37-39.
[24] Ibid., 58.
[25] Ibid., 67-68.
[26] Ibid., 69.
[27] Ibid., 72-78.

The Spread of the Gospel

Acts 13:1	Antioch of Syria
Acts 15:39	Cyprus
Acts 15:41	Syria and Cilicia
Acts 16:6-7	Phrygia and Mysia
Acts 17:13	Berea
Acts 20:1-2	Macedonia and Greece
Romans 15:19	Jerusalem to Illyricum (which includes Dalmatia)
Corinthians	Corinth
2 Corinthians 1:1	Achaia
2 Corinthians 8:1	Macedonia
2 Corinthians 10:16	The regions beyond Corinth
Ephesians	Ephesus
Philippians	Philippi
Thessalonians	Thessalonica
Hebrews 13:24	Italy
1 Peter 1:1	Pontus, Galatia, Cappadocia, Asia, and Bithynia

The History of Churches

The Bogomils

Bogomils is the name given to the true believers in Bosnia, Bulgaria and Armenia from the first to the tenth centuries

Paulicians was the original name that was given to the Bogomils

They are sometimes referred to as the Cathari because of their pure lifestyles

The name Bogomil is derived from the Bulgarian *Bog z'mlui*, signifying 'God have mercy'

By 1240, Bogomilian doctrines had spread over all Europe and the number of believers was between two and one-half and three million

The membership of Bogomil churches was divided into two classes. The *Credentes* were regular believers and the *Perfecti* were the leaders, mainly pastors, missionaries and women who assisted them.

The History of Churches

The Bogomils

There were two sects of these believers, one in Bulgaria and another in Bosnia

The sect in Bulgaria only had a few manuscripts of the Bible, so they were somewhat influenced by the bad doctrine of the Manichaeans. As they got more manuscripts, their theology became increasingly sound.

The Bosnia sect had more access to the completed Word of God and were a sounder group

Many Slavonic kings were converted and became Bogomils

The Bosnian Bogomils were also very evangelistic and sent missionaries throughout Europe

Some Bogomil missionaries went near Albi, France and the converts there became the Albigenses

Common Beliefs of the Bogomils

These are some of the common beliefs that all the Bogomils shared

They believed

Only saved persons are to be baptized

Salvation is not tied to the Lord's Supper and baptism

Adherence to church independence

Freedom of conscience in religious worship

They opposed

Infant baptism (Paedobaptism)

A church hierarchy

Any worship of the Virgin Mary or the saints

The History of Churches

Chapter 20

The Waldenses

Do not suppose that the Paulicians, who became known as Bogomils in the Balkan States, are the only ones that constitute an unbroken line of churches that stayed true to New Testament doctrine and practice. They weren't. There were hosts of others in many locations. Dr. Carl Deimer's quote bears repeating, "In every century you can find groups who were against the Roman Catholic Church including the whole idea and all for which it stood." [1] The Paulicians, some of whom became known as Bogomils, were in the east, the Waldenses and Albigenses were in the heart of Europe and the Welsh Baptists were in Wales. These and others all had direct stems back to the original church established personally by Jesus Christ in Jerusalem, Israel.

If one branch of the stem was severed, the line remained unbroken because other branches of the stem were firmly intact. Furthermore, long before some of the branches were destroyed, they had cast forth seeds of their own kind and those seeds had sprouted and were thriving in other locations. The unbroken line was proliferating itself. A Frenchman may have a child who begets a French child, who moves to another country and begets yet another French child. The original Frenchman may meet a premature death; however, the French line continues in the children. In a parallel sense, true churches have continued from that first one in Jerusalem to the present. From the start true churches have reproduced generation after generation of spiritual children who remained true to the teachings of Jesus and the apostles. While some churches departed from the faith and ceased to remain in the true line of churches, those that remained true to New Testament doctrine and practice proliferated and reproduced themselves in Bulgaria, Croatia, Italy, France, Wales, Germany, England and many other places. Large communities of these churches developed. As they migrated to far-away places, they often lost contact with other churches of their kind; yet regardless of where they were, they remained true to core issues. They constitute one family or unbroken line of New Testament Christians and churches.

It is true that they have been sorely misrepresented by their enemies who exercised every imaginable and cruel effort to destroy them as well as documents relating to them. [2] In spite of such efforts, there is too much evidence to deny them.

TRUE BELIEVERS THROUGHOUT EUROPE

In our last chapter, mention was made of the fact that the Bosnian Bogomils were very evangelistic. They sent missionaries throughout Europe, particularly into Lombardy and the South of France. "Brethren from Bosnia and other Balkan countries, making their way through Italy, came into the south of France, **finding those who shared their faith everywhere.**" [3] (Emphasis mine.) This westward evangelistic movement by the Bogomils was going on in the eleventh century and these Bogomils were enormously successful. Their success was largely due to the receptive hearts they found as they moved westward. By 1240 "the Bogomilian doctrines had spread over all Europe," and Bogomil believers numbered between two and one-half and three million. [4] Note well: though the Bogomils were great instruments of God in the spread of true New Testament Christianity across central and Western Europe, what they taught and practiced was not new to the inhabitants they found there. When the Bogomils arrived, they found people "everywhere" who already believed and practiced what they did. This was especially the case in the mountainous areas where large numbers of the inhabitants did not profess the Catholic faith. Believers were "scattered throughout the south of France, the valleys of the Pyrenean Mountains, the valleys of Piedmont and the country of Milanese . . . ." [5]

There are many so-called *scholars* who would have us believe that the Paulicians, the Albigenses, the Waldenses, the Anabaptists and other non-Catholic groups that flourished throughout Europe for centuries all originated with some man in the same way that Lutherans originated with Luther, Presbyterians with Calvin and Anglicans with Henry VIII, but community after community of true believers and churches are traceable to no man. They existed here and there by various names all the way back to Christ and New Testament days, when their enemies in Antioch of Syria mocked them with the name *"Christians,"* **Acts 11:26**. It is true that many of them identified with famous personalities who led great revivals and growth among them. To contend that those famous Christian leaders founded the Christian groups associated with them is only an imaginative leap. It is akin to claiming that America was founded by Abraham Lincoln because he was a famous American. The fact is that America existed for a long time before Lincoln was born. It is likewise true that many Christian groups true to the faith existed long before someone came to them, embraced what they believed and became a famous leader among them. Such is the case with Peter Waldo and the Waldenses. The evidence points to the fact that the Waldenses were the ones who converted Waldo and taught him most of what he later propagated with such eloquence and influence. He was a member of the Waldenses and their greatest leader, but he was not their founder. The Waldenses were there a long time before Waldo was born.

True New Testament Christianity spread across central and Western Europe

---

PETER WALDO

Peter Waldo is mentioned at this point because he is so commonly misunderstood to be the founder of the Waldenses. It is good to understand who he was and see him in proper perspective. He is called by a variety of names including Waldo, Valdesius and Waldensis. [6] Peter was a wealthy and distinguished merchant in Lyons, France. He was aroused to see his need of salvation by the sudden death of one of the guests at a feast he had given. He began to read the Scriptures and soon received Christ as his personal Savior. In 1173 after reading **Matthew 19:21**, he made sure the financial state of his wife, then sold the rest of his belongings and gave the money to the poor. After seven years of devoted study of the Scriptures, Peter began to travel and preach. Companions known as *Poor Men of Lyons* joined with him, and soon he had a large following. This drew the ire of the Catholic Church under Pope Alexander III. Waldo and his followers were driven out of Lyons by Imperial edict and excommunicated in 1184. They scattered into surrounding countries and continued to preach salvation by grace through personal faith in Christ. [7]

With the passing of time Waldo became so influential that he became inseparably associated with the Waldenses. Many who wish to deny the earlier existence of Waldensian Christians and churches prior Waldo claim that Peter is the founder of the Waldenses. The facts simply will not substantiate that claim; substantial evidence refutes it.

THE NAME AND ORIGIN OF THE WALDENSES

It is claimed by some that the Waldenses derived their name from Waldo. That is not the case. "The name Waldenses was originally applied to the inhabitants of the valleys of the Alps, but, in after times, it was applied to that class of Christians, everywhere, who embraced the same views with the inhabitants of the valleys." [8] The English word *valley* comes from the Latin word *vallis*. In French and Spanish the word is *valle* and in Italian it is *valdeci*. The people in the Piedmont and other valleys of the Alps were called *Vaudois* or *Waldenses* meaning "men of the valleys." [9] Long before Peter Waldo, multitudes in the areas where he and his followers preached were already sympathetic to his beliefs. There is far greater reason to believe that Peter received his sir-name from the Waldenses than to believe that they received their name from him.

As Waldo's evangelists travelled two by two clad in woolen garments with wooden shoes or barefoot, "They penetrated Switzerland and Northern Italy. Everywhere they met with a hearty response. The principal seat of the Waldenses became the slopes of the Cottian Alps and East Piedmont, West Provence and

Dauphiny. Their numbers multiplied into thousands." [10] They became so strong and numerous that at times the Roman Catholics used the name to embrace all sects which opposed their doctrine. [11] There were multitudes of Waldenses, but not every set of believers and churches outside the Roman Church were Waldenses. It is true that largely due to the success of Peter Waldo and his evangelists, the name Waldenses was understood to encompass vast numbers of believers and churches over a very broad area. Let it not be forgotten that "it is a historical fact, fully made out, that the name Waldenses was applied to the inhabitants of the valleys, as a religious community" [12] long before Peter Waldo.

Dr. Alexis Muston is arguably the world's foremost authority on the Waldenses. He wrote the most complete and comprehensive history in existence on this huge group of Christians and churches. He said, "The Vaudois of the Alps are, in my opinion, primitive Christians, or descendants and representatives of the primitive church, preserved in the valleys from the corruptions successively introduced by the Church of Rome into the religion of the gospel. It is not they who have separated from Catholicism, but Catholicism which has separated from them by changing the primitive church." [13] He went on to say that the independence of the diocese of Milan where many of the Christians of the Alps lived, as well as the opposition of the episcopate of Turin to image worship in the ninth century, must have contributed to the security of the Waldenses in those regions. Dr. Muston also embraced the position that the great influence of Peter Waldo is "not sufficient to prove that the Vaudois of the Alps derive their origin from him. Many circumstances, on the contrary, seem to establish their existence anterior to his time." [14] "There are some who believe the Vaudois to have enjoyed the uninterrupted integrity of the faith even from apostolic ages .... At least it may be pronounced, with great certainty, that they had been long in existence before the visit of the Lyonese reformer." [15]

The Waldenses themselves, as well as a host of other scholars, believed in their own antiquity. [16] In 1689 one of their most notable leaders, Henri Arnold, said, "The Vaudois are in fact descended from those refugees from Italy, who, after Paul had there preached the gospel, abandoned their beautiful country and fled, like the woman mentioned in the Apocalypse, to these wild mountains, where they have to this day handed down the gospel, from father to son, in the same purity and simplicity as it was preached by St. Paul." [17] Even the Calvinist reformer of the 16th century, Theordore Beza, said, "As for the Waldenses, I may be permitted to call them the very seed of the primitive and purer Christian Church." [18] Eminent scholar Dr. G.H. Orchard contended that the lineage of the Waldenses is directly connected to the Novatians and Donatists, who were powerful bodies of dissidents in Italy and Africa, bodies which never became a part of the state church. Under the influence of Augustine who could endure no rival, emperors Theodosius and Honorius "in 413, issued an edict declaring that all persons rebaptized, and the rebaptizers, should be both punished with death." [19] Dr. Orchard went on to say, "These combined modes of oppression led the faithful to abandon the cities, and seek retreats in the country, which they did, particularly in the valleys of Piedmont, the inhabitants of which began to be called Waldenses." [20]

No honest person or true scholar can say the Waldenses originated in the 1170 with Peter Waldo. No proof has been found linking them to a person or date short of Jesus Christ, and the evidence points to their perpetuity from the first century.

Waldenses means "men of the valleys"

WHAT THE WALDENSES BELIEVED

The usual practice of the Catholics was to condemn and discredit every church or movement that refused to fall into lock step with them. Within the ranks of the Cathari there were serious falsehoods; however, the Catholics exaggerated these. [21] In their efforts to discredit the Waldenses and justify their atrocities against them, the Catholics falsely and maliciously branded the Waldenses as Manichaeans and the worst of the Cathari. The truth is that the doctrines of the Waldenses "had no connection with Manicheism." [22] They "were distinct from the Cathari and other sects in origin and doctrine" but shared with them the condemnation of the Catholic Church. [23]

Keep in mind that the term Waldenses is generic. It is a name that was given to many people living in widely separate lands with customs and doctrines that varied. It should not be assumed that all Waldenses over time and in different locations believed and practiced exactly alike. For example, "it is possible that some of the Italian Waldenses practiced infant baptism but there is no account that the French Waldenses or the Waldenses proper, ever practiced infant baptism." [24] (That should not be a surprise in view of the differences seen over the years and from church to church among Baptists. Sometimes segments of churches in sound groups depart completely into error.) It should also be kept in mind that on core issues almost all of the Waldenses were in harmony. The doctrine and practices listed here are typical of the great majority of Waldensian churches whenever and wherever they were found.

The Waldenses were committed to the Scriptures as the ultimate rule of faith and practice; and no authority of any man, however eminent, was allowed to set aside the authority of Scripture. Thus they saw no need for special confessionals or sets of rules outside the Scriptures. They held Christ as the supreme example of conduct. They believed in the indwelling of the Holy Spirit and leaned heavily on His leadership for a clearer understanding of the Scriptures; however, they staunchly rejected the idea that He gives new revelation. They also believed in the free exercise of one's conscience in matters of religion and rejected all efforts of coercion in such matters. They believed in self-defense (even with weapons), were exceedingly cautious about oaths in the name of God and categorically rejected the pomp, ceremony and salvation theology of the Catholic Church. To the Waldenses, salvation was possible only through a personal relationship with Jesus Christ by faith. Thus they rejected institutional salvation through the church by any form of rituals or sacraments, including baptism and the Lord's Supper. They believed in the autonomy of each local church and rejected an episcopate and a church hierarchy. They were highly evangelistic, lived remarkably pure and holy lives and highly valued education. [25]

The Waldenses also "believed that everyone should have the Bible in his own tongue" [26] and translated portions of the Scriptures into their tongue, a practice that highly infuriated the Catholic hierarchy. Key positions of the Waldenses were (1) the deity of

Christ, (2) salvation exclusively by grace through faith in Jesus Christ, (3) direct relationship to God apart from a hierarchy or episcopate, (4) the autonomy of the local church, (5) the sole authority of Scripture, (6) baptism and the Lord's Supper as ordinances and not sacraments and (7) the daily practice of New Testament teachings. [27]

> **The Waldenses believed in salvation only through Jesus Christ by faith**

A GLIMPSE INTO THE LIFE OF THE WALDENSES

The Waldenses were extraordinary people who lived simple, ordinary, godly lives. Even their enemies repeatedly confessed to their upright character. For example, Claudius Seisselius, the Archbishop of Turin said, "Their heresy excepted, they generally live a purer life than other Christians. They never swear except by compulsion and rarely take the name of God in vain. They fulfill their promises with punctuality; and live, for the most part, in poverty. . .In their lives and morals they were perfect, irreprehensible, and without reproach to men, addicting themselves with all their might to observe the commands of God." [28]

During the time of a great persecution of the Waldenses of Merindol and Provence, a number of young doctors from Sorbonne in Paris, the apex of Catholic schooling and theology of the day, were sent to investigate the Waldensian heresy. One of those young doctors publicly avowed that during his time among the Waldenses, he had "understood more of the doctrine of salvation from the answers of little children in their catechisms than by all the disputations which he had ever heard." [29] It would be fitting to conclude this chapter by quoting the report of a Catholic monk who was sent to investigate one region of the Waldenses. The following is his report.

"Their clothing is of the skins of sheep - they have no linen. They inhabit seven villages, their houses are constructed of flint stone, having a flat roof covered with mud, which, when spoiled or loosed by the rain, they again smooth with a roller. In these they live with their cattle, separated from them, however by a fence. They also have two caves set apart for particular purposes, in one of which they conceal their cattle, in the other themselves when hunted by their enemies. They live on milk and venison, being, through constant practice, excellent marksmen. Poor as they are, they are content, and live in a state of seclusion from the rest of mankind. One thing is very remarkable, that persons externally so savage and rude, should have so much moral cultivation. They know French sufficiently for the understanding of the Bible and the singing of Psalms. You can scarcely find a boy among them, who cannot give you an intelligent account of the faith which they possess. In this indeed, they resemble their brethren of the valleys. They pay tribute with a good conscience, and the obligations of the duty is peculiarly noted in their confessions of faith. If, by reason of civil wars, they are prevented from doing this, they carefully set apart the sum, and at the first opportunity they send it to the king's tax gatherers." [30]

The Waldenses were godly, peace-loving people, yet they were hated by the Catholics and treated like vicious criminals. In the next chapter, we shall look at their spiritual kinsmen, the Albigenses and the Welsh Baptists. We shall also examine some of the extreme measures against them by the Catholics.

---

[1] Carl Deimer, Professor, *History of Christianity II*, Video Lecture 3, Liberty University DLP, 2004.

[2] John T. Christian, *A History of the Baptists*, vol. 1, (Texarkana, Ark.-Tex.: Bogard Press, 1922), 3.

[3] E.H. Broadbent, *The Pilgrim Church,* (Grand Rapids, Michigan: GOSPEL FOLIO PRESS, 1999), 107.

[4] L.P. Brockett, *The Bogomils of Bulgaria and Bosnia; or the Early Protestants of the East,* (Philadelphia: American Baptist Publications Society, 1879. Classic Reprints #43 by Vance Publications, Pensacola, FL., 2001), 37.

[5] D.B. Ray, *Baptist Succession: A Hand-book of Baptist History,* (Parsons, Kansas: Foley Railway Printing Company, 1912),155.

[6] Christian, 69.

[7] Broadbent, 114-115.

[8] D.B. Ray, *Baptist Succession: A Hand-book of Baptist History,* (Parsons, Kansas: Foley Railway Printing Company, 1912), 153.

[9] Ibid., 154-155.

[10] Christian, 70.

[11] Ray, 153.

[12] Ibid., 154.

[13] Alexis Muston, *The Israel of the Alps: A Complete History of the Waldenses and Their Colonies,* vol. 1, (London: Blackie & Son, Paternoster Buildings, E.C., 1875, reprinted Paris, Arkansas: The Baptist Standard Bearer, Inc.), 17.

[14] Ibid., 17-18.

[15] Ray, 154-155.

[16] Christian, 70.

[17] Broadbent, 114.

[18] Christian, 73-74.

[19] George Herbert Orchard, *A Concise History of Baptists,* CD Rom, version 1, (Paris, Arkansas: The Baptist Standard Bearer, Inc., 2005), 179.

[20] Ibid.

[21] Philip Schaff, *History of the Christian Church,* vol. 5, (Peabody, Massachusetts: Hendrickson Publishers, 2002), 470.

[22] Ray, 156.

[23] Schaff, 493.

[24] Christian, 77.

[25] Broadbent, 119-121.

[26] Earle E. Cairns, *Christianity Through the Centuries: A History of the Christian Church,* 3rd ed., (Grand Rapids, Michigan: Zondervan, 1996), 222.

[27] Deimer.

[28] Christian, 75.

[29] Ibid.

[30] Ibid., 76.

The Waldenses

Waldenses is the name given to the true believers who lived in the valleys of the Alps. Later it was applied to Christians in general with the same beliefs.

The English word valley comes from the Latin word *vallis* (*valle* in French and Spanish; *valdeci* in Italian). Vaudios or Waldenses means "men of the valleys."

There is evidence that points to their perpetuity from the first century.

The Waldenses were extraordinary people who lived simple, godly lives. Even their enemies repeatedly confessed to their upright character.

In 1180, Peter Waldo began to travel and preach. Companions known as *Poor Men of Lyons* joined with him, and soon he had a large following. Waldo became so influential, that in time, he became inseparably associated with the Waldensenes.

Common Beliefs of the Waldenses

They believed

Salvation was possible only through a personal relationship with Jesus Christ by faith

The Scriptures are the ultimate rule of faith and practice

Christ is the supreme example of conduct

The indwelling of the Holy Spirit (gave them clearer understanding of the Scriptures)

Free exercise of one's conscience in matters of religion

Self-defense (even with weapons)

Exceedingly cautious about oaths in the name of God

The autonomy of the local church

Everyone should read the Bible in their own language

They opposed

The Holy Spirit giving new revelation

Institutional salvation through the church by any form of rituals or sacraments

Chapter 21

Albigenses and Welsh Baptists

The Roman state-church was powerful, but it did not conquer everyone. The Roman state-church grew to become the Catholic Church and claimed to be the exclusive and only true church of Jesus Christ; however, claims do not always constitute reality. The truth is that the Catholics are the ones who departed from Christ and His teachings, and many of the Christians and churches that stayed true to Him are the ones the Catholics did their best to destroy.

In this book we have given brief consideration to some of those groups of churches which never aligned with the drifting churches that banded into the Roman state-church and in time became the Catholic Church. We've taken brief looks at the Montanists, Novatians, Donatists, Paulicians, Bogomils and Waldenses. There were others.

THE ALBIGENSES

Previous mention has been made that both the Bosnian and Bulgarian Bogomils were very evangelistic. Some of their members dedicated themselves to vocational ministry, particularly for evangelistic and missionary work. These were called the *Perfecti* and a great many of them migrated across Europe making converts wherever they went. Though both the Bosnian and the Bulgarian

Bogomil missionary works were widespread, their greatest impact was in and around Southern France. When they arrived, they found kindred spirits already there in abundance. These people and churches had never aligned with the state church. They had roots back to the first century churches through the Montanists, Novatians and Donatists. They readily amalgamated into one people, the Bosnian Bogomils with the Waldenses and the Bulgarian Bogomils with the Albigenses. As time progressed, these two large communities of believers and churches became very closely associated. They were often seen as one group of heretics by the Catholics who persecuted them mercilessly.

C. Schmidt expressed Catholic sentiments. He called the Albigenses "the heretics – and more especially the Catharist heretics – of the south of France in the 12th and 13th centuries." [1] Schmidt went on to admit that the designation of their origin is "hardly exact." "The name Albigenses does not appear until after the Council held at Lombers near Albi about the middle of the twelfth century." [2] It appears that the great number of believers and churches in this area were Waldenses and given the name Albigenses in this region due to their proximity to the city of Albi. The Waldensian movement had extended into Southern France from Italy. [3] In this area and in Toulouse, where their numbers were greatest, they were also called Bougres because of the influence of the Bulgarian Bogomils on them. [4] "Though these eminent witnesses for the truth are now termed, generally, Waldenses and Albigenses, yet they were formerly known by a variety of names – some derived from their teachers, some from their manner of life, some from the places where they resided, some from the fate they suffered, and some from the malice of their enemies. The valley of Piedmont first gave them the name Vallenses, Waldenses, or Vaudois, a name which since has been employed to distinguish them as a primitive church. Those in the south of France were termed Albigenses, or Poor Men of Lyons, from their residence in and about Albi and Lyons. In like manner they were called Picards, Lombards, Bohemians, etc., from the countries in which they dwelt. The epithets Cathari and Peterines were applied to them as terms of reproach; and that of Lollards, either from the same cause or from a Waldensen pastor, Walter Lollard, who flourished about the middle of the thirteenth century." [5]

The unmistakable point is that these people were very numerous and widespread. "In the year 1200, both the city of Toulouse, and eighteen other principal towns in Languedoc, Provence, and Dauphine, were filled with Waldenses and Albigenses." [6] Catholic persecution soon followed; and as we shall see, they were slaughtered and driven out. Before we examine this terrible time, it would be wise to pause and examine what these people taught and practiced. Let us see just what it was that made them so dangerous. What made them so worthy of wholesale slaughter and the meanest, cruelest, most outlandish and inhumane persecution that this world has ever known?

The Albigenses had roots back to the first century churches

ALBIGENSE/WALDENSE BELIEFS AND PRACTICES

As in any large movement of Christians, there was not 100% unanimity in the beliefs and practices of the Albigenses and Waldenses. Just as some Baptists do today, some Albigenses and Waldenses held beliefs contrary to the clear teachings of Scripture and to others who wore their name. That does not make all Baptists or Albigenses/Waldenses guilty. Those out of line with core New Testament doctrine and practices were the small minority, and they were on the fringes of the movement as a whole. Many historians, including some modern Baptist historians, find a few bad apples in a trainload of good apples and reject the whole load.

"It must never be forgotten that on account of persecution they scarcely left a trace of their writings, confessional, apologetic or polemical; and the representations which Roman Catholic writers, their avowed enemies, have given them, are highly exaggerated." [7] This point is well seen in a book on the Waldenses written by Pius Melia in 1870. Melia did his best to justify the Catholic atrocities against the Waldenses and Albigenses. He contended that the cruel efforts against them were justified because some of their numbers were lawbreakers. He brought up the Inquisitors whom he called "righteous" (a description truly out of touch with reality), who in 1400 in the depth of winter forced believers into the deep mountains where 80 of them froze to death. He also wrote of the Catholic justices, who in December 1475 in Susa (Switzerland), condemned mountain believers to be burned at the stake. He then quoted Pope Innocent VIII, who in 1487 wrote a letter saying such action was justified because, "The heretics have endeavoured to draw the faithful into their errors, have despised the censures of the Church, robbed the goods, and destroyed the homes of the Inquisitor, killed his servant, made war against their temporal Masters, and committed a great many other like abominations." [8] It should be obvious to any honest person that these Waldensen and Albigensen believers were not criminals. Melia failed to mention that the Catholics made the laws; and that in many cases where these believers committed acts of violence, they were fighting in self defense for their families, property and lives. He also overlooked that in any society, a few criminals can be found; and that it is prejudice and bigotry to damn every person in that society because of the wrong-doing of a few. It is not difficult to see that underlying the entire effort against the Waldenses and Albigenses was their refusal to bow the knee to Rome. As Dr. Christian put it, their persecutors "did not tax them with immoralities, but they were condemned for speculations, or rather for virtuous rules of actions, which the Roman Catholics accounted heresy." [9]

There is ample evidence, even from their persecutors, to get a clear picture of what the vast majority of rank and file Waldenses and Albigenses believed. They said:

1. A Christian church should consist of good people.

2. A church has no power to frame any constitutions.

3. It was not right to take oaths.

4. It was not lawful to kill mankind.

5. A man ought not to be delivered up to the officers of justice to be converted.

6. The benefits of society belong alike to all members of it.

7. Men are saved by grace through faith alone, without works.

8. The church ought not to persecute any, even the wicked.

9. The Law of Moses was no rule for Christians.

10. There was no need for priests, especially the wicked ones.

11. There was no need for sacraments.

12. The orders and ceremonies of the Church of Rome were futile, expensive, oppressive and wicked.

13. Baptism is by immersion.

14. Infant baptism is wrong. [10]

Dr. D. B. Ray summarized Waldensen/Albigensen beliefs and practices in this manner:

1. They possessed the Baptist peculiarity of regarding Jesus Christ as their founder and head.

2. They regarded the Bible alone as containing their rule of faith and practice.

3. They taught repentance, faith, baptism and the Lord's Supper in that order.

4. They believed in baptism by immersion of only those who professed salvation by grace through personal faith in Jesus Christ.

5. They believed in equal rights and privileges for all under the law.

6. They observed the Lord's Supper as a memorial feast, not as a salvation-giving sacrament.

7. They were against religious persecution. [11]

CATHOLIC PERSECUTION OF THE ALBIGENSES AND WALDENSES

Let this section be prefaced with the realization that the persecutions and atrocities against these believers who refused to align with the Catholic Church are far, far too numerous to cover with much depth. At this point we can touch only a few cases and neither of these in much detail. It should be kept in mind that these are but the tip of a huge iceberg. Whole communities of these believers were completely wiped out; whole regions were purged of them. At the same time they flourished in other communities and regions. Sometimes they even returned to where their forefathers were annihilated and flourished there again. It can be said without possible refutation that the rugged Alps truly proved to be a place of refuge for these people of God, who staunchly refused to depart from New Testament doctrine and practice and join the Church of Rome.

Such was the case "in Languedoc and Provence in the South of France where there was a civilization in advance of other countries. The pretentions of the Roman Church to rule had been generally opposed and set aside there. The congregations of believers who met apart from the Catholic Church were numerous and increasing." 12 In 1209 Pope Innocent III declared a crusade against Raymond VI, the ruler of Provence who had not enforced the Pope's order to banish the heretics from his country. The populace and most of the leadership of the region were on the side of the Waldenses and Albigenses. The Pope offered *Indulgences* to all who would take part in the crusade. The prospect of money in addition to an open license to sin (the essence of an *Indulgence*) attracted hundreds of thousands of men. Led by Simon de Montfort, a seasoned military leader of ruthless cruelty, "the most beautiful and cultivated part of Europe at that time was ravaged, becoming for twenty years the scene of unspeakable wickedness and cruelty, and was reduced to desolation." 13 Even Dr. Schmidt, who was decisively pro-Catholic, wrote, "This implacable war, which threw the whole of the nobility of the north of France against that of the south and destroyed the independence of the princes of the south and destroyed the brilliant Provencal civilization, ended, politically in the treaty of Paris (1229), but did not extinguish the heresy, in spite of the wholesale massacres of heretics during the war." 14 Perhaps Mr. Schmidt did it unwittingly, nonetheless he confirmed the obvious. Under a small umbrella of protection (the treaty of Paris) from persecution by the Catholic Church, the Albigenses and Waldenses of south France prospered. The Pope couldn't stop the prosperity of these New Testament Christians ("heretics") through his legates and Catholic evangelists, so he and his Catholic supporters declared war on them. The Catholics mercilessly burned them at the stake *en masse;* looted, took and destroyed their property; pillaged the land into total ruin and did their best to blacken the good name of these godly people; however, they failed to extinguish them.

For decades to come, the Catholics hunted these New Testament Christians as though they were vicious, wild, dangerous beasts. They weren't. Before the end of the 13th century, new political powers who knew the work ethic of these believers were in charge of this area. The new political powers recruited them to return in sizeable numbers. [15] The relentless carnage by the Catholics continued until the population of New Testament Christians in this immediate area was largely depleted.

There were many Waldensians and New Testament believers by other names in a great number of other locations. As one of them who became a turncoat inquisitor said of them before he died in 1259, "there is scarcely any land in which this sect does not exist." [16] Wherever they were and by whatever names these believers were called, the rulers from Rome pursued them with the intent of annihilation by whatever means it took, however foul. In a later chapter, we shall look more thoroughly into this claim; but for now we take a brief look at distant cousins who were in the same unbroken line of believers who taught and practiced New Testament Christianity from the first-century forward.

The Catholics inflicted massive destruction upon the Albigenses, but they failed to extinguish them

---

THE WELSH BAPTISTS

In approximately 63 A.D., the New Testament book of Philippians was written by Paul while he was a prisoner in Rome. He was under the constant custody of Caesar's royal Praetorian guards. He had an enormous impact and reached many of his guards with the gospel. These Roman soldiers from across the empire cycled in and out of Rome back to their homelands taking the gospel with them. Paul said, *"But I would ye should understand, brethren, that the things which happened unto me have fallen out rather unto the furtherance of the gospel; So that my bonds in Christ are manifest in all the palace, and in all other places,"* **Philippians 1:12-13**. Among those whom he reached with the gospel were Pudens and Claudia, **2 Timothy 4:21**. Pudens and Claudia were Welsh.

The Welsh people were a tribe of Great Britain. About 50 B.C. the Romans invaded the British Isle but were unable to fully conquer the Welsh. The Romans made peace and dwelt among the Welsh people for many years. During that time many Welsh soldiers joined the Roman army and large numbers of Welsh families visited the grand capital city of Rome. Welsh records indicate that Pudens and Claudia, along with other converted Welshmen, took the gospel home; and thousands of Welsh people were converted to the pure strain of New Testament Christianity. About the year of A.D. 180, the Welsh king Lucius became the first king in the world to embrace New Testament Christianity. [17]

Long before churches on the European Continent, in the East and in North Africa began their steady departure from New Testament doctrine and practice, pure New Testament Christianity was flourishing among the Welsh people. "It is well known to all who are acquainted with the history of Great Britain, that Carleon, in South Wales, was a renowned city in past ages, and a notable place for religion. In the tenth persecution under Diocletian, the pagan Roman Emperor, many of the seed of Gomer suffered much. No less than three of those martyrs were citizens of Carleon; Julius, Aaron, and Amphibal, Baptist ministers. Many of the Welsh writings which were more valuable than the precious gold, were destroyed at that time, which was about the year of 285." [18] Please note that this was a third of a century before Constantine made Christianity the religion of Rome in the creation of a state church. Here was a large flourishing community of believers and churches practicing New Testament Christianity from the first century forward. They never were a part of the departure from Scripture to tradition. They never were a part of the state church and never were a part of the Catholic Church. To deny this unbroken line is to deny the facts. The Vale of Carleon is situated in the foothills between England and the mountainous parts of Wales. One Welsh historian wrote, "It is our valley of Piedmont; the mountains of Merthyn Tydfyl, our Alps; and the crevices of the rocks, the hiding places of the lambs of the sheep of Christ, where the ordinances of the gospel, to this day have been administered in their primitive role, without being adulterated by the corrupt Church of Rome." [19]

As expected, the growing Church of Rome couldn't bear the thought that anyone claiming to be Christian would reject its claims and refuse to join their ranks. By the late sixth century, she was nearing full-fledged status as the Roman Catholic Church. "In 593 Gregory, bishop of Rome sent Austin the Monk into England, to bring the Saxons into conformity to the Church of Rome." [20] When he reached Wales at the beginning of the seventh century, there was in Bangor "a college containing 2100 Christians who dedicated themselves to the Lord, to serve him in the ministry." [21] The area from Bangor on the north to Carleon on the south was a stronghold of New Testament Christianity. They baptized only believers by immersion and immediately rejected Austin's Catholic brand of Christianity via sacramental ritualism through the Church with its corrupt idea of a hierarchy. According to Henry D'Anvers' *Treatise on Baptism* published in London, England in 1674, pages 329-336, Austin said that if these Welsh Baptists "would not take peace with their brethren, they should receive war with their enemies: And if they disdain to preach with them the way of life to the English Nation, they should suffer by their hands the revenge of death: and which Austin accomplished accordingly, by bringing the Saxons upon them to their utter ruin." [22]

That was the Roman Catholic way: *convert them or kill them.* It happened for centuries all over the world. Thankfully we have reached an era in which it is politically impossible for them to exercise such brutal power in many places in the world; however, let it never be forgotten that this is the official Catholic mindset. It is a mindset that brought unimaginable torture to millions of New Testament Christians for centuries and produced a trail of blood that should sicken every civilized human.

In spite of it all, God has preserved His people. An unbroken line of daughter churches has come from that original seed church in Jerusalem, Israel. Here and there a stem, a population, has flourished and then been extinguished; but always the line has continued in some other place. The words of Jesus remain true and His promise is historically traceable, *"I will build my church; and the gates of hell shall not prevail against it,"* **Matthew 16:18**. We have briefly traced that unbroken line through three distinct developments: the Bogomils in the East, the Waldenses and the Albigenses in the heart of Europe and the Welsh Baptists in the Western British Isle.

Atrocities against these and other groups of believers continued, and major developments began to dramatically change the face of the Western world. In coming pages we shall follow these lines as their positions remained firm and their names changed in the midst of a wicked world in major flux.

---

[1] C. Schmidt, *Encyclopaedia Britannica*, vol. 1, s.v. "Historie de la secte des Cathares ou Albigenses," (Chicago: London: Toronto, William Benton, Publisher, 1960), 528.

[2] E.H. Broadbent, *The Pilgrim Church,* (Grand Rapids, Michigan: GOSPEL FOLIO PRESS, 1999), 109.

[3] John T. Christian, *A History of the Baptists*, vol. 1, (Texarkana, Ark.-Tex.: Bogard Press, 1922), 62.

[4] Schmidt.

[5] D.B. Ray, *Baptist Succession: A Hand-book of Baptist History,* (Parsons, Kansas: Foley Railway Printing Company, 1912), 157.

[6] I.K. Cross, *The Battle for Baptist History,* (Columbus, Georgia: Brentwood Christian Press, 1990), 64.

[7] Christian, 61.

[8] Pius Melia, *The Origin, Persecutions, and Doctrines of the Waldenses,* (London: James Toovey, 1870; Pensecola, FL, Classic Reprints, No. 58, Vance Publications, 2002), 63-64.

[9] Christian, 60.

[10] This list is adapted from Dr. Christian's *A History of the Baptists*, page 61.

[11] Ray, 323-339.

[12] Broadbent, 110.

[13] Ibid.

[14] Schmidt.

[15] Alexis Muston and W. Hazlitt, *The Israel of the Alps: A History of the Persecution of the Waldenses,* (London: Savill & Edwards, Printers, 1852), 27.

[16] Broadbent, 112.

[17] Cross, 37-38.

[18] Ray, 74.

[19] Ibid.

[20] Ibid., 69

[21] Ibid., 70.

[22] Ibid.

The Albigenses

Albigenses is the name given to the true believers who lived near Albi in southern France.

The name Albigenses originated in the twelfth century, but they had roots back to the first century churches through the Montanists, Novatians and Donatists.

They were also called Bougres because of the influence of the Bulgarian Bogomils on them.

Because of the intense persecution against them, there is almost no trace of their writings.

The Pope couldn't stop the prosperity of these New Testament Christians, so he declared war. The Catholics inflicted massive destruction upon the Albigenses, but they failed to extinguish them.

The History of Churches

The Welsh Baptists

Welsh Baptists is the name given to the true believers who lived in Wales (south-western part of Great Britain).

While Paul was a prisoner in Rome, he shared the gospel with Caesar's Praetorian guards, which included Pudens and Claudia (they were Welsh).

Pudens and Claudia, along with other converted Welshmen, took the gospel home, and thousands of Welsh people were converted to the pure strain of New Testament Christianity.

This was a large flourishing community of believers and churches practicing New Testament Christianity from the first century forward.

About the year of A.D. 180, the Welsh king Lucius became the first king in the world to embrace Christianity.

Chapter 22

The Reign of Terror

Webster says simply that *terrorism* is "the use of force and threats to frighten people into obeying completely." [1] Never in the history of mankind has there been a reign of terror as massive and long-running as the one by the Catholic Church. That state church which grew to be the Catholic Church with the Roman Catholic division rising to supremacy was the greatest terrorist organization this world has ever known. This church was bloodthirsty, money-hungry and compulsively domineering beyond what words can adequately communicate. Words such as cruelty, sinister, immoral, unprincipled and merciless describe the Catholic Church. Lying, the use of brute force, injustice and the lust for absolute power and control were its hallmarks; and the church did what it did in the name of the God of the Bible.

The church's deception of Basil, a physician and Bogomil leader in Bulgaria late in the eleventh century, illustrates a total lack of principles, which was characteristic of the Catholic Church both East and West. The life of Basil was a model of godliness, and his influence was tremendous. Alexius Comnenus I, a hater of all non-Catholics, was the Bulgarian king at the time. Under the pretense of deep interest in a better understanding of Bogomil doctrine, Alexius set a trap to destroy Basil and as many Bogomils as possible. He expressed a willingness to embrace the views of the Bogomils and invited Basil to expound Bogomil doctrine before the imperial cabinet. To draw him out, Alexius questioned Basil on many fine points. Suddenly he threw open a fake wall behind which a scribe had been taking notes. Alexius accused Basil of heresy and summoned the officers of his court to bind Basil in irons. Alexius then used Basil's testimony to round up as many Bogomil followers as possible; and after much abuse and mockery, he burned them all to death at the stake. Alexius' devilish daughter wrote gleefully of the event in a book she titled *Alexiad.* Dr. L.P. Brockett wrote these words, "We cannot bring ourselves to lay before our readers the description she gives so minutely and with such evident enjoyment of the preparations for the holocaust in the hippodrome – the crackling of the fire and the shrinking of the poor human bodies wasted by fasting, but still sustained by unfaltering trust in their Saviour as they come nearer to the flames, the turning away of their eyes, and finally the quivering of their limbs as the fire scorched and shriveled their flesh." [2]

Keep in mind that Basil's story presented here is not an isolated event. To the contrary, this kind of persecution began shortly after Constantine created the state church (early in the fourth century) and escalated for centuries. At one point it was the common mode of operations across most of Eastern and Western Europe, including the British Isles. Only when the Protestant Reformation succeeded in breaking down the Roman Catholic monopoly to some extent (sixteenth and seventeenth centuries) did Catholic terrorism abate; however, even then it did not completely end. Even today in some parts of the world, Catholics continue to employ force to impose themselves on others.

THE TOOLS OF THEIR TRADE

It will be timely at this point to briefly review how the Catholics postured themselves to destroy all opposition as they gained increasing power. The marriage of the church to the state set the stage for their power grab. Once the organized group of churches (which saw themselves as the one and only true church) was recognized by the secular state as the true church, it had civil, secular power to enforce its wishes. It was the desire of Constantine and later emperors, as well as the desire of the organized church hierarchy, to force every person and church to be a part of the organized church. Those that refused had the combined power of the organized church and the state against them. As the church grew stronger and the state grew weaker (a steady trend for 900 years), the church began to increasingly tell the state who to oppress and persecute. Furthermore, as the state-church connection strengthened, the number of Catholics in the general populace increased. Over time most of the Feudal lords and landholders, most of the political magistrates and most people of means and power were Catholics. The church and state became almost inseparable. The laws were made by Catholics and enforced by Catholics. It was heresy punishable by torture and probable death to not be a Catholic. Those who found themselves at odds with the Church were automatically at odds with the civil authorities because often the civil authorities were also church authorities: judges, prosecuting attorneys, executioners. There was no jury system, and Catholic civil authorities carried out the decisions (including punishments) of the Catholic Church (ecclesiastical) authorities. The situation was a true monopoly. Those at odds with the law faced a stacked deck. There was no justice; the whole system was pro-Catholic. Additionally, there was no appeal. The head of the whole system was the pope, who was the author and monarch of the system. Appealing to him was akin to a German Jew appealing to Adolph Hitler about executions in the gas chambers.

Excommunication, the Interdict and the Ban

You will recall that Pope Gregory VII (Hildebrand) succeeded in instituting three tools designed to destroy all opposition to the Catholic Church. First, he formally legalized the practice of **Excommunication**. This meant the church could take away one's salvation. Second, he made the **Interdict** a matter of Catholic Law. The Interdict expanded the church's excommunication power making it possible for the church to send a whole nation or populace of people to hell. Third, he also made the **Ban** a part of Catholic law. The ban gave the church power (enforced by civil authorities) to run an excommunicated person out of the territory and exile him.

These moves, and others like them, put more power into the hands of the Catholics and made it legal for them to punish all who did not embrace their views. For example, as in the case of Basil, a person could be honorable, pure and law-abiding, yet be excommunicated, banned or burned at the stake because he believed in salvation by personal faith in Jesus Christ and not by baptism and the Lord's Supper.

> **The ban gave the church the power to exile an excommunicated person**

Legates

Legates were also the brain-child of Gregory VII. They were appointed by him (and following popes) to carry out his wishes. Legates carried the personal power and authority of a pope and took precedence over all other Catholic authorities. They were very much like human bloodhounds. In the name of the pope, they spread across of Europe hunting for heretics, especially for leaders of non-Catholic churches and movements. They had free rein wherever they went, whether in kings' palaces or with secular rulers. They made demands and threatened to remove from power those who refused. The legates were bullies. They were hated even by Catholics, both ecclesiastical and secular. Furthermore, they were almost universally corrupt. The vast majority of them were known even among their Catholic peers for their immorality, drunkenness and overbearing ways. [3] It is not difficult to see where the Waldenses, the Bogomils and other believers and churches that were not a part of the Catholic system stood when they were subjected to the power of these corrupt and brutal bullies.

> **Legates carried the personal power and authority of a pope**

The Inquisition

At the fourth Lateran Council in 1215 the Roman Catholic Church instituted courts of Inquisition and gave them the power to hunt and torture heretics. [4] Terrorism took a mighty leap forward. Ecclesiastical officials now had legal power to torture and do every damnable thing imaginable to any non-Catholic and they had the power of the state behind them. Simply being a non-Catholic was adequate grounds for the rankest persecution and torture; no crime, just not being a Catholic.

In each district where the Inquisitors went, they set up business in either a Dominican or Franciscan monastery which became both the court and the prison where the crimes against humanity were carried out. Kings such as Louis VIII of France subsidized and supported them. Their power literally became absolute. It was a crime to oppose the Inquisition and the decisions of the Inquisitors were arbitrary. "The Inquisition was not bound by the ordinary rules of procedure in the inquiries: the accused was surprised by a sudden summons, and as a rule imprisoned on suspicion. All the accused were presumed to be guilty, the judge being at the same time the accuser. Absence was naturally considered as contumacy, and only increased the presumption of guilt by seeming to admit it. The accused had the right to demand a written account of the offences attributed to him, but the names of the witnesses were withheld from him . . . Heretics or persons deprived of civil rights (infames) were admitted as witnesses in cases of heresy. Women, children of slaves could be witnesses for the prosecution, but not for the defense." [5] Records exist showing the testimony of children as young as ten. No witness might refuse to testify under pain of being considered a heretic. The Inquisitors made the accused swear to name all who were partners with them in their heresy and to name all whom they suspected to be heretics. Witnesses were tortured in order to get them to say what the Inquisitors wanted to hear and all confessions extorted in the prison chambers had to be *freely* confirmed by the witness. Not one of these mock trials could be considered litigious because any lawyer defending the accused would have been guilty of heresy. There was never one case of an acquittal. Depending on the whim of the Inquisitors, the accused could be sentenced to perpetual imprisonment with on-going degrees of punishment in the deepest dungeon, with single or double fetters, and with the bread and water of affliction. The mortality rate for these was very high. Some of the accused were handed over to secular authorities. This was, in effect, "equivalent to a sentence of death, and of death by fire." [6]

The Inquisitors were professional assassins, serial killers, wholesale murderers for hire. They are the ones who hunted down the Waldenses and Albigenses in Southern France and the surrounding area and did more to eradicate the unbroken line of New Testament believers and churches than Catholic war against them ever could. [7]

It was in Spain that the Inquisition gained its greatest strength. On May 26, 1232, Inquisitors were sent to Aragon by Pope Gregory IX. Over the years a series of political developments led Spain in a radical pro-Catholic direction and in 1480 King Ferdinand and Queen Isabella, apart from the help of the papacy, founded a national Inquisition in Spain "directed against local heretics." [8] The Spanish Inquisition's purge against non-Catholics is one of the most gruesome, inhumane, uncivilized, barbaric campaigns against humanity that has ever occurred.

When the Dominican Inquisitors from Spain arrived in the regions east of the Adriatic Sea (Balkan states), they found immediate resistance from the believers and churches which flourished there. In 1234 Gregory XI orchestrated a crusade against the region and Bosnia was laid waste by fire and sword. In spite of tremendous violence against them, the believers and churches in Bulgaria, Rumania, Slavonia and Dalmatia gained strength.

The Inquisition was strong in France and in Italy. In Savoy it constantly carried out atrocities against the Waldenses of the Alps, but in Sicily the Waldenses and the Fraticelli were too strong and the Inquisition was not successful. Different popes made many efforts in Germany to introduce the Inquisition against the large numbers of non-Catholics who flourished there, believers whom they branded as heretics; however, German sentiment against the papacy was growing and the Inquisition was not widely embraced. Pope Urban VI's attempt to plant the Inquisition permanently in Germany succeeded only briefly. The Waldenses were strongest in Bohemia and in 1247 Pope Alexander IV introduced the Inquisition which attacked with a vengeance. For 100 years the Inquisitors did their dirty work in Bohemia; however, the Waldenses and other New Testament lines of Christians and churches continued to flourish.

It is hard to believe that humans did to other humans what the

Catholics did to non-Catholics through the Inquisition. It is also very difficult to see how current generations can ignore and overlook these atrocities and so passionately embrace Catholicism.

The Inquisitors were professional assassins and serial killers for hire

---

TERRORIST METHODS

Almost every method of intimidation and torture known to humanity at that time was used at one time or another by the Catholics to frighten people into obeying completely. No gutter was ever too deep for them, no practice too evil or macabre. This section of our book will doubtless be sickening and very distressing to some. It is hard to imagine that these things happened at all, let alone in the name of God by people claiming to be Christians; but they did. The documentation is there. In abundance!

Tactics

A book of this nature does not allow time to examine each torture tactic, although it is eye-opening to mention some of the most popular and common types. They include, but were not limited to:

- Ripping out teeth/nails

- Beating

- Blinding

- Boiling

- Bone breaking

- Branding and Burning

- Castration

- Choking

- Cutting

- Disfigurement

- Dislocation

- Drowning

- Flagellation, whipping and beating

- Flaying

- Roasting

- Genital mutilation

- Limb/finger removal

- Starvation

- Tongue removal

- Disemboweling

- Compression of the limbs by special instruments or ropes

- Injection of water, vinegar or oil into the body

- Application of hot pitch [9]

Tools

A large number of sinister tools and machines were used by the Catholics to impose terrible tortures upon those whom they had arbitrarily declared to be heretics. [10] A brief explanation is given for better understanding. Please do not assume these were all of the tools used by the Catholic persecutors against their victims.

- **Boot or Spanish boot** – High boots were made of spongy leather and placed on the victim's feet. He was then tied onto a table near a large fire. A quantity of boiling water was poured on the boots, which penetrated the leather, ate away the flesh, and often dissolved the bones of the victim.

- **Branding irons** – These tools were used to burn victims.

- **The collar** – A heavy (11 pounds) spiked metal collar was used for fitting around the neck of the victim. It usually resulted in infections and a slow, agonizing death.

274

- **Ducking stools** – A ducking stool was a chair-like device which was used for drowning women. Suspects were bound to the device and thrown into a deep lake or river. Those who floated were considered full of the devil and those who drowned were considered innocent.

- **Foot press** – This press was used for crushing feet.

- **Heretic's fork** – This was a length of metal with two opposing bi-pronged forks as well as an attached belt or strap. One end was pushed under the chin and the other into the sternum, the strap fixed the device to the neck. This effectively immobilized the head at a total extension of the neck, and caused great pain. [11]

- **The maiden** – This was an iron cabinet with a hinged front. The torturer would interrogate the victim and torture or kill by piercing the body with sharp objects, such as knives, spikes or nails while the victim was forced to remain standing. The condemned would bleed profusely and weaken slowly, eventually dying because of blood loss or asphyxiation. Most iron maidens were made so the sharp points did not pierce vital organs. This assured that the victim would not die immediately and that the torturous death would be prolonged. [12]

- **Pillory** – This was a kind of scaffold in a public place with a wheel. The victim was attached to the wheel which turned and exposed him to the crowd which looted and tormented him.

- **Scavenger's daughter** – This was a machine for compressing the body rather than stretching it.

- **The Brank** – This was a locking iron muzzle, metal mask or cage which encased the head and prevented the victim from speaking. There was an iron curb projecting into the mouth which rested on the top of the tongue. Some models had iron spikes that pierced any time the victim attempted to speak. This device was also known as **Scold's bridle** and the **Gossip's bridle**.

- **Stocks** – Victims were held by their hands and feet in a public area.

- **Thumbscrew** – This was a portable device used to crush fingers and toes.

- **The wheel** – This was a device used to stretch, break and rip apart the victim. Sometimes the victim was dragged by a horse(s) until totally mutilated.

Two of the most common, yet macabre and inhuman means of torture and death, deserve special treatment. They are *Burning at the Stake* and *The Rack*. Before explaining each, let it be known that all of these tortures were both physical and psychological. Catholic legates, Inquisitors and their civil cohorts routinely forced parents to watch their children tormented and murdered by these means in order to force a *confession*. Likewise, children were forced to watch their parents suffer and die. These cruel and uncivilized tactics were used against mates, friends and neighbors. This was truly terrorism of the first rank!

Burning at the Stake

Burning at the stake was the most popular and common means of Catholic torture and killing. It not only destroyed the so-called heretic, it also sent a chilling message to all others who dared stand against the Catholic Church. This method of torture and execution had been practiced long before there was a Catholic Church; however, the Catholics made it their method of choice. It is noteworthy that the later Protestant state churches burned many people at the stake.

There were three methods of burning at the stake. The first method is the one that is best understood. As the word indicates, a *stake* was used in this method. The stake was driven into the ground and the victim was tied to it, usually with ropes which kept him from escaping. Chains or iron hoops were also used to secure the victim. Wood was piled around the stake and set on fire. A second method was very similar to the first. The main difference is that the wood was piled higher to hide the victim. This was the method of choice in killing witches. The third method of burning at the stake involved a ladder which was attached to a frame above the fire. The victim was tied to the ladder which was swung down into the flame. Some were arranged so that the victim could be lowered and raised in and out of the flames several times to insure a slow death. This method was popular in Germany and in the Nordic countries. [13]

Sometimes multiple victims were burned to death in a common fire. This necessitated a large fire, which proved to be a blessing to the victims. Rather than dying slow, agonizing deaths, the victims of large fires generally died of carbon monoxide poisoning rather than from the flames; however, many executioners were horribly cruel. They prepared small fires which brought great suffering and agony for long periods of time before the death of the victim. In slow deaths, victims would die from heatstroke, loss of blood plasma and shock.

Many readers have encountered the word *faggot*. Faggots were small bundles of sticks and straw. Like torches, they could be easily lit and fed against the body of a victim, particularly the feet and calves. The agony and prolonged suffering of the victim was obvious. If allowed, friends and family members would add additional firewood as quickly as possible to avoid a prolonged death by the martyr.

"Some sources state that it was more normal for the stake to be at the centre of a large ring or pile of wood with a gap left for the condemned to be led to the stake. Once they were tied to the stake and the gap filled with wood, the condemned would be hidden from sight. When this method of execution was applied with skill, the condemned's body would burn progressively in the following sequence: calves, thighs and hands, torso and forearms, breasts, upper chest, face; and then finally death. On other occasions, people died from suffocation with only their calves on fire. . . . In many burnings a rope was attached to the victim's neck passing through a ring on the stake and they were simultaneously strangled and burnt." [14]

By law, victims were sometimes strangled before being burned at the stake

---

The Rack

"The **rack** is a torture that consists of an oblong rectangular, usually wooden frame, slightly raised from the ground, with a roller at one, or both, ends, having at one end a fixed bar to which the legs were fastened, and at the other a movable bar to which the hands were tied. The victim's feet are fastened to one roller, and the wrists are chained to the other. As the interrogation progresses, a handle and ratchet attached to the top roller are used to very gradually stepwise increase the tension on the chains, inducing excruciating pain. By means of pulleys and levers this roller could be rotated on its own axis, thus straining the ropes until the sufferer's joints were dislocated and eventually separated.

Additionally, once muscle fibers have been stretched past a certain point they lose their ability to contract, thus victims who were released had ineffective muscles as well as problems arising from dislocation. One gruesome aspect of being stretched too far on the rack is the loud popping noises made by snapping cartilage, ligaments or bones. Eventually, if the application of the rack is continued, the victim's limbs are ripped right off. One powerful method for putting pressure upon a prisoner was to merely force him to view someone else being subjected to the rack. A person stretched on the rack presented a spectacle of the body in pain." [15]

The rack was commonly used by the Inquisitors to force a confession from an accused heretic. It was the tool of choice for the Spanish Inquisitors. Not only was the rack gruesome in its cruelty against a victim, it was also a major psychological weapon. It is not difficult to imagine the psychological affect it had on multitudes that were forced to watch others on the rack. They would make up lies, accuse neighbors and friends and say or do just about anything they thought might keep them off the rack.

What a disgraceful heritage! Yet it is the heritage of Ferdinand and Isabella, Torquemada and Ximenez and many other famous Catholic heroes. [16]

MAJOR MOVEMENTS AGAINST
NEW TESTAMENT CHRISTIANS

As you have followed this story, you have no doubt become aware that Catholic persecution was not merely a movement against a few individuals. It was against movements, communities of believers and churches like the Bogomils, the Waldenses and the Albigenses. The Catholics took out every one they possibly could, but they concentrated on leaders of these sects. Many stories could be told

278

of military actions into different areas, all with the specific intent of eradicating non-Catholic believers who were all considered to be heretics. What you are about to read is a brief, but typical, description of one Catholic effort to annihilate non-Catholics.

Waldenses flourished and won many to Christ in the valleys and mountains around La Torre, Italy, an area under the Catholic jurisdiction of Turin. In 1655 the Catholics ordered the Waldenses out of most areas in the region and into a restricted area. Under threat of death, they were to clear the area within three days and sell all of their lands within 20 days. The movement was designed to destroy them.

Meanwhile the Catholics moved in with an army that grew to over 15,000 and began to seize the goods and property of the Waldenses. Throughout a series of battles, the Waldenses withstood them. After repeated defeats, the Catholic general (Gastaldo) on Wednesday morning, April 21, 1655 announced to the Waldenses that he was now ready to receive deputies. The innocent Waldenses sent deputies to whom the general apologized and made promises of peace. The Waldenses took him at his word and emerged from their mountain strongholds. "On Saturday, 24th April, 1655, at four o'clock in the morning, the signal for a general massacre of the Vaudois was given to the traitorous troops, from the tower of the castle of La Torre." Here is the account that was written of the events that transpired. "Young children . . . were torn from their mothers' arms, dashed against the rocks, and their mangled remains cast on the road. Sick persons and old people, men and women, were burned alive in their houses, or hacked in pieces, or mutilated in horrible ways, or flayed alive, or exposed bound and dying in the sun's noontide heat, or to ferocious animals; some were stripped naked, bound up in the form of a ball, the head forced down between the legs, and then rolled over precipices; some of these poor creatures, torn and mangled by the rocks, but stayed in their downward progress by the branch of a tree, or other prominence, were seen, forty-eight hours later, still lingering in all the torments of pain and famine.

Women and girls, after being fearfully outraged, were impaled on pikes, and so left to die, planted at angles on the road; or they were buried alive; or, impaled as above, they were roasted before a slow fire, and their burning bodies cut in slices, by those *soldiers of the faith*, as by cannibals. After the massacre, such children as survived, as could be seized, were carried off, and cast, like lambs into a slaughter-house, into the monasteries and convents and private abodes of the propagandists. Next, after massacre and abduction, came incendiarism: monks and priests, and other zealous propagandists, went about with lighted torches and projectiles, burning down the houses, previously ensanguined by the soldiers with the blood of their owners and their families. . . . Here, a father had seen his children cut in pieces by the sword, or absolutely torn limb by limb by four soldiers; there the mother had seen her daughter cruelly massacred before her face, after having been cruelly outraged; there the sister had seen her brother's mouth filled with gunpowder, and the head then blown to atoms. . .Of these, the eyes were torn from the head; of those, the nails from the fingers; some were tied to trees, their heart and lungs were cut from them, and they were thus left to die in anguish. . .not a single cottage was left." [17]

Stunning! Unbelievable! Horrendous! But, typical of the way Catholics treated those who didn't submit to and become one of them! Their efforts were not always to this magnitude; but even when the scale was smaller, the way they treated their victims was essentially the same. Misters Muston and Hazlitt go on to say that when word of this massacre spread across Europe, the perpetrators sent out a narrative printed in Italian, French and Latin in which they "charged the Vaudois with bringing all the mischief upon themselves." [18] It seems that when the Catholics attacked and someone defended himself, in the eyes of the Catholics, that *someone* was the perpetrator and any harm that might follow was justified.

For hundreds of years the Roman Catholic Church was the greatest terrorist organization the world has ever known. They tortured and slaughtered humans by the millions. Many of those they murdered were our spiritual forefathers, members of a line of believers and churches that are continuously traceable all the way back to the church Jesus personally established in Jerusalem, Israel.

In our next chapter we shall look at a development that changed the face of Europe forever and toppled the papacy from its position of absolute domination and control.

[1] *Webster's New World Dictionary with Student Handbook: Young People's Edition*, s.v. "terrorism," (Nashville, Tennessee: The World Publishing Company, 1973), 719.

[2] L.P. Brockett, *The Bogomils of Bulgaria and Bosnia; or the Early Protestants of the East*, (Philadelphia: American Baptist Publications Society, 1879. Classic Reprints #43 by Vance Publications, Pensacola, FL., 2001), 46-51.

[3] Philip Schaff, *History of the Christian Church,* vol. 5, (Peabody, Massachusetts: Hendrickson Publishers, 2002), 784.

[4] *Webster's*, s.v. "Inquisition," 366.

[5] P. Fredericq, *Encyclopaedia Britannica*, vol. 12, s.v. "History of the Inquisition in the Middle Ages," (Chicago: London: Toronto, William Benton, Publisher, 1960), 378-379.

[6] Ibid., 379.

[7] C. Schmidt, *Encyclopaedia Britannica*, vol. 1, s.v. "Historie de la secte des Cathares ou Albigenses," (Chicago: London: Toronto, William Benton, Publisher, 1960), 529.

[8] Fredericq, *Britannica*. 380-383.

[9] *Middle Ages Torture* (http://www.middle-ages.org.uk/middle-ages-torture.htm).

[10] Ibid.

[11] *Wikipedia,* (en.wikipedia.org/wiki/Heretic's_fork).

[12] Ibid., /wiki/Iron_maiden_(torture_device).

[13] *A History of Violence,* (home.comcast.net/~burokerl/burning_at_the_stake.htm).

[14] *Wikipedia,* (en.wikipedia.org/wiki/Execution_by_burning).

[15] Ibid., /wiki/Rack_(torture).

[16] Earle E. Cairns, *Christianity Through the Centuries: A History of the Christian Church*, 3rd ed., (Grand Rapids, Michigan: Zondervan, 1996), 260-262.

[17] Alexis Muston and W. Hazlitt, *The Israel of the Alps: A History of the Persecution of the Waldenses,* (London: Savill & Edwards, Printers, 1852), 131-141.

[18] Ibid., 141.

Tools of Torture

These are the two of the most common, yet macabre and inhuman means of torture and death used by the Catholics against their victims.

Burning at the Stake

This was the most popular and common means of Catholic torture and killing. It not only destroyed the so-called heretic, it also sent a chilling message to all others who dared stand against the Catholic Church. There were three methods to do this.

1. The stake was driven into the ground and the victim was tied to it, with either ropes, chains or iron hoops. Wood was piled around the stake and set on fire.

2. This was similar to the first method. The main difference is that the wood was piled higher to hide the victim. This was the method of choice in killing witches.

3. The victim was tied to the ladder which was swung down into the flame. The ladder could be raised or lowered to insure a slow death

The "law" required that victims be strangled before burning at the stake, but many were deliberately burned alive."[1]

The Rack

The rack was commonly used by the Inquisitors to force a confession from an accused heretic. A person is laid on a wooden frame and their hands and feet are tied to it. By using pulleys and levers, the victim is stretched, which can cause excruciating pain and dislocate joints.

A prisoner can be pressured by forcing him to look at victim on the rack, which showed a person that was writhing in pain.[2]

[1] *A History of Violence*,
(home.comcast.net/~burokerl/burning_at_the_stake.htm).

[2] *Wikipedia*, (en.wikipedia.org/wiki/Rack_(torture_device)).

Chapter 23

Ripe for Violence and War in the Name of God

The Crusades were military campaigns carried out by the Roman Catholic Church in the eleventh, twelfth and thirteenth centuries against those whom it perceived as enemies of the cross of Christ. The better-known Crusades were against the Muslims who held Jerusalem; however, there were also Crusades against Christians whom the Catholics deemed to be heretics. [1] In reality the Crusades were holy wars by professing Christians.

Widespread misunderstandings and misconceptions about the Crusades cause many people to view them in a glamorous and romantic way. It is important at this point in our book to gain a clear and general understanding of this history-changing phenomenon which was orchestrated by the Roman Catholic papacy. "There were seven greater Crusades, the first beginning in 1095, the last terminating with the death of St. Louis, 1270." [2] During and after this time, there were other minor expeditions against the Muslims, in addition to Crusades against supposed Christian heretics.

In this chapter we will look at the background that led to the Crusades against the Muslims.

THE STATE OF THE ROMAN CATHOLIC PAPACY

Long before Constantine established a state church, many churches strayed from the Scriptures as their sole authority for doctrine and practice, and embraced tradition as an equal or superior authority. Many of these were the bigger, more powerful churches of that day, and they steadily gravitated together into a structured entity. This entity of churches was not yet formally organized; however, those who constituted it increasingly saw it as one unit, one church, a Catholic Church with a capital "C." Furthermore, this movement of churches and the leaders viewed themselves as the true Christian Church and all others as heretical. This group was tenaciously committed to unity within the *Church,* which they viewed as one. They felt it their right and responsibility to force other Christians and churches into conformity with them.

Constantine viewed this informal entity as *the church.* When he wed this *church* to the Roman state, *the church* instantly had law, authority and the power of secular government behind it. Constantine wanted all Christians and churches to be a part of this state church. Since they were within his political domain, he considered it his right to control the religious lives of all his subjects. Being a part of the Roman state meant being a part of the Roman religion. He made Christianity the official Roman religion; not the Christianity of Jesus Christ and the New Testament, but the new brand of compromised *Christianity* that had developed. Already the leadership of this informal entity of compromised churches insisted that every Christian and church should be a part of it. With the formalization of the state church union, it became possible for church and state officials to force dissenters to either join the state church or face persecution. Yes, the use of deadly force became legally possible. Ecclesiastical wishes were enforced by sheriffs, police and other civil authorities.

Over the next few centuries this entity, which became formalized into a state church, continued to grow and strengthen. At the beginning of the seventh century, its power became adequately consolidated to the point that it could be rightfully called the Roman Catholic Church. For the next 600 years it grew into a powerful and rich force which dominated the entire Western World.

This new entity and force was not without enemies and trouble. The following list is not all-inclusive, but briefly describes the state church's primary forces of opposition.

Secular Opposition

From the time of Constantine onward, virtually all secular powers resented and opposed the power and the wealth of the state church. For example, the Roman Emperor, Julian the Apostate, opposed what Constantine had done and the growth of power in the bishops in Rome; but with the Empire in decline and the capital so far away in Constantinople, he was too weak to do much about it.

Furthermore, the new Germanic powers that over-ran the western part of the Empire were leery about too much power in the hands of the state church and its head bishop. Many of these leaders liked what the bishop of Rome and his church could do for them; they didn't like the inordinate power and influence that he had.

Religious Opposition

From before the time of Constantine, there were many Christians and churches that did not support the drift of the bigger, more influential churches into an informal organization which became accepted as one true church. When this informal organization was formalized into the state church, these dissenters never became a part of it. Already, mention has been made of the Montanists, the Novatians and the Donatists. There were also the Welsh Baptists and the Paulicians. These Paulicians became forerunners of later non-affiliated groups such as the Bogomils, the Waldneses and the Albigenses.

Additionally, there were struggles within the state church for dominance and supremacy. Churches in other cities claimed they were at least equal, if not superior, to Rome. Because of her connection to Paul, the church in Antioch claimed superiority to Rome. Jerusalem saw herself as the mother church. Alexandria was strong and affirmed roots to John Mark. Beginning with Constantine's move, Roman emperors resided in Constantinople and claimed the church there to be the head church. They all presented opposition to the church in Rome.

Pressure from the eastern rank of the state church was especially great against Rome with her papacy. Both the bishops of Rome (popes) and the bishops of Constantinople (patriarchs) wanted dominance. These two dominant flanks of Catholicism were antagonistic and made it a point to oppose each other doctrinally and practically at almost every possible junction. As previously discussed, on July 16, 1054, each side excommunicated the other in a permanent schism. This was less than fifty years before the first Crusade against the Muslims.

> **Churches in other cities claimed they were at least equal, if not superior, to Rome**

Islam

With the birth of Islam early in the seventh century, more pressure was mounted against the state church. By that time it had become the Roman Catholic Church, and the papacy ruled it. Islam exploded on the scene, and within 100 years it had conquered much of the east, most of North Africa, much of Spain and was putting pressure on the Roman Catholic world from both the east and the west.

It is noteworthy that the Eastern Catholic Empire had been rapidly losing its hold on its territories to the Muslims. Antioch and Edessa were lost to Islam in 1086. In spite of their past differences, Eastern Catholic leaders appealed to the West for help against the Muslims. Constantinople had been close to capture by the Muslims, and earlier popes (with the ulterior hope of "subjection of Eastern churches to the dominion of the Apostolic see" [3]) had urged all Christians to come to the rescue. The real reason seems to have been defense; however, religion was used as justification for the appeal.

Nationalism

By the end of the eleventh century, Feudalism had begun to give way to Nationalism in Europe. Nations had begun to form. Feudal lords began to see themselves as a part of a bigger entity, a general jurisdiction under a king. States such as France, Spain, England, Scotland, Wales, Germany, Greece, Hungary, Italy and others emerged. The papacy had long assumed supreme authority over all of Europe; every secular power was subject to the pope. Through the years, more and more of the secular rulers resented the external authority of the pope over them. Henry IV insisted on appointing and governing church officials in the Holy Roman Empire which he governed. Through the Catholic network of feudal lords and government officials in the Holy Roman Empire, in 1076 Pope Gregory VII succeeded in bringing Henry IV into submission. Henry II of England (1154-1189) defied papal power. Under the bare-knuckles politics of Pope Alexander III, Henry II buckled and was brought into submission. These cases illustrate the growing spirit of nationalism which made it increasingly difficult for the popes to maintain their stranglehold on Europe.

Corruption Within the Roman Catholic Church

- **Financial exploitation**

  Previous mention has been made of ways the popes financially exploited the people, including their own bishops, priests and individual churches: annates, collations, commendations, expectancies, reservations, *Jus Spoliorum,* tithing, dispensations and indulgences. By these and other heavy-handed means, the papacy grew extremely wealthy; however, such wealth, especially by exploitation, generated jealousy and resentment.

- **Financial corruption**

  Furthermore, throughout the hierarchy of the Roman Catholic Church and especially at the headquarters in Rome, there was enormous corruption. Monasteries became rich and notorious for lives of pleasure, excess and immorality. The headquarters at Rome were even more corrupt and immoral than the operations downstream. While multitudes of people throughout the empire lived in abject poverty and misery, their religious leaders lived in luxury and excess. Kings and landlords were taxed to the breaking-point by the popes, who in turn squandered that money on lavish buildings and on all of the material pleasures their hearts desired. One who was oppressed could not afford to resist, lest he be excommunicated or run the risk of having the pope orchestrate attacks against him by other lords.

- **Immorality**

  Legates, Inquisitors, bishops, monks and other church officials who were supposed to be holy men of God and sworn to celibacy, were sexually promiscuous. In fact, it was common for them to use their elevated positions to force sex with females of their choosing. Homosexuality was rampant.

  For the most part holiness and justice were unknown in the papal system. Greed, abuse of power, cruelty and hypocrisy were the hallmarks of this evil system. It was this wicked poison within the house of Catholicism, particularly the papacy, which gave rise to the hermits from whom grew monasticism. Soon after their inception, the monasteries became equally corrupt, leading to monastic reforms. Once the Lord said of Israel, *"Ye will revolt more and more: the whole head is sick, and the whole heart faint. From the sole of the foot even unto the head there is no soundness in it; but wounds, and bruises, and putrifying sores: they have not been closed, neither bound up, neither mollified with ointment,"* **Isaiah 1:5-6.** Surely this is a perfect description of the Roman Catholic Church, especially in the eleventh century.

Papal Prestige

The fact is that in the eleventh century the papacy needed a better image. The papacy was born during the reign of Gregory I (590-604). He was the first Roman bishop to bring almost all of the political entities of Western Europe under his control. In spite of the opposition to it from many sides, the papacy continued to expand and strengthen until 1215; however, such external tyranny coupled with internal corruptions could not last forever. The popes were shrewd and would stop at nothing to hold on to their position of power. In the Crusades against the Muslims, they found the ideal vehicle, a popular political move to take attention off their sinful, corrupt selves. For a while their ploy produced astounding success.

> **The papacy continued to expand and strengthen until 1215**

A FIELD RIPE FOR EXPLOITATION

During the latter part of the eleventh century, Europe was truly a field ripe for exploitation, and the popes capitalized on the situation in royal fashion. There are many reasons why Catholic Europe unified so intensely in military efforts against the Muslims.

A Land of Glamour and Romance

From the early days of Christianity, a pilgrimage to Jerusalem was the goal of many professing Christians. There was a romance about it. "The Holy Land became to the imagination a land of wonders, filled with the divine presence of Christ. To have visited it, to have seen Jerusalem, to have bathed in the Jordan, was for a man to have about him a halo of sanctity." [4] The accounts of those who visited there were met in convents and the open streets with open-mouthed curiosity. Many viewed the Holy Land as a place where they could find God and find relics. Multitudes wanted to go there; the Crusades provided the opportunity.

A Spirit of Revenge

Furthermore, resentment and a spirit of revenge were latent throughout Europe. As early as 841, Muslims had captured Rome and sacked St. Peter's Basilica. In 846 they threatened Rome a second time. [5] In the seventh century the Muslims had taken the Holy Land, and through the years Muslim leaders had periodically persecuted Christian residents of Palestine as well as the pilgrims who went there. Early in the eleventh century, Catholic barons, princes, bishops and monks had begun to lead organized pilgrimages to the Holy Land with as many as 12,000 at a time. Pilgrims who made the journey were forced to pay a fee to enter Jerusalem. One group of pilgrims led in 1092 by Eric, king of the Danes, was met by savage Seljukian Turks who captured, imprisoned and sold many of them into slavery. [6] Reports of this kind of treatment by the Muslims made it back home and infuriated the people of Europe. They were ready for revenge.

Opportunity and Freedom

Some saw a trip to the Holy Land as an opportunity for starting a profitable trade in silk, paper, spices and other Eastern products.

Between 1188 and 1270, the kings of France joined with the pope in granting Crusaders "exemption from debt, freedom from taxation and the payment of interest." [7] A better economic status was a great incentive for supporting the Crusades.

Adventure and License to Sin

Some of Europe's most eminent men went on the Crusades, but so also did "the lowest elements of European society – thieves, murderers, perjurers, vagabonds, and scoundrels of all sorts." [8] They received indulgences (blank checks to sin) and were promised eternal life. Eugenius (1146) extended eternal life to the parents of those taking part in a Crusade. Innocent III included those who built ships and contributed in any way to the Crusades. [9]

The Crusades were glorified. Participants were glorified as martyrs. The cross was the badge of the Crusaders, and those who went were called soldiers of the cross. The Muslims were depicted as the vilest of pagans (enemies of Christ) and Crusaders were told that there was no sin in killing them. They were told that they profited by killing these pagans, and that Christ would be glorified when they did. [10] For the average European who had lived an uneventful life of hard labor and who had never been very far from his birthplace, the prospect of travel and adventure to a glamorous place like Jerusalem was awesome. The offer of eternal life and a document that would allow him to sin with no consequence made the prospect extremely appealing.

In November of 1095 the famous Council of Clermont in Southern France decreed the first Crusade. Pope Urban II was present and preached a fiery sermon which reverberated among Catholics throughout the Roman Catholic Church. He called the Turks an accursed race and accused them of devastating the kingdom of God by fire, pillage and sword. He said the short way to an incorruptible crown was a trip to the Holy Land to fight the pagans. He stirred the crowd of thousands of Catholic churchmen and lords into a frenzy saying, "God wills it, God wills it!" [11] Soon Catholic Europe was electrified. "A new passion had taken hold of its people. A new arena of conquest was opened for the warlike feudal lord, a tempting field of adventure and release for knight and debtor, an opportunity for serf and villain. All classes, lay and clerical, saw in the expedition to the cradle of their faith a solace for sin, a satisfaction of Christian fancy and a heaven-appointed mission. The struggle of states with the papacy was for the moment at an end. All Europe was suddenly united in a common and holy cause, of which the supreme pontiff was beyond dispute the appointed leader." [12]

Popular current belief is that the virtuous Catholic popes cared so much about Jerusalem that they were righteously determined to liberate it from the wicked Muslims. Such was hardly the case. The fact is that the rule of the popes was seriously sagging and badly needed a boost. The popes found that boost, the cause that could unite Europe behind them, in the liberation of Jerusalem from the Muslims. The Crusades were a political move by the popes to help their own cause, not a move motivated by righteous love for Jerusalem and the Holy Land.

In our next chapter we will take a brief look at five of the Crusades against the Muslims. We will also consider the major impact the Crusades had on the course of history. In later chapters we will also consider Catholic Crusades against our Christian forefathers whom the Catholics accused of being heretics.

Due note should be taken of the fact that the Crusades were exclusively a Roman Catholic movement. There were multitudes of believers scattered across Europe who were not a part of it.

---

[1] *Webster's New World Dictionary with Student Handbook: Young People's Edition*, s.v. "crusade," (Nashville, Tennessee: The World Publishing Company, 1973), 173.

[2] Philip Schaff, *History of the Christian Church,* vol. 5, (Peabody, Massachusetts: Hendrickson Publishers, 2002), 215.

[3] Ibid., 225.

[4] Ibid., 222.

[5] Ibid., 221.

[6] Ibid., 223.

[7] Ibid., 217.

[8] Ibid., 216.

[9] Ibid., 217.

[10] Ibid., 218.

[11] Ibid., 229

[12] Ibid., 231.

Enemies of the Catholic Church

Secular Opposition

From the time of Constantine onward, virtually all secular powers resented and opposed the power and the wealth of the state church. The new Germanic powers that over-ran the western part of the Empire were leery about too much power in the hands of the state church and its head bishop.

Religious Opposition

From before the time of Constantine, there were many Christians and churches that did not support the drift of the bigger, more influential churches into state churches. There were struggles within the state church for dominance and supremacy. Churches in other cities claimed they were at least equal, if not superior, to Rome. The bishops of Rome (popes) and the bishops of Constantinople (patriarchs) were antagonistic and made it a point to oppose each other doctrinally and practically at almost every possible junction.

Islam

Islam exploded on the scene, and within 100 years it had conquered much of the east, most of North Africa, much of Spain and was putting pressure on the Roman Catholic world from both the east and the west.

Nationalism

By the end of the eleventh century, Feudalism had begun to give way to Nationalism in Europe. Nations had begun to form. The growing spirit of nationalism made it increasingly difficult for the popes to maintain their stranglehold on Europe.

The History of Churches

Corruption Within the Catholic Church

Financial Exploitation

The popes financially exploited the people, including their own bishops, priests and individual churches, through amates, collations, commendations, expectancies, reservations, *Jus Spoliorum*, tithing, dispensations and indulgences. Such wealth, especially by exploitation, generated jealousy and resentment.

Financial Corruption

Monasteries became rich and notorious for lives of pleasure, excess and immorality. The headquarters at Rome were even more corrupt and immoral. Kings and landlords were taxed to the breaking-point by the popes, who in turn squandered that money. The oppressed could not afford to resist, lest he be excommunicated.

Immorality

It was common for church officials to use their elevated positions to force sex with females of their choosing. Homosexuality was rampant. Greed, abuse of power, cruelty and hypocrisy were the hallmarks of the papal system.

Papal Prestige

The papacy was born during the reign of Gregory I. The papacy continued to expand and strengthen until 1215. Such external tyranny coupled with internal corruptions could not last forever. The popes were shrewd and would stop at nothing to hold on to their position of power.

The History of Churches

Exploitation by the Catholic Church

A Land of Glamour and Romance

A pilgrimage to Jerusalem was the goal of many professing Christians. There was a romance about it. Many viewed the Holy Land as a place where they could find God and find relics. Multitudes wanted to go there; the Crusades provided the opportunity.

A Spirit of Revenge

Resentment and a spirit of revenge were latent throughout Europe. In the seventh century the Muslims had taken the Holy Land, and through the years Muslim leaders had periodically persecuted Christian residents of Palestine as well as the pilgrims who went there. Reports of this kind of treatment by the Muslims made it back home and infuriated the people of Europe. They were ready for revenge.

Opportunity and Freedom

Some saw a trip to the Holy Land as an opportunity for starting a profitable trade in silk, paper, spices and other Eastern products. A better economic status was a great incentive for supporting the Crusades.

Adventure and License to Sin

Eugenius extended eternal life to the parents of those taking part in a Crusade. Participants in the Crusades were glorified as martyrs. The Muslims were depicted as the vilest of pagans (enemies of Christ), and Crusaders were told that there was no sin in killing them. They were also told that they profited by killing these pagans and that Christ would be glorified when they did.

294

Chapter 24

The Iron Fist Cracked

Now that you have an understanding of what brought about the Crusades, it is time to examine the actual campaigns. You will recall that there were seven greater Crusades, plus several lesser Crusades against the Muslims. There were also Catholic Crusades against true Christians whom the Catholics considered to be heretics.

In this chapter we will look at five of the greater Crusades against the Muslims. These are indicative of the Crusades as a whole and are sufficient to give an understanding of their character.

A BRIEF LOOK AT FIVE CRUSADES
AGAINST THE MUSLIMS

The First Crusade (1095-1099)

Pope Urban II instigated this Crusade and appointed Peter the Hermit to be his personal representative. Peter saw no value in training, weapons or armaments. He was sure that God would miraculously give the Crusaders victory. Multitudes of men, women and children gathered in Lorraine and at Treves in France and demanded that Peter the Hermit lead them immediately to Jerusalem. They set forth in unwieldy bands. The first band of over 12,000 under the leadership of Walter the Penniless made it safely through Hungary but was attacked by Muslim Turks and almost totally destroyed at Belgrade. Only a few stragglers reached Constantinople. The second band of 40,000 was led by Peter himself. They too made it through Hungary, but in Bulgaria they encountered much the same fate as the first band. Only 7,000, all in pitiful condition, made it to Constantinople. The emperor transported them across the Bosporus, where they awaited the arrival of the regular army. While they waited, they plundered the countryside. A rumor that the vanguard had captured the Turkish capital at Nicea lured them into a nearby plain, where they were surrounded and massacred by the Turkish Cavalry. "Their bones were piled into a ghastly pyramid . . . Walter fell in the battle; Peter the Hermit had fled back to Constantinople . . . A third swarm, comprising fifteen thousand, mostly Germans under the lead of the monk Gottschalk, was massacred by the Hungarians." [1] This first encounter suggested to the Turks that they didn't need to worry so much about the Western Crusaders. They were a joke to the Turks. [2]

The Turks misjudged the situation. There were serious military people in Greece who were eager to make their presence known. In the absence of a central commander, each military man did as he saw fit. There was no coordinated command and strategy. Some 50,000 European soldiers gathered at Constantinople. The patriarch of Constantinople panicked; he mistakenly thought they had come to take revenge on him for excommunicating the pope. [3] Each of three armies found a way to cross the Bosporus, and by 1097 the first army had made its way to Nicea. They found the Turkish army on rest and relaxation. Because of his experience with Peter the Hermit, the sultan scorned the Crusaders. Almost without a fight, the Crusaders took the Turkish capital which was full of the families of the Turkish soldiers. When the Turks realized what had happened and responded, the Crusaders cut off heads of the Turkish wives and children and threw them over the walls. The Turkish soldiers broke off the fight and planned an ambush in the plains of Turkey. The Turks met the first Christian army on the plains and defeated them; however, the second army appeared on the horizon, and shortly thereafter the third army appeared. The Turks were defeated. [4]

Within a year the Crusaders were nearing Antioch. One route to the city was around the mountains. A large number of the

Crusaders decided to take that long or northern route. There was a shorter route through a narrow mountain pass called the Syrian Gates. This area was in the hands of Arabs, who were sure the Crusaders were not dumb enough to attempt this route of sure slaughter. They made no attempt to defend it, especially when they saw large numbers taking the longer route. The fact is that some of the Crusaders did take the short or eastern route. The Arabs planned a pitched battle against the Crusaders who were coming around the mountains; however, the smaller band of Crusaders arrived early. They found Antioch unprotected and took the city. The Arabs were cut off and defeated; they retreated into the mountains. The Crusaders entered the city, but were quickly surrounded by the returning Arabs. During the siege, the Crusaders ran out of supplies and food and were "forced to eat horse flesh, camels, dogs, and mice and even worse." [5] Peter Barthelemy claimed that he had a vision about the lance that pierced Jesus. According to his vision, the lance was buried under their feet. Every Crusader became an instant digger. A lance head was found and brought to Peter, who proclaimed it to indeed be the very lance that pierced Jesus. He claimed that the Savior's blood was still on it. The excitement was electric. In the absence of a supreme commander, 50,000 Crusaders grabbed their swords and shields and charged the Arabs, who left their women and children in their tents and fled. One Crusader reported that when they found the women in their tents, they did nothing evil to them except to pierce their bellies with their lances. [6]

By 1099 these Crusaders had made it to Jerusalem. After several failed visions and attempts to take the city by miraculous means, they finally built ramps, scaled the walls, took the city and killed every resident who did not claim to be a Christian. This included surviving warriors, women, children and Jews. They now controlled a corridor from Jerusalem to Constantinople in which they built thirteen castles to protect and hold the route.

> **Peter Barthelemy had a vision about the lance that pierced Jesus**

The Second Crusade (1147-1149)

The second Crusade was a debacle. It was prompted by the fall of Edessa in 1144. Edessa was the outer citadel of the Crusader's earlier conquests. The Turks overran the city and massacred its inhabitants. [7] Soon they were threatening Jerusalem. Pope Eugenius III saw this threat and commissioned a charismatic monk, Bernard of Clairvoix to preach the Crusade. Bernard did so with spectacular results. Within a few months he had King Louis VII of France and Emperor Konrad III of the Holy Roman Empire (mainly Germany) in place to lead the Crusade along with 70,000 men including 7,000 knights. [8] The two sovereigns could not work together. They finally arrived at Jerusalem but decided to attack Damascus before moving against Edessa. The whole effort failed and the weakness of the Crusaders was underscored. The Muslims took Jerusalem in 1187 and Europe was convinced that there must be a third Crusade.

The Third Crusade (1190-1193)

This Crusade is probably the most famous of all. It was led by Richard the Lionheart and called *the Crusade of the Kings*.

Richard the Lionheart (Richard I of England) was a most charismatic figure: tall, strong, charming, brave and daring. He was also hot-headed and selfish. To the Arab soldiers he was very intimidating. Richard was a military man. He sold whatever was necessary and raised the money for this campaign. Leading this Crusade with Richard was Philip Augustus, king of France, and Frederick Barbarossa (Fred the Red), head of the Holy Roman Empire. The administrative-minded Philip was the opposite of Richard. These two clashed; and Philip, who was afraid of Richard, left his troops and returned to France. Frederick was 70 years old and fat, but he led 100,000 troops. When he came to a shallow river in Asia Minor (Turkey), he failed to take off his armor before crossing. He fell off his horse and drowned. His son continued with Richard but decided to pickle his dad in a water-tight coffin filled with vinegar and take him into battle. Ultimately he took Frederick back to Germany for burial. The effect of all these developments was that Richard was in full control of the Crusaders.

Opposing him was Saladin the Egyptian, who had taken Jerusalem. He was respected on both sides for his integrity. After many confrontations, Saladin succeeded in holding Jerusalem. He and Richard entered into negotiations, and a treaty was signed allowing Saladin to run Jerusalem, but he would allow Christian pilgrimages. The Christians would have to pay a tax. [9]

Like the previous two, this Crusade was a failure.

> **This famous Crusade was led by Richard the Lionheart**

The Fourth Crusade (1200-1204)

Ironically this Crusade never directly involved the Muslims. The Turks were threatening Constantinople, and the patriarchs were asking for Western help. At the same time they were hedging their bets by acting friendly toward the Turks. These Easterners envisioned the day when they would not have Western help. The earlier Crusaders had noticed this friendliness toward the Muslims and were suspicious. They were as angry with the Eastern Catholics as they were with the Muslims.

Upon ascending the papal throne, Pope Innocent III gave himself to reviving the Crusader spirit. He strong-armed most of the Catholic leaders of Europe to get behind a fourth Crusade and dispatched legates to stir up the cause. He offered indulgences, eternal life and full protection to all Crusaders. Thousands were recruited to follow the nobles who led the campaign. The Crusaders mustered at Venice from which they planned to sail to Constantinople. The Venetian Grand Council "agreed to provide ships for 9000 esquires, 4500 knights, 20,000 foot-soldiers, and 4500 horses, and to furnish provisions for nine months for the sum of 85,000 marks;" [10] however, the Crusaders had only 50,000 marks. One of the Venetians, Henry Dandolo, proposed that the balance would be eliminated if the Crusaders would aid in capturing Zara, the Christian capital of Dalmatia and the chief market on the east coast of the Adriatic Sea. Zara was the main economic competition of the Venetians. The Crusaders agreed and completely destroyed Zara, a community completely free of Muslims. Meanwhile the rightful emperor of Constantinople had been overthrown, blinded and imprisoned by his brother. Greek messengers appeared at Zara and appealed to the Venetians and Crusaders to attack Constantinople. This suited the private ambitions of the Venetian merchants; it would effectively eliminate their competition.

The Venetians delivered the Crusaders to Constantinople and told them they would have to pay for return passage; earlier they had volunteered to transport them to Constantinople for free. The Crusaders had no money and were enraged at the whole picture. The Venetians pointed out that there was plenty of wealth in Constantinople which was theirs for the taking. The violence, plunder and pillage that followed were far more than an attack to restore the rightful emperor. Constantinople was looted and ruined.

The fourth Crusade was really not a Crusade at all. There never was a battle against the Muslims, although the blows inflicted by the Crusaders against their Catholic kinsmen in Constantinople paved the way for its fall to the Turkish Muslims. [11]

The Children's Crusade (1212)

The Children's Crusade is one of the most pathetic spectacles this world has ever witnessed. It ended in the total ruin of approximately 30,000 children, mostly French and German.

The Crusade started with a 12-year old French boy named Stephen, who claimed he had a vision in which Christ appealed to him to rescue the holy places. Word of the vision, fanned with priestly zeal, spread across Europe. Catholic children from all over the continent joined the effort. The idea was picked up by a 10-year old German boy named Nicholas. Men and women, good and bad, joined the effort

Those with Stephen rallied at Marseilles, expecting the waters of the Mediterranean Sea to part for them. Two slave traders named Hugo Ferreus and William Procus offered to convey them across the Mediterranean "for the sake of God and without price." Seven vessels set sail; two shipwrecked on San Pietro off the coast of Sardinia. "The rest reached the African shore, where the children were sold into slavery." [12]

Another group, under an anonymous leader, rallied at Cologne before passing through Eastern Switzerland and across the Alps to Brindisi. They sailed for Jerusalem never to be heard of thereafter.

The group with Nicholas reached Genoa in August of 1212. When the waters of the Mediterranean failed to part, they pressed on to Brindisi. Many died on the way, and those who made Brindisi were swallowed up in the population.

> **This Crusade ended in the total ruin of about thirty thousand children**

LASTING IMPACTS FROM THE CRUSADES AGAINST THE MUSLIMS

The Crusades against the Muslims failed in three respects: (1) The Holy Land was not won, (2) the advance of Islam was not permanently checked and (3) the schism between the East and the West was not healed. Even so they resulted in many changes, some for the better and some for the worse.

Negative impacts

- The Crusades were a personal disaster for most of the Crusaders. The vast majority of them starved, froze, were killed in battle or died of disease or in some other horrible way.

- All kinds of vices developed in the Crusader camps and were brought back to Europe.

- The schism between the Eastern Catholics and the Western Catholics widened as a result of the Crusades. To this day, there remains a deep resentment and distrust between the two sides.

- The Crusades galvanized deep hatred, distrust and resentment in the minds of Muslims for Christianity and Christians.

- The papacy made great financial profit off the Crusades. In exchange for the guarantee of straight passage to heaven for all Crusaders, they had to leave all of their possessions, including lands, to the papacy. By the end of the Crusades, the papacy owned about one third of all the land in Europe. [13]

- The Crusades brought about the rapid development of the system of papal indulgences. This development grew exponentially, and quickly became a means of control and income for the Catholics. Worst of all, the Crusades were used to lure Catholics into fighting against true Christians and churches throughout Europe. These true New Testament Christians were viewed as heretics to be destroyed. [14]

- The Crusades gave birth to Catholic military orders: the Templars and the Hospitallers. [15] The Roman Catholic Church now had its own standing army, which it thereafter consistently used to persecute, oppress, maim and kill. The army was especially used against dissenters.

Positive impacts of the Crusades that cracked the iron papal fist

- New learning was introduced from the East. The learning of the Eastern Catholics as well as the Arabs had been far superior to the West. The Easterners had copies of Greek and Latin manuscripts and were schooled in the languages of the Scriptures. Crusaders were exposed to this knowledge and some secured copies of the Scriptures and brought them back to the West. [16]

- This proved to be an eye-opening experience and gave rise to an age of scholasticism. This natural education of so many of the laity, coupled with a sudden new interest in secular things, began to undermine the power of the ecclesiastical hierarchy. [17] Some within the Roman Catholic Church started to see how far away from New Testament Christianity they were. Like a seed sprouting in a giant rock, the light of truth began to penetrate the enormous darkness of the Roman Catholic Church. No immediate change would be forthcoming, but a small seed entered the iron fist. It would eventually produce a huge crack called the Protestant Reformation.

- The Crusades greatly fostered the rise of nationalism in Europe; and more than any other factor, nationalism became the undoing of absolute domination by the papacy.

o Feudalism was weakened. Many of the knights and nobles who went on Crusades never returned. Also large numbers sold their lands to peasants or wealthy middle class townsmen to raise money for the Crusades. They had nothing to bring them back. Cities controlled by feudal lords were able to buy charters, providing them with self-government. The prolonged absence of so many lords and knights (in many cases it was permanent) gave sovereigns a rare opportunity to extend their authority. Furthermore, the channeling of so many resources, so much money and so much attention and energy into the Crusades led to a rise in national feeling that eventually weakened papal power. Kings were able to centralize their control with the aid of a growing middle class, which favored a strong centralized nation-state under a monarch in order to provide the security and order so essential to business. [18] The Crusades thus resulted in a spirit of nationality in the people and kings of Europe which consolidated the nations into the form which they have since retained with little change. [19]

o As a direct result of the Crusades, growing cities (and commerce between them) began to replace the small, isolated, self-contained kingdoms of the feudal lords. Immediately after the first Crusade, Italian cities like Venice began regular trade with the East. People returning from the Crusades wanted the luxuries they had seen in the East. [20] Commerce would never stop growing. Cities flourished and a new middle class began to emerge. [21] Early foundational steps to a nationalistic Europe under the control of heads of state, instead of iron-fisted rule by a single pope, were being taken. The iron fist now had a slight crack. It would take many struggles and many years for Europe to throw off iron-fisted papal domination, but the Crusades had cracked the fist and initiated the process.

The popes saw the Crusades as a way to divert attention away from their wicked and overbearing ways and a means of rallying Europe behind them. They orchestrated the Crusades as a means of enhancing their prestige, galvanizing their power and protecting their dynasty. They succeeded for a while, but the whole effort ultimately backfired. The very effort they initiated introduced ideas and dynamics in Europe that would ultimately liberate their captives.

It should be pointed out that it was the popes whose motives were sinister. As earlier mentioned, their agenda was protection of their dynasty. The liberation of Jerusalem from the Muslims was merely a means toward that end. It is doubtless true that many who went on Crusades went for the wrong reasons: to avoid debt, for adventure, to receive eternal life from the pope and other corrupt reasons; however, that does not mean that every Crusader was corrupt. The intentions of many of the Crusaders were pure and lofty.

> **The Crusades gave rise to an age of scholasticism**

[1] Philip Schaff, *History of the Christian Church,* vol. 5, (Peabody, Massachusetts: Hendrickson Publishers, 2002), 231-233.
[2] Carl Deimer, Professor, *History of Christianity I,* Video Lecture 19, Liberty University DLP, 2004.
[3] Ibid.
[4] Ibid.
[5] Schaff, 236.
[6] Ibid.
[7] Ibid., 252-253.
[8] Ibid., 254.
[9] Deimer, Lecture 20.
[10] Schaff, 271.
[11] Deimer, Lecture 20.
[12] Schaff, 268.
[13] Deimer, Lecture 20.
[14] Schaff, 290-291.
[15] Justo L. Gonzalez, *The Story of Christianity,* vol. 1, (San Francisco: HarperCollins Publishers, 1984), 299-300.
[16] Deimer, Lecture 20.
[17] Schaff, 292.
[18] Earle E. Cairns, *Christianity Through the Centuries: A History of the Christian Church,* 3rd ed., (Grand Rapids, Michigan: Zondervan, 1996), 216.
[19] Schaff, 292.
[20] Ibid.
[21] Gonzalez, 300.

Crusades Against the Muslims

The First Crusade (1095-1099)

Pope Urban II instigated this Crusade to Jerusalem. With no training, sixty-seven thousand men, women and children set forth to march to Jerusalem. All but seven thousand were massacred. After this, fifty thousand European soldiers marched to Nicea and defeated the Turkish army. By 1099, the Crusaders had made it to Jerusalem and took the city.

The Second Crusade (1147-1149)

A second Crusade was started when the Turks massacred the inhabitants of Edessa. Pope Eugenius III commissioned Bernard of Clairvoix, a monk, to preach the Crusade. He got seventy thousand soldiers from France and Germany to retake Edessa. The two groups could not work together, so the whole effort failed. The Muslims retook Jerusalem in 1187.

The Third Crusade (1190-1193)

This Crusade is probably the most famous of all. It was led by Richard the Lionheart and called the *Crusade of the Kings*. He failed to retake Jerusalem, which was held by Saladin the Egyptian. Richard entered into negotiations and a treaty was signed allowing Saladin to run Jerusalem, but he would allow Christian pilgrimages for a tax.

The Fourth Crusade (1200-1204)

Pope Innocent III decided to revive the Crusader spirit because the Eastern Catholics were acting friendly toward the Turks. The Venetian merchants transported them by ship to Zara, where it was completely destroyed. They were then taken to Constantinople, which was looted and ruined.

The Children's Crusade (1212)

A 12-year old French boy named Stephen claimed he had a vision in which Christ appealed to him to rescue the holy places. Catholic children from all over the continent joined the effort. It ended in the total ruin of approximately thirty thousand children, mostly French and German.

The History of Churches

305

Lasting Impacts from the Crusades

The Crusades against the Muslims failed in three respects:

1. The Holy Land was not won
2. The advance of Islam was not permanently checked
3. The schism between the East and the West was not healed

Negative Impacts

The vast majority of the Crusaders starved, froze, were killed in battle or died of disease

All kinds of vices developed in the Crusader camps and were brought back to Europe

The schism between the Eastern Catholics and the Western Catholics widened

The Crusades galvanized deep hatred and distrust in the minds of Muslims for Christianity

The papacy made great financial profit off the Crusades

The Crusades brought about the rapid development of the system of papal indulgences

The Crusades gave birth to Catholic military orders: the Templars and the Hospitallers

Positive Impacts

New learning was introduced from the East

The Crusades greatly fostered the rise of nationalism, which became the undoing of absolute domination by the papacy

Chapter 25

The Tide Turned

The Crusades against the Muslims greatly fostered the nationalization of Europe, and no dynamic brought about the demise of papal domination like European nationalism. Nations formed and kings grew stronger. More and more they challenged popes and won. The trend was gradual but unrelenting. Though they would remain rich and powerful beyond ordinary comprehension, the popes would cease to be the absolute dictators of Europe. Time would diminish Catholic power and control. It would also greatly reduce the papacy's ability to sweep the wealth of Europe into its coffers.

Furthermore, with nationalization, Catholic legates, inquisitors and armies would not enjoy the free reign they had known for so many centuries. They'd still persecute, maim and kill, especially in some countries like Italy and Spain, but not with unlimited freedom. The persecution of New Testament Christians and churches would continue and come from new sources, but not with universal and unabated ferocity by the Catholics.

Things were changing in Europe, but slowly. Before conditions improved for those multitudes of poor Christians who followed first-century doctrine and practices, they got worse. With legates, Crusades and the Inquisition, the papacy made their existence extremely perilous. Before turning our attention to the loss of papal power, we shall take a brief peek at open war against primitive Christians and churches.

CATHOLIC WAR AGAINST GOD'S PEOPLE

The Holy Wars (Crusades) of the popes against the Muslims held a mystique of wanderlust and adventure. An opportunity to go to the Holy Land to rescue Jerusalem and the holy shrines from those *awful, devilish pagans* had a pious appeal. The cause seemed noble. Catholics from across Europe answered the call to go and fight the enemies of God.

The popes were enterprising souls with a vast empire of wealth and control. They would do whatever it took to foster and preserve their position. The Crusades against the Muslims temporarily elevated papal prestige to an all-time high. The popes were quick to capitalize on this tidal wave of popularity and harness it against those whom they hated the most, the dissenters, those Christians who from the first century had refused to leave the doctrine and practices of the New Testament.

Hundreds of years of persecution had failed to stop these primitive Christians. Century after century, they had converted people from all walks of life including multitudes of Catholics whom they promptly re-baptized. Kings, legates, bishops and whole regions were brought to salvation by these followers of Christ, who went by many names but whose beliefs were essentially the same: the ultimate authority of the Scriptures, salvation exclusively by personal faith in Jesus Christ, baptism by immersion only after salvation, the priesthood of every believer, the autonomy of the local church and the deity of Jesus Christ. Their numbers grew and their communities were found throughout the land; however, these New Testament believers were generally more numerous in mountainous areas where they could hide and find natural protection in rugged, inaccessible areas. The Cottian Alps proved to be their best stronghold.

Though the Crusades were not successful in the Holy Land, the popes found them to be an enormously successful means of raising an army. Men could (1) fight the enemies of God, (2) receive eternal life for doing so and (3) receive indulgences or an ahead-of-time license to cover whatever sins they might commit. The popes quickly capitalized on the prevailing climate and began to organize Holy Wars (Crusades) against *heretics* (those primitive Christians who refused to yield to Catholicism).

308

The Crusades were not successful in the Holy Land

CRUSADES AGAINST DISSENTERS

The Crusade Against the Albigenses (1209)

Mention has been made of Pope Innocent III. In 1209 he proclaimed a Crusade against Raymond VI who ruled in Provence. The Catholics considered Toulouse the center of heresy. [1] The pope had demanded that Raymond banish the heretics who flourished there (Albigenses), who were responsible for Europe's most beautiful and prosperous economy. When Raymond stalled, Innocent proclaimed a Crusade, which resulted in the devastation of Provence. "Indulgences, such as had been given to the Crusaders who went at great risk to themselves to rescue the Holy Places in Palestine from the Muslim Saracens, were now offered to all who would take part in the easier work of destroying the most fruitful provinces in France. This, and the prospect of booty and license of every kind, attracted hundreds of thousands of men." [2] As they marched through the region, the Catholic Crusaders under the leadership of the cruel general Simon de Montfort ravaged the land. "The ears, noses, and lips of prisoners were cut off." [3] At the town of Beziers, none was spared. At "La Minerva, about 140 believers were found, women in one house, men in another, engaged in prayer as they awaited their doom. De Montfort, had a great pile of wood prepared, and told them to be converted to the Catholic faith or mount the pile." All burned to death. [4]

Crusades against the Albigenses continued for thirty years; at their end, the region was a spectacle of desolation. [5]

The Crusade Against Bosnia (1238)

In spite of major Catholic efforts to prevent it, the *heresy* of the Bogomils "grew and increased, like the waters of Noah's flood." [6] Emboldened by the success of the Crusade against Provence, Pope Gregory IX proclaimed a Crusade against Bosnia. Under the leadership of the king of Sclavonia, Bosnia was *purged*. "No troubadour has sung, no historian recorded, the barbarities and atrocities of this war of extermination: we know only that many thousands were enrolled among the glorious army of martyrs." [7] In 1240 Pope Gregory congratulated the Sclavonian king for "wiping out the heresy and restoring the light of Catholic purity." [8]

The Crusade Against Savoy (1486)

In the 15th century, Waldenses were flourishing in Savoy on the western flank of the Alps. In 1486 Pope Innocent VIII issued a bull of extermination against them "by which he enjoined all temporal powers to take arms for their destruction. He summoned all Catholics to a crusade against them, 'absolving beforehand all who should take part in this crusade from all ecclesiastical penalties, general or special, setting them free from the obligation of vows which they might have made, legitimating their possession of goods which they might have wrongfully acquired, and concluding with a promise of the remission of all sins to every one who should slay a heretic. Moreover, he annulled all contracts subscribed in favour of the Vaudois, commanded their domestics to abandon them, forbade any one to give them any assistance, and authorized all and sundry to seize upon their goods." [9] Thousands volunteered: "persons ambitious of distinction, vagabonds, fanatics, men without lawful employment, needy adventurers, plunders of every description, and pitiless robbers and assassins." [10] This horde of marauders, in company with 18,000 regular troops furnished jointly by the king of France and the sovereign of Piedmont, marched into Savoy. This Crusade had nothing at all to do with the loyalty of these primitive Christians to their civil authorities. The charge against them in Pope Innocent's bull of extermination was that they converted others to their doctrine and practice, and "that their principal means of seduction was their great appearance of sanctity." [11] What a picture! Kill and exterminate hard-working, law-abiding, peaceful, solid citizens simply because they believe and teach that salvation is by faith in Jesus Christ and not through any church! What a crime! In the name of God send a whole army to a flock of harmless, highly productive sheep! The whole Crusade was absurd, but weren't they all?

The Massacre of the Whole Population of Val Louise (1488)

In some cases, Crusades such as the one against Savoy failed. God repeatedly seemed to intervene on behalf of His remnants of New

Testament Christians; however, under the direction of the popes, Catholic exterminators incessantly pursued non-Catholics. Catholic atrocities in Dauphiny illustrate the point. By the end of 13th century, Catholic legates had killed New Testament Christians and depopulated many of the Dauphiny valleys such as the Durance. Over the years, Waldenses communities had begun to recover in these rugged mountains. When the Catholic Crusaders failed in Savoy, they moved against a strong community of Waldenses at the town of Briancon. The believers retreated to a large mountain cave high above the city. The Catholic commander, La Palud, and his forces sealed off the entrance of the cave with wood and set it on fire. More than 3,000 Waldenses, the whole population of Val Louise, were massacred including "400 little children smothered in their cradles, or in the arms of their mothers." [12]

CRUSADES AND CONQUEST

Crusades became an ugly tool to be employed for many vile purposes, including conquest. For example, in 1207 a German abbot, Gottfried, visited eastern Prussia. Two native princes were soon converted to Catholicism. The Catholics saw an opportunity to extend their domain, and an abbot named Christian was made bishop of Prussia (1212-1215). In 1217 Honorius III ordered a Crusade which was renewed by Gregory IX in 1230. Teutonic knights "ready enough to further religious encroachment by the sword, promised, as they were, a large share in the conquered lands" carried on continual wars from 1230 until 1283. [13] They literally took over this territory.

It is well known that the goal of explorers such as Columbus, Cortés and Coronado was conquest. What is not so readily acknowledged is the religious connection behind these efforts. These explorers were to make Catholics of those whom they conquered, and their method was *conversion by the sword*. They took the wealth (the real objective) of those they conquered, and forced (yes, forced) them to become Catholics. For example, when the Spanish Conquistador Hernán Cortés and his Catholic strong-men reached Mexico City, Moctezuma II and the Aztec Indians welcomed them with great pomp. The Spaniards seized Moctezuma II and brutally conquered the Aztecs in the name of

God. Their practice was to give the chiefs a chance to be converted. If a chief failed to convert, he was burned at the stake. If he converted, he was choked to death for having resisted. [14] This mode of operation by Catholic conquerors explains how Latin and South America became predominately Catholic.

Advancing the cause of Catholicism was ever at the heart of the Catholic demagogues. Ferdinand and Isabella bankrolled Columbus. The spoils would go to them and Catholicism would prosper. "Columbus signed an agreement April 17, 1492, to devote the proceeds of his undertaking beyond the Western seas to the recovery of the holy sepulcher. Before his fourth and last journey to America he wrote to Alexander VI renewing his vow to further furnish troops for the rescue of the sacred locality." [15]

THE LOSS OF PAPAL PRESTIGE AND POWER

The Weakness of Boniface VIII (1294-1303)

A pope was expected to die in office; however, the hermit pope, Peter de Murphone (Coelestin V) abdicated. [16] This raised questions of the legitimacy of his successor, Boniface VIII. [17]

Under Boniface's reign, England and France were heading toward war, a war that Boniface did not want. He wanted English and French tax money to go to Rome and not to the war effort. Boniface ordered the war efforts to cease and threatened both England and France with interdicts. In the latter quarter of the eleventh century, Gregory VII had backed down Henry IV of England. Other European kings had been forced into submission to previous popes; however, times had changed and the nations were not as impotent as before.

King Edward I of England ignored Boniface's interdict. King Philip IV of France informed Boniface that he not only was continuing preparations for war, but that France was also stopping all monetary payments to the papacy. Furthermore, Philip began to support Boniface's rivals, who were saying that Boniface was not a genuine, legitimate pope.

Pope Boniface VIII promptly issued his famous papal bull, *unam sanctum* (one sanctuary) of 1302. The position of the popes had long been that, "If the sacred chair is vacant, the empire lacks the dispenser of salvation; if the throne is empty, the Church is defenseless before her persecutors. It is the duty of the Church's ruler to maintain kings in their office, and of kings to protect the rights of the Church." The bull of Boniface asserted the supremacy of the papacy "to both swords, the spiritual and the temporal, with the one ruling the souls of men and with the other their temporal concerns." [18] It demanded that everyone must submit to the pope to be saved. *Unam sanctum* also illustrates the totalitarian mindset of the Roman Catholic Church. When Boniface placed France under an interdict, Philip tried to seize the pope. Boniface escaped but died within a month. [19]

Do not mistakenly assume that this affront of the papacy by the English and the French meant immediate relief to primitive Christians. It most assuredly did not. What it did mean is that a turning point had been reached. At that time, none of the multitudes of suffering saints realized the slightest relief. In fact, in their desperation to hold on to power, the Catholics actually got worse. The days of the Inquisition were the worst of all, although it is doubtful that any measure of religious freedom the world has known since would ever have been possible apart from the cracks that began to widen in the papal iron fist in the thirteenth century.

> *Unam sanctum* declares that the Pope has ultimate supremacy over both the spiritual and temporal worlds

The Big Papal Schism

What the affront to Pope Boniface VIII by England and France did is further weaken the papacy. There was only one pope between Popes Boniface VIII and Clement V. During this period, the papacy had become submissive to French interests. Pope Clement V decided to move the papal office to Avignon, France, which is just across the border from Italy. He also selected enough French cardinals to guarantee that the next pope would be French. For the next 69 years (1309-1377), the papacy fell largely under

French control. (This period is known to Catholics as *the Babylonian Captivity*.) It is not difficult to imagine how the king of England and other kings felt about this arrangement. Tremendous division within Catholicism grew. Catholic Europe was in an uproar.

In 1378 Pope Gregory XI moved the papal office back to Rome; however, the cardinals were mostly French. The cardinals elected Urban VI only after he promised to take the papacy back to Avignon. After they elected Urban, he staunchly refused to leave Rome. The French cardinals then met and elected another pope who moved back to Avignon. Now the Catholic Church had two popes, each claiming to be the Vicar of Christ. Since a pope is the only one who can order and confirm a bishop, each time a bishopric became empty, two bishops were appointed. A council was called in 1409 to resolve the matter and both popes were removed. Pope Alexander V was elected as the real pope; however, because the council was not called by a pope, neither the pope in Rome nor the pope in Avignon would step down. Now there were three popes. [20] Another council was called which deposed all three and elected Pope Martin V who was backed by the Holy Roman Emperor. [21] This move effectively re-established the papacy in Rome.

Obviously, bickering and division such as this further weakened and deteriorated the papacy. Over time, its stranglehold on the political life of Europe would be broken and eventually that would lead to political protection for those who were not a part of Catholicism. As positive as this change was, it would be much, much later before religious freedom from a state church would become a reality in the world.

Appalling Immorality

It is hard to imagine any group of humans being any more immoral than the popes, bishops and other Catholic leaders who posed as holy men of God. Rank immorality had been a long-time tradition of the Catholic hierarchy; however, 904-963 is known as the Pornocracy. During that time of anarchy and confusion, ten popes reigned. [22] Most of them were removed by murder and treachery. This period was also called *the Rule of the Harlots* because, in most

314

cases, it was wicked women behind the throne who ran the papacy. All of them were promoting either their husbands or their sons. [23]

At the same time the popes and the church officers were promoting salvation through the Church over which they presided, they were living lives of ultimate self-indulgence. While they were mercilessly and inhumanely torturing godly men and women, and burning many of them at the stake, they were personally behaving with immoral abandon beyond adequate description. They acted as if there is no God and that morality doesn't matter. For example, Pope John XII (955–963) "was said to have turned the Basilica di San Giovanni in Laterano into a brothel and was accused of adultery, fornication, and incest." He "was an immoral man and whose palace was likened to a brothel. The bishop of Cremona, Luitprand said, 'No honest lady dared to show herself in public, for Pope John had no respect either for single girls, married women, or widows – they were sure to be defiled by him, even on the tombs of the holy apostles, Peter and Paul.' Pope Boniface VIII maintained his position through lavish distribution of stolen money. He was quoted saying, 'to enjoy oneself and lie carnally with women or with boys is no more a sin than rubbing one's hands together.' Pope John XXIII was said to have seduced and violated three hundred nuns. He must have had a strong and insatiable libido, for he kept a harem of no less than two hundred girls. He was called 'the most depraved criminal who ever sat on the papal throne.' A Vatican record says this about him, 'His lordship, Pope John, committed perversity with the wife of his brother, incest with holy nuns, intercourse with virgins, adultery with the married, and all sorts of sex crimes . . . wholly given to sleep and other carnal desires, totally adverse to the life and teaching of Christ . . . he was publicly called the Devil incarnate.' Pope Pius II was said to have been the father of many illegitimate children. He spoke openly of the methods he used to seduce women, and he encouraged young men to also seduce women and even offered to instruct them in methods of self-indulgence." [24]

It should not be difficult for any sane-thinking person to see why a mighty ground-swell of sentiment against the totally corrupt, immoral and bankrupt papacy would develop and grow. Even Catholics found it deplorable. The whole system was a reproach.

A TURNING POINT HAD BEEN REACHED

The vast bulk of raw power was still in the hands of the papacy and the Roman Catholic Church, but it wasn't what it had once been. It would take centuries before those outside Catholicism would feel much relief, and millions more would die at the hands of the Roman executioners; however, a turning-point had been reached. At this early stage, the rulers of Europe who opposed Rome did so primarily over power and control, not over theology. Reformers began to appear on the scene in increasing numbers, but the sad truth is that most of them did not oppose the evil theology of Rome; they were only interested in reforming the rampant corruption that marked this perverted entity. Most of the kings and reformers who opposed Rome also opposed and persecuted first-century, New Testament Christians and churches. For hundreds of years to come, those in the unbroken line of true churches continued to routinely face merciless atrocities; however, multitudes of them remained true to the faith that was once delivered to the saints.

---

[1] Philip Schaff, *History of the Christian Church,* vol. 5, (Peabody, Massachusetts: Hendrickson Publishers, 2002), 507-508.

[2] E.H. Broadbent, *The Pilgrim Church,* (Grand Rapids, Michigan: GOSPEL FOLIO PRESS, 1999), 110.

[3] Schaff, 512.

[4] Broadbent, 111.

[5] Schaff, 508-509.

[6] L.P. Brockett, *The Bogomils of Bulgaria and Bosnia; or the Early Protestants of the East,* (Philadelphia: American Baptist Publications Society, 1879. Classic Reprints #43 by Vance Publications, Pensacola, FL., 2001), 73.

[7] Ibid., 75.

[8] Ibid.

[9] Alexis Muston, *The Israel of the Alps: A Complete History of the Waldenses and Their Colonies,* vol. 1, (London: Blackie & Son, Paternoster Buildings, E.C., 1875, reprinted Paris, Arkansas: The Baptist Standard Bearer, Inc.), 31.

[10] Ibid.

[11] Ibid., 32.

[12] Ibid., 42-44.

[13] Schaff, 432-433.

[14] Carl Deimer, Professor, *History of Christianity II,* Video Lecture 24, Liberty University DLP, 2004

[15] Schaff, 215.

[16] Ibid., 208-210.

[17] Deimer, *History of Christianity I,* Video Lecture 23.

[18] Schaff, 777.

[19] Deimer.

[20] Ibid. Lecture 23.

[21] *Wikipedia,* (en.wikipedia.org/wiki/Pope_Martin_V).

[22] Ibid., /wiki/List_of_sexually_active_popes.

[23] Deimer, Lecture 16.

[24] *Roman Catholicism,* (www.eaec.org/cults/romancatholic.htm).

Crusades Against Dissenters

The three papal inducements to join a Crusade were:

1. Men could fight the enemies of God
2. Receive eternal life for doing so
3. Receive indulgences to cover whatever sins they might commit

The Crusade Against the Albigenses (1209)

Pope Innocent III wanted to remove the heretics from Toulouse, so he proclaimed a Crusade against the ruler of Provence. It lasted for thirty years, and the region was decimated.

The Crusade Against Bosnia (1238)

Pope Gregory IX proclaimed a Crusade against Bosnia to remove the Bogomils. After about two years under the leadership of the king of Sclavonia, Bosnia was *purged*.

The Crusade Against Savoy (1486)

Waldenses were flourishing in Savoy on the western flank of the Alps. Pope Innocent VIII issued a bull of extermination against them because they were converting people to their doctrine. A hoard of marauders and eighteen thousand French troops marched into Savoy to exterminate the Waldenses. This Crusade failed.

The Massacre of the Whole Population of Val Louise (1488)

The Crusaders moved against a strong community of Waldenses at the town of Briancon. When the believers retreated to a large mountain cave, the Catholic forces sealed off the entrance with wood and set it on fire. More than three thousand Waldenses were massacred.

Chapter 26

Reform and Reformers

The utter corruption and depravity of the papacy caused even Catholics to revolt. Bishops and lower level church officials throughout the system resented the cancer at the top. Though most of them were also corrupt and immoral, they didn't like the exploitation and oppression of the pope. Furthermore, civil leaders throughout Europe hated the heavy-handed, dictatorial power of the papacy over them. Resistance among civil leaders grew everywhere.

REFORM

It was generally agreed in most quarters that fundamental change must occur. The pope could not continue as the ecclesiastical and political dictator of Europe. The corruption and financial exploitation of the masses by the papacy must be addressed; however, there was not a general consensus as to how the Roman Catholic ecclesiastic-political system should be reformed. (It should be kept in mind that during the Middle Ages, the Roman Catholic Church dominated the political entities of Europe. Until the time of Boniface VIII at the end of the 14th century, popes had their way and subdued kings and other political leaders who might challenge them.) Viewpoints on reform fell loosely into three categories.

Classical Reformation

Some reformers believed the Roman Catholic Church had lost its way and ceased to be the true church of Jesus Christ. They wanted to do away with the Catholic Church altogether and start over. They wanted to reform the church to what it was when Constantine first wed it to the state. They were not against all that the Roman Catholic Church had become; however, they felt the solution was the initiation of a new, purer church as it was before exploitation, immorality and corruption became so rampant. They believed the state church, which became the Roman Catholic Church, had at one time been the true church. They also believed that it had lost its way and was no longer the true church.

The classical reformers were neither against a state church, nor many of the corrupt doctrines and practices of the Catholics. They continued to embrace universal church theology, baptismal regeneration, infant baptism and many other unscriptural positions. These reformers saw themselves as re-establishing the true church, which had died mainly because of corruption. They agreed that some Roman Catholic Church theology was bad, but they believed most Catholic theology was sound. To them, the thing that had ruined the Catholic Church was bad practices, not bad theology.

This idea of reform ignored altogether the concept of perpetuity or an unbroken line of true churches from Christ forward. Perpetuity as guaranteed by Jesus Christ in **Matthew 16:18** means the line of true churches will continue unbroken until Jesus' return. It does not allow for the line to be broken and then later restarted. The thinking of the classical reformers was out of step with the teaching of the Bible on the issue of perpetuity.

Protestant reformers such as Luther, Zwingli and Calvin were classical reformers.

Radical Reformation

The radical reformers really were not reformers in the true sense of the word. They were reformers only in the sense that they said change needed to come. Their intent was neither to reform and clean up the Roman Catholic Church nor to start a new church.

320

They simply wanted a return to first-century, New Testament Christianity. They believed the Roman Catholic Church should go. They did not seek its reformation; they thought it should be abandoned. They saw Roman Catholicism as evil, fraudulent and a reproach to true Christianity. They had no interest in reforming a church that never was legitimate. They embraced only the Scriptures as the rule for doctrine and practice. They fully rejected tradition and all of the Scripture-contradicting beliefs and practices that had entered Christendom as a result thereof. They also rejected the concept of *church* as seen by Constantine and totally refused the idea of a state church.

This group insisted on the core beliefs of the New Testament and thought all churches should return to first-century, New Testament doctrine and practice. The Waldenses, Anabaptists and other practitioners of New Testament Christianity constituted an unbroken line of churches that had existed from the time of Christ. The radical reformers simply embraced and championed the beliefs and practices of true churches that had existed from the start.

For centuries, primitive Christians and churches had been the primary objects of Roman Catholic scorn and persecution. It is not difficult to see why they did all they could legitimately do to escape the cruel, merciless false church that had for centuries tormented and murdered their kind in the name of Christ. With all their might, they resisted Catholic efforts to destroy them and they were encouraged when mighty men of God such as John Wycliffe and John Huss rose up and championed their causes against the Catholics. Often they saw hope for themselves in movements against Catholicism. In their desperation and desire for relief, sometimes they were deceived by thinking reformers were like them. (Some reformers were, but some were not.) Sometimes they joined reformers and reform movements only to find, after great hurt, that the reformers did not share their first-century, New Testament convictions. They were often used and betrayed by those who were no more than classical reformers. Their experience with Martin Luther is a case in point. "There never was a moment when Constantinianism stood unchallenged. In the company of the 'heretics' the New Testament was honored . . . a Church based on personal faith will challenge the concept of a Church embracing all. The battle between these two concepts of the Church had been raging for twelve centuries when Luther put the trumpet of reform to his lips." [1] For a while many primitive Christians thought Luther was one of them and supported him. After a while his true colors surfaced, and these primitive Christians withdrew their support. It would be totally dishonest to say they were Protestants simply because they were briefly involved with Martin Luther. They were continuously around in great numbers long before the first Protestant reformer. They were not breaking away from the Catholic Church; they were never a part of it. They were not out to start a reformation of new churches; they thought the reformers were finally returning to the true unbroken line of New Testament doctrine and practice. Sadly they were wrong. Most of the reformers proved to be very similar to the Catholics in doctrine and practice. That includes their oppressive approach toward all who failed to join them. Because of the brief involvements of some of these primitive Christians with classical reformers, many shallow-thinking historians identify them and their churches as Protestants. They were not. They were people of the unbroken line, people who had embraced the core doctrine and practices of the New Testament from the start. In their desperate need for freedom from Rome's tyranny, they supported some of the reformers whom they mistakenly thought to have embraced their cause. It is not honest to deny them as people of the unbroken line and accuse them of being no more than reformers.

> **Radical reformers wanted to return to first-century, New Testament Christianity**

Counter Reformation

The counter reformers merely wanted to clean up the inside of the Roman Catholic Church; they did not want to destroy it. These were those who were against starting any church outside the Catholic Church.

REFORMERS

Keep in mind that the chief force undermining the papal monopoly was growing nationalism and an intensifying desire for political independence from the papacy. The reformers themselves were not interested in political independence; they were consumed with the evils of Catholicism, particularly those of the papacy. As corruption in the Catholic system grew worse, the numbers of reformers swelled and their voices became louder. Sympathy and passion for reform spread. The response of the papacy was to destroy the reformers. The popes turned on reformers with the same ferocity that they had exercised for centuries against those primitive Christians who had refused to embrace Catholicism. The situation became increasingly hostile and bloody and eventually erupted into open war.

A history of this sort would be incomplete without at least a brief look at some of the early reformers. Keep in mind that a few of these reformers were either originally a part of the line of true churches reaching back to Christ or became a part of it. (Those who became a part of the unbroken line did so by trusting Christ as personal savior, by embracing New Testament doctrine and practices and by believer's baptism by immersion.) Other reformers never became a part of the unbroken line of true churches. Instead, they broke with Catholicism and started some new movement or *church*. There is a vast difference. No new movement or church that started short of Jesus Christ could ever be considered a part of the unbroken line. To be a part of the unbroken line of true churches, it is vital to tie into the doctrine and practice of Jesus Christ. Sadly, most of the reformers merely wanted to clean up the filth of the Catholic Church or start a new church very much like the Catholic Church. They were not interested in a return to the pure teachings of the New Testament. In fact, most of them rejected and wanted no part of those primitive Christians who were there and who had been there all along.

The early reformers and reform efforts we are about to examine by no means constitute a complete list, although it is sufficient to shed light on the spirit of reform that intensified in the medieval world which found itself enslaved to Catholicism.

Councilor Efforts

Counter reformers within the Catholic Church thought reform could come through councils. Popes were to call councils, but a group of cardinals called a council at Pisa in 1409. It was called to deal with three issues: reform, heretics and the papal schism. Reform was never addressed. Another council was held at Constance (1414-1418). The same three issues were on the agenda. It resulted only in the burning of John Huss at the stake and more confusion over who was pope. A third council at Pavia (1423) failed. Several councils were called between 1431 and 1445. Only a pope could legitimately call a council and under pressure during this period, popes did call councils. When the bishops arrived, the pope would often dismiss them and call for re-convening in another city. [2] The popes thus thwarted all efforts toward reform until 1460, at which time Pope Pius II published the papal bull *Execrabilis*. This bull says that an attempt to reform the papacy through a council is heresy. It said the monarchical form of government in the church was the one given through Peter. This bull says popes receive their "authority directly from Christ without mediation." [3] In spite of continued corruption, this bull ended efforts to reform the papacy through councils.

> *Execrabilis* declares that reforming the papacy
> through a council is heresy

William of Ockham (1300-1345)

William of Ockham was an intellectual Franciscan monk who studied at Oxford in England. He attacked the wealth and lavish lifestyle of the papacy by arguing that Christ and the apostles did not own property either individually or corporately. [4] He taught that Christ alone is the head of the church and questioned the theological basis of the papacy. [5] After being persecuted in England because of the questions he raised about the legitimacy of the papal system, he fled to France where he thought his views would be welcome.

Ockham was excommunicated, [6] but his voluminous writings paved the way for reformation and encouraged others to stand against the papacy.

John Wycliffe (1329-1384)

John Wycliffe was also an Oxford scholar. He lived when the papacy was divided between Rome and Avignon. The French and English were at war; the French popes of that era were supporting the French against England. Wycliffe preached against the pope's secular sovereignty and wrote a tract calling the pope, "the anti-Christ, the proud, worldly priest of Rome." [7] He said the pope had no more power to bind and loose than any other priest. He also said that if pressed by necessity, temporal lords could seize the possessions of the clergy. Furthermore Wycliffe attacked the whole concept of the seven sacraments. He was especially outspoken against transubstantiation, [8] which had been officially decreed in 1215. [9]

John Wycliffe was particularly passionate about the authority of the Scriptures. He taught that the Scriptures were the sole authority for doctrine and Christian living. With vigor he attacked the belief that tradition be considered with Scripture as authoritative. In his book *Of the Truth of Holy Scripture* (1378), he taught that the teachings of the Scriptures are the final word on every subject. Both he and his Catholic opponents recognized the far-reaching consequences of this teaching. Furthermore, Wycliffe rejected the allegorical method of exegesis (interpreting Scriptures by reading hidden, subjective meanings into them) which was common of that era. He said Scripture should be interpreted by Scripture, and that the primary and literal sense of a text should first be taken before moving to figurative meanings and applications. Wycliffe also rejected the concept of the universal Catholic Church. [10]

The time was ripe for the message of John Wycliffe. Englishmen resented the collusion between Rome and the French enemy. They did not like the papal hierarchy and welcomed the stance of Wycliffe against the Roman Catholic Church. He defended England's right against foreign encroachment and assailed much of the doctrine of Catholicism. When local church authorities rose up against Wycliffe, the duke of Lancaster protected him. [11] Pope

Gregory XI condemned Wycliffe and demanded that he be imprisoned; however, Wycliffe was viewed as an English patriot, and the nobility of England stood with him against the pope.

"In his sermons, tracts and larger writings, Wycliff brought Scripture and common sense to bear . . . Wycliff is the foremost religious pamphleteer that has arisen in England." [12] Wycliffe's greatest impact came by his giving the English-speaking people their first Bible in their own tongue. The popes had realized that when any people receive the Scriptures in their own tongue, those people invariably becomes more antagonistic toward the papacy and the Roman Catholic Church. "The Council of Toulouse, 1229, had forbidden the use of the Bible to laymen." [13] The papacy thus considered it heresy to translate the Bible into any language. [14] Wycliffe's translation was from the Latin Vulgate. It stands forth as the champion of the open Bible and of the concept that the Bible is a book for every man. Few acts have had the impact of Wycliffe's gift of the Bible to English-speaking people. It is one of history's most definitive events in breaking the Catholic stranglehold. That break was not completed overnight, but Wycliffe's English Bible was a huge contribution.

> **The Council of Toulouse, 1229, had forbidden the use of the Bible to laymen**

The Lollards

Among John Wycliffe's numerous contributions was his commitment and approach to evangelism. Wycliffe taught young men and sent them two-by-two throughout England. They went forth teaching, preaching and winning souls to Christ. They were known as Lollards. As early as 1300, the name Lollard was used in reference to some in England regarded as heretics by the Roman Catholics. [15] Obviously the positions espoused by John Wycliffe did not originate in England with him. They were already latent in the society before he was born. It cannot be said that Wycliffe started a new movement in England; the movement was already there before he was born. He merely became a champion of the movement and gave it great identity.

The teachings of John Wycliffe found sympathy not only with the nobility of England but also with believers who already existed there. The nobles were attracted to Wycliffe because his stance helped them in gaining political independence from the papacy. Primitive Christians were drawn to Wycliffe because they heard in him many of the truths they had long embraced.

The Lollards were enormously successful in England. "It was said that two men could not be found together and one not be a Lollard or a Wycliffite." [16] Because of the success of the Lollards, the House of Commons presented petitions to King Henry IV asking for the modification of laws against them. His answer was a signed warrant for the burning at the stake of Thomas Badly, who was accused of denying transubstantiation. Sir John Oldcastle (Lord Cobham), who was a distinguished soldier, was a Lollard. When Henry V came to the throne, he seized Sir John's castle and burned him at the stake. After Oldcastle's death, "a law was passed that whoever read the Scriptures in English would forfeit land, chattels, goods, and life, and be condemned as a heretic to God, an enemy to the crown, and a traitor to the kingdom; that he should not have any benefit of sanctuary; and that, if he continued obstinate, or relapsed after being pardoned, he should first be hanged for treason against the king, then burned for heresy against God." [17]

John Huss (1374-1415)

Nationalism was also growing in Bohemia and the Czechs wanted out from under the domination of Germany and Rome. Universities had come on the scene and there was an exchange of scholars between the University of Oxford and the University of Prague.

John Wycliffe was held in the highest regard in Bohemia and was sometimes called the fifth evangelist. Wycliffism spread and John Huss who was born ten years after the death of Wycliffe became its chief spokesman. "Wycliffism passed out of view in England; but Hussitism, in spite of the most bitter persecution by the Jesuits, has trickled down in pure though small streamlets into the religious history of modern times, notably through the Moravians of Herrnhut." [18]

Like Wycliffe, John Huss was an avid student of the Scriptures. Both embraced the core doctrine and practices of New Testament Christianity. Huss became head of the philosophy department at the University of Prague and pastor of the Bethlehem Church. The building was a large, three-story cube with no floor. It was open with a pulpit halfway up one side wall. Huss preached to hundreds. "His sincere faith and striking abilities, with his eloquence and charm of manner, worked mightily among people already prepared by labors of the Waldenses who had been before him." Multitudes were saved and the country soon became polarized between the German element that supported Rome and the Czechs who supported the teachings of Wycliffe. [19] Many Catholic efforts were launched against Huss but he was relatively safe in Bohemia.

Eventually the pope publicly burned Wycliffe's writings, excommunicated Huss and summonsed him to appear before the Council of Constance. [20] The king of Bohemia, the nobility, the university and the majority of the people supported Huss and his teaching. He was relatively safe in Bohemia and did not want to go to Constance. Huss knew the Catholics killed those whom they excommunicated. The Holy Roman Emperor, Constance Sigismund, promised Huss safe conduct and a right of passage to and from the conference; however, the emperor did not have the means necessary to guarantee Huss' safety. When Huss arrived in Constance, the Catholics immediately threw him in prison. The bishop simply said, "We do not keep our word to heretics." [21] John Huss was then condemned by the Council, and on July 6, 1415, he was burned at the stake. [22]

Those in Bohemia who embraced first-century Christianity became known as Hussites. John Huss' followers were called Bohemian Brethren. They were angry over what happened to their leader and carried on the movement with the sword. They struck fear into the hearts of the Germans. [23]

OBSERVATIONS

John Wycliffe and John Huss Embraced New Testament Doctrine and Practice

It should be observed that both Wycliffe and Huss simply plugged into the primitive Christian positions which were already there; they did not originate new doctrine or practices. Neither started a new church or movement. Rather they became a part of the unbroken line of doctrine and practice that dated back to Christ. They were radical reformers.

It is not difficult to see that through these men the unbroken line of true churches continued. Each connected to a line and community of believers whose spiritual lineage connected back to the first century.

There Were Many Other Reformers

It should also be observed that there were other reformers. Some were classical, some were radical and many were counter. All of them put pressure on the papacy.

All Efforts Toward Reform Met with Total Resistance and Intensified Persecution

Let it finally be observed that all efforts toward reform brought resistance from the papacy. The popes did not want reform or change in any form or fashion. As far as they were concerned, it was not going to happen and they would do whatever it took to stop it. Like a cornered animal under attack, the greater they felt the threat to be, the more vicious and radical their opposition and resistance efforts became. They intensified the Inquisition. Jesuits were dispatched to hunt and kill reformers and dissenters. Crusades were mustered. When the Protestant Reformation began, a Catholic army was raised to squelch it.

Life for all who either opposed or who refused to be a part of Catholicism actually got worse.

The Roman Catholic Church Could Not Stop Reform

The movement to change the system would not be denied. The Catholic Church was hopelessly corrupt in both composition and practice. Nationalism had arrived. Secular leaders would no longer tolerate domination and merciless exploitation from the Catholic Church and the popes who master-minded such evil, domination and exploitation.

In our next chapter we shall see how the spirit of reform matured into a full-fledged Protestant Reformation.

---

[1] Leonard Verduin, *The Reformers and Their Stepchildren,* (Grand Rapids, Michigan: William B. Eerdmans Publishing Company, 1964), 35.

[2] Carl Deimer, Professor, *History of Christianity I,* Video Lecture 24, Liberty University DLP, 2004.

[3] Philip Schaff, *History of the Christian Church,* vol. 6, (Peabody, Massachusetts: Hendrickson Publishers, 2002), 420.

[4] Ibid., 191.

[5] Deimer.

[6] Schaff.

[7] Ibid., 316.

[8] Schaff, 336-337.

[9] Deimer.

[10] E.H. Broadbent, *The Pilgrim Church,* (Grand Rapids, Michigan: GOSPEL FOLIO PRESS, 1999), 138-140.

[11] Schaff, 317.

[12] Ibid., 319.

[13] Ibid., 341.

[14] Deimer.

[15] Schaff, 350.

[16] Broadbent, 141.

[17] Ibid., 142.

[18] Schaff, 358.

[19] Broadbent, 143.

[20] Ibid.

[21] Deimer.

[22] Broadbent, 144.

[23] Deimer.

Reformation of the Catholic Church

It was generally agreed that fundamental change must occur in the Catholic Church. These were three different viewpoints on the needed change.

Classical Reformation

This group wanted to reform the church to what it was when Constantine first wed it to the state. They thought that bad practices, not bad theology, had ruined the Catholic Church. They continued to embrace universal church theology, baptismal regeneration, infant baptism and many other unscriptural positions.

Radical Reformation

This group insisted on the core beliefs of the New Testament and thought all churches should return to first-century, New Testament doctrine and practice.

Counter Reformation

The counter reformers merely wanted to clean up the inside of the Roman Catholic Church; they did not want to destroy it. They were against starting any church outside the Catholic Church.

Reformers of the Catholic Church

Councilor Efforts

Counter reformers thought reform could come through councils. A group of cardinals called a number of councils to deal with reform, heretics and the papal schism. Finally, Pope Pius II published the papal bull *Execrabilis* which declared that reforming the papacy through a council is heresy.

William of Ockham (1300-1345)

He was an intellectual Franciscan monk who taught that Christ alone is the head of the church. He attacked the wealth of the papacy by arguing that Christ and the apostles did not own property. His voluminous writings paved the way for reformation and encouraged others to stand against the papacy.

John Wycliffe (1329-1384)

He was an Oxford scholar who believed in the authority of the Scriptures. He assailed much of the doctrine of Catholicism and was defended by the duke of Lancaster when the local church rose up against him. His greatest impact was giving the English-speaking people their first Bible in their own tongue.

The Lollards

They were young men sent out two-by-two throughout England, teaching, preaching and winning souls to Christ.

John Huss (1374-1415)

He lived in Bohemia and embraced the core doctrine and practices of New Testament Christianity. He was the pastor of the Bethlehem Church and multitudes were saved. When he went to the Council of Constance, he was thrown in prison and then burned at the stake.

Chapter 27

The Protestant Reformation

The intent of this historical account is to present a balanced picture. Deliberate effort has been made to avoid undue emphasis on Catholicism or Protestantism. Both of these definitive movements were players on the stage. There are many who take the position that in Christendom there are only two divisions: Catholics and Protestants. That is untrue. As we have already seen, there is a third group called first-century New Testament Christians: those who, from Christ to the present, stayed true to *"the faith which was once delivered unto the saints,"* **Jude 3**. An intelligent understanding of professing Christendom from Jesus to the present would not be possible apart from a working knowledge of all three. The main intent of this book has been to view the years with the New Testament Christians in mind; however this account is not only about them. It is designed to also present a *working knowledge* of their counterparts and the events of time which so dramatically impacted and molded them.

The New Testament Christians were here by varying names long before there was a reformation with its Protestants. These New Testament Christians pre-date Protestantism, which makes it impossible to call them Protestants. A large number of New Testament Christians were doctrinally and practically sound. In their efforts to liberate themselves from the awful tyranny of Catholic oppression, some of these primitive Christians became involved with various elements of Protestantism; but they were not Protestants. Long before the Protestants initiated their reform efforts, these primitive Christians were already on the scene. They were neither trying to get out of Catholicism (for they had never been in it) nor attempting to start a new church (for they were already a part of the unbroken line of churches established by Jesus Christ).

The Protestant phenomenon was such a massive historical occurrence with world-wide implications that it must be given treatment. In view of the totalitarian and corrupt entity which Catholicism became, the Protestant Reformation was a natural development in the history of Christendom. Already we've heard the calls for change and examined a few of the early movements toward reform. In this chapter we shall look mostly at the classical reformers and those who are the true Protestants. This will help us better identify and understand the line of New Testament churches that continued right through this era. It is not too difficult to differentiate them from the Protestants. The Protestants surely identified them and engaged in the same oppressive tactics against them that had long been employed by the Catholics.

Christendom is composed of New Testament Christians, Catholics and Protestants

---

CLASSICAL VERSUS COUNTER REFORM

Keep in mind that classical reformers had in mind the replacement of the medieval Roman Catholic Church with a new church closely akin to the state church of Constantine. Conversely, the counter reformers wanted to keep and clean up the medieval Roman Catholic Church. They were not opposed to the doctrine or the theological practices of Catholicism. They opposed both the corruption and the absolute power of the papacy. Even those political states that were staunchly Catholic did not want the pope dictating their politics and taking their money.

As nationalism strengthened throughout Europe, two main directions with regard to Christianity emerged. Those nations such as Spain that desired counter reform became independent from the papacy but stayed staunchly Catholic. Those nations desiring classical reform became independent from the papacy and formed new state churches very similar to the Roman Catholic Church. These were the Protestants.

From a geographical standpoint, those nations north of the Alps generally became Protestant, while those nations south of the Alps generally remained Catholic. There were Catholic and Protestant populations within each nation. In each case, one side or the other prevailed and the nation became known as Catholic or Protestant. Spain, France, Italy and Ireland were predominately Catholic while Germany, Switzerland, England, Scotland and the Scandinavian countries were predominately Protestant. In addition to Catholics and Protestants in all of the emerging nations, there were large and widespread communities of New Testament Christians who were neither Catholic nor Protestant. Among these there were great leaders who preached New Testament doctrine and practices and who preached against the evils of Catholicism. Even though they were not trying to clean up the Catholic Church or out to start some new church, history has identified these as radical reformers. They were simply the people of the unbroken line who wanted nothing more than liberty to practice their faith.

GROUNDWORK FOR REFORMATION

We've seen two of the early radical reformers, John Wycliffe (England) and John Huss (Bohemia). Remember that these were not true reformers; they were simply leaders who preached the core doctrine and practices embraced by primitive, New Testament Christians from the time of Jesus onward. They actually identified with the communities of primitive Christians in their locales; and because of their immense successes, those communities assumed their names. In both cases, the Catholics rigorously opposed them and made every effort to stop them, although both were popular with the people and had limited support within the nobility.

John Wycliffe's prolific writings influenced multitudes. His translation of the Bible put the Scriptures into the hands of the common English-speaking man. "The translation of the Bible had its due effect, and great numbers came to acknowledge it as the only guide for faith and conduct." [1] The Scriptures have an enlightening power. King David observed, *"The commandment of the LORD is pure, enlightening the eyes,"* **Psalm 19:8**. In the light of the Scripture, the peasants of England realized that *"God is no respecter of persons,"* **Acts 10:34**. They woke up to the fact "their enslavement under their luxurious rulers was irreligious because it was unjust." [2] A Peasant Revolt led by Wat Tyler erupted (1377-1381). Since the nobility and the church owned the land and ruled the peasants primarily as slaves, the revolt united the nobility against the peasants. This rebellion marked the beginning of the end of serfdom in medieval England; [3] although, since it was largely the peasants who had embraced the positions of John Wycliffe, strong measures were taken to put down Wycliffe's movement. Remarkably Wycliffe died a natural death in 1384, but his followers met with increasing oppression from the Roman Catholics.

A similar scenario occurred in Bohemia. After John Huss was burned at the stake, many of his followers fought for the cause he championed. For a while, Jan Žižka led a successful warfare with the small town of Tabor as its military and spiritual center. Nobility and peasantry united; but the pope raised crusades against them, and the Hussites were eventually defeated. [4]

In both cases, the success of these primitive Christians was relatively short-lived. The Catholics were able to subdue them, but they were not able to squelch the demand for change and reform that was growing in these countries and others across Europe. In the cases of Wycliffe and Huss, the desire was simply the freedom to preach the Christ of the Bible and His teachings. They were not looking to start a new church; they wanted a revival of the original church.

Others who called for change had different motives. Some differed slightly with Rome's theology, but most wanted a new, reformed church. They wanted a church much like the Roman Catholic Church in doctrine and practices, but one without the corruption. Their success did not come altogether as a result of their theology or their reform efforts. The nationalistic desire of the nobility and political leaders throughout the land to be free from the yoke of papal oppression was the central driving force for reformation. Some of these strong lords were willing to back and protect reformers, not because they were sympathetic to their religious messages, but because they saw in the reformers the possibility of throwing off the papal yoke.

The desire of New Testament churches is revival, not reform

MARTIN LUTHER

Such was the case of Martin Luther, the famous German reformer. By the beginning of the sixteenth century, Spain had become united and was the strongest nation in Europe. France and England had distanced themselves politically from the pope. Other emerging nations were exercising greater independence from Rome, and the papacy was feeling the financial impact. As other nations drew away from the papacy, the pope increased pressure on Germany for revenues. The bishops were putting extreme pressure on the German people for money. [5] The huge drain of money from Germany to Rome had a major negative impact upon the German economy.

Frederick III

At the time (early sixteenth century), Frederick III, Elector of Saxony, was highly regarded for his intelligence, wisdom and piety. Though Frederick was a staunch Catholic, he was impressed with the new learning and enlightenment of his day. The Crusaders had brought copies of the Greek New Testament from Constantinople, and a renaissance of learning and culture was flourishing in Europe. Less emphasis was being placed on God, and a much more humanistic view of life was becoming the norm. In 1502 Frederick founded the University of Wittenberg. [6]

Wittenberg

Martin Luther was born in 1483 to strict German parents who gave him pious training. In 1501 he entered the best university in Germany (Erfurt) to study law. Erfurt was close to Bohemia, and Luther was exposed to the influence of John Huss. During the summer of 1505, at a time of great fear during a lightning storm,

Luther vowed to become a monk if God would spare his life. Early in his life, Luther had seen the emptiness of Catholic theology. During a trip to Rome, he became especially disillusioned when he saw other priests rush through the mass. They were paid per mass, and Luther realized that the whole operation was no more than a money-making scheme. In 1511 he moved to Wittenberg, where he lived in an Augustine monastery and earned a doctor of theology degree in the university. Luther became intensely interested in the gospel. Neither the pope nor his Augustine mentors had been able to give him peace about his personal salvation. He began to study the Bible in the original languages and as he studied Romans, he realized that justification before God is possible only by faith. In 1515 Luther accepted justification by faith and determined to stand for Christ regardless of the cost. He became a professor at the University of Wittenberg. [7]

Frederick III was highly impressed with Luther and became his protector. [8] It would have been impossible for Luther to succeed apart from the protection he received from Frederick. For example, when John Huss was to appear before the Catholics, they burned him at the stake. When Frederick saw that the Catholics were about to kill Martin Luther, he kidnapped Luther and hid him for a year at Wartburg castle. He did so at great risk to his own life; however, he had enough military strength and backing from other German nobility to succeed. [9]

Luther was able to succeed because of protection from Frederick III

Indulgences

The sale of indulgences became the catalyst for the open fracture of the corrupt Catholic Church. Remember that a Catholic *indulgence* is essentially a grant from the Church to sin. Webster says that in the Roman Catholic Church, an indulgence is "a freeing from all or part of the punishment due in purgatory for a sin." [10]

As Luther continued his professorship at Wittenberg, Pope Leo X, one of the most worldly, avaricious and extravagant of all the popes, was building St. Peter's Basilica at an enormous cost. This unscrupulous pope issued a papal bull for the sale of indulgences to raise money for the project. Spain, England and France ignored the bull; but the weak German ruler, Maximilian, yielded to the pope. Pope Leo divided Germany into three districts and for a price appointed Albert Archbishop of Mainz and Magdeburg. The utterly corrupt Albert borrowed heavily from a bank in Augsburg to pay for the bishoprics. In an agreement with the pope, Albert had permission to keep half the money from indulgence sales. The Augsburg bank backed the arrangement. Archbishop Albert appointed Johann Tetzel his commissioner and Tetzel employed sub-agents. [11] Tetzel traveled with great pomp and circumstance through Germany, extravagantly lauding the pope's bull. The people were piously enticed to purchase indulgences for their own benefit and for the benefit of their departed relatives and friends "whom they might release from their sufferings in purgatory 'as soon as the penny tinkles in the box.'" [12]

Luther's 95 Theses

This occurred where Luther lived; he was witness to the lurid activity. November 1 was the Catholic all saints day (when all the saints were to be recognized); and according to this satanic teaching, on the night before (Halloween) evil spirits came out of their graves to revel. Luther had been working on an answer and affront to the evils he saw in Catholicism. He organized them in the form of *95 Theses* which he nailed on the main door of the Wittenberg Church on the night of October 31, 1517. He chose that date because the feast that was held at the church on this occasion attracted professors, students and people from all directions. The theses attacked the under pins of Catholicism, including purgatory as well as the position of the pope. In short, his *95 Theses* said that salvation is only by the blood of Jesus Christ, and that it cannot be purchased. [13] They were quickly printed, and within three months they were circulating throughout Europe. "They sounded the trumpet of the Reformation. They found a hearty response with liberal scholars and enemies of monastic obscurantism, with German patriots longing for emancipation from Italian control, and with thousands of plain Christians . . . ." [14]

CATHOLIC RESPONSE AND
THE BREAK WITH ROME

Excommunication

Many agreed with Luther, but many did not. He was immediately attacked by Johann Tetzel, who besides being the chief seller of indulgences, was also prior of a Dominican convent, a doctor of philosophy and a papal inquisitor. The Catholics, especially the Dominicans, were determined to silence Luther; however, Frederick III of Saxony kept Luther from falling into their hands. Tetzel and others blasted Luther, but Luther continued to write. In 1520 he published *The Address to the German Nobility,* in which he demolished the pope's claim that Rome had spiritual power over temporal authority. Soon he wrote *The Babylonian Captivity* in which he challenged the sacramental system of Rome. Later that year, he wrote *The Freedom of the Christian Man,* in which he challenged the theology of Rome and advocated the priesthood of every believer.

In June of 1520, Pope Leo X excommunicated Luther with the papal bull *Exsurge Domine.* Luther received the bull which declared him a heretic and answered it with a tract in which he mocked Pope Leo X, called him the Antichrist and denounced him as "a hardened heretic, an antichristian suppresser of the Scriptures, a blasphemer. . . ." [15] In turn the pope ordered Luther's writings to be burned. At 9:00 a.m. on December 10, 1520 in the presence of a large number of professors and students, Luther burned the papal bull together with papal decretals, the canon law and other Catholic writings.

The Diet of Worms

In 1521 the pope demanded that Charles V, Emperor of the Holy Roman Empire, force Luther to a diet (a formal assembly) or hearing in the city of Worms. By that time, Luther had become so overwhelmingly popular that the Catholics feared to do him bodily harm. Charles, along with letters of safe conduct from Frederick and other German noblemen, guaranteed Luther the protection of the Empire. It was on April 17-18, 1521 that Luther defended his anti-Catholic writings before the notables of his world, most of whom were bent on his destruction. He defended his stance, refused to recant and uttered the famous words, "Here I stand. I cannot do otherwise. God help me! Amen."

The Edict of Worms

A few days later the Edict of Worms was passed. It made Luther an outlaw and placed Frederick in jeopardy from his Catholic neighbors. [16] It was at this time when Frederick kidnapped Luther to Wartburg in an effort to insure his safety. The pope officially demanded the German emperor to end Luther and his movement; however, the torch had been lit and would not be extinguished. German nobles took sides. Luther and others continued to write.

The German Peasants

Many of the peasants were primitive Christians. They were often called Anabaptists and in some circles they are known as *the medieval underworld.* This group pre-existed the Reformation and "had its own power and momentum quite apart from Luther . . . It may safely be said that a person could not spend the span of a human life anywhere in Europe without coming into contact personally with the 'heretic.'" [17] "There is every reason to believe that the Reformers were at the first sympathetic toward much of the old heritage of the 'heretic.' They said things that cheered the hearts of people who had been conditioned" by centuries of first-century doctrine and practice. At first they thought the Reformers were the answers to their prayers."[18] They thought Luther was coming to their side and supported his efforts in an uprising against the nobility. They were mistaken. When Luther was weak, he needed them, but he was not willing to alienate the nobility. He did not think the Reformation could survive without the backing of the nobility. Luther needed the support of the strong and wealthy more than he needed the support of the weak peasants who were more compatible to his doctrine. He turned on the peasants and advised a wholesale suppression of their uprising. Thousands of them perished in the widespread bloodshed of the Peasants' War of 1523-1525. [19] This had the impact of making Luther's Protestant Reformation an upper class movement and gave it power to succeed against the Catholics.

> ### Thousands of peasants perished in the Peasants' War of 1523-1525

The Augsburg Confession

After years of struggle and Catholic efforts to eradicate Lutheranism, a conference was convened in Augsburg, Germany in the summer of 1530. On June 21 through a series of remarkable events, the Augsburg Confession was signed by seven German princes. This document established Lutheranism. [20] In 1531 a group of princes sympathetic to Lutheranism organized the Schmalkaldic League for mutual defense. The Protestant Reformation would not be terminated.

THE REFORM WILDFIRE

Scandinavia

Lutheranism quickly spread to Scandinavia. Denmark followed Luther's reforms. Norway was close behind followed by Iceland, Sweden and Finland. Luther's ideas also spread in Scotland and England.

The Swiss Reformation

- **Huldreich Zwingli** (1484-1531)

    Another major Protestant reformer was an extremely immoral man named Huldreich Zwingli. He professed Christ and became a reformer through academia; he argued that everything should be measured by the Bible. Luther's teachings and the activities in Germany had produced a major uproar in Switzerland. In 1523 at Zwingli's suggestion, the government of Zurich ordered a public debate. The purpose of the debate was to settle the controversy between the reformers and the Catholics on the sole basis of the Scriptures. In preparation for the debate, Zwingli prepared his famous *Sixty-seven Conclusions*. His positions were very similar to those of Luther; he argued against the mass, purgatory and images. The city council of Zurich declared Zwingli the winner of the debate and thus became reformed.

Though there were similarities, Zwingli differed sharply with Luther. Luther taught that there is a very real presence of the very body and blood of Christ in the celebration of the Lord's Supper. Zwingli argued that the bread and wine are only symbolic of Christ's body and blood. This was almost identical to the position taken by John Calvin. [21] Because of political risk, in his public debates, Zwingli was unwilling to take a strong stand against Christ being literally in the Lord's Supper. The result was the loss of some of his strongest followers.

Like Luther, Zwingli maintained the union of church and state and infant baptism.

- **John Calvin**

John Calvin carried on the Reformed movement and is best known for his sovereign grace theology, which is built primarily around five main theological assumptions:

o   The total depravity of man

o   Unconditional election

o   Limited atonement

o   Irresistible grace

o   The perseverance of the saints

Calvin was an attorney headquartered in Geneva. At 26 he published a work titled *Institutes of the Christian Religion,* which had lasting and profound influence. He was also a debater. Like Zwingli, he was intolerant of all who disagreed. Both were advocates of a state church and both followed the Catholic practice of persecuting their enemies, even to the death. [22]

The Anglican Reform

- ### Henry VIII

  The reformation in England was political, not theological. King Henry VIII was regarded as a defender of the Catholic religion; however, he was motivated by the state side and not the church side. Henry wanted a son. His father, Henry VII, wanted his sons to marry royalty. Henry VII's oldest son, Arthur, married Catherine of Aragon (Spain). Arthur died and Henry VII insisted that his younger son, Henry VIII marry Catherine. Catholicism prohibited such marriages, but Henry arranged a papal dispensation. When no surviving males were born to this union, Henry VIII wanted to get rid of Catherine so he could marry the younger and prettier Anne Boleyn. While Henry was still married to Catherine, Anne became pregnant by him. Henry sought an annulment from the pope, who refused it on the grounds that a child (Mary who became queen of Scotland) had already been born to Henry and Catherine. Henry had Mary declared an illegitimate child and promptly married Anne. Elizabeth was born to Henry and Anne; but when Anne had no male child, Henry had her beheaded and married Jane Seymour. [23] She died from an infection shortly after giving birth to Edward. [24] Three years later Henry married Anne of Cleves. The marriage was annulled after six months. [25] A few weeks later, he married Catherine Howard. She was found guilty of treason because of infidelity and was beheaded. [26] Henry then married Catherine Parr, who outlived him. [27]

- ### The Act of Supremacy

  Immediately after his marriage to Anne Boleyn, Henry declared the *Act of Supremacy*. It simply said that the king of England was also the head of the Church of England. The pope promptly excommunicated Henry VIII and Anne Boleyn.

  After the death of Henry VIII, England vacillated between Catholicism and Protestantism. Henry's son, Edward VI, brought in many aspects of Protestantism; but he was followed by Mary, Queen of Scots. She made it her business to rid England of Protestantism and is known as *Bloody Mary*. *Foxes*

Book of Martyrs was written during Mary's rule. Her purge actually brought many sympathizers to the Protestant cause.

Elizabeth followed Mary to the English throne. In 1559 Elizabeth renewed the *Act of Supremacy* and reversed everything Mary did. The pope declared Elizabeth illegitimate and sent the Spanish Armada to remove her from the throne. The Armada was destroyed in the English Channel by the smaller English vessels. [28]

The new Protestant English Church was called Anglican. Doctrinally it is almost identical to the Roman Catholic Church.

CONCLUSION

Keep in mind that the Protestant Reformation was one of the most comprehensive events in the history of the Western world. This study is only a very brief summary. It is important to know something of it; however, the Protestant Reformation is not the path of primitive, New Testament Christians who have existed since Christ. The Protestants are newcomers. They didn't leave the Catholic Church and join the unbroken line of true churches. To the contrary, they left the Catholic Church and started new churches. Jesus promised that churches like the church He initiated would continue in an unbroken line until His return. There is a big gap of almost 15 centuries between Jesus and the start of the Protestant churches. It is therefore impossible that a Protestant church could constitute the church which Jesus Christ said would prevail continuously until His return.

It is not the intent of this book to dwell in depth with churches outside that unbroken line; however, at least a functional, working knowledge of auxiliary people and events helps provide a better, clearer understanding of those churches in the unbroken line.

In our next chapter, we shall take a brief look at the history of the Bible following the canonization of the New Testament. That chapter will be followed with information about those Christians and churches of the unbroken line during and after the Protestant Reformation.

1 E.H. Broadbent, *The Pilgrim Church,* (Grand Rapids, Michigan: GOSPEL FOLIO PRESS, 1999), 141.

2 Ibid.

3 *Wikipedia,* (en.wikipedia.org/wiki/Peasants'_Revolt)

4 Broadbent, 144-145.

5 Carl Deimer, Professor, *History of Christianity II,* Video Lecture 4, Liberty University DLP, 2004.

6 Philip Schaff, *History of the Christian Church,* vol. 7, (Peabody, Massachusetts: Hendrickson Publishers, 2002), 132.

7 Deimer, Lecture 6.

8 Schaff.

9 Ibid., 330-340.

10 *Webster's New World Dictionary with Student Handbook: Young People's Edition*, s.v. "indulgence," (Nashville, Tennessee: The World Publishing Company, 1973), 361.

11 Schaff, 148-152.

12 Ibid., 153.

13 Deimer, Lecture 6.

14 Schaff, 167.

15 Ibid., 247-248.

16 Gordon Rupp, *The Reformation Crisis,* ed. Joel Hurstfield, (New York: Harper & Roe Publishers, 1965), 25-26.

17 Leonard Verduin, *The Reformers and Their Stepchildren,* (Grand Rapids, Michigan: William B. Eerdmans Publishing Company, 1964), 36.

18 Ibid.

19 Schaff, 440-449.

20 Ibid., 698-699.

21 Ibid., 669-678.

22 Deimer, Lecture 9.

23 Ibid., Lecture 11.

24 *Wikipedia,* (en.wikipedia.org/wiki/Jane_Seymour).

25 *Ibid.,* /wiki/Anne_of_Cleves.

26 *Ibid.,* /wiki/Catherine_Howard.

27 *Ibid.,* /wiki/Catherine_Parr.

28 Deimer, Lecture 11.

Martin Luther

Year	
1483	Martin Luther was born in Eisleben to strict German parents who gave him pious training (November 10, 1483)
1501	Luther entered the best university in Germany (Erfurt) to study law
1502	Frederick III, Elector of Saxony, founded the University of Wittenberg
1505	At a time of great fear during a lightning storm, Luther vowed to become a monk if God would spare his life
1511	Luther moved to Wittenberg, where he lived in an Augustine monastery and earned a doctor of theology degree in the university. Luther became intensely interested in the gospel.
1515	Luther accepted justification by faith and determined to stand for Christ regardless of the cost
1517	95 Theses - Luther had been working on an answer and affront to the evils he saw in Catholicism. He organized them in the form of 95 Theses, which he nailed on the main door of the Wittenberg Church. (October 31, 1517)

The History of Churches

Martin Luther

Year	
1520	Luther published The Address to the German Nobility in which he demolished the pope's claim that Rome had spiritual power over temporal authority
	Soon he wrote The Babylonian Captivity in which he challenged the sacramental system of Rome
	Later that year, he wrote The Freedom of the Christian Man in which he challenged the theology of Rome and advocated the priesthood of every believer
	Pope Leo X excommunicated Luther with the papal bull *Exsurge Domine* (June 1520)
	In the presence of a large number of professors and students, Luther burned the papal bull together with papal decretals, the canon law and other Catholic writings (December 10, 1520 at 9:00 a.m.)
1521	Diet of Worms - The pope demanded that Charles V, Emperor of the Holy Roman Empire, force Luther to a diet (a formal assembly) or hearing in the city of Worms

The History of Churches

Martin Luther

Year	
1521	Luther defended his anti-Catholic writings before the notables of his world most of whom were bent on his destruction. He uttered the famous words, *"Here I stand. I cannot do otherwise. God help me! Amen."* (April 17-18, 1521)
	A few days later, the Edict of Worms was passed. It made Luther an outlaw and placed Frederick in jeopardy from his Catholic neighbors
1523	Peasants' War (1523-1525) - They thought Luther was coming to their side and supported his efforts in an uprising against the nobility. He turned on the peasants and advised a wholesale suppression of their uprising.
1525	Thousands of them perished.
1530	The Augsburg Confession was signed by seven German princes. This document established Lutheranism (June 2, 1530)
1531	A group of princes sympathetic to Lutheranism organized the Schmalkaldic League for mutual defense. The Protestant Reformation would not be terminated.
1546	Luther died in Eisleben on February 18, 1546

The History of Churches

King Henry VIII

King Henry VIII was regarded as a defender of the Catholic religion. However, he was motivated by the state side and not the church side. His father, Henry VII, wanted his sons to marry royalty. Here are his wives.

Catherine of Aragon (Spain) - Wife of Henry's older brother, Arthur. When Arthur died, Henry married her at the request of his father. Henry was 17 years old. She had no male heirs and one daughter named Mary. He had Mary declared an illegitimate child and annulled their marriage. (married June 1509 - 1533) [1]

Anne Boleyn - They were secretly married after she became pregnant with Elizabeth. She had no male child and only one daughter. She was found guilty of adultery, incest and high treason. Anne was beheaded. (married Jan 1533 - May 1536) [2]

Jane Seymour - Henry married her eleven days after Anne's execution. She died shortly after she gave birth to a male child named Edward. (married May 1536 - Oct 1537) [3]

[1] *Wikipedia*, (en.wikipedia.org/wiki/Henry_VIII_of_England).

[2] Ibid., /wiki/Anne_Boleyn.

[3] Ibid., /wiki/Jane_Seymour.

King Henry VIII

Anne of Cleves - Three years later, Henry married Anne of Cleves. The king's chancellor, Thomas Cromwell, urged this match. After six months, the marriage was annulled. (married Jan 1540 - July 1540) [4]

Catherine Howard - They were married a few weeks after the annulment from Anne. Henry was 49 years old and she was around 19. She was found guilty of treason because of infidelity. She was beheaded at the Tower of London. (married July 1540 - February 1542) [5]

Catherine Parr - She was noticed by Henry at his daughter's (Mary) house. They were married at a small ceremony. Henry died in January 1547 at the age of 55, while she died in September 1548 at the age of 36. (married July 1543 - January 1547) [6]

The reformation in England was political, not theological. In 1534, Henry broke away from the Roman Catholic Church by declaring the Act of Supremacy, which made him the *Supreme Head of the Church of England*. The pope promptly excommunicated Henry and Anne Boleyn.

The History of Churches

[4] Ibid., /wiki/Anne_of_Cleves.

[5] Ibid., /wiki/Catherine_Howard.

[6] Ibid., /wiki/Catherine_Parr.

Chapter 28

Getting Bibles into the
Hands of the People

The Bible is God's self-revelation. It is the owner's manual of Christianity. Without it Christians have no compass. **Psalm 119:130** declares of God, *"The entrance of thy words giveth light; it giveth understanding unto the simple."* Truth liberates from the darkness of ignorance and the bottomless pit of evils that accompany it. The whole Christian case rises or falls on the Bible. Christianity is what God says it is in the Bible. Without the Bible, Christianity is nothing more than what man says it is, and every man has his own opinions. The Bible makes Christianity static; tradition makes it evolutionary. Satan has always sought to loose Christianity from its underpinnings. Throughout the centuries, there has been an on-going battle for the Bible.

Satan has used an endless parade of men and methods to keep the Word of God from men; however, in spite of hundreds of years of enormous efforts to keep it from the people, he has failed. It has reached the masses and no book has come even close to impacting as many lives as the Bible has. Since the finalization of the New Testament almost two millennia ago, nothing has been more instrumental than the Bible in changing the course of human history. Furthermore, the Old Testament of the Bible was the chief player on life's big stage for almost two millennia prior to the New Testament.

The first recorded attack by Satan was against the Word of God. He first questioned it and then outright denied it, **Genesis 3:1-4**. He has never stopped this practice. Since the inception of Jesus' church in Jerusalem, the history of the Bible is intricately woven into the history of the world. Already we have spoken of its completion and canonization. Now we will briefly summarize how God has preserved His Word through the centuries and brought it to modern man, particularly in the English language.

> **Through the centuries, there has been an on-going battle for the Bible**

THE LIGHT EXTINGUISHED

The Dark Ages

The period of time between the fall of Rome in 410 and the revival of learning that emerged from the Crusades is generally known as the Dark Ages. The dating of the Dark Ages has always been fluid, but there is little question that the invention of the mechanical printing press by Johannes Gutenberg in 1439 and his printing of the Bible in 1454-1455 [1] was a break-through in opening the eyes of the world. It is not coincidental that this era known as the Dark Ages represents the apex of the Catholic Church. Catholicism ruled with a heavy hand during the Dark Ages. The bishops of Rome insisted that they had an exclusive claim on God and that they served as his mouthpieces (the Vicars of God). [2]

The Scriptures Forbidden to the Common Man

In the latter part of the Dark Ages, Catholic policy forbade Bible reading by the common man. The Catholic Church also censored many other books. [3] Catholic apologists deny this reality; however, the proof is undeniable. No less a scholar than Philip Schaff wrote, "The synod of Toulouse, 1229, presided over by the papal legate, celebrated the close of the Albigensian crusades and perfected the code of the Inquisition. It has an unenviable distinction among the great synods on account of its decree forbidding laymen to have the Bible in their possession." [4] Canon 14 from the Synod of

Toulouse forbade the laity to have in their possession any copy of the books of the Old or New Testaments in the vulgar tongue, with the exception of the Psalms and a few passages dealing with Mary. [5] The vulgar tongue means a language common among the people. [6] In 1234 the Synod of Tarragona issued a similar prohibition. Furthermore, through the years since those synods, the Catholic Church has maintained a critical view of Bibles and materials published outside its jurisdiction. [7] It cannot be successfully denied that the Catholic Church has a history of suppressing efforts to put the Bible into the hands of the masses of ordinary people.

The Bible in Greek

For hundreds of years, the only copies of the Scriptures were handwritten. Those copies were almost exclusively in Hebrew, Greek or Latin. Furthermore, there were only a few full copies. (A full copy was called a codex.) Spread throughout the East and West were "approximately 5,000 Greek manuscripts which contain all or part of the New Testament." [8] There were many other fragments. Most of these were in the hands of the state church authorities, but not all. The primitive Christians had limited copies.

Early Translations of the Bible

By 405 Jerome had translated the Bible into Latin. Prior to Jerome, there were many Latin translations; Jerome's assignment was to produce a standardized Latin translation. [9] During the early centuries, translations of portions of the New Testament also appeared in Syriac, Coptic, Gothic, Armenian, Georgian, Ethiopic, Old Slavonic and other languages. [10]

Prior to the arrival of a Greek New Testament in the West, one of the most notable translations of the Bible was by John Wycliffe. Wycliffe was a mighty champion of the Scriptures "as the primary and absolute authority in matters of faith and morals, and maintained the desirability of its being made generally accessible to Christians." [11] By 1384 John Wycliffe and his associates had translated the Bible into English. [12] These translations are from Latin and they closely follow the Vulgate. [13] Since the translations were not from the original languages, they contained many errors.

354

They also came forth at a time when the papacy, which opposed the availability of the Scriptures to the common man, ruled with an iron fist. Nevertheless, Wycliffe's translation was a tremendous contribution to English-speaking people and planted the seed for future translations.

> **By 405 Jerome had produced a standardized Latin translation of the Bible**

THE GREEK NEW TESTAMENT OF ERASMUS

Erasmus

Desiderius Erasmus (1465-1536) was a monk who wanted to reform the Catholic Church from within. He was also an outstanding Greek scholar. Erasmus produced a critical edition of the Greek New Testament which was published by Johann Froben in Basel on March 1, 1516. This was the first edition of the Greek New Testament. [14] Prior to Erasmus' work, the New Testament was available to Westerners only in Latin, primarily the Vulgate translation of Jerome, which is one step removed from the original tongue. Erasmus' work gave scholars the ability to study the Word of God directly from the original language. Due to Erasmus' limited number of source manuscripts (no more than five), his Greek New Testament contained many errors (many of which were later corrected). Even so, his Greek New Testament was a huge step in ultimately bringing the Scriptures to the common man. It gave other scholars the tool they needed to translate the Bible into vulgar or common languages. After Erasmus' Greek New Testament was published in 1633 by an enterprising publisher named Elzevir, it became known as *Textus Receptus*. Other Greek texts based on far more sources have since emerged; however, none have revealed substantial errors in *Textus Receptus*, which continues to be regarded by many as reliable and authoritative. It is noteworthy that Erasmus was branded as a heretic; however, he remained Roman Catholic. [15]

The moveable type printing press produced momentous consequences for Western culture and civilization. "Before 1500 Bibles had been printed in several of the principle vernacular

355

languages of Western Europe – Bohemian (Czech), French, German, and Italian." [16] It was Erasmus' production of the Greek New Testament that paved the way for accurate translations of the Bible. That document gave Greek scholars a direct link to the original language of the New Testament; no longer were they dependent upon a secondary source.

> **Textus Receptus is the first edition of the Greek New Testament**

Luther

While Martin Luther was kidnapped for his own safety at Wartburg, he translated the New Testament into German directly from Erasmus' work. The Bible had already been translated into German directly from the Latin Vulgate. The impact of the Latin Vulgate-based translation was minimal. Luther's Bible was first printed in 1534, and the impact was phenomenal. He "brought the teaching and example of Christ and the Apostles to the mind and heart of the Germans in life-like reproduction. . . He made the Bible the people's book in church, school, and house . . . Hereafter the Reformation depended no longer on the works of the Reformers, but on the book of God, which everybody could read for himself as his daily guide in spiritual life." [17]

THE BIBLE IN ENGLISH

The English language has become the dominant language for much of the world. The far reaches of the old British Empire, modern international travel, America's affluence and other factors have contributed to that reality. This day, in almost any nation on earth, large numbers of people speak English in addition to their native tongues. People around the world are eager to learn English. In the sixteenth century, one could scarcely have imagined the profound and lasting impact of a Bible in the English language.

There were nine English translations prior to the King James Bible; however, none compares to it in terms of style and impact. To better understand and appreciate the enormously successful King James Bible, it is important to know something about the English Bibles that preceded it.

The Wycliffe Bible

Mention has been made that John Wycliffe was the first to translate the entire Bible (Old and New Testaments) into English. He had no Greek or Hebrew texts, and thus translated from the only source available to him, Jerome's Latin Vulgate. Wycliffe's Bible is also known as the Lollard Bible. [18]

The Wycliffe Bible is the first English translation of the Bible

---

The Tyndale Bible

Though the Bible existed in English earlier, "No part of the English Bible was printed before 1525, no complete Bible before 1535, and none in England before 1538." [19] With the availability of Erasmus' Greek text of the New Testament and a Hebrew text published in 1488, William Tyndale resolved to first translate the New Testament into English. Resistance was so strong in England that in 1524 Tyndale resorted first to Hamburg and finally to Wittenberg. Catholic enemies found him and stopped his work at Wittenberg; but Tyndale escaped to Worms, where he finished the first translation of the New Testament into English directly from Greek.

The translation was smuggled into England where it was an instant success. He began work translating the Old Testament; but "on May 21, 1535, Tyndale was treacherously kidnapped and imprisoned in Belgium. On October 6, 1536, he was tried as a heretic and condemned to death. He was strangled and burned." [20]

The Tyndale story is powerful and well illustrates both the liberating power of God's Word, and the intense desire of the Catholic Church to suppress it. The case of William Tyndale contradicts the Catholic claim that it has never opposed the dispersion of the Bible to the common man. If they approved of Tyndale's efforts to translate the Bible into English for the common man, why would they hunt him down and mercilessly kill him as though he was a vicious criminal?

The Coverdale Bible

Tyndale's Bible was the first to be translated into English from the original language; however, he was able to complete only the New Testament. Myles Coverdale was the first to publish a complete English Bible. In 1533 King Henry VIII established the Church of England and in 1534 the Upper House of Convocation of Canterbury petitioned the king to commission a translation of the Bible into the vulgar English tongue. [21] Coverdale's Bible was really a translation of translations. His sources consisted primarily of "Luther, the Zurich Bible, the Latin Version of Pagninus, the Vulgate, and, in all likelihood, the English translation of Tyndale." [22]

Matthew's Bible

The large sale of Tyndale's New Testament and the success of the Coverdale Bible convinced London booksellers that a new and profitable business was open to them. The hope of financial gain was quick to bring out another English translation. It came out in the name of Thomas Matthew; however, it is believed that this name was an alias for John Rogers, a friend and coworker of Tyndale. This Bible was primarily a compilation of the works of Tyndale and Coverdale. It was printed in 1537. [23]

The Great Bible

Ironically Tyndale's work was circulating with the king's permission in the Coverdale and Matthew Bibles. King Henry VIII wanted a large Bible with copies placed in churches so it would be accessible to the public. Previous English Bibles were private endeavors; however, this new Bible was commissioned by the king with the backing of ecclesiastical authority. It had the distinction of being the first *duly authorized* version. It first appeared in April of 1539 and was called the Great Bible because of its immense size. [24] The Great Bible is known by several different names: the Cromwell Bible, the Cranmer Bible, the Whitechurch Bible and the Chained Bible. It was called the

Chained Bible because copies were chained to secure structures within the various churches. [25] The Great Bible is the first to subdivide chapters into verses.

The Second Matthew Bible

A rival edition of the Great Bible was also privately published in 1539. It was really a piracy of the existing Matthew Bible. A Greek scholar named Richard Taverner acted as editor and merely made revisions. This Bible can hardly be called a new translation. [26]

The Geneva Bible

During the brief reign of the Catholic queen Mary Tudor (Bloody Mary), every effort was made on her part to erase Protestantism from England. Many English reformers fled to Geneva, Switzerland. Among them was William Whittingham, the brother-in-law of John Calvin. He translated what is known as the Geneva Bible. The New Testament was completed in 1557, and the complete work was done 1560. The text of the Geneva Bible was readily acceptable, although the Calvinist notes made it unacceptable for official use in England. [27]

The Geneva Bible is sometimes called the Breeches Bible, in view of its translation of **Genesis 3:7**, *"They sewed fig leaves together and made themselves breeches."*

The Bishop's Bible

Archbishop Matthew Parker saw the superiority of the Geneva Bible, which quickly became a rival to the Great Bible. Queen Elizabeth had come to the English throne, and steps were soon taken to revise the Great Bible. [28] The revision would replace both the Great Bible and the Geneva Bible. Like the Great Bible, the Bishop's Bible used verse divisions. The Bible was divided into parts and distributed to scholars for revision. Since Bishop Parker served as editor and most of the revisers were bishops, it was called the Bishops' Bible. It was published in 1568 and is the first Bible to be translated by a committee. [29]

The Douay-Rheims Bible

The Douay-Rheims Bible was the first Roman Catholic translation of the Bible into English. It was a reaction to the success of the other English Bibles and an attempt by the Catholics to hold their positions. The New Testament was published in 1582 at the English College of Rheims, and the Old Testament at Douay in 1609-1610. It was "merely a secondary rendering from the Latin Vulgate, and in many places it suffered like these from extreme literalness and stilted and ambiguous renderings." [30]

THE KING JAMES BIBLE

The Inception at Hampton Court

After the death of Queen Elizabeth in 1603, King James VI of Scotland became the King of England. He called a conference at Hampton Court in 1604 to hear the complaints of the Puritans. A large number of Anglican bishops, clergymen and professors were present along with four Puritan leaders, including John Rainolds, who was president of Corpus Christi College. At that meeting, Rainolds suggested the need for a uniform, standard translation of the Bible. King James picked up the idea and initiated the project. [31]

The Best of the Best

Through the previous translation efforts, the English Bible had undergone a purification process. The newer translations incorporated the improvements of those before. King James was determined that the best of both scholarship and style be integrated into this new translation. He brought the best scholars of England into the project, experts in Hebrew and Greek from Oxford, Cambridge and other places. Modern critics with biases against the King James Bible have disputed those translators; however, when they are examined man-by-man, skepticism against them proves absolutely unfounded. [32] Even those who reject the King James Bible as archaic generally concede that it is a very accurate translation. Furthermore, the sublime beauty of the King James Bible speaks for itself.

Scholars and Sources

With the full authority and support of the King of England, the work of translation was begun. All of the translators were Englishmen except one, and all were members of the Anglican Church. Including those who oversaw the project, there were 47 translators. [33] They were all men. They were divided into six companies; each company was given a section of the Bible for translation. A huge number of resources were available to them. They had the entire Old and New Testaments in the original tongues, the Masoretic Text, the Septuagint and virtually all translations in all languages, including all previous English translations. They had access to a library containing extensive commentaries. [34]

Fifteen general rules were given to govern the translators. [35] Their main policy was to let the truth of the original texts rule. As much as possible, the Bishops' Bible was to be followed "and as little altered as the truth of the original will permit." [36] To the maximum extent possible, the King James Bible was to be a literal, word-for-word translation. When the Bishops' Bible did not convey exactly the correct meaning, other translations could be consulted. Hebrew and Greek words having no direct equivalent in English were to be italicized.

> **Forty-seven men translated the King James Bible**

The 1611 and Subsequent Editions

The translation was finalized and first published in 1611. There was immediate criticism when it was released, but it was short-lived. Since its initial release, the King James Bible has gone through many revisions and editions. The better revisions have been to correct and upgrade spelling, punctuation, grammar and formatting, including page layouts and type styles. The fourth revision, edited by Benjamin Blayney, was published by Oxford University Press in 1769. It was similar to a third revision by Francis Parris, published by Cambridge University press in 1762. Both "the Parris and Blayney editions modernized, standardized, and corrected the text, punctuation, spelling, and italics." [37] The

Blayney edition was superior to that of Parris and has become the standard among King James Bible printings. This 1769 edition is the one commonly used today. In the years that have followed 1769, numerous new English translations have flooded the market. To date, none has proven to the masses that it is superior to the King James Bible. "There can be no denying that the Authorized Version has historically been viewed as the standard Bible – in every century." [38]

An Extraordinarily Unique Success

"The KJV was a startling success. It had the 'wisdom, grace and beauty of previous translations, and possessed an eloquence which even unbelievers are forced to acknowledge.' H. L. Mencken has said this about the KJV: 'It is the most beautiful of all the translations of the Bible, indeed, it is probably the most beautiful piece of writing in all the literature of the world. Many learned but misguided men have sought to produce translations that should be mathematically accurate and in the plain speech of every day. But the AV (Authorized Version, another name for the KJV) has never yielded to any of them, for it is palpably and overwhelmingly better than they are . . . Its English is extraordinarily simple, pure, eloquent and lovely. It is a mine of lordly and incomparable poetry at once the most stirring and the most touching ever heard of. In speaking of the requirements laid down by James, Alistair McGrath says, in what is almost an oxymoron: 'It attained literary elegance by choosing to avoid it.' And Gustavus S. Paine, in speaking of the readability of the KJV, says, 'Rhythm in the days of King James was important, not merely as a source of pleasure to the ear, but as an aid to the mind. Generations to come would learn to read by puzzling out vss. in the Bible that for many families would be the whole library. But at the time of translation, a Bible 'appointed to be read in the churches' was made to be listened to and remembered. Its rhythms were important as a prompting to the memory. From every viewpoint, the KJV is a masterpiece of translation. It is very accurate. Its 'readability' is superb. It is understandable by the people in the pew, young and old alike. It is sublime and creates a sense of reverence conducive to worship. It is written in beautiful cadences and rhythms that made it nearly singable and easy to memorize. It is ideally suited to use in the church and in the home. It evokes emotions in keeping with the nature of the text." [39]

Phenomenal World-Wide Success

The impact of the King James Bible upon the world could hardly be overstated. It became the undisputed Bible of non-Catholic Christianity. Britain established a world-wide empire; and wherever Englishmen went, the King James Bible went. It came to America and became America's Bible. America became a super-power, and America's Bible was there wherever she went. English missionaries took it to Africa and Burma and a host of other places, it was the textbook of great preachers such as Charles Spurgeon and Billy Graham, armies of soldiers took it to their foxholes, and it became plentiful and inexpensive. Copies sold by the millions, and most English-speaking homes had multiple copies. For almost 400 years, it has consistently been the world's best-selling book. It became unquestionably the Bible of the home as well as the church. For centuries school teachers used it in public classrooms to teach English, morals and culture; private teachers still do. Alexander Cruden developed a concordance, making it easy to study and reference. For hundreds of years, the King James Bible has been the most studied book in the world. Countless millions of people have come to know Jesus Christ as personal Savior as a direct result of the King James Bible, and this day it is still a viable player in the marketplace.

God's Word into the Hands of the Masses of Common People

More than any other event in the history of mankind, the production of the King James Bible put the Word of God into the hands of the people, not only clerics and church officials but also common, ordinary people. **Psalm 12:6-7** says of God, *"The words of the LORD are pure words: as silver tried in a furnace of earth, purified seven times. Thou shalt keep them, O LORD, thou shalt preserve them from this generation for ever."* God promised to preserve His Word. It is quite obvious that God used the King James Bible to both get His Word to masses of people worldwide and to preserve it. It is not His only means of accomplishing these objectives, but it must be regarded as one of His chief means of doing so.

[1] *Wikipedia,* (en.wikipedia.org./wiki/Gutenberg_Bible).

[2] *The Catholic Encyclopedia,* (www.newadvent.org/cathen/15403b.htm).

[3] The Catholic Index of Prohibited Books is a list of books forbidden by the Roman Catholic Church. Visit *The Catholic Encyclopedia.* (www.newadvent.org/cathen/07721a.htm).

[4] Philip Schaff, *History of the Christian Church,* vol. 5, (Peabody, Massachusetts: Hendrickson Publishers, 2002), 812.

[5] Edward Landon, *A Manual of Councils of the Holy Catholic Church,* vol. 2, (Edinburgh: 1909), 171-172.

[6] *Webster's New World Dictionary with Student Handbook: Young People's Edition,* s.v. "vulgar," (Nashville, Tennessee: The World Publishing Company, 1973), 778.

[7] For a good summary of the Catholic stance see Michael Scheifler's *Bible Light Homepage* (www.aloha.net/~mikesch).

[8] Bruce Manning Metzger, *The Text of the New Testament,* 2nd ed., (New York and Oxford: Oxford University Press, 1968), 36.

[9] Ibid., 72-78.

[10] Ibid., 67-86.

[11] F.F. Bruce, *The Books and the Parchments,* (Old Tappan, New Jersey: Fleming H. Revell Company, 1984), 212.

[12] *Wikipedia,* (en.wikipedia.org./wiki/John_Wycliffe).

[13] Schaff, vol. 6, 342.

[14] Kurt and Barbara Aland, *The Text of the New Testament,* 2nd ed., (Grand Rapids: William B. Eerdman's Publishing Company, 1989), 3.

[15] Carl Deimer, Professor, *History of Christianity II,* Video Lecture 4, Liberty University DLP, 2004.

[16] Metzger, 95.

[17] Schaff, vol. 7, 341.

[18] *Encyclopaedia Britannica,* vol. 3, (Chicago, London, Toronto: William Benton, Publisher, 1960), 531.

[19] Ibid.

[20] Laurence M. Vance, *King James: His Bible and its Translators,* (Pensacola, Florida: Vance Publications, 2006), 78-79.

[21] Vance, 79.

[22] *Britannica,* 532.

[23] Ibid.

[24] Ibid.

[25] Vance, 80.

[26] *Britannica.*

[27] Vance, 80-81.

[28] *Britannica.*

[29] Vance, 81.

[30] *Britannica.*

[31] Vance, 11-23.

[32] Vance, 23-35.

[33] Ibid., 30-31.

[34] Ibid., 41.

[35] For a complete listing of those rules see *King James: His Bible and its Translators* by Laurence M. Vance, pages 46-46.

[36] Vance, 84.

[37] Ibid., 65.

[38] Ibid., 110.

[39] Herman Hanko, *Our Venerable King James Bible,* (Lansing, Illinois: Peace Protestant Reformed Church), 4-5. (www.peaceprc.org/ourvenerablekjv.pdf).

The History of Bible Translations

Year	
405	Jerome translated the Bible into a standardized Latin version
410	Dark Ages - The time period from the fall of Rome in 410 to the revival of learning that emerged from the Crusades
1229	Synod of Toulouse - The papal legate forbade the layman from possessing the Bible
1234	Synod of Tarragona - It issued a similar prohibition against the possession of Bibles
1384	Wycliffe Bible - English translation from the Latin Vulgate by John Wycliffe and his associates. It is also called the Lollard Bible.
1439	First Printing Press - The invention of the mechanical printing press by Johannes Gutenberg
1454	Gutenberg Bible - The printed version of the Latin Vulgate translation
1516	Greek New Testament - Desiderius Erasmus wrote this version based on a limited number of source manuscripts. It was called the *Textus Receptus* when it was published in 1633.
1525	Tyndale Bible - William Tyndale wrote this New Testament English translation based on Erasmus' Greek text and a Hebrew text

The History of Churches

The History of Bible Translations

Year	
1534	German Bible - Martin Luther translated the New Testament into German directly from Erasmus' work
	The Upper House of Convocation of Canterbury petitioned the king to commission a translation of the Bible into the vulgar English tongue. It would be done by Myles Coverdale.
1535	Coverdale Bible - Myles Coverdale was the first to publish a complete English Bible. The sources included the Zurich Bible, the Pagninus Bible, the Vulgate and probably the Tyndale Bible.
	May 21, 1535 - Tyndale was kidnapped and put in prison in Belgium
1536	October 6, 1536 - Tyndale was found guilty of being a heretic and was put to death by strangulation and burning
1537	Matthew's Bible - Published under the pseudonym of Thomas Matthew, this complete English Bible is primarily a compilation of the works of Tyndale and Coverdale
1539	Great Bible - This is the first duly authorized English Bible which appeared in April 1539. King Henry VIII wanted a large Bible with copies placed in churches so it would be accessible to the public. It was called the Great Bible because of its immense size. It was the first Bible to subdivide chapters into verses.
	Second Matthew Bible - A rival edition of the Great Bible which was really a piracy of the existing Matthew Bible. Richard Taverner acted as editor and merely made revisions.

The History of Churches

The History of Bible Translations

Year	
1560	Geneva Bible - William Whittingham, the brother-in-law of John Calvin, was an English reformer which fled to Geneva, Switzerland. He translated this English version of the Bible. The Calvinist notes made it unacceptable for official use in England.
1568	Bishop's Bible - Matthew Parker, Archbishop of Canterbury, served as editor for this revision of the Great Bible. It was called the Bishop's Bible because most of the revisers were bishops. It is the first Bible to be translated by a committee.
1582	Douay-Rheims Bible - This was the first Roman Catholic translation of the Bible into English. It was an English translation from the Latin Vulgate.
1603	After the death of Queen Elizabeth in 1603, King James VI of Scotland became the King of England
1604	King James VI called a conference at Hampton Court in which the Puritan leader John Rainolds suggested the need for a uniform, standard translation of the Bible. King James picked up the idea and initiated the project.
1611	King James Bible - Forty-seven men working in six groups created this English translation from manuscripts in the original tongues
1769	Benjamin Blayney edited the fourth revision of the King James Bible. This edition is the one commonly in current use.

Chapter 29

Anabaptists

Anabaptists is the historical name of a movement of primitive, New Testament Christians. It is also descriptive of their best-known practice. *Baptist* means *baptizer,* and *ana* means *anew.* The Anabaptists baptized anew all who came to them with invalid baptisms. Bystanders, especially their enemies, tagged them with the name *Anabaptists* or re-baptizers.

Anabaptist is not a name they gave themselves; they actually resented it. They did not see themselves as re-baptizers; they were simply baptizers or Baptists. To their way of thinking, those who had been *baptized* before salvation had never been baptized at all. They believed that in order to have a valid baptism, a person must first have personal faith in Jesus Christ as his Savior. Therefore baptized babies, those who experienced a ritualistic church baptism void of true repentance and faith in Christ, or anyone baptized before he personally trusted Christ, really had not been baptized at all. When these primitive Christians baptized such ones, it was not a re-baptism; it was simply a baptism. It is not difficult to see why they took exception to the tag *ana.* Even so, others called them *Anabaptists* and that name speaks much about their beliefs.

> **Baptist means *baptizer,* and ana means *anew***

THE ORIGIN OF THE ANABAPTISTS

People of the Unbroken Line from Christ

"The beginnings of the Anabaptist movement are firmly rooted in the earlier centuries." [1] The famous Lutheran historian, John Laurence Mosheim said, "The true origin of that sect which acquired the denomination of Anabaptists by their administration anew the rite of baptism to those who came over to their communion, and derived that of *Mennonites* from the famous man to whom they owe the greatest part of their present felicity, is hidden in the depths of antiquity, and is, of consequence, extremely difficult to be ascertained." [2] Anabaptists did not view themselves as a new sect. Records testify that people believing and practicing exactly what they believed and practiced had been around since the time of the New Testament. In fact "for more than twelve centuries baptism in the way taught and described in the New Testament had been made an offense against the law, punishable by death." [3] "The Mandate of Speier, April 1529, declares that the Anabaptists were hundreds of years old" [4] and "Cardinal Hosius, a member of the Council of Trent, A.D. 1560, in a statement often quoted, says, 'If the truth of religion were to be judged by the readiness and boldness of which a man of any sect show in suffering, then the opinion and persuasion of no sect can be truer and surer than that of the Anabaptists since there have been none for these twelve hundred years past, that have been more generally punished or that have more cheerfully and steadfastly undergone, and even offered themselves to the most cruel sorts of punishment than these people.'" [5]

The Anabaptists Did Not Originate with Ulrich Zwingli

There are historians who contend that the Anabaptist movement had its origin in Zurich, Switzerland in January of 1525. They argue that the movement was born out of dissatisfaction with Ulrich Zwingli by a small band of his radical followers over his refusal to take a public stand in favor of Scriptural baptism. George Blaurock, Conrad Grebel and others met at the home of Felix Manz and exchanged baptisms. These extremely bold and zealous men, who went forth with enormous success, were supposedly the original Anabaptists. [6] It is true that these

370

outstanding men, who embodied the essence of Anabaptist doctrine and practice, bolstered the Anabaptist movement. It is also true that primitive, New Testament Christians, straight on doctrine and practice, including baptism, predated Manz, Blaurock and Grebel by centuries. All Manz and the others did was theologically come to where multitudes had already been for hundreds of years.

They Did Not Originate with the Münster Rebellion

The origin of Anabaptists is also misrepresented by those who connect them to the infamous Münster Rebellion of 1524. Most historians agree that the rebellion grew more out of the desperation of feudalism with its slavery and oppression of poor people, than out of religious convictions. [7] It is true that religious issues became mixed therein, and some Anabaptists were involved, but the facts verify that the main line of German Baptists descended from the ancient Waldenses centuries before the Münster Rebellion.

They Are Descendents of the Waldenses

In reality, the Anabaptist movement was the continuation of that unbroken line of Christians and churches from Christ forward. Throughout the centuries, these believers had been called Anabaptists, not because they constituted a movement, but because of their practice of requiring proper baptism of those who came to them. During the time in history when the Western World was desperately trying to free itself from Catholic tyranny through a Reformation, these people and churches emerged as a movement and were tagged with the name Anabaptists because of their baptismal practices. Many of them were simply Waldenses who were given a new name. "Roman Catholic historians and officials, in some instances eye-witnesses, testify that the Waldenses and other ancient communions were the same as the Anabaptists" [8] "It is a well-known fact that the Dutch, or German, Baptists were called 'Anabaptists' and Waldenses interchangeably." [9] Mosheim, who was no friend of Baptists, said German Anabaptists, who were sometimes known as Mennonites, were right when they claimed "their descent from the Waldenses, Petrobrusians, and other ancient sects. . .Before the rise of Luther and Calvin, there lay concealed, in almost all the countries of Europe, particularly in Bohemia, Moravia, Switzerland, and Germany, many persons, who adhered tenaciously to the following doctrine, which the Waldenses, Wickliffits, and Hussites, had maintained." [10] He then proceeded to enunciate some of that doctrine.

> **Waldenses were also known as Anabaptists because of their baptismal practices**

A Movement Does Not Necessarily Originate with a Well-Known Leader

"It will be remembered that the same class of people who were called Baptists in England, and Anabaptists in Germany, were also called Mennonites, not that he [Menno Simons] was their founder, but because he united with them, and became one of their most powerful and influential ministers." [11] What an important observation to keep in mind! Weak thinkers and those with an agenda often jump to premature or unfounded conclusions by tying an entire movement to one of its powerful leaders. Menno Simons of the Netherlands (1496 – 1561) was an Anabaptist, but he no more originated the Anabaptists than Abraham Lincoln originated the United States. D.B. Ray quotes leading authorities of the Dutch Reformed Church in their *Religious Encyclopedia* regarding the unbroken line. "We have now seen that the Baptists who were formerly called Anabaptists, and, in latter times, Mennonites, were the original Waldenses; and who have lone, in the history of the church, received the honor of their origin. On this account, the Baptists may be considered as the only Christian community which has stood since the days of the apostles, and as a Christian society, which has preserved pure the doctrines of the Gospel through all ages." [12]

Let it also be observed that "The modern Mennonites are wholly different from the ancient Mennonite Anabaptists." [13] Over time the Mennonites accepted pouring and also left their roots in other areas; however, Menno Simons embraced Anabaptist doctrine and practices.

RIGOROUS PERSECUTION BY STATE CHURCHES

In many heads there exists a myth that religious liberty and tolerance came with the birth of Protestant churches. Few beliefs are farther from the truth.

The Roman Catholic Stance Against All Dissenters

As we have already seen, every effort was made by the Roman Catholic Church to silence and destroy the reformers. "The laws of pagan Rome and Christian Rome were alike severe against every open dissent from the state religion." [14] The Catholic position is reflected in their champion, Thomas Aquinas, who taught that "the rites of idolaters, Jews, and infidels ought not to be tolerated, and that heretics or corrupters of the Christian faith, being worse criminals than debasers of money, ought (after due admonition) not only to be excommunicated by the church, but also be put to death by the state." [15] The differing positions of the reformers were of little interest to the Catholics; anyone seeing anything different from Catholicism was a threat that must be terminated. Therefore, Catholic oppression and violence against all forms of opposition intensified as the Reformation grew.

The Multiplication of State Churches

One might imagine that the various reformers would have seen the gross evils that accompany a state church. Such was not the case. Those who pulled the plug on Catholicism promptly plugged their new church into the state. The state church arrangement never missed a beat. When Martin Luther broke with the Catholics, his new Lutheran Church became the state church of a large part of Germany. He had the backing of that segment of the nobility which stood with him against Rome. When Ulrich Zwingli broke with Catholicism and established the Reformed Church, he had the backing of the political powers in Zurich, Switzerland. Political governmental power went with them as their movements grew and encompassed greater geographical areas. When King Henry VIII broke with the papacy, he established the Anglican Church in England; from the point of inception, it was the state church of England. In all cases, the state backed the church and enforced ecclesiastical decisions.

The Protestant Stance Against All Dissenters

The hypocrisy of Protestant leaders in denying to those who differed with them the same rights they sought from Catholicism is glaring, although they "felt it their duty to God and to themselves to suppress and punish heresy as well as civil crimes." [16] Like the Catholics, these new state churches and their leaders became vicious and merciless in dealing with those who opposed them. A comprehensive presentation of evidence to support this claim is beyond the scope of this book, but evidence abounds. The Anabaptists, usually regarded as radicals and extremists by all sides, were targets of Protestants and Catholics alike.

Most Anabaptists were peasants, and Luther always feared that they might join some new radical leader in a rebellion against the sadistic oppression of them by the nobility. The theological issue that caused his great hatred toward them was their requirement of personal faith in Christ prior to baptism. That stance forbade infant baptism, which Luther approved. [17] Luther wrote a tract to refute them. [18] Since he could find no New Testament Scripture to justify violence against peaceful disagreement (Anabaptists), Luther, like other reformers, used the Old Testament. By branding them as seditionists, he felt justified in calling "for the punishment for blasphemy found in the Mosaic Law." [19]

Mention has been made of Zwingli and the small band of radical followers who broke with him over baptism and other issues. These young men, known as Swiss Brethren, baptized themselves and started a new, free church outside the jurisdiction of Zwingli's new state church. Zwingli regarded this as civil and ecclesiastical disobedience punishable by death. He had Konrad Grebel jailed and drowned six others, including Felix Manz. [20] Georg Blaurock became an Anabaptist. "On the same day that Manz was drowned (January 5, 1527), Blaurock was stripped to the waist and beaten with rods until the blood ran down his back." [21] Two and one-half years later, Blaurock and a co-worker were tortured in an effort to gather information about other Anabaptists in the area. They were then burned at the stake. [22]

In England the story is the same. The Anglicans were not tolerant of other religious persuasions. English monarchs differed in some regards; however, their desire for a uniformity of belief moved them with varying intensity to seek out and eradicate perceived treason in England. "Individuals of contrary belief were targeted, apprehended, imprisoned, interrogated, and sometimes executed." [23] One such individual was John Bunyan, who wrote the famous *Pilgrim's Progress* while serving time in a Bedfordshire County prison. He was there for violations of the *Conventicle Act* which prohibited the holding of religious services outside the auspices of the established Church of England. [24] The infamous Tower of London was primarily a fortress, but it also served as a place of execution and torture. [25] *The Book of Martyrs* by John Foxe, first published in 1563, is a gut-wrenching account of men and women who died for the faith. Many of them were in England in the last century before the book was published. The truth is that the Anglicans were no more tolerant of religious positions contrary to their own than the Catholics, the Lutherans or those in the Reformed Church. Where there were state churches, there was no religious liberty.

THE PROLIFERATION OF THE ANABAPTISTS

In spite of great efforts on many fronts to discredit and eradicate Anabaptists in the sixteenth century, they spread rapidly. In many provinces, there was grassroots sympathy for the doctrine and practices taught by the Anabaptists; and it is said that sometimes a congregation was established within a few hours after the arrival of an Anabaptist preacher. In Germany, Switzerland and Austria, the strength of the Anabaptists surpassed that of the Lutherans and the Zwinglian movements in terms of adherents. It is not difficult to understand the jealousy of the Lutherans, the Reformed Church and the Catholics alike against the Anabaptists, whom they saw as a great threat. Anabaptists were hunted as though they were dangerous, wild beasts. Soldiers were sent to hunt and kill them on the spot without trial or sentencing. Laws were passed making it a crime to be an Anabaptist, prices were placed on their heads, and it became a crime to offer food or shelter to an Anabaptist. Thousands of them were systematically executed. Massacres occurred but still they multiplied. [26]

Georg Cajacob Blaurock

Mention has been made of Georg Cajacob, who became known as Blaurock because he wore a blue coat. This huge and bold man won great numbers of disciples wherever he went. Shortly before his martyrdom, he became pastor of an orphaned church in the Adige Valley of Austria. The Anabaptist pastor was burned at the stake on June 2, 1529. Blaurock preached up and down the Inn and Etsch river valleys where converts increased steadily. [27]

Balthasar Hubmaier

Balthasar Hubmaier (1481-1528) is regarded by many as the most important Anabaptist of all. Hubmaier was born a peasant, but eventually earned a doctorate in theology at Ingolstadt as a vintage Catholic. In 1522 Hubmaier was converted and became an Anabaptist. He wrote a tract titled *Concerning Heretics and Those Who Burn Them.* In it he presented the Anabaptist position and said that those who burn heretics are the real heretics. He also wrote a book titled *The Christian Baptism of Believers* in which he refuted Zwingli's positions on baptism. [28] In Zurich, Hubmaier was jailed and persecuted on the rack. After being released, he traveled as far as Nikolsburg, Austria. In eighteen months, he made and baptized over 6,000 converts. [29] Hubmaier was captured and taken to Vienna, where he was burned at the stake. A few days later, a stone was tied around the neck of his wife, and she was thrown from a bridge into the Danube where she drowned. [30]

> **Balthasar Hubmaier is regarded by many as the most important Anabaptist of all**

Johannes (Hans) Denck

Johannes (Hans) Denck was a brilliant young man, who early in his life identified with the Lutherans. He soon saw their hypocrisy in advocating justification by faith while living impure lives. His insistence on purity earned him scorn and exile. In Augsburg, Denck met Balthasar Hubmaier, who led him to be baptized and join the Anabaptists. Persecution arose in Augsburg. Denck moved to Strasbourg, where the Anabaptist brethren were numerous, influential and viewed simply as Baptists. [31] Denck is known as one of the best Anabaptist theologians. [32]

Michael Sattler

The striking testimony of Michael Sattler had an awesome impact. Sattler was a Benedictine monk who converted to Anabaptist and began a successful ministry in South Germany near Schleitheim. Sattler is believed to be the author of a confessional which set forth Anabaptist positions. He was apprehended by the Catholics who sentenced him to death at Rottenburg. The sentence read, "Michael Sattler shall be committed to the executioner. The latter shall take him to the square and there first cut out his tongue, and then forge him fast to a wagon and there with glowing iron tongs twice tear pieces from his body, then on the way to the site of execution five times more as above and then burn his body to powder as an arch-heretic." [33] The Catholics did it. They cut out Sattler's tongue to keep him from speaking, dragged him through the city in an ox cart and stopped periodically to dig out hunks of his flesh with hot pokers. They then tied him to a stake in such a way that they could lower him into the flames and raise him out again. Sattler got wind of the Catholic plans and promised his followers that if God's grace was sufficient, he'd bring the tips of his forefingers together. As the Catholics held Sattler in the flames, the ropes burned off and Sattler brought the tips of his fingers together. [34]

Menno Simons

Earlier mention was made of Menno Simons. After a group of radicals took over the city of Münster for 18 months, congregations of Anabaptists everywhere were falsely accused and persecuted with greater violence than ever before. Some Anabaptists were involved; however, as indicated earlier, the Münster Rebellion was mainly a political event. It grew out of the desperation of peasants for relief from servitude, rather than out of theological convictions. Nonetheless, the event made the nobility of Germany, Austria and Switzerland very leery of all peasant movements, including religious movements such as the Anabaptists. Luther assumed that any peasant movement would ultimately lead to rebellion.

In the face of the greatest of dangers, Menno Simons visited and encouraged the scattered and harassed remnants. [35] He worked in the Netherlands until 1543, when he was declared an outlaw, and a price was placed on his head. Any who might shelter him was condemned to death, and prisoners who might deliver him into the hands of the executioner were promised pardon. Simons was forced to leave the Low Countries and eventually found refuge under the protection of Count Alefeld in Fresenburg, Holstein. Melchoir Hoffman, another Anabaptist, had earlier introduced the Anabaptist message extensively into the Netherlands. [36] Large numbers of Anabaptist brethren joined Simons in Holstein. In Fresenburg, Simons was supplied with a means of printing. His writings were widely circulated and had a major impact outside the area. [37] No person had greater influence in the Lowlands than Menno Simons. [38]

It should be stated again that those listed here constitute only a very small fraction of the great number of early Anabaptist leaders.

OBSERVATIONS

Long before Luther, Zwingli or Calvin, communities of primitive, New Testament Christians and churches abounded from the Balkans to the British Isles and from Scandinavia to the Mediterranean. They especially abounded in the Alps. These believers and churches went by a variety of names. There were some within these communities who were too far from the New Testament to be called true believers and churches; however, within these ranks, there were many who maintained the pure doctrine and practices of the New Testament.

Among these were those early Christians who refused to identify with the churches that embraced tradition over Scripture and became the Roman state church of Constantine. That state church went on to become the Roman Catholic Church, but those early believers never were a part of it. Almost from the start, the state church began to persecute them, and they were forced into the Alps for safety and survival. They did survive and abundantly reproduced themselves, even in the face of great adversity. They progressed through the ages by many names such as Montanists,

Novatians, Donatists, Paulicians, Bogomils, Albigenses, Waldenses, Brethren, Mennonites and Anabaptists. As we shall see in the next chapter, *Ana* was dropped, and they were simply called Baptists. Their name changed with the times, but their doctrine and practices remained essentially the same and they constitute an unbroken line from Christ forward.

Many things can be said of these people, but it cannot be legitimately said that they are newcomers. They certainly did not originate with the Protestant Reformation, and they were in no sense Protestants. They are the people who confirm the words of Jesus' prophecy, *"I will build my church; and the gates of hell shall not prevail against it,"* **Matthew 16:18**. They constitute proof that **Ephesians 3:21** is right. God has received *"glory in the church by Christ Jesus throughout all ages."* Some of the early churches began a steady departure from the Scriptures, became the state church and turned absolutely corrupt and godless. By no stretch of the imagination could that drift of churches be considered the true line which Jesus promised. In spite of enormous efforts to eradicate them, there remained an unbroken line of churches that kept believing in the sole authority of the Scriptures, the deity of Christ, salvation exclusively by personal faith in Jesus Christ, the autonomy of the local church, holy living and the second coming of Christ. They were beaten and battered and they left a trail of blood, but they survived and they are still here.

---

1 John T. Christian, *A History of the Baptists,* vol. 1, (Texarkana, Ark.-Tex.: Bogard Press, 1922), 83.

2 John Laurence Mosheim, *An Ecclesiastical History, Ancient and Modern,* Archibald Maclaine, translator, (New York: Harper and Brothers, Publishers, 1871), 127.

3 E.H. Broadbent, *The Pilgrim Church,* (Grand Rapids, Michigan: GOSPEL FOLIO PRESS, 1999), 172.

4 Christian.

5 Ibid., 85-86.

6 William R. Estep, *The Anabaptist Story: An Introduction to Sixteenth – Century Anabaptism,* 3rd ed., (Grand Rapids: William B. Eerdmans Publishing Company, 1996), 11-15.

7 D.B. Ray, *Baptist Succession: A Hand-book of Baptist History,* (Parsons, Kansas: Foley Railway Printing Company, 1912), 142-143.

[8] Christian, 85.

[9] Ray, 147.

[10] Mosheim, 128.

[11] Ray, 149.

[12] Ibid., 150.

[13] Ibid.

[14] Philip Schaff, *History of the Christian Church,* vol. 7, (Peabody, Massachusetts: Hendrickson Publishers, 2002), 53.

[15] Ibid., 55.

[16] Ibid., 51.

[17] John S. Oyer, *Lutheran Reformers Against Anabaptists,* (Paris, Arkansas: The Baptist Standard Bearer, Inc., 1964), 114-139.

[18] Schaff, 606-611.

[19] Oyer, 138.

[20] Carl Deimer, Professor, *History of Christianity II,* Video Lecture 13, Liberty University DLP, 2004.

[21] Estep, 51-52.

[22] Ibid., 53.

[23] Sarah Covington, *The Trail of Martyrdom: Persecution and Resistance in Sixteenth-century England,* (South Bend, Indiana: University of Notre Dame press, 2003), (www.bibliovault.org/BV.book.epl?BookId=5883).

[24] *Wikipedia,* (en.wikipedia.org/wiki/The_Pilgrim's_Progress).

[25] Ibid., /wiki/Tower_of_London.

[26] *Mennonites in Europe,* (www.anabaptists.org/writings/excerpts/meneu-1.html).

[27] Estep, 52-53.

[28] *Balthasar Hubmaier,* (www.mainstreambaptists.org/mbn/hubmaier.htm).

[29] Deimer, Lecture 14.

[30] Broadbent, 175.

[31] Ibid., 179.

[32] Deimer.

[33] Estep, 57.

[34] Deimer, Lecture 13.

[35] Broadbent, 200.

[36] Estep, 152-160.

[37] Broadbent, 207.

[38] Estep, 160-176.

The Origin of the Anabaptists

People of the Unbroken Line from Christ

Anabaptists did not view themselves as a new sect. Records testify that people believing and practicing exactly what they believed and practiced had been around since the time of the New Testament.

They Did Not Originate with Ulrich Zwingli

There are some historians who contend that the Anabaptist movement started in 1525 when a small band of Ulrich Zwingli followers were upset that he refused to take a public stand in favor of Scriptural baptism. These zealous men who went forth with enormous success were supposedly the original Anabaptists.

They Did Not Originate with the Münster Rebellion

The infamous Münster Rebellion of 1524 grew from the desperation with slavery and oppression rather than religious convictions.

They Are Descendents of the Waldenses

In reality, the Anabaptist movement was the continuation of that unbroken line of Christians and churches from Christ forward. Throughout the centuries these believers had been called Anabaptists because of their practice of requiring proper baptism of those who came to them.

Anabaptist Leaders

Georg Cajacob Blaurock

This bold man won great numbers of disciples wherever he went. Shortly before his martyrdom, he became pastor of an orphaned church in the Adige Valley of Austria.

Balthasar Hubmaier (1481-1528)

He is regarded by many as the most important Anabaptist of all. He was born a peasant, earned a doctorate in theology as a Catholic, and then was converted to an Anabaptist. He wrote a tract and a book about the Anabaptist doctrines. He made and baptized over 6,000 converts in Austria. He was then captured and burned at the stake.

Johannes (Hans) Denck

As a Lutheran, Johannes Denck met Balthasar Hubmaier who led him to be baptized and join the Anabaptists. Denck is known as one of the best Anabaptist theologians.

Michael Sattler

Sattler was a Benedictine monk who converted to Anabaptist and had a successful ministry in South Germany. He was apprehended by the Catholics and horribly tortured in public. As he was being burned at the stake, he made a hand gesture that indicated that God's grace was sufficient.

Menno Simons (1496 - 1561)

Menno Simons visited and encouraged the scattered and harassed remnants from the Münster Rebellion. He moved to Holstein where his writings were widely circulated and had a major impact outside the area.

Chapter 30

Baptists

At this point, a reminder of the focus of this book is in order. The point has been repeatedly made that throughout history from Jesus Christ to the present, there has always been an unbroken line of Christians and churches that stayed true to New Testament doctrine and practices and which never became a part of a union of churches which united with the state and went on to become the Catholic Church. There is zero reason to assume that at some point all churches ignored New Testament warnings against false teachers and drifts from the truth and went into apostasy. (*"For I know this, that after my departing shall grievous wolves enter in among you, not sparing the flock. Also of your own selves shall men arise, speaking perverse things, to draw away disciples after them. Therefore watch, and remember, that by the space of three years I ceased not to warn every one night and day with tears,"* **Acts 20:29-31**. *"For the time will come when they will not endure sound doctrine; but after their own lusts shall they heap to themselves teachers, having itching ears; And they shall turn away their ears from the truth, and shall be turned unto fables. But watch thou in all things, endure afflictions, do the work of an evangelist, make full proof of thy ministry,"* **2 Timothy 4:3-5**). Yes, some did go into apostasy, but not all! Why shouldn't we believe what history confirms, that many believers and churches stayed true to and earnestly contended for, *"the faith which was once delivered unto the saints"* and did not succumb to *"certain men crept in unawares, who were before of old ordained to this condemnation, ungodly men, turning the grace of our God into lasciviousness, and denying the only Lord God, and our Lord Jesus Christ,"*

Jude 3-4? The unspoken assumption of a large number of modern church historians is that at one point or another, all Christians and churches departed from the New Testament way, became hopelessly corrupt in doctrine and in practice and had to ultimately return to the New Testament way. As we have seen in these chapters, that is an invalid assumption.

RECAP

The Unbroken Line

We know that during His earthly ministry Jesus Christ personally established His church in Jerusalem, Israel. At that time, He promised its perpetuity until His return, **Matthew 16:18-19**. Especially through the ministry of the Apostle Paul (but not limited to him), New Testament churches rapidly proliferated across Asia Minor, around the Aegean Sea, into Rome which was the nerve center of the Empire, across North Africa, around the Fertile Crescent, into Europe and as far west as Wales (**Acts**).

The Route It Has Taken

An unbroken line of churches true to the New Testament way can be traced through Macedonia, **2 Corinthians 8:1**, into the Balkan States, and from there through missionaries to the Alps in and around Southern France, Switzerland and Northern Italy. When Bogomil missionaries arrived in Central Europe from Bulgaria and Bosnia, they found great communities of people who already believed as they did. This second branch of the unbroken line of true New Testament churches is the one that had, under great persecution from the state church of Constantine, migrated westward and populated Europe with New Testament churches. As the Church in Rome grew stronger, these churches found their greatest stronghold in the relative protection of the Cottian Alps. Through the centuries, they went by many names such as Cathari, Paulicians, Waldenses and Albigenses. "It is a significant fact well established in credible history that even as far back as the fourth century, those refusing to go into the Hierarchy, and refusing to accept the baptism of those baptized in infancy, and refusing to

384

accept the doctrine of 'Baptismal Regeneration' and demanding rebaptism for all those who came to them from the Hierarchy, were called 'Anabaptists.' No matter what other names they then bore, they were always referred to as 'Ana-Baptists.' Near the beginning of the sixteenth century, the 'Ana' was dropped, and the name shortened to simply 'Baptist,' and gradually all other names were dropped." [1]

The unbroken line can be traced from Jerusalem, both through the eastern Balkan States to the Anabaptists in Europe, and through the center of Europe itself to the Anabaptists. The great communities of Waldenses, especially the pre-Reformation Waldenses, were for the most part Anabaptists. They definitely were never a part of the Catholic line; and the fact that the state church (which became the Catholic Church) persecuted them mercilessly from its start is irrefutable testimony that they were never a part of Catholicism. We have seen how the unbroken line made it to the days of the Reformation; we know also that the churches of the unbroken line were not break-aways from Reformation churches. To the contrary, they had been there all the time; and many of the reformers joined and became a part of the unbroken line. It was not (except in a few cases of deception), the other way around.

Furthermore, we have seen that a third branch of the unbroken line came through Wales. Through the ministry of the Apostle Paul, certain Welsh people were reached with the gospel message while on military duty in Rome. These went back home to Wales and established great and flourishing Christian communities. When Catholicism later arrived in Wales, Christianity suffered greatly under the usual Catholic onslaught against all non-Catholics; however, New Testament Christianity survived in the British Isles and eventually made its way to America. [2]

BRITISH BAPTISTS

With this background in mind, it is now time to take a more specific look at post-Reformation Baptists or the continuation of the unbroken line through and past the Reformation particularly in Britain.

Early British Baptists

Baptists in Britain predate John Wycliffe, who lived and died in the fourteenth century. Historians both sympathetic to Baptists, as well as those who were not, testify to the existence of those who embraced Baptist beliefs all the way back to John the Baptist. [3] In addition to the early arrival of New Testament Christianity in Wales, John Foxe recorded how it came to England in the latter half of the second century. [4] Foxe also recorded many of the efforts of Emperor Diocletian to destroy the early Christians in England. [5] The point is that Christians who embraced and practiced the positions set forth in the New Testament were in England and Wales hundreds of years before Wycliffe or the later Protestant Reformation. Thomas Crosby gave most of his life to a study of the existence of Baptist people and their principles in England. At first he surmised that they originated in England with John Wycliffe; however, after years of research and careful study, he wrote these words, "The true Christian doctrine, and form of worship, as delivered by the Apostles, was maintained in England, and the Romish government and ceremonies, zealously withstood, till the Saxons entered into Britain, about the year 448." [6] Mr. Crosby went on to elaborate that these "English Baptists" practiced baptism of only believers by immersion. As previously mentioned, in 597 Pope Gregory sent the monk, Austin, to convert the British to the Catholic brand of Christianity. When he failed to do so by persuasion, he turned to persecution. He succeeded in officially bringing England and Wales into Catholicism; however, he never succeeded in eradicating true New Testament Christianity from England or Wales. [7] A thousand years later, when John Wycliffe arrived on the scene, Anabaptists were still there practicing New Testament doctrine and practices. Before Wycliffe, an eloquent Dutchman named Walter Lollard came to England from the Waldenses. His followers rapidly increased; and it is said that within a few years, more than one-half of the people of England became Lollards. [8] The evidence strongly indicates that it was their influence that turned John Wycliffe from Catholicism.

> **New Testament Christians were in England hundreds of years before Wycliffe**

Specific Churches in England

In spite of great persecution and enormous efforts to eradicate England of these people with distinctly Baptist beliefs, they multiplied. "The followers of Lollard and Wycliff united and in a short time England was full of the 'Bible Men'. . .The Lollard movement was later merged into the Anabaptist" [9] and over time they became known simply as Baptists. Well before the Protestant Reformation, Baptist churches existed in many places in England. There was an organized Baptist church in London led by Simon Fish in the year 1525." [10] Both native Baptists and immigrants from the Continent, particularly Holland, organized Baptist churches. New churches (sometimes called *conventicles*) sprang up in London, Kent, Feversham, Maidstone, Eythorne, Essex, Bocking, Lansdowne and many other places. [11]

Every English regime hated and persecuted the Baptists. They were a thorn-in-the-side of a nation with a state church (Anglican). When parents will not baptize their children into the church, it is impossible for the state to control religion in that country. Even in the face of severe persecution, "the Baptists continued to multiply; foreigners continued to stream into the country, as many as 4,000 resided near Norwich, many of them were Baptists. Moreover churches were formed. Of these still existing it is alleged that Faringdon was founded in 1576; Crowle and Epworth both in 1597; Dartmouth, Oxford, Wedmore, Bridgewater, all in 1600. That is to say there were conventicles in at least nine counties outside London, where churches still exist as their direct successors." This was written in London on April 11, 1902. [12]

John T. Christian said, "At best the distinction between the names Baptists and Anabaptists is technical" and went on to cite a document by Sir William Cecil, an official of Queen Elizabeth, which called all of them "Baptists." Dr. Christian then said, "It is therefore scientifically correct to call these people Baptists." [13]

As we are about to see, most modern historians, including Baptists, erroneously argue that Baptists originated in England out of the initial efforts of John Smyth.

THE JOHN SMYTH CONTROVERSY

Baptists were always independent churches. An examination of their ancestry back to Christ shows that they never were a part of a state church. A strong doctrinal position of Baptists (by whatever name) has always been the autonomy of each church. Each Baptist church was independent of both the civil government and all other churches. Furthermore, each church was congregational in internal government.

Separatists

Toward the end of the sixteenth century, another independent group emerged in England. They were called *Separatists* and believed in congregational government. Because of their popular leader, Robert Browne, they were also called *Brownists* and they soon numbered in the thousands. [14] Like the Baptists, the Separatists were proponents of a *Free Church* without control from either the Anglican Church or civil government. Under severe persecution, Browne eventually broke and returned to the Church of England; however, his followers continued the Free Church movement. They were hunted and persecuted. Some were burned at the stake. Still the movement continued. [15]

The Separatists were not Baptists, but some Baptists became involved with them. Baptists held firmly to the position that in order for one to be a member of a church, he had to be saved and baptized by immersion. [16] The independent Separatists "baptized infants, one of whose parents (or whose guardian) was a believer." [17] In this case, as was so often the case, the number one dividing issue was baptism. One group stands out from all others through the centuries and it is that group that perennially insisted that in order to be a member of a church a person must (1) be saved and (2) be baptized by immersion (3) by the authority of a legitimate church. Their enemies called them Anabaptists and eventually dropped the *Ana*.

John Smyth

One of those in the Separatist movement was John Smyth. In 1606 he formed a Separatist church in Gainsborough, England. [18]

There are major conflicts in the stories of his pastorate at Gainsborough. Supposedly on the night of March 24, 1606, he was baptized in the Don River. Two years later (1608), he moved his whole church of about eight people to Amsterdam, Holland, where his group united with an existing Separatist church whose pastor was named Ainsworth. Smyth opposed infant baptism, and he and his party were soon excluded from Ainsworth's church. Smyth and his followers proceeded to baptize themselves (Smyth reportedly baptized himself, an act called se-baptism) and formed a new church. A split soon developed in Smyth's new church, and he along with 24 others were excluded. Smyth and those who sided with him repudiated their baptisms and the organization of his church as invalid. They then sought membership in one of the Mennonite churches in Amsterdam. After much internal strife among the Mennonites over Smyth and his followers, they were received into this church whose mode of baptism was sprinkling. Shortly thereafter (1610), Smyth died as a Mennonite in Holland, and the remnant of his church that had stayed with him became extinct. [19] In 1611 or 1612, Thomas Helwys, who had originally paid the passage of the entire church from England to Holland, took the other remnant of Smyth's church back to England. There he was apprehended by the king and died in prison. [20] Before his death, Helwys formed a new church in London, which is claimed by some to be the first General Baptist church in England. [21]

John Smyth Was Not a Baptist

It is quite obvious that there is no valid reason to believe that John Smyth was ever a Baptist. The church he organized and moved to Holland was a Separatist church, not a Baptist church. Dutch Baptists were everywhere in Holland. Instead of going to one of their churches for a valid baptism, Smyth baptized himself (some say Helwys baptized him). Neither self-baptism (se-baptism) nor baptism by a Separatist would make Smyth a Baptist. He could have received a valid baptism and become a Baptist, but he didn't. "Smyth and his church thought they had the right to originate baptism among themselves." [22] Like many later Christians, they completely ignored perpetuity which is the fact that legitimacy comes from Christ through His unbroken line of true, New Testament churches. No person is to simply trust Christ and then start baptizing people on his own. Doing so ignores perpetuity and the authority which Jesus gave to His church to baptize. To be valid, baptism must be administered by legitimate authority. Jesus gave that authority to His church, not to individuals independent of church authority. *"Go ye therefore, and teach all nations, baptizing them in the name of the Father, and of the Son, and of the Holy Ghost: Teaching them to observe all things whatsoever I have commanded you: and, lo, I am with you alway, even unto the end of the world. Amen,"* **Matthew 28:19-20**. That command by Jesus was to His church corporate, which would continue in an unbroken line until His return. He did not give the authority to baptize to individuals acting apart from church capacity. Smyth missed that and thought the authority to baptize rested in individuals (him), not in a legitimate church.

William H. Whitsitt, Leader of the Assault on Baptist Heritage

In spite of the facts about Smyth and Helwys, Dr. William H. Whitsitt, who became the third president of the Southern Baptist Theological Seminary in Louisville, Kentucky (1895), contended that there is no unbroken line of true churches back to Christ. Overlooking overwhelming historical evidence of the continuous practice of baptism by immersion from Christ to his time, Dr. Whitsitt said that immersion was not practiced in England before 1641. He therefore summarily wrote off all of the dissenters prior to that time as illegitimate Christians and churches. With the same stroke of his pen, he banished all of the great historians as unscientific because they did not cite enough primary sources in their histories. Many of these historians lived on or near location, often very near in time to the people and events of which they wrote. They gave their lives to research and documented proofs about those faithful primitive, New Testament Christians who sealed their testimonies with their blood. In spite of that reality, Dr. Whitsitt is considered by many to be imminently smarter and far more knowledgeable that the combined lot of his predecessors. Because of him and his following of modern scholars who say there was no Baptist immersion before 1641, we should all disbelieve the promise of perpetuity made by Jesus in **Matthew 16:18** and affirmed by Paul in **Ephesians 3:21**, reject the irrefutable evidence of New Testament Christians through the ages, and say that Baptists are nothing more than a band of Protestant new-comers who originated in England only after 1641 out of the groundwork laid by John Smyth. [23]

Baptist Heritage Does Not Rise or Fall on John Smyth

The history of Baptists (in England or elsewhere) does not rest on John Smyth. Whether he was a Baptist or not is inconsequential to the unbroken line of New Testament churches back to Christ. Long before Smyth was born and long after he died, New Testament churches existed. They were called by a variety of names (Baptists, Anabaptist, Waldenses, etc.), but they were the same spiritual line of people regardless of time or location. If Smyth never existed, the history of the unbroken line of true churches would be unharmed. They didn't start with Smyth, and they didn't end with him. "The baptism of Smyth did not affect the baptism of the Baptist churches of England. It has been affirmed that the General Baptist churches of England originated with this church of Smyth's; that this was the mother church of Baptists; and even that the Baptist denomination originated here in the year 1609 . . . The Baptist historians of England are singularly unanimous on this point. 'If he (Smyth) were guilty of what they charge him with,' says Crosby, ''tis no blemish on the English Baptists; who neither approved any such method, nor did they receive their baptism from him.'" [24] The Smyth issue "does not in the least interfere with the overwhelming, historical facts that the English Baptists had their origin originally from the ancient Welsh Baptist churches planted in the apostolic age." [25]

As we have already seen, persons embracing Baptist views existed in England and Wales as far back as the first century. They were generally scorned as Anabaptists. We have spoken of Walter Lollard, a German preacher who came to England about 1315. His great success produced a great company of followers called Lollards. John Wycliffe was deeply involved with this movement and his followers were not only called Wycliffites, they were more commonly called Lollards. The Lollards Tower in London is testimony to the long line of Baptists in England long before John Smyth. [26] Particularly in the last 300 years prior to John Smyth,

Baptists had streamed into England from the Continent. Furthermore, some independent groups in England realized the illegitimacy of their baptisms and actually went to Holland to receive valid baptisms. They returned to England to propagate streams of Baptist churches. [27]

OBSERVATIONS

The unbroken line of New Testament Christians and churches from Christ to the present has been viciously attacked and denied; however, the evidence supports their case. The unbroken line leads from **Matthew 16:18** to the Baptists in England. That spiritual line of people has somehow, through the centuries, stayed true to the core doctrine and practices of the Scriptures. They have always insisted in the sole authority of the Scriptures in matters of doctrine and practice, the deity of Christ, salvation by grace through personal faith in Christ, the priesthood of every believer, the autonomy of each local church, holy living and freedom of conscience. These biblical positions always excluded tradition as a rule of doctrine or practice, institutional salvation in any form, a hierarchy within or outside a church and a state church. It necessitated the re-baptism of all who came with anything short of baptism by immersion as a believer in Jesus Christ. This consistent position throughout the centuries gained them their most common name, *Anabaptists*. In time the *Ana* faded and this unbroken line of churches became known simply as Baptists. They are neither newcomers nor Protestants. They originated with Jesus Christ, not in England; but they flourished in England and came to America via English soil.

In our next and final chapter, we will trace them to America. We shall also consider their tremendous contribution to the religious liberty that is known today in much of the world.

1 J.M. Carroll, *The Trail of Blood,* (Lexington, Kentucky: Ashland Avenue Baptist Church, 1992), 39.

2 Ibid., 43-44.

3 John T. Christian, *A History of the Baptists,* vol. 1, (Texarkana, Ark.-Tex.: Bogard Press, 1922), 171-175.

4 John Fox, *Christian Martyrology,* (London, Paris and New York: Fisher, Son, & Co., 1840), 102-103.

5 Ibid., 77-79.

6 Thomas Crosby, quoted in *A History of Baptists* by John T. Christian, 177.

7 Christian, 178-181.

8 Ibid., 184.

9 Ibid., 187.

10 Fox, 264.

11 Christian, 196-198.

12 Ibid., 209.

13 Ibid., 205-206.

14 E.H. Broadbent, *The Pilgrim Church,* (Grand Rapids, Michigan: GOSPEL FOLIO PRESS, 1999), 251.

15 Ibid., 252-253.

16 Carl Deimer, Professor, *History of Christianity II,* Video Lecture 17, Liberty University DLP, 2004.

17 Broadbent, 251.

18 Christian, 223.

19 D.B. Ray, *Baptist Succession: A Hand-book of Baptist History,* (Parsons, Kansas: Foley Railway Printing Company, 1912), 133-135.

20 Deimer.

21 Ray, 135.

22 Christian, 225.

23 I.K. Cross, *The Battle for Baptist History,* (Columbus, Georgia: Brentwood Christian Press, 1990), 131-141.

24 Ibid.

25 Ray, 141.

26 Lollards Tower, The Archbishop of Canterbury, (www.archbishopofcanterbury.org/943).

27 Ray, 136-139.

Baptist Heritage

Apostolic Age - The ancient Welsh Baptist churches originated in this time period. This is the beginning of the English Baptists. The unbroken line leads from Matthew 16:18 to the Baptists in England.

Emperor Diocletian, who reigned from A.D. 284 to 305, tried many times to destroy the Christians in England. This is proof that Christians were in England at an early time.

Anabaptists - They believed in the re-baptism of all who came with anything short of baptism by immersion as a believer in Jesus Christ. In time, the Ana faded and they became Baptists. They originated with Jesus Christ, not in England.

True believer's biblical positions:

Included
Insistence in the sole authority of the Scriptures in matters of doctrine and practice
The deity of Christ
Salvation by grace through personal faith in Christ
The priesthood of every believer
The autonomy of each local church
Holy living and freedom of conscience

Excluded
Tradition as a rule of doctrine or practice
Institutional salvation in any form
A hierarchy within or outside a church and a state church

394

Chapter 31

Baptists in America

That there are multitudes of Baptists in America who practice primitive, first-century New Testament Christianity is currently observable and indisputable. To trace the roots of these believers and their churches back to Rhode Island is necessary, but not adequate, to connect them to the unbroken line that originated with Jesus Christ. For American Baptist churches and their offspring to be legitimate, they must be connected by doctrine and practice to that line of pre-America churches which is traceable back to Christ.

Evidence has been presented in this book which supports the claim of an unbroken line of New Testament churches from Christ to Britain. In this final chapter, we shall show how these primitive Christians reached America and flourished here. It is also fitting that we deal briefly with one of their greatest contributions to America and the modern world: *freedom of religion*.

BRITISH BAPTISTS

In chapter 30, we dealt specifically with how Baptists reached Britain and became established there. They staunchly allowed only those who were saved and baptized by immersion to be members into their churches. [1] Baptism by immersion only after salvation was their chief earmark; and they believed salvation comes only by grace through personal faith in Jesus Christ who died, was buried and rose again. In Britain there were tens of thousands of New Testament Christians and hundreds of churches connecting back to the apostles. That was particularly the case in Wales and England. ² They were called Lollards, Brethren, Anabaptists and other names; however, over the years they became known simply as Baptists.

Two leading groups of Baptists emerged in England. One group believed Christ died for everyone; they were called General Baptists. The second group believed Christ died only for the elect; these were called Particular Baptists.

> **British Baptists were also known as Lollards, Brethren, and Anabaptists**

CONDITIONS IN ENGLAND

Keep in mind that England was officially Anglican. A state church existed, and a state church always seeks to force its positions and will upon the entire populace. A measure of religious tolerance existed in England; however, there was no freedom of religion. England was Anglican, and other religious groups were persecuted. In terms of doctrine and practice, Anglicanism is mostly Catholicism by a different name.

There arose a group within the Anglican Church that wanted to stay in the church and purify it. Those of this very zealous and strict sect were called Puritans. When King James I arrived from Scotland (1603), a large number of Puritans presented him with a list of reforms which they wished to see instituted in Anglicanism as soon as possible. These reforms, known as the Millenary Petition, called for the removal of lingering Catholic practices such as making the sign of the cross at baptism and reading from the Apocrypha during church services. The Puritans also argued that no popish opinion should be taught or defended. They said clergy should be allowed to marry and argued that excommunication end as a political weapon. King James did not prove to be a friend to the Puritans. ³

During the reigns of King James and Queen Elizabeth, another group of Puritans called Separatists determined that they would not violate their own consciences by outwardly conforming to Anglican laws while they were secretly fighting to reform the Anglican Church. These chose not to conform and left the Anglican Church altogether. They paid the heavy price of fines, imprisonments, expulsions and executions. [4]

There was on-going religious strife and division in England. From one political regime to the next, religious stances and politics swung from one extreme to another like a great pendulum. Queen Mary (Bloody Mary) ruled England and Ireland from July 19, 1553 until November 17, 1558. She was passionately Catholic and sought to purge her domain of all non-Catholics. [5] Her reign was a nightmare for primitive Christians. At her death her half sister, Elizabeth I, became queen of England and Ireland and ruled until March 24, 1603. She was Anglican but much more tolerant than her predecessors. Puritans, Separatists, Baptists and others flourished under her reign. She was followed by King James I (1603-1625). He was a strong Anglican and determined to put down the Puritans and the Separatists. [6] King James I was followed by King Charles I (1625-1649) who was openly sympathetic to Catholicism and came down hard on non-Catholics, especially Puritans. At that time, there was an anti-king sentiment in England. That sentiment was also in the Parliament. The Puritans were staunch Calvinists, as were the Scottish Presbyterians. The discontented Parliament dismissed King Charles I in 1649 and appealed to the king of Scotland for help. He invaded and Charles I was beheaded. England then went through a Commonwealth (1649-1660), two pro-Catholic kings (Charles II [1660-1685] and James II [1685-1688]) before William and Mary (1689-1702) came to power. The *Act of Toleration* was passed in 1689. It brought a measure of freedom of religion to England. [7]

During those years before the *Act of Toleration,* life in England was perilous for those who were not a part of the state church. Many non-compliant ministers were shot, either in their homes or churches. Some were dragged into the streets and stabbed to death. Groups of New Testament believers were herded into church buildings where the doors were locked and the buildings set on fire. Thousands were driven into rivers and lakes with spears, swords, axes, guns and other dangerous weapons. Women were tied to posts and stripped to the waist. Their breasts were cut off, and they were left to bleed to death. [8]

| **The official Church of England was Anglican** |

THE GLAMOR OF A NEW WORLD

It is not difficult to see why so many people would be eager to leave England for a new start in the *New World* that had been discovered. Constant turmoil and frequent persecution (there was also widespread poverty and many social ills), coupled with the prospect of a new life of freedom in the new world, appealed to the masses. This was true in England, but it was also true on the Continent. Waves of people, including Baptists, began to migrate to America. The Virginia Colony at Jamestown was established May 14, 1607. [9] The Plymouth Colony of Plymouth, Massachusetts was an English colonial venture from 1620-1691. [10] As these colonies continued to spring up, more Baptists and others began to reach American shores. The unbroken line of New Testament churches extended itself to America. While New Testament churches continued in England and many other European locations, they sprang up in America. There was no break in the line.

STATE CHURCHES IN AMERICA

Do not assume that all who fled to America had in mind freedom of religion in this new world. They did not. The vast majority of those who came sought relief from the oppression of the state church which had abused them in the old world. They were not against the concept of a state church; they simply wanted their church to be the state church. They didn't want to be oppressed; they wanted to be the oppressors. Most of them held the hypocritical position that it is perfectly acceptable to force religious positions on everyone in the populace as long as they are your positions.

Upon arrival in America, the Puritans promptly made theirs the state religion of the New England colonies (Massachusetts,

Connecticut and New Hampshire). The southern colonies (Virginia, Maryland, the Carolinas and Georgia) established Anglican church-state unions. The middle colonies (New York, Pennsylvania, Delaware and New Jersey) were more pluralistic and open to different views.

These state churches promptly adopted the same vicious practices of those from whom they fled. For example, when a Baptist church was established in Boston, the Puritan General Court passed laws that allowed Puritan leaders to seize Baptist property. They nailed shut the doors of the Baptist church and ordered all citizens of Massachusetts to baptize their babies. "In Virginia the situation was just as bad. Their charter demanded that all of the inhabitants conform to the Episcopalian beliefs enforced in England. A 15 pound tax was assessed each person to pay for the salary, land and cattle of the ministers. Penalties for fines as much as 20 pounds were prescribed against anyone who failed to attend church or spoke negatively against a preacher of the state-sponsored Anglican or Episcopal Church. A fine of 2,000 pounds of tobacco was decreed against any adult who would not have his child baptized. One thousand of those pounds went to the informer." [11]

A specific case in point is that of Pastor John Clarke, Deacon John Crandall and Elder Obadiah Holmes, who went from Rhode Island to Lynn, Massachusetts to visit one of their aging, blind members, William Witter. They were Baptists. On Sunday Pastor Clarke preached to a small group who came to Witter's house to worship. During the sermon, two constables entered the house and arrested Clarke, Holmes and Crandall. The three were forced against their wills to attend a Puritan worship service, where they refused to remove their hats. For disrespect they were taken to a Boston prison. Later they were tried. Clarke was fined twenty pounds, Holmes thirty pounds and Crandall five pounds. Friends paid the fines of Clarke and Crandall, but Holmes said he had done nothing wrong and refused to have his fine paid. After two months Holmes "was marched to a public place, the Boston Common; there, in a merciless manner, he was publicly flogged with thirty lashes from a three-braided whip, thus receiving ninety stripes . . . Following the public beating of Holmes, two bystanders, John Hazel and John Spur, approached Holmes and shook his hand. As a result of this encouraging gesture, both men were arrested and later fined for giving aid and comfort to a lawbreaker. Hazel was an elderly man and – perhaps due to the grueling ordeal of incarceration – died before he arrived home following his release." [12]

ROGER WILLIAMS

The popular but mistaken concept is that Roger Williams was the first to plant a true and enduring Baptist church in America. Williams was a Puritan living in England who, like many Puritans, concluded that the Anglican Church could not be reformed. On April 7, 1630 with attorney John Winthrop as their governor, a group of Puritans known as the Massachusetts Bay Company left Southampton, England for America with the intent of creating "a true Church of England." [13]   They had no plans for religious liberty; to the contrary they planned to set up a pure Anglican state church in America. All citizens would be required to be a part of it and subject to its laws and control. Regardless of their church affiliation, such was the intentions of almost all of those early settlers who migrated to America.

Six months after Winthrop arrived in Salem Harbor, Roger and Mary Williams sailed from Bristol and joined Winthrop at Salem. The winter of 1631 was vicious in New England; however, large numbers of Puritans continued to flee England for a new beginning in the new world. Roger and Mary Williams soon made their way into the new city of Boston. Roger was a well-educated minister with a good reputation and was soon asked to be parish minister. He turned down the offer. He was becoming more and more convicted that there must be immediate and complete separation from the Church of England.   This stance was unpopular with Governor Winthrop and most of the people who believed a successfully reformed Anglican Church in America would translate into church reformation in England. Williams' consistent and vocal stance brought him disfavor in Boston. He and Mary moved to nearby Salem, where he was quickly embraced; however, due to pressure from Boston, Salem turned against Williams, who moved to Plymouth. In Plymouth, Williams and his ideas became well known.   He spoke and wrote of Puritan

injustices, especially against the Indians.   He argued that King
Charles I had no right to give anyone exclusive title to anything in
America from 40 to 48 degrees latitude.   Williams argued that the
Indians were people too, with real rights, and that they should be
treated in a Christian manner.   He exposed vast differences
between Puritan thought and activities and the teachings of true,
biblical Christianity.   He taught that "the magistrate hasn't any
authority to punish those who break the commandments dealing
with a man's relationship to God." [14]

In Plymouth, Williams assisted the minister of the church.
Williams was highly disappointed when members of the Plymouth
church traveled to England and attended Anglican services but
were not reprimanded upon return.   In late 1633, he resigned his
post with the Plymouth church and returned to Salem. [15]

The Plymouth authorities were glad to see him go. He continued
his outspoken ways and became well-known in the colony. His
talk didn't sit well with the Puritans, especially their civil and
ecclesiastical leaders. The General Court of the colony moved
against Williams. A series of encounters and debates ensued.
Williams challenged almost everything and "cast doubt on nearly
everything that Massachusetts held dear: its charter, its General
Court, its churches, its land and most of all its promise." [16] At the
conclusion of their fourth meeting, the General Court ordered
Roger Williams to depart the jurisdiction. Plans were to ship him
back to England, although in January of 1636 he hastily left his
wife and home in Salem and slipped into the snowy woods in
hopes of reaching Narragansett Bay. He became lost in the woods
but was rescued by Indians, with whom he spent the winter near
present-day Bristol, Rhode Island. When spring came, some of his
followers learned of his whereabouts and joined him. The group
moved to a spring of fresh water in what is currently Providence,
Rhode Island and established a town. [17]

Williams became convinced that baptism is only by immersion to
believers.   "Ezekiel Holliman baptized Williams and Williams
baptized the others and in 1639 they formed a society which some
call a church. A few months after this Williams withdrew from the
church believing that he was not scripturally baptized since
Holliman wasn't baptized when he baptized Williams. He never

joined any other church but considered himself a seeker the rest of his days." [18] Within four months, the Roger Williams church (if it ever was a church) ceased to exist and came to nothing. It never produced any offspring [19] and "it is evident that Roger Williams was never a member of any true, legitimate Baptist church." [20] The First Baptist Church of Providence, Rhode Island claims to be the first Baptist church in America with the year of its founding being 1638. Evidence is quite conclusive that the Providence church was re-established at some point in time after 1639; that is the year the church effort of Roger Williams started and failed. [21]

Even though Roger Williams cannot be rightfully viewed as the founder of a true, legitimate Baptist church in America, he was a man greatly used of God to establish liberty of conscience in this country. The world is indebted to him. "He and Dr. Clark worked together to finally secure a charter for the colony of Rhode Island guaranteeing religious liberty." [22]

Roger Williams was never a true Baptist

JOHN CLARKE

From as early as 1630 and onward, the number of Baptists in America was growing rapidly. They were a thorn in the side of the Presbyterian Puritans. Thomas Hooker of Connecticut wrote to Thomas Sheppard of Cambridge, "I like those Anabaptists and their opinion every day worse than the other . . . unless you be very watchful you will have an army in the field before you know how to prepare or to oppose." [23] The Baptist stance against infant baptism was a catalyst issue even as it had been through the centuries. Persecutions against them escalated in 1635. On November 13, 1644, the General Court of Massachusetts passed a law for their suppression. [24]

John Clarke was born in Bedfordshire, England in 1609. He was highly educated and was a doctor who also became a preacher. He "received his baptism and ordination in London, in a church whose succession extends in a regular line back to the apostolic age . . . He came to this country, as a Baptist minister, from London . . .

He settled, at first, in Massachusetts; but fled from persecution, and arrived in Rhode Island in March, 1638; and in the same year established the first Baptist church on the continent of America, Newport, R.I." [25] Dr. Clark remained pastor of the Newport church until his death.

On March 28, 1638, Dr. Clark and his colleagues purchased land and obtained a deed from the Indians. [26] "The colonists sent him to England in 1651 for a better charter for Rhode Island. He couldn't receive it from Cromwell, but he did from Charles II twelve years later in 1663. This charter granted political and religious freedom to Rhode Island. He was a leader among the Baptists and in the government of Rhode Island." [27] It should be noted that Dr. Clarke's efforts in England to secure the Rhode Island charter took years and reduced him to financial poverty. Without the help of Roger Williams' support and fund-raising efforts back home, it would have been virtually impossible for Dr. Clarke to succeed. [28] The world is surely indebted to both Dr. John Clarke and to Roger Williams who were true pioneers of religious liberty.

> **Rhode Island was granted political and religious freedom by Charles II**

THE SPREAD OF BAPTIST CHURCHES IN AMERICA

It is a mistake to assume that there were no Baptists in America prior to John Clarke's church in Newport, Rhode Island. Baptists were continually migrating to America from England and other European countries. It should not be difficult to understand that it took time for them to establish churches, especially in view of the political climate against them at that time. The Puritans and others persecuted Baptists and all others who did not submit to them. "As Baptist sentiments have ever been wont to, from the days of John the Baptist, so in America they prevailed in spite of oppressive persecution. In the following order they appear in the different United States. Rhode Island, 1638-56; Massachusetts, 1663-6; Pennsylvania, 1711-46; New Jersey, 1712-47; New York, 1724-48; Connecticut, 1726-50; South Carolina, 1738-45; and thus onward to the present time." [29]

Delaware

Baptists came to Delaware from Wales. "In the spring of the year 1701, several Baptists, in the communities of Pembroke and Caermarthen, resolved to go to America; and as one of the company, Thomas Griffith, was a minister, they were advised to be constituted into a church; they took the advice; the instrument of their confession was in being in 1770." [30]

Massachusetts

Massachusetts Baptist churches began in Boston.

Virginia

The first Baptist church in Virginia was planted by Dutton Lane and Daniel Marshall. Marshall received his baptism in regular order from a regular Baptist church in the Philadelphia association.

Pennsylvania

Pennsylvania Baptist churches originated through the ministry of Thomas Dungan. Dungan left Rhode Island, apparently with other Baptists, and planted a Baptist church. This church soon merged with another which came to the area. The second church was made up of Welsh emigrants from Lower Dublin (a township in Pennsylvania). They were regular Baptists. The first church in Philadelphia was organized in 1698 of English Baptists, some of whom were of Hansard Knolly's church in London.

Maryland

A Baptist church was planted in Maryland in 1742 in the home of Henry Sator, a layman.

North Carolina

In North Carolina, Paul Palmer, a native of Maryland who was baptized at the Welsh Tract Baptist Church in Delaware, planted a Baptist Church in 1727.

South Carolina

Many of the earliest settlers in South Carolina were Baptists. Many of them came as colonists from England; some came from Maine due to Puritan persecution. Under the leadership of a minister named William Screven, they planted a Baptist church in the Charleston area.

Maine

As early as 1647, there were several persons professing to be Baptists in and around Kittery, Maine the oldest town in the province. The nearest Baptist church was in Boston. Upon the advice of Isaac Hull, who was pastor of the Boston church, the Maine Baptists united with the Boston church, which then authorized them as a new and separate Baptist church in Kittery. The Boston church ordained and licensed William Screven to be their pastor; he is the same pastor who later planted the first Baptist church in South Carolina.

New York

A Baptist church was planted in New York about 1712 by a minister named Valentine Wightman. Wightman was from a Baptist church in North Kingston, Maine. The North Kingston church was originated in a revival held by a minister named Baker from Newport, Rhode Island.

Georgia

Georgia Baptists have their roots in the Baptists of Charleston, South Carolina. [31]

Kentucky

John Gano was a prominent Baptist minister who traveled almost the length of the east coast evangelizing and planting churches. Kentucky was the last place he visited before his death. He "had an active part in influencing Baptist concerns for religious liberty as the Continental Congress hammered out the new constitution." [32]

It is not at all difficult to see how the unbroken line of primitive, first-century, New Testament churches reached America and proliferated.

> **Baptists were continually migrating to America from England**

WELSH MINISTERS

The number of Welsh ministers who came to America to start Baptist churches is impressive: Tomas Griffith, John Mills, Morgan Edwards, Samuel Jones, Abel Morgan, William Davis, Davis Evans, Nathaniel Jenkins, Griffith Jones, Caleb Evans, Elisha Thomas and Enoch Morgan just to name a few. There were also many others from London and other English locations. [33] The unbroken line of perpetuity is clear.

"By 1707 Baptists had formed an association of churches . . . The Philadelphia Association originated with churches planted by members from Wales. The association was formed originally of only five churches: Lower Dublin, Piscataway, Middleton, Cohansey, and Welsh Tract." [34] The strongest of these churches was the Welsh Tract Baptist Church that purchased a large track of land on the Delaware River near present-day Newcastle. Many evangelists went forth from this church, including John Gano who baptized George Washington. [35]

FREEDOM OF RELIGION

In view of this brief look at the history of Christendom from the Church in Jerusalem onward, each of us should have a far greater appreciation for religious liberty. This great blessing is currently taken for granted by far too many. Let us not forget that liberty of conscience has been a Baptist position from the start and that freedom of religion is an American peculiarity. Thankfully other nations have adopted this position; however, it started in America. Furthermore, it became a reality mainly because of efforts by the Baptists.

Before and into the Revolutionary War, the colonists were divided on the issue of freedom of religion. The middle colonies were more tolerant. In the southern colonies and in New England, the state church mentality prevailed. All who failed to fully support the official religious positions of civil authorities were oppressed and persecuted. Baptists and Quakers were required to register annually with civil authorities. The charters granted by the King of England spelled out laws governing the colonies. Only the Rhode

Island charter granted freedom of religion. In all other cases, civil authorities had the power to make laws and dictate the religious lives of the people. The church-state mentality governed the American colonies. Everyone was considered to be a subject of the Church of England. Those of other persuasions were law breakers. Specific punishments were imposed against those who violated religious laws. Activities such as preaching ideas contrary to Anglican doctrine, failure to attend church, failure to baptize your baby, disrespect for a clergyman and "preaching the gospel of the Son of God" [36] were punishable by fines, public whippings and imprisonment. Everyone had to pay taxes to support the official church and her ministers. Baptists, especially Baptist preachers, were main targets of the colonial establishments.

Due to the constant efforts of Roger Williams and the courageous and tenacious labors of Dr. John Clarke, on July 8, 1663, King Charles II of England signed the Rhode Island charter. It was truly a monumental act and marked a new era in the history of mankind. Rhode Island became the first place on earth of significant size and endurance to experience official, government-sanctioned freedom of religion. In part the charter reads, ". . . that a most flourishing civil state may stand and best be maintained, and that among our English subjects, with a full liberty in religious concernments . . . That our royal will and pleasure is, that no person within the said Colony, at any time hereafter, shall be any wise molested, punished, disquieted, or called into question, for any difference in opinion in matters of religion . . . ." [37]

The next year, King Charles II granted a similar charter for the whole of Carolina. In those early days, New Jersey was divided into two halves. The West New Jersey half passed their own liberty of religious conscience law in 1677. In 1670 William Penn published his manifesto titled *The Great Cause of Liberty of Conscience.* In it he made clear that religious liberty includes the right to visibly worship according to one's conscience. When Penn's own colony (Pennsylvania) was established in 1682, liberty of religious conscience was written clearly into the charter. [38]

In spite of these great strides, freedom of religion was not yet universal in America. Colonies like Virginia and Massachusetts staunchly held to a state church ideology. Rigid ecclesiastical laws were passed and enforced. Baptists were oppressed. For example, "The Rev. James Ireland was thrust into prison for preaching in Virginia, and while in jail an effort was made to destroy his life by putting powder under the floor of his cell, but it was unsuccessful; then his enemies tried to suffocate him by filling his little room with the stifling fumes of burning brimstone and pepper pods; and finally his physician and jailor conspired to poison him . . . he never recovered." [39] Even under such adverse conditions during his five months in prison, Rev. Ireland preached through his prison bars to listening crowds. He led to Christ many of his cell-mates, who were sent to harass him. [40]

With the coming of the Revolutionary War and the birth of a new nation, the issue of freedom of religion came to a head. Would the United States of America embrace a state church or would this new nation grant freedom of religion to all her citizens? During and following the war, great Baptist patriots such as Isaac Backus, Lewis Craig, John Waller, John Weatherford, John Gano and a host far too great to name, gave themselves tirelessly to the cause of religious liberty. [41] Many Baptist preachers served as chaplains in the Continental Army; hundreds of Baptist soldiers distinguished themselves as the best soldiers in Washington's army.

After the war when the Continental Congress convened to draw up a constitution (1787), freedom of religion was by no means a certainty. Baptists had proliferated; there were tens of thousands of them scattered throughout the colonies. It was vital to them that religious liberty be made a part of the founding documents of the United States of America. For example, John Leland was a very influential Baptist preacher in Virginia who was nominated to be a delegate to the Virginia convention for ratification of the U. S. Constitution. James Madison was also a candidate for the delegate spot. Leland met with Madison and told him that the Virginians would not approve the Constitution without a guarantee of religious liberty. By this time Baptists dominated Virginia. Madison, a gifted speaker, assured Leland that he would fight for this cause. Leland graciously stepped aside allowing the more persuasive and articulate Madison to attend the convention in his place. [42] The battle for religious liberty was intense. As late as 1775, nine of the thirteen colonies still had officially established churches supported by tax revenues. At the time of the

Constitutional Convention, Massachusetts, New Hampshire and Connecticut maintained established churches. The Constitution proper did not fully clarify and guarantee the issue of religious tolerance. "Some delegates to the Constitutional Convention would not agree to ratify the Constitution without a guarantee that a written Bill of Rights would be speedily enacted to secure religious and other important individual liberties." [43]

"Virginia ratified the Constitution July 28, 1788. Within a year Madison went to congress and helped draw up the Bill of Rights, fulfilling the promise made to Leland." [44] It was not until the meeting of the first United States Congress in 1789 that the ten amendments known as the Bill of Rights were added to the Constitution. They were introduced by Thomas Jefferson, a long-time friend and admirer of the Baptists. Only the Baptists had fought for religious liberty as guaranteed in the first amendment. The Puritans of Massachusetts opposed it and refused to ratify the Bill of Rights. The Congregationalists, the Episcopalians (American Anglicans) and the Presbyterians all opposed the first amendment; however, the Bill of Rights came into effect on December 15, 1791, having been ratified by three-fourths of the States. [45]

That precious and rare first amendment reads, "Congress shall make no law respecting an establishment of religion, or prohibiting the free exercise thereof; or abridging the freedom of speech, or of the press; or the right of the people peaceably to assemble, and to petition the Government for a redress of grievances." [46]

It is doubtful that any of us fully comprehend the magnitude of that amendment!

The first amendment of the Constitution grants freedom of religion

---

1 Carl Deimer, Professor, *History of Christianity II,* Video Lecture 17, Liberty University DLP, 2004.

2 John T. Christian, *A History of the Baptists,* vol. 1, (Texarkana, Ark.-Tex.: Bogard Press, 1922), 172-175.

3 Edwin S. Gaustad, *Liberty of Conscience: Roger Williams in America,* (Grand Rapids: William B. Eerdmans Publishing Company, 1991), 10-11.

4 Ibid., 12.

5 *Wikipedia,* (en.wikipedia.org./wiki/Mary_I_of_England).

6 Deimer.

7 Ibid.

8 Edgar C. Carlisle, *Our Religious Freedom, a Baptist Trophy,* (Johnson, Kansas: IBO Press, 1979), 16-19.

9 *Wikipedia,* (en.wikipedia.org/wiki/Jamestown,_Virginia).

10 Ibid., /wiki/Plymouth_Colony.

11 Carlisle, 29-30.

12 Louis Franklin Asher, *John Clark (1609-1676) Pioneer in American Medicine, Democratic Ideals, and Champion of Religious Liberty,* (Pittsburgh, Pennsylvania: Dorrance Publishing Co. Inc., 1997), 57-64.

13 Gaustad, 21.

14 Edward H. Overbey, *A Brief History of the Baptists,* (Little Rock, Arkansas: The Challenge Press, 1974), 81.

15 J. Stanley Lemons, *The First Baptist Church in America,* (Providence, Rhode Island: The Charitable Baptist Society, 2001), 4.

16 Gaustad, 38.

17 Lemons, 5-8.

18 Overbey, 81.

19 W.A. Jarrel, *Baptist Church Perpetuity,* (Dallas, Texas: Published by the author, 1894), 383.

20 D.B. Ray, *Baptist Succession: A Hand-book of Baptist History,* (Parsons, Kansas: Foley Railway Printing Company, 1912), 111-112.

21 I.K. Cross, *The Battle for Baptist History,* (Columbus, Georgia: Brentwood Christian Press, 1990), 152-153.

22 Ibid., 153.

23 Christian, 368.

24 Ibid., 369.

25 Ray, 121.

26 Cross, 154.

27 Overbey, 80-81.

28 Gaustad, 188-194.

29 D.C. Haynes, *The Baptist Denomination its History, Doctrines, and Ordinances,* (New York: Sheldon, Blakeman & Co., 1856), 52.

30 Jarrel, 393.

31 Ibid., 392-397.
32 Cross, 157.
33 Ray, 122-125.
34 Cross, 157.
35 Ibid.
36 James R. Beller, *The Baptist History Workbook,* (Arnold, Missouri: Prairie Fire Press, 2002), 215.
37 Asher, 79.
38 Gaustad, 194-196.
39 Cross, 159.
40 David Gibbs, Jr. and David Gibbs III, *Understanding the Constitution: Ten Things Every Christian Should Know About the Supreme Law of the Land,* (Seminole, Florida: The Christian Law Association, 2006), 85.
41 Beller, 216-219.
42 Ibid., 220-221.
43 Gibbs, 83.
44 Ibid., 221.
45 *Wikipedia,* /wiki/United_States_Bill_of_Rights.
46 *The Constitution of the United State of America,* The Bill of Rights, Amendment I.

Reigning in England

Starting Year	Num Years	Ruler	
1553	5	Mary I	She was passionately Catholic and sought to purge her domain of all non-Catholics. She was also known as Bloody Mary.
1558	45	Elizabeth I	She was Anglican but much more tolerant than her predecessors. Puritans, Separatists, Baptists and others flourished under her reign.
1603	22	James I	He was a strong Anglican and determined to put down the Puritans and the Separatists.
1625	24	Charles I	He was openly sympathetic to Catholicism and came down hard on non-Catholics, especially Puritans. The discontented Parliament dismissed King Charles I in 1649 and appealed to the king of Scotland for help. He invaded, and Charles I was beheaded.

Reigning in England

Starting Year	Num Years	Ruler	
1649	11	Common wealth	Parliament appointed the Council of State to govern the land as a Commonwealth. [1]
1660	25	Charles II	During this pro-Catholic king's reign, the *Clarendon Code* (anti-Puritan laws) was passed. [2]
1685	4	James II	This pro-Catholic king believed in absolute monarchy. He tried to establish freedom of religion in England by passing the *Declaration of Indulgence*, which removed punishments from Catholics and Protestant dissenters. [3]
1689	13	William III Mary II	Under their reign, the *Act of Toleration* was passed. This act brought a measure of freedom of religion to England.

The History of Churches

[1] *Wikipedia*, (en.wikipedia.org/wiki/English_Council_of_State).

[2] Ibid., /wiki/Charles_II_of_England.

[3] Ibid., /wiki/James_II_of_England.

First Baptist Churches

City, State	Years	Planted by
Massachusetts	?	These churches began in Boston.
Virginia	?	Dutton Lane and Daniel Marshall. Marshall received his baptism from a Baptist church in the Philadelphia association.
Kittery, Maine	1647	William Screven, who was ordained and licensed by the Boston church.
Charleston, South Carolina	?	William Screven. Many of the church members came as colonists from England; some came from Maine due to Puritan persecution.
Pennsylvania	?	Thomas Dungan. He left Rhode Island with other Baptists to plant a church. They merged with a church in the area that was made up of Welsh emigrants from Lower Dublin (a township in Pennsylvania).

First Baptist Churches

City, State	Years	Planted by
Philadelphia, Pennsylvania	1698	English Baptists, some of whom were of Hansard Knolly's church in London.
New York	1712	Valentine Wightman. He was from a Baptist church in North Kingston, Maine.
North Carolina	1727	Paul Palmer, who was baptized at the Welsh Tract Baptist Church in Delaware.
Maryland	1742	Henry Sator, a layman.
Georgia	?	They have their roots in the Baptists of Charleston, South Carolina.
Delaware	1770	Thomas Griffith. Members were from Pembroke and Caermarthen in Wales.

The History of Churches

Maps

Europe and the Mediterranean Area
(1st Century)

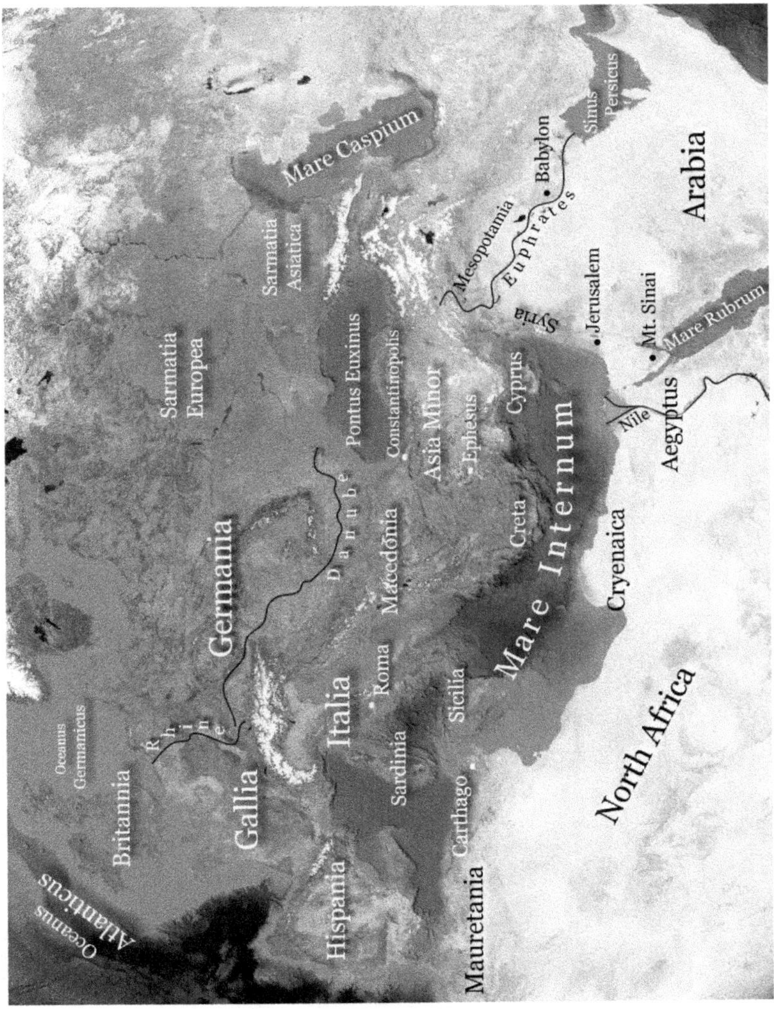
Mare Caspium
Sinus Persicus
Babylon
Arabia
Mesopotamia
Euphrates
Sarmatia Asiatica
Jerusalem
Syria
Mt. Sinai
Mare Rubrum
Sarmatia Europea
Pontus Euxinus
Constantinopolis
Asia Minor
Ephesus
Cyprus
Mare Internum
Nile
Aegyptus
Germania
Danube
Macedonia
Creta
Cryenaica
Oceanus Germanicus
Rhine
Italia
Roma
Sicilia
Britannia
Gallia
Sardinia
Carthago
North Africa
Oceanus Atlanticus
Hispania
Mauretania

Mediterranean Area

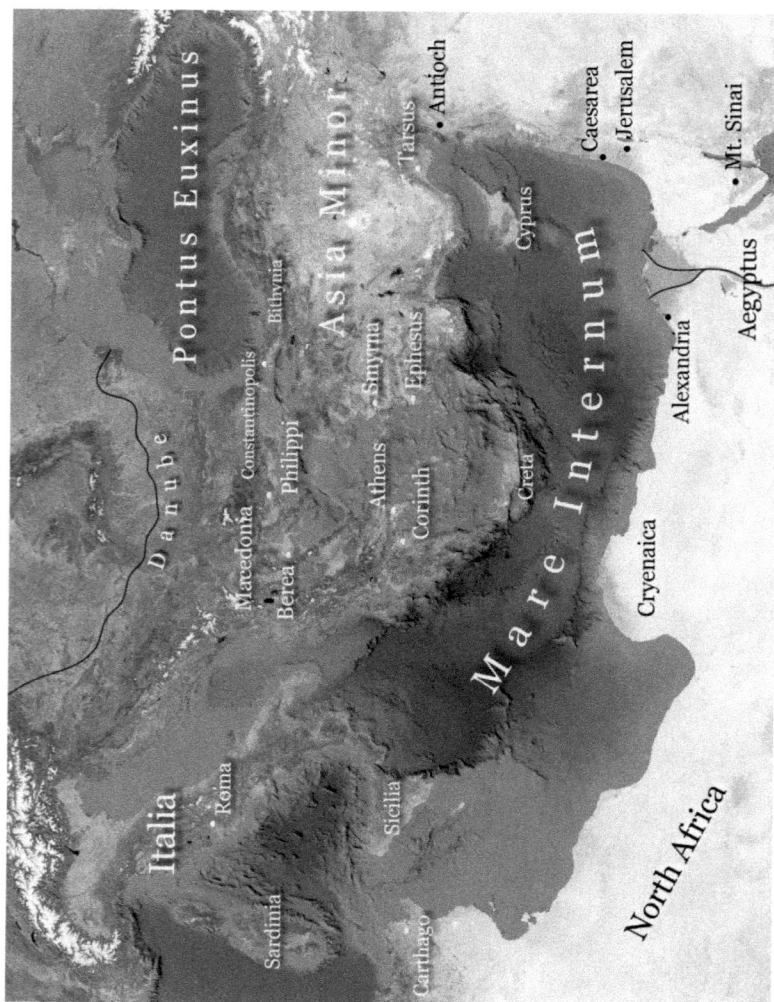

Asia Minor

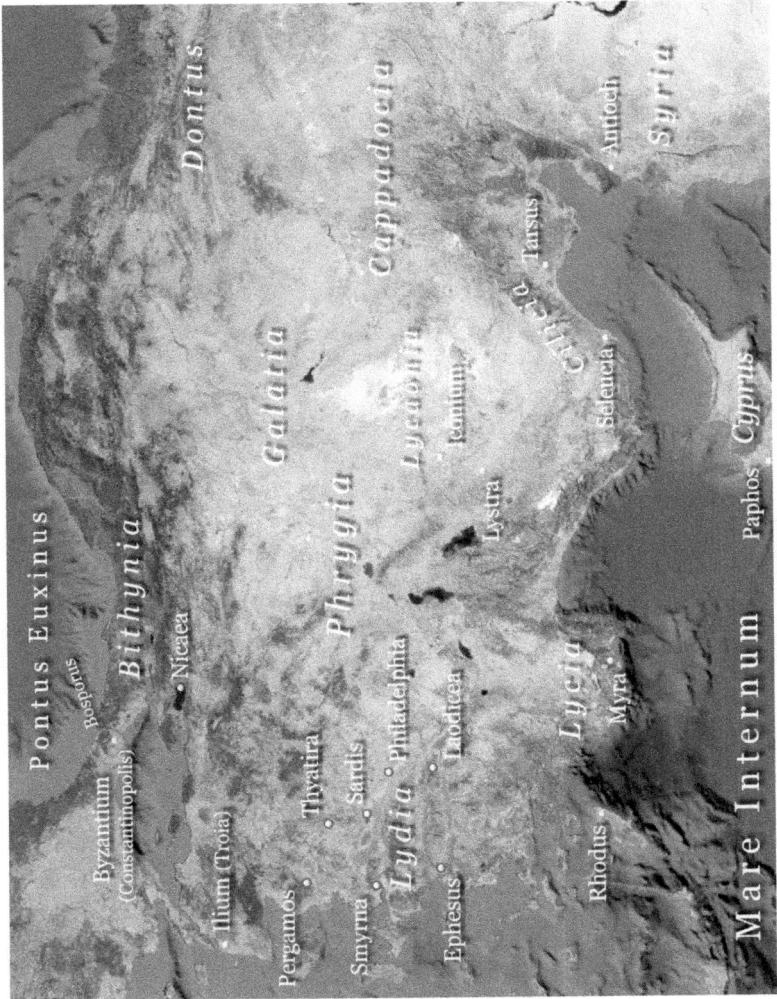

Italy and France

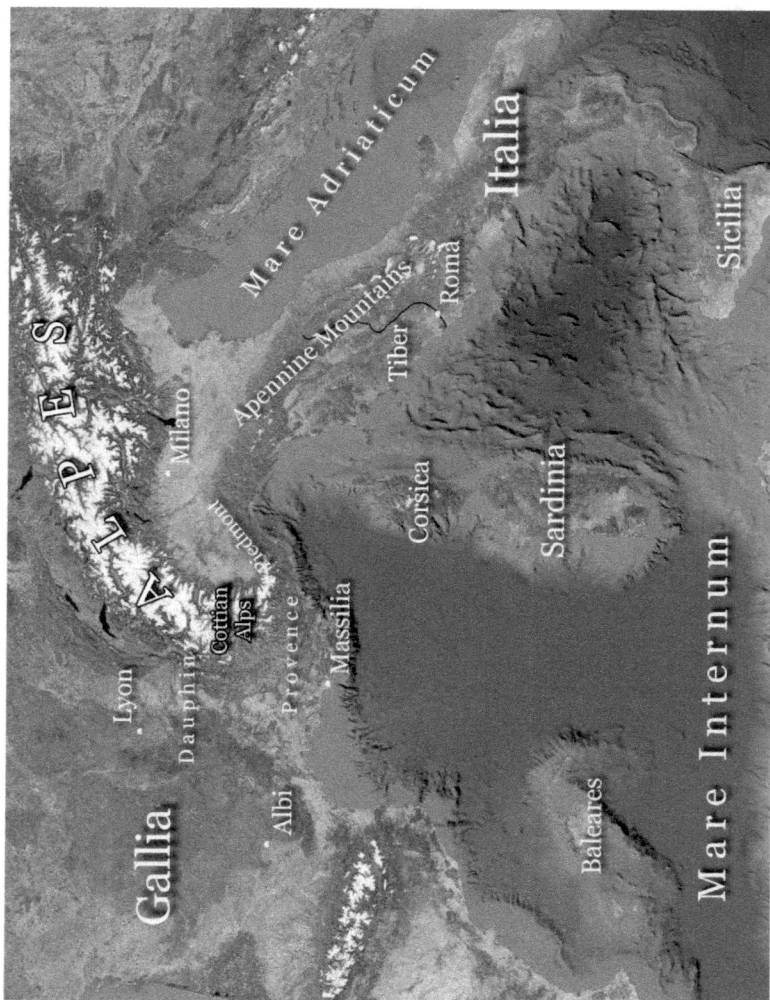

Europe and the Mediterranean Area
(15th Century)

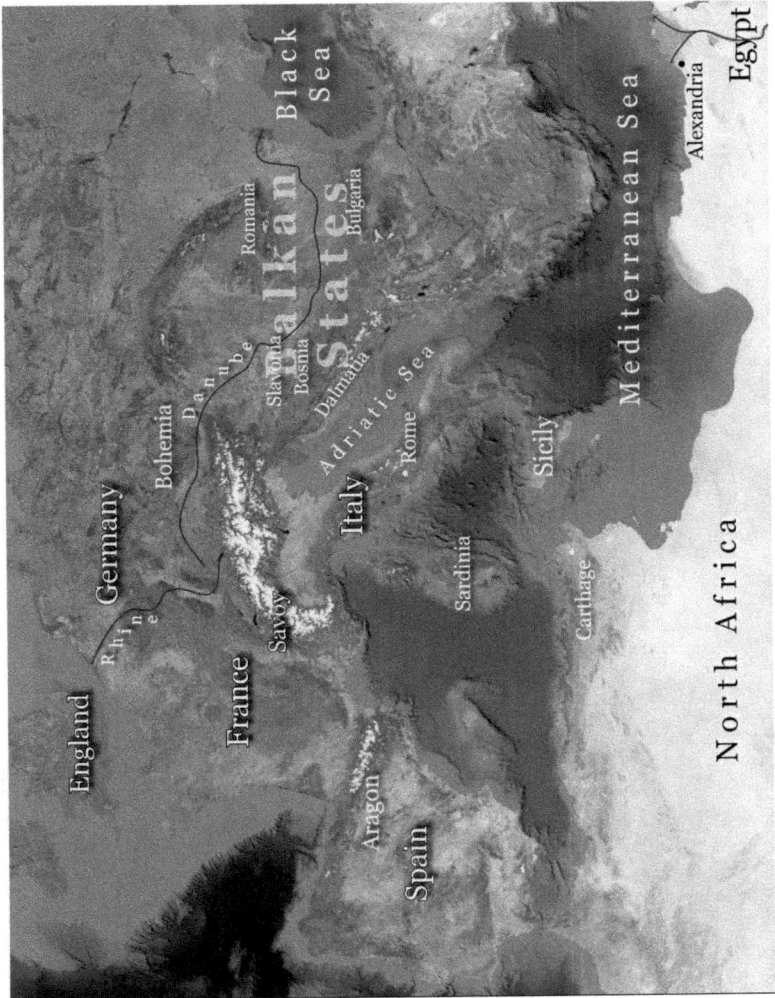

Balkan States

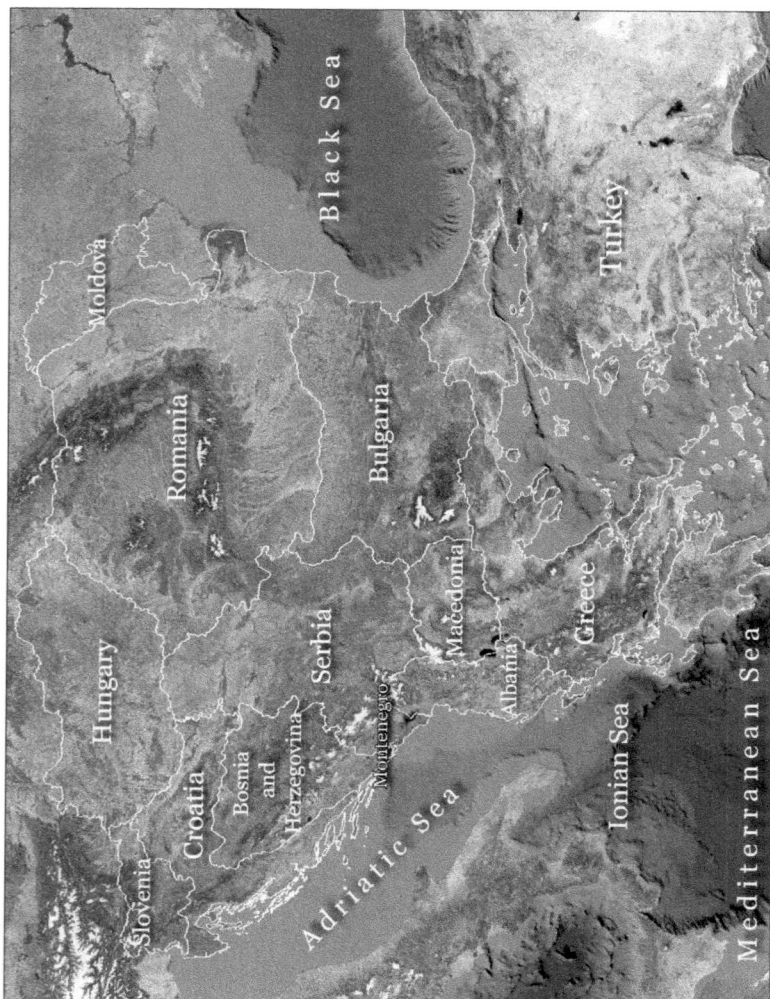

France, Germany and England

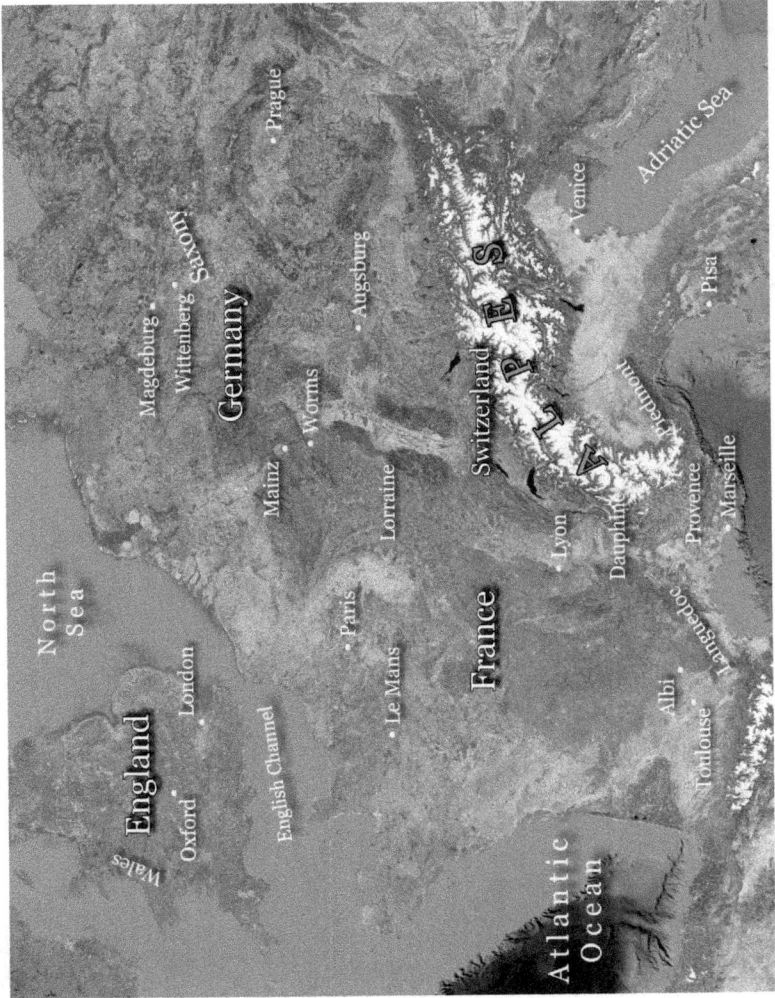

British Isles

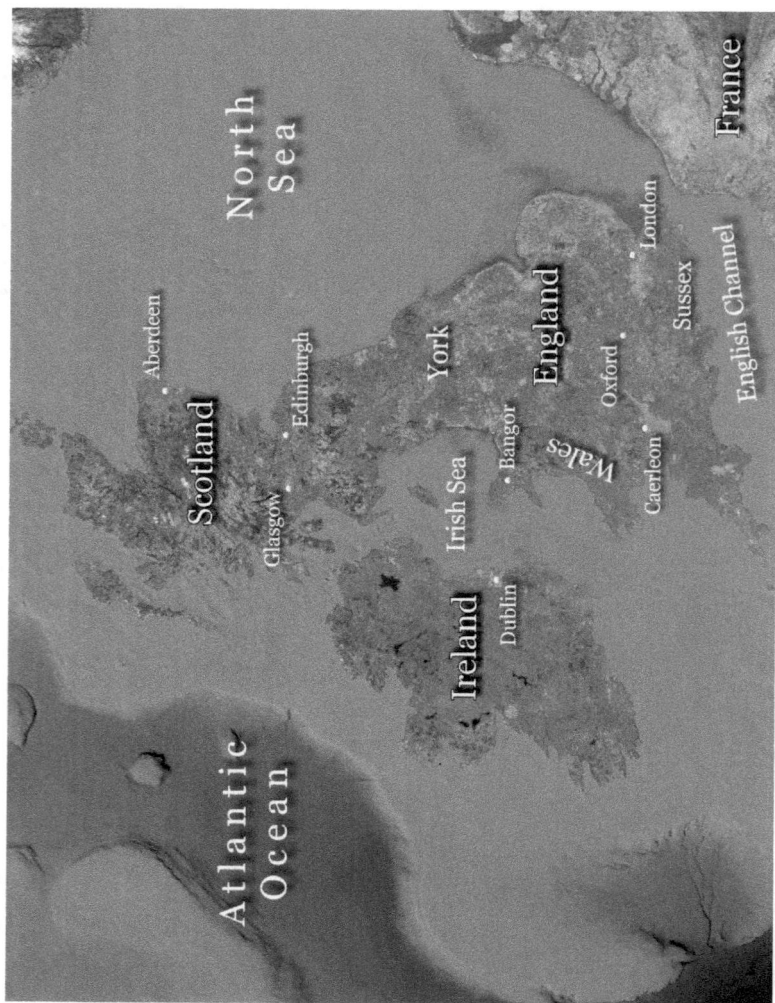

England and Wales

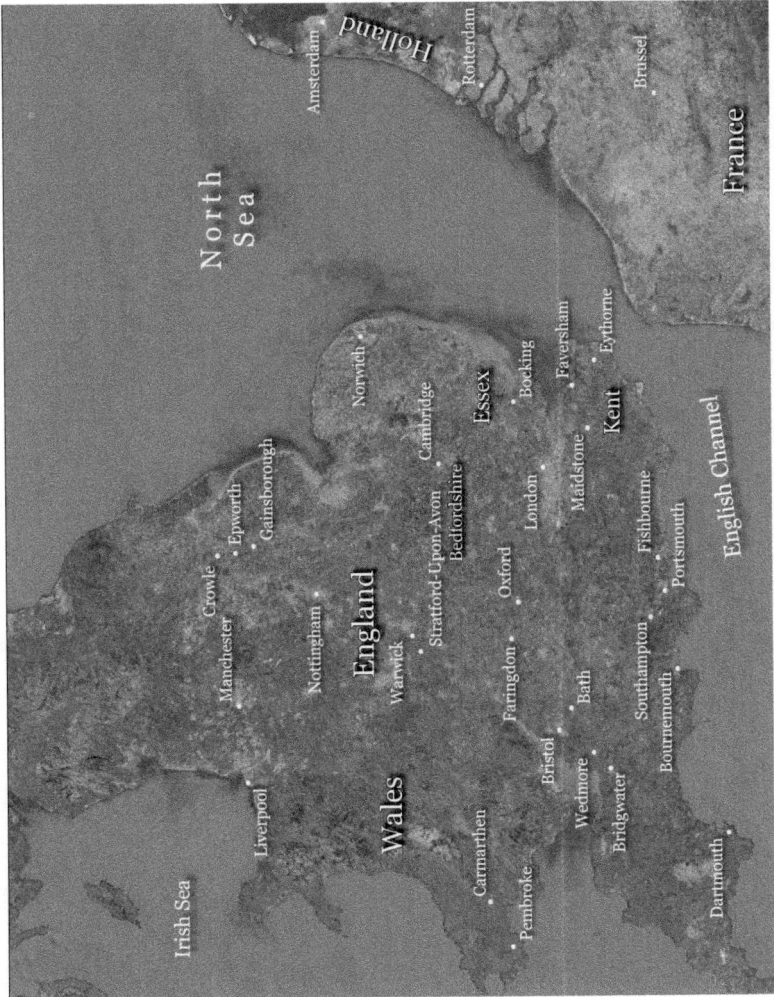

America
Original 13 States

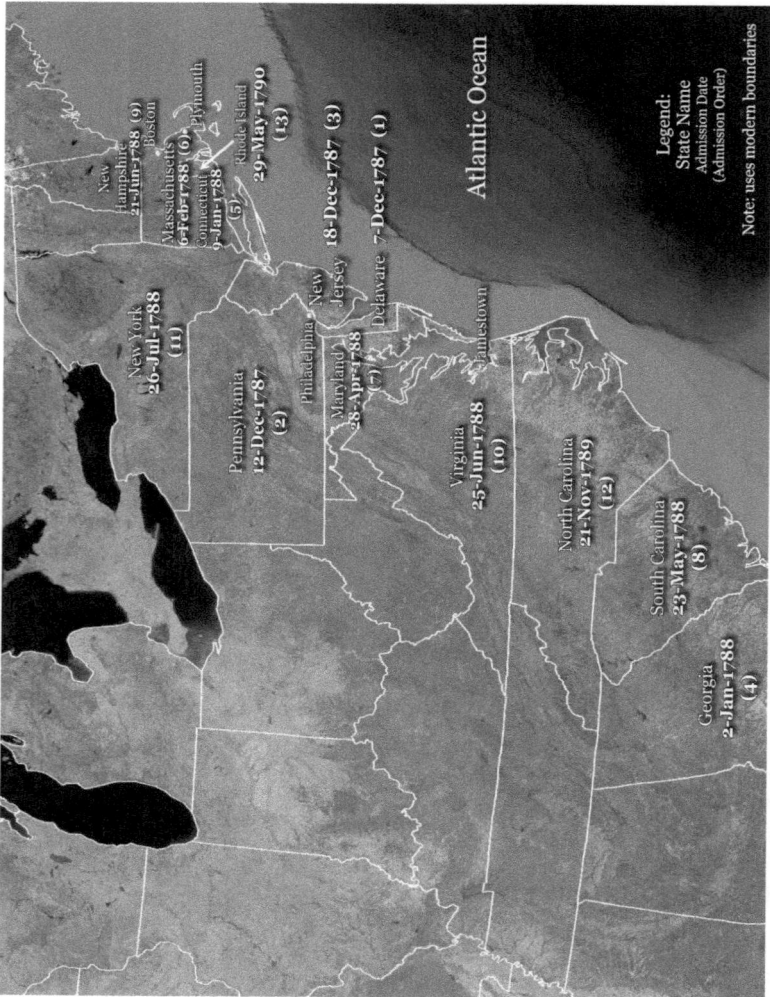

Bibliography

Aland, Kurt and Aland, Barbara. *The Texts of the New Testament.* Grand Rapids: William B. Eerdmans Publishing Company, 1995.

Asher, Louis Franklin. *John Clark (1609-1676) Pioneer in American Medicine, Democratic Ideals, and Champion of Religious Liberty.* Pittsburg, Pennsylvania: Dorrance Publishing Co. Inc., 1997.

Athanasius. *Nicene and Post-Nicene Fathers.* 14 vols. Peabody, Massachusetts: Hendrickson Publishers, Inc., 2004.

Beller, James R. *The Baptist History Workbook.* Arnold, Missouri: Prairie Fire Press, 2002.

Benedict, David. *History of the Donatists.* Paris, Arkansas: The Baptist Standard Bearer, 1875.

Broadbent, E.H. *The Pilgrim Church.* Grand Rapids, Michigan: GOSPEL FOLIO PRESS, 1999.

Brockett, L.P. *The Bogomils of Bulgaria and Bosnia; or the Early Protestants of the East.* Philadelphia, Pennsylvania: American Baptist Publications Society, 1879.

Bruce, F.F. *The Books and the Parchments.* Old Tappan, New Jersey: Fleming H. Revell Company, 1984.

_____. *The New Testament Documents: Are They Reliable?* Downers Grove, Illinois: InterVarsity Press, 1981.

Cairns, Earle E. *Christianity Through the Centuries.* Grand Rapids, Michigan: Zondervan, 1996.

Carlisle, Edgar C. *Our Religious Freedom, a Baptist Trophy.* Johnson, Kansas: IBO Press, 1979.

Carroll, J.M. *The Trail of Blood.* Lexington, Kentucky: Ashland Avenue Baptist Church, 1992.

Carson, D.A., Moo, Douglas J. and Morris, Leon. *An Introduction to the New Testament.* Grand Rapids: Zondervan, 1992.

Cathcart, William. *Baptist Encyclopaedia.* Paris, Arkansas: The Baptist Standard Bearer, 1887.

Christian, John T. *A History of the Baptists.* 2 vols. Texarkana, Texas-Arkansas: Bogard Press, 1922.

Clarke, Kent D. *The Canon Debate.* Peabody, Massachusetts: Hendrickson Publishers, Inc., 2004.

Covington, Sarah. *The Trail of Martyrdom: Persecution and Resistance in Sixteenth-century England.* South Bend, Indiana: University of Notre Dame Press, 2003.

Coxe, A. Cleveland. *Ante-Nicene Fathers.* 10 vols. Peabody, Massachusetts: Hendrickson Publishers, Inc., 2004.

Cross, I.K. *The Battle for Baptist History.* Columbus, Georgia: Brentwood Christian Press, 1990.

Deimer, Carl. *Church History* seminary courses. Lynchburg, Virginia: Liberty University, 2004.

Encyclopaedia Britannica. Chicago: William Benton Publishers, 1960.

Estep, William R. *The Anabaptist Story: an Introduction to Sixteenth-Century Anabaptism.* 3rd ed., Grand Rapids: William B. Eerdmans Publishing Company, 1996.

Ferguson, Everett. *The Canon Debate.* Peabody, Massachusetts: Hendrickson Publishers, Inc., 2004.

Foxe, John. *Foxe's Book of Martyrs.* Grand Rapids, Michigan: Fleming H. Revell, 2000.

_____. *Christian Martyrology.* London: Fisher, Son, & Co., 1840.

429

Fiensy, David A. *The College Press NIV Commentary: New Testament Introduction.* Joplin, Missouri: College Press Publishing Company, 1997.

Fredeircq, P. *Encyclopaedia Britannica.* Chicago: William Benton Publishers, 1960.

Gaustad, Edwin S. *Liberty of Conscience: Roger Williams in America.* Grand Rapids: William B. Eerdmans Publishing Company, 1991.

Gibbs, David Jr. and Gibbs, David III. *Understanding the Constitution: Ten Things Every Christian Should Know About the Supreme Law of the Land.* Seminole, Florida: The Christian Law Association, 2006.

Gonzalez, Justo L. *The Story of Christianity.* 2 vols. San Francisco: HarperCollins Publishers, 1984.

Graves, J.R. *Old Landmarkism: What Is It?* Texarkana, Texas: Bogard Press, 1880.

Hanko, Herman. *Our Venerable King James Bible.* Lansing, Illinois: Peace Protestant Reformed Church.

Haynes, D.C. *The Baptist Denomination its History, Doctrines, and Ordinances.* New York: Sheldon, Blakeman &Co., 1856.

Holy Bible: King James Version. Nashville: Broadman & Holman, 1987.

Landon, Edward. *A Manual of Councils of the Holy Catholic Church.* Edinburgh, 1909.

Lemons, J. Stanley. *The First Baptist Church in America.* Providence, Rhode Island: The Charitable Baptist Society, 2001.

Link, Hans-Georg. *New International Dictionary of New Testament Theology.* Grand Rapids: Zondervan, 1986.

Jarrel, W.A. *Baptist Church Perpetuity*. Dallas, Texas: Published by the author, 1894.

Margoliouth, David Samuel. *Encyclopaedia Britannica*. Chicago: William Benton Publishers, 1960.

Melia, Pius. *The Origin, Persecutions, and Doctrines of the Waldenses*. London: James Toovey, 1870.

Menzies, Allan. *Ante-Nicene Fathers*. 10 vols. Peabody, Massachusetts: Hendrickson Publishers, Inc., 2004.

Metzger, Bruce M. *The Canon of the New Testament: Its Origin, Development and Significance*. Oxford: Clarendon Press, 1997.

_____. *The Text of the New Testament*. Oxford: Oxford University Press, 1968.

Mikhail, Labib. *The Jerusalem Connection*. March, 2002.

Mohammed. *The Koran*. Elmhurst, New York: Tahrike Tarsile.

Morey, Robert. *The Islamic Invasion: Confronting the World's Fastest Growing Religion*. Las Vegas, Nevada: Christian Scholars Press, 1992.

Mosheim, John Laurence. *An Ecclesiastical History, Ancient and Modern*. New York: Harper and Brothers, Publishers, 1871.

Muston, Alexis. *The Israel of the Alps: A Complete History of the Waldenses and Their Colonies*. London: Blackie & Son, Paternoster Buildings, E.C., 1875.

_____ and Hazlitt, W. *The Israel of the Alps: A History of the Persecution of the Waldenses*. London: Savill & Edwards, Printers, 1852.

Orchard, Herbert George. *A Concise History of Baptists*. Paris, Arkansas: The Baptist Standard Bearer, Inc.

431

Overbey, Edward H. *A Brief History of the Baptists*. Little Rock, Arkansas: The Challenge Press, 1974.

Oyer, John S. *Lutheran Reformers Against Anabaptists*. Paris, Arkansas: The Baptist Standard Bearers, 1964.

Patterson, Morgan W. *Baptist Successionism: A Critical View*. Valley Forge, Pennsylvania: Judson Press, 1969.

Ray, David Burcham. *Baptist Succession: A Hand-book of Baptist History*. Parsons, Kansas: Foley Railway Printing Company, 1912.

Reese, Edward. *The Chronological Bible*. Nashville, Tennessee: E.E. Gaddy and Associates, Inc. Publishers, 1997.

Rupp, Gordon. *The Reformation Crisis*. New York: Harper & Roe Company, 1965.

Rutherford, John. *The International Standard Bible Encyclopaedia*. 4 vols. Grand Rapids: Wm. B. Eerdmans Publishing Co., 1956.

Schaff, Philip. *History of the Christian Church*. 8 vols. Grand Rapids: WM. B. Eerdmans Publishing Company, 1955.

Schmidt, C. *Encyclopaedia Britannica*. Chicago: William Benton Publishers, 1960.

Smith, Sheldon. *The Sword of the Lord*. Murphreesboro, Tennessee: The Sword of the Lord Publishers, February, 2002.

Strong, James. *Strong's Greek Dictionary of the New Testament*. New York: Abingdon Press, 1958.

Tacitus. *Documents of the Christian Church*. Oxford: Oxford University Press, 1999.

Tertullian. *Ante-Nicene Fathers*. 10 vols. Peabody, Massachusetts: Hendrickson Publishers, Inc., 2004.

Thiessen, Henry Clarence. *Introduction to the New Testament.* Peabody, Massachusetts: Hendrickson Publishers, Inc., 2002.

Thompson, J.E.H. *The International Standard Bible Encyclopaedia.* 4 vols. Grand Rapids: Wm. B. Eerdmans Publishing Co., 1956.

Towns, Elmer. *Theology for Today.* Orlando, Florida: Harcourt Custom Publishers, 1997.

Trajan. *Documents of the Christian Church.* Oxford: Oxford University Press, 1999.

Ulrich, Eugene. *The Canon Debate.* Peabody, Massachusetts: Hendrickson Publishers, Inc., 2004.

Vance, Laurence M. *King James: His Bible and Its Translators.* Pensacola, Florida: Vance Publications, 1960.

Verduin, Leonard. *The Reformers and Their Stepchildren.* Grand Rapids: William B. Eerdmans Publishing Company, 1964.

Vine, W.E. *An Expository Dictionary of New Testament Words.* Nashville: Thomas Nelson Publishers, 1985.

Vineyard, Jim. *Fundamental Baptist World Missions.* January, 2002.

Wigram, George V. and Winter, Ralph D. *The Word Study Concordance.* Wheaton, Illinois: Tyndale Publishing House, 1978.

Webster's New World Dictionary with Student Handbook: Young People's Edition. Nashville, Tennessee: The World Publishing Company, 1973.

About the Author

LESTER HUTSON served as a Baptist pastor for over 60 years. He is now Senior Pastor of Northwest Baptist Church in Houston. He does limited work as a field representative for the Christian Law Association and conducts a limited number of seminars, revivals and other such engagements. He continues to write and is the author of numerous books including *Basic Bible Truths,* an internationally used soul-winning method.

www.lesterhutson.org

www.ingramcontent.com/pod-product-compliance
Lightning Source LLC
Chambersburg PA
CBHW062355090426
42740CB00010B/1291